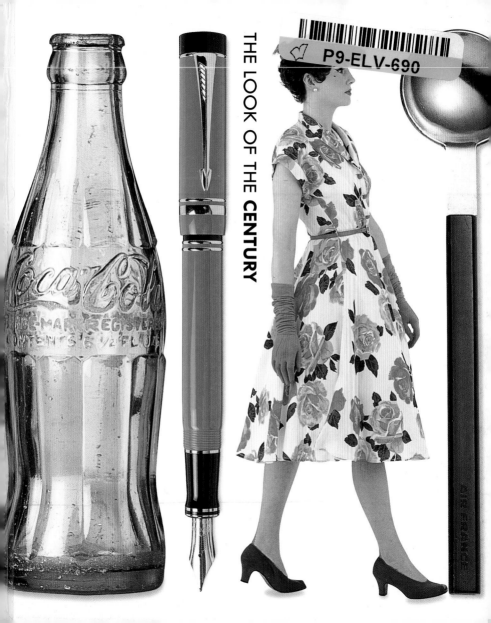

THE LOOK OF THE **CENTURY**

AIR FRANCE

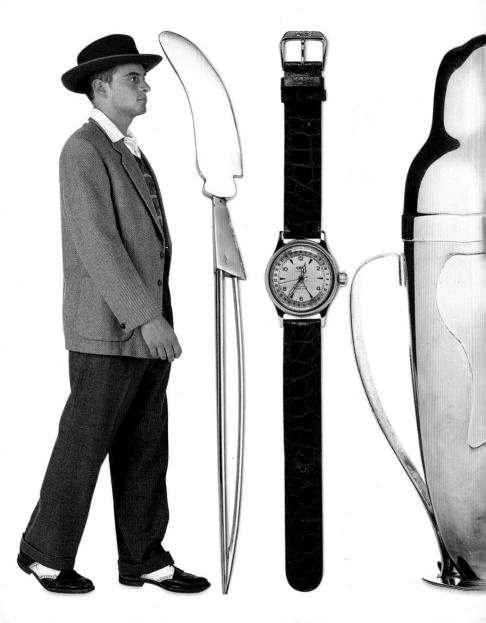

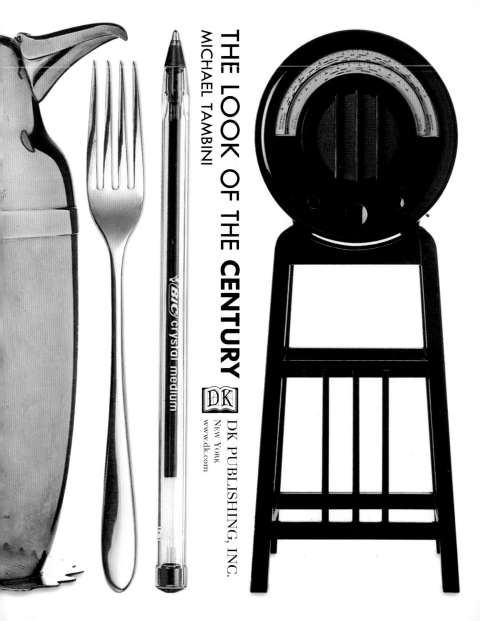

MICHAEL TAMBINI

THE LOOK OF THE **CENTURY**

DK

DK PUBLISHING, INC.
NEW YORK
www.dk.com

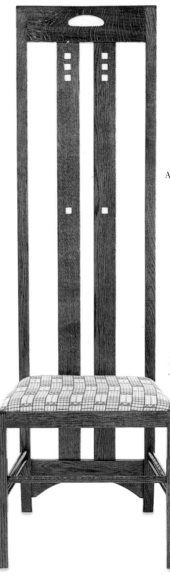

A DK PUBLISHING BOOK
www.dk.com

First American Edition, 1996
First Paperback Edition, 1999
2 4 6 8 10 9 7 5 3

Published in the United States by DK Publishing, Inc.
95 Madison Avenue, New York, New York 10016

DK Publishing books are available at special discounts
for bulk purchases for sales promotions or premiums.
Special editions, including personalized covers, excerpts
of existing guides, and corporate imprints can be
created in large quantities for specific needs. For
more information, contact Special Markets Dept.
DK Publishing, Inc./95 Madison Ave.
New York, NY 10016/Fax: 800-600-9098.

Library of Congress Cataloging-in-Publication Data
Tambini Michael.
The look of the century / [Michael Tambini]. -- 1st American ed.
    p. cm
Includes biographical references and index.
ISBN 0-7894-4635-9
1. Design. Industrial--History--20th century. 1. Title.
TS171.T35 1996
745.2'09' 04--dc20   96-11806
                                                          CIP

Reproduced by Colourscan, Singapore
Printed and bound in Italy by
Lego, Vicenza

Senior Editors Janice Lacock, Louise Candlish
Senior Art Editor Tracy Hambleton-Miles
Project Editor Jo Marceau
Art Editor Dawn Terrey
Editors Jane Sarluis, David T. Walton
Designer Carla De Abreu
Design Assistant Stephen Croucher

Senior Managing Editor Sean Moore
Art Director Peter Luff

Production Manager Meryl Silbert
Picture Researcher Jo Walton
DTP Designer Zirrinia Austin

Photography Dave King, Steve Gorton,
Andy Crawford

Consultants Robert Opie,
Professor Jonathan M. Woodham

National Design Museum Review Panel
Susan Yelavich, Assistant Director for Public
Programs *Gillian Moss*, Curatorial Chair, and
Assistant Curator, Textiles Department
Deborah Sampson Shinn, Assistant Curator,
Department of Applied Arts and Industrial
Design *Joanne Warner*, Assistant Curator,
Wallcoverings Department *Caroline Mortimer*,
Special Assistant to the Director

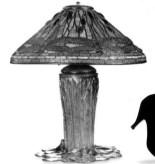

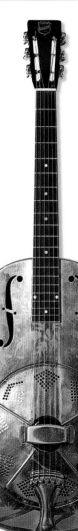

CONTENTS

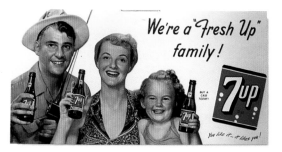

FOREWORD

The word "man-made" must characterize the look of much of our environment over the past hundred years. Human inventiveness and, increasingly, human consumption of products invented by others has gathered pace, even though the great powerhouse of the last decades of the century — Japan — has deliberately slowed the galloping mania of shorter and shorter product lifecycles. Its falter resulted from the great recession of the 1980s, and almost coincides with the first of the movements that have targeted conspicuous waste: greenism, anti-exploitationism, portent of gloomism. This reevaluation of the need for products is the moral lens through which we can look at the environment and the artifacts that we have made for a century.

Are we proud of this century? Have most lives been improved by it? And, especially interesting to the designer, have we changed most people's capacity to judge the aesthetics and the functional achievements of the common culture? This book's look at the products of a century shows stylistic movements in the form and the detail of products, just as clearly as an examination of a century of painting, literature, or fashion would. Every one of those movements threw up style leaders, and these are inevitably the declared heroes of our look at the century. There is, of course, a vastly larger number of unsung heroes who are the engineers and designers of the great majority of the artifacts — which are the real landscape of the time. Our heroes are often only the greenhouse keepers, breeders of the new flora in that landscape.

Even so, it is the greenhouse that makes the brightest colors and the rarest blooms and so inevitably we look for them to give this book the focus and the brightness that will form our remark on what a century has done.

On perhaps a more prosaic level, there are changes in the size of common products and the effect of manufacturing technology on their availability — through the cost, longevity, and form of things. The radio exemplifies this perfectly. Originally, it was wooden-cased; then in everlasting Bakelite;

later, it was vastly changed in size to hand-held; and by 2000 it will still be available but virtually absent from sight — the only trace a slender wire and a plug in the ear. We've seen incomprehensible prejudices that affected many products' looks overnight: as recently as the 1950s, it was *de facto* forbidden to make anything other than park railings in the color green — the omnipotent buyers dictated it to be unlucky — until Citroën sold a 2-CV, and then anything could be green. And as the century closes, the greatest effect on how things look is undoubtedly from man's inhumanity to man — the computer. Of course, we all know how laborsaving and entertaining they are, but their inhumanity lies in their theft of many personal skills and, of course, jobs.

All that aside, their effect on product form and construction is profound and highly visible. If you can imagine it, if you can depict it on your screen, then you can have it. The look of communications has changed and is still dramatically changing, the demands of the media far outstripping the producer's ability to care for long about the look. The message — and its effectiveness — is the force. But the optimists among us know that there are more and more young — and older — designers who are skilled and who can use these tools. For the form maker of the commonplace, we've had a good — the best — century.

KENNETH GRANGE
FOUNDER OF PENTAGRAM DESIGN, LONDON

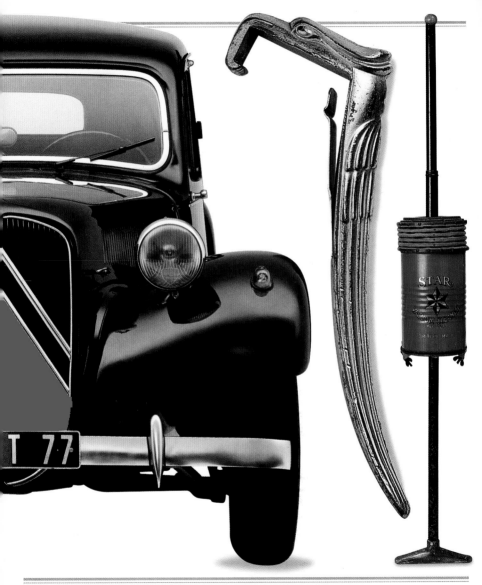

INTRODUCTION

Our world is changing at a dizzying speed, and technology is racing ahead so quickly that many of us are overwhelmed by the multitude of new designs and inventions that are available: videophones, cable television, solar-powered cars, virtual reality, the Information Superhighway… Yet so many of the things we take for granted, or even feel are becoming outmoded, were the stuff of dreams just 100 years ago. In fact, change has been this century's only constant. As well as the technical advances that science has contributed to the product designs of the 20th century, designers and craftspeople have also been influenced by a bewildering succession of movements, from Art Nouveau to postmodernism, Bauhaus to Psychedelia. Some, such as De Stijl, were relatively short-lived and affected only a limited number of countries. Others, such as Art Deco, lasted longer and had international exponents. The following pages, which are divided by decade, give a concise introduction to the most important of these movements and their key designers, as well as some of the most interesting developments and innovations from each era.

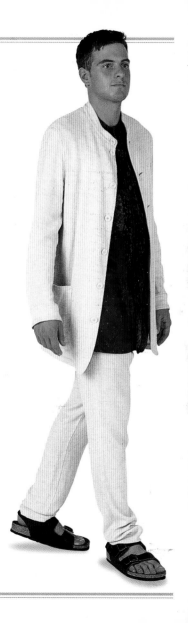

1900–09

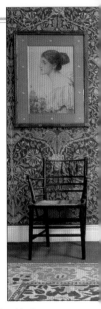

At the dawn of the 20th century, a frenetic series of momentous advances in technology was making a major impact on society. The internal combustion engine, the electric motor, and the rudiments of telecommunication allowed manufacturers to aspire to hitherto unimaginable heights of efficiency. Previously handmade goods could now be made more quickly and cheaply by machine, undermining the role of craftsmanship. The machine was also revolutionizing the domestic world and, with the advent of the radio, telephone, and television, it was to completely redefine "communication" at home and at work. The assembly line drastically accelerated the production of vehicles, making the automobile affordable to a much wider market. In 1903, the Wright brothers realized the centuries-old dream of flight by traveling 131 feet (40 meters) through the air in their gas-driven biplane.

Gustav Stickley chair

This beautifully crafted wooden and leather chair was made in 1904–05. Typical of Stickley's work, it was produced using mechanical processes.

Arts and Crafts interior

The walls of this room at Wightwick Manor in Wolverhampton, England, are lined with William Morris' Honeysuckle printed linen; other items are by his followers.

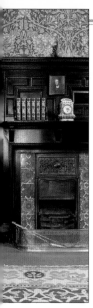

Just six years later, Louis Blériot flew his little monoplane 26 miles (42 kilometers) across the English Channel from France to England. Within 30 years, flight would be available to anyone with money, with regular passenger flights crossing the world.

ARTS AND CRAFTS MOVEMENT

Although a product of the Victorian age, the Arts and Crafts movement left a legacy that extended deep into the 20th century. The primary concern of its central figures was that "machine-age" manufacturers were driven by quantity rather than quality. The movement's most influential designer and theorist was William Morris (1834–96). His company, Morris and Co., produced a wide range of items, including furniture, stained glass, wallpaper, fabrics, and pottery. For Morris, art and craft had equal status and his designs utilized the skills of craftsmen and artists in collaboration. Arts and Crafts work is characterized by medieval and gothic references; Morris wanted the craftsman's hand visible in the work, differentiating it from the machine-made. The robust, simply constructed furniture left the joints exposed, and in metalwork the hand of the craftsman was visible in the textural hammerwork. Morris believed that good design was uplifting and would contribute to a happier society – a belief shared by the modernists in the 1920s. Although the Arts and Crafts movement began in Britain, there were European and American counterparts. Workshops, or guilds, following Morris' precepts sprang up in many countries. While American designers, such as Gustav Stickley, followed the British model closely, many Europeans moved away from the fundamental tenets of the Arts and Crafts movement and more readily embraced Art Nouveau and modernism.

Blériot's Type XI airplane

The airplane that Louis Blériot flew over the English Channel in 1909 was constructed from linen stretched over a wooden frame, supported by wire struts.

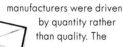

ART NOUVEAU

By 1900, the dominant movement of the decade, Art Nouveau, was already established, born of the Arts and Crafts movement and the 19th-century Aesthetic movement. Its exponents were much more willing to embrace the use of new materials and mass production than their Arts and Crafts counterparts. While they also drew on the past, they shared an enthusiasm for the future that set them apart from the preceding movement. The name is derived from art dealer Samuel Bing's shop, *L'Art Nouveau*, which opened in Paris in 1895. Leading designers from around Europe were invited to display their work there, including the Belgian Henry van de Velde (furniture), the American Louis Comfort Tiffany (glassware), and Frenchmen Emile Gallé (glassware) and René Lalique. The latter was one of the key exponents of Art Nouveau. His exquisite jewelry, often based on plant or insect motifs, used glass, semi-precious stones, and gold. Although Art Nouveau developed in idiosyncratic ways in many countries (it was closely related to Jungendstil in Germany, Secession in Austria, and Stile Liberty in Italy), the fluid, organic style is easily recognizable. The dominating characteristic is the whiplash curve that influences both the form and the surface decoration of the object. Its organic fluidity was inspired by nature, particularly plant-life. There are also references to past traditions, such as Celtic art and Rococo, to be found in the style. Art Nouveau could be interpreted either naturalistically or abstractly and its principles could be applied to the design of anything from architecture to jewellery. The most important work took place in France, Belgium, Austria, and Scotland.

THE GLASGOW SCHOOL

In Scotland, the Glasgow School, a small, but widely recognized group of designers, led by the architect and designer Charles Rennie Mackintosh, was producing work that combined the functionalism of the Arts and Crafts movement with the exuberance of Art Nouveau. Its work fused a geometric format with a flowing linear pattern based on organic form.

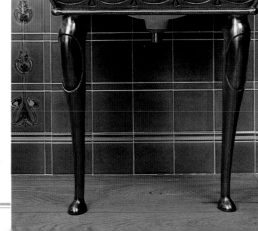

Porte Dauphine Metro entrance

Architect Hector Guimard designed a series of ornate entrances for the Paris Métro in cast iron and glass. Some remain intact today.

Cast-iron washstand

This highly ornate British wash basin, dating from 1903 to 1911, demonstrates the curving, organic lines of Art Nouveau. Its majolica tiles are typical of the period.

1910–19

Josef Hoffmann was one of the leading figures in the group of Viennese artists and architects known as the Vienna Secession. Although most of the art of the Secession was fundamentally Art Nouveau in style, its design is remembered for a more geometric approach to decoration. The Secession published its own journal, *Ver Sacrum*, and held regular exhibitions showing work from many international artists.

WIENER WERKSTÄTTE

In 1903, Hoffmann formed the Wiener Werkstätte with Koloman Moser. This association of workshops owes much to the Arts and Crafts guilds. The Wiener Werkstätte was responsible for producing fine pieces of jewelry, metalwork, textiles, furniture, and architecture. Its designers occupied ground between the decorative Art Nouveau and the austerity of modernism, which was beginning to influence the design of objects.

THE MACHINE AESTHETIC

As the century progressed, designers became less concerned with the crafts aesthetic and favored instead the aesthetic of the machine. In 1917, a group of Dutch painters, architects, designers, and philosophers formed a collective called De Stijl ("The Style"). Moving away from natural form in architecture and design, the De Stijl group attempted to find a visual language to express a new machine aesthetic by using a limited color palette and geometric shapes and

Excelsior Auto-cycle
By 1914, all the major components of the modern motorcycle were already in place; the designs that followed represented a process of refinement.

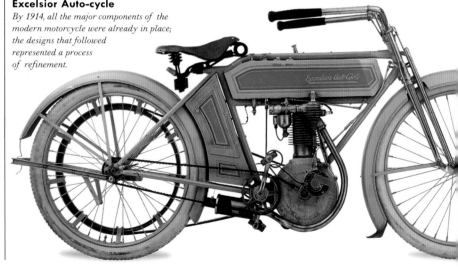

Coca-Cola bottle
*Based on the shape
of the cola nut, the
Coca-Cola bottle was
redesigned in 1915
and has remained
virtually unchanged
ever since.*

lines alone. Of all the work, perhaps Gerrit Rietveld's Red-and-blue chair of 1918 comes closest to achieving this aim. Constructed from standardized lengths of machine-finished wood, it is devoid of all unnecessary ornamentation. De Stijl's influence extended throughout Europe, particularly to the constructivists in Russia and the Bauhaus in Germany. In Italy, the futurists, who included poet Filippo Marinetti (1876–1944) and artist Giacomo Balla (1871–1958) also glorified the machine.

MASS PRODUCTION

The industrialist Henry Ford had founded the Ford Motor Company in 1903, and over the next few years he developed a system of mass production that was to have a permanent effect on the design process: the standardization of parts for easy assembly and, in 1913, the moving assembly line. When these principles were applied to the Model T Ford, it was so successful that by the 1920s every second car on the world's roads was a Model T. Mass production made goods affordable to a much wider market, but also left factory workers with a feeling of alienation. Their role in manufacturing was reduced to an anonymous, repetitive task. Some now took up William Morris' argument that the only escape was a return to craftsmanship; but the momentum of mass production was not to be resisted and, in fact, increased as the century progressed.

However, the quality of life of the average worker began to be improved by the introduction of a plethora of time- and laborsaving devices, such as washing machines, hair dryers, and irons.

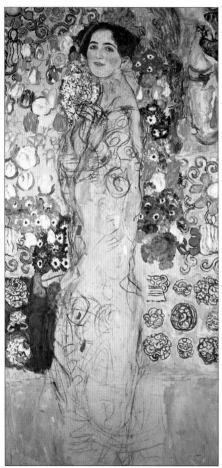

Gustav Klimt, *Portrait of a Lady*, 1917–18
Austrian artist Klimt provided a bridge between fine art and Art Nouveau. His richly decorative paintings, with large blocks of flat pattern and heavy use of gilt, were firmly based in the traditions of the Vienna Secession.

ELECTRICITY

The majority of these newfangled devices did not really save time, but they did save labor, making housework less tiring. Many of them were electrically operated. A relatively new commodity at the beginning of the century, electricity was as yet unavailable to most homes. However, the promise of a clean, odorless energy source, bright lighting at the flick of a switch, and the attraction of new inventions like the electrically powered vacuum cleaner made electricity such a worthwhile investment that it was quickly accepted throughout the Western world.

THE BIRTH OF CORPORATE IDENTITY

In Germany at this time, Peter Behrens became artistic director of the electrical manufacturer AEG (Allgemeine Elektricitäts-Gesellschaft). The company recognized the need to unify its design, and Behrens' standardization and interchangeability of components were crucial to AEG's success. The clearest example of this are his kettle designs from 1909, which allowed for 80 variations from just three basic models. Behrens also ensured

Hoffmann's metalwork
This silver bowl was made by architect and designer Josef Hoffmann in 1917. Much of Hoffmann's furniture has similarities with that of the Scot Charles Rennie Mackintosh. Both utilized geometry and the repeat pattern in their work.

that there was continuity in all other elements of the company's output, from architecture to advertising. AEG had taken on a corporate identity – a practice copied by other companies later. Behrens employed some of the most avant-garde designers, including Walter Gropius, Mies van der Rohe, and Le Corbusier. Their work has had an enormous impact on product design and greatly influenced the debate about art and technology.

THE BAUHAUS

In 1919, an art school was formed in Germany known as the Bauhaus. Under the directorship of Walter Gropius it became one of the most influential design institutions of the century, active until 1933. Its simple aim was to train artists to work for industry; and although its achievements can easily be exaggerated, it has left a lasting

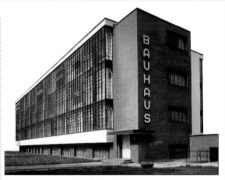

The Bauhaus building
Walter Gropius designed the new school building at Dessau in 1925. It has become a symbol of modernism, with its emphasis on steel, glass, and concrete, and has had a great impact on the development of 20th-century architecture.

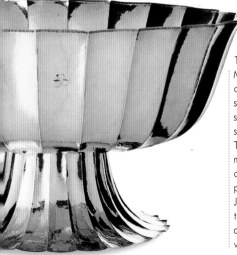

impression on 20th-century design. Using modern industrial materials, stripped down to their basic elements and without added decoration, Bauhaus designers attempted to make products that avoided historic reference. Their aspirations were not always achieved. Marcel Breuer's famous Wassily chair has many of the characteristics associated with the Bauhaus style – made from tubular steel and with a stripped-down geometric form. Yet its construction still owes more to the craftsman than the machine. The Bauhaus' greatest success was its teaching methods, which have been copied the world over. Gropius attracted highly respected painters, including Wassily Kandinsky (1866–1944), Josef Albers, and Paul Klee (1879–1940), to teach the foundation course. Celebrated architects such as Marcel Breuer and Mies van der Rohe also taught at the school.

1920–29

At the influential 1925 *Exposition Internationale des Arts Décoratifs et Industriels Modernes* held in Paris, the Swiss architect Le Corbusier designed one of the pavilions, naming it *L' Espirit Nouveau.* This was a model of modernism: its plain white walls, concrete frame, and large expanses of glass were unified by an uncompromising geometry. The inside was decorated with commercially available, unpretentious furniture including the bentwood Thonet armchair (see p.57). However, the *Exposition* is remembered less for the functionalism of Le Corbusier's contribution and more for the look that the rest of the exhibits in the other pavilions encapsulated. For it was from this exhibition that the term "Art Deco" was derived.

ART DECO

This decorative style was inspired by non-western art, particularly that of Africa and Egypt, made popular by the discovery in 1922 of Tutankhamun's tomb by Howard Carter. Diaghilev's Ballets Russes (which first danced in Paris in 1909) and the cubist paintings of Pablo Picasso (1881–1973) and Georges Braque (1882–1963) captured the imagination of designers. However, Art Deco was not a design movement, but rather a shared approach to styling. The interplay of geometric forms; abstract patterns of zig-zags, chevrons, and sunbursts, rendered in brilliant colors; and the use of bronze, ivory, and ebony were all common features. Criticized by

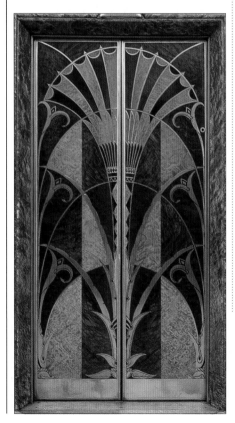

Art Deco doors
These beautiful elevator doors are from the Chrysler building in New York (see right). They are inlaid with wood veneers and brass, and were designed by the architect William van Alen.

Chrysler building, New York
The headquarters of the American motor manufacturer was a stunning example of the mainstream acceptance of Art Deco in America. The upper floors were clad in metal, reflecting the company's product.

some for its opulence, it was seen to distract from the purist theories expounded by the modernists. Furniture designers such as Jacques-Emile Ruhlmann (who designed the interior of one of the pavilions at the 1925 Paris Expo) used exotic veneers and ivory inlays in a rich, decorative scheme. He was inspired by 18th-century design, but updated the look by using geometry and modern materials.

Art Deco did not remain the preserve of the wealthy. Indeed, new, inexpensive materials such as Bakelite were flexible and popular. In Britain, Wells Coates used Bakelite to great effect in his radio designs (see p.91). In architecture, colored glass and chromium created the Art Deco look at relatively low cost and was used successfully in public buildings such as the Odeon theaters. The cinema itself played an important role in popularizing the Art Deco style,

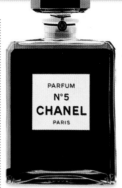

Chanel No 5
The world's most famous perfume was launched by Chanel in 1921. Its name came from the fact that Coco Chanel had allegedly rejected four other scents by perfumer Ernest Beaux before settling on his fifth.

through the exterior architecture and the plush interiors of the picture palaces. In New York, the greatest monument to Art Deco architecture was William van Alen's Chrysler building. This extraordinary skyscraper expresses the glamour of Art Deco both in its interior and exterior decoration and forms. The semi-circular pinnacles were faced in Nircosta metal to create gleaming white surfaces reminiscent of platinum (the metal most frequently chosen for contemporary jewelry).

Many famous designers who had made their names with products featuring the Art Nouveau style now adapted their designs to the new look. For example, René Lalique switched from his trademark organic-looking jewelry to Art Deco glassware, including car mascots, perfume bottles, and statuettes.

1920s' FASHION

In the 1920s, the Charleston became the first of many dance crazes to sweep America. To perform such energetic dancing, dresses had to be worn shorter to allow for greater freedom of

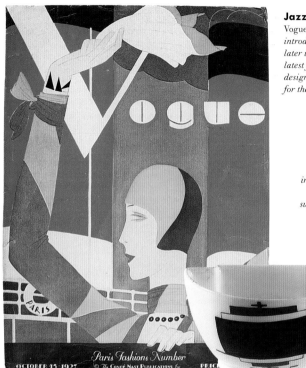

Jazz Age fashion
Vogue *was one of the magazines that introduced women, first in the US and later in Europe and Australia, to the latest fashions. This stylized cover was designed by Eduardo Benito in 1927 for the Paris fashions issue.*

Suprematist ceramics
Kazimir Malevich designed and Ilia Chashnik decorated this quite impractical porcelain cup in 1923, in line with the ideas of the Russian suprematist movement. Produced for the State Porcelain Factory, it was intended for export and exhibition in western Europe.

Paris Fashions Number

OCTOBER 15 1927 © The Condé Nast Publications Inc. PRIC

movement. Young women, known as "flappers," began to cut their hair into short bobs, and often wore cloche hats or berets. Designer Coco Chanel created a look to accompany women's new-found sense of confidence. Adapting men's clothes, she promoted a flat-chested, boyish silhouette, frequently worn with flamboyant costume jewelry, but above all designed for comfort and style, and to radiate youth. It perfectly reflected the spirit of the new era.

THE JAZZ AGE

Popular entertainment also influenced public taste. Jazz, which evolved in New Orleans at about the turn of the century, was now mainstream popular music. With the development of swing in Chicago, there were large ensembles playing with written orchestration. Benny Goodman, Count Basie, Artie Shaw, and Glenn Miller were all major musicians. The interior of Radio City Music Hall in New York, which opened in 1932, was designed in an Art Deco style by Donald Deskey using a jazz motif. Similar patterns were used in textiles, wallpaper, and ceramics.

SUPREMATISTS, CONSTRUCTIVISTS, AND VKHUTEMAS

In Russia, a desire similar to that of the Dutch De Stijl designers (see p.16) inspired a number of artists, among them the painter Kazimir Malevich, to attempt to find a universal relationship between geometric forms and pure color. Their work, termed suprematism, was more concerned with aesthetics and geometry than with functionality. It was superseded by less abstract constructivist design. The constructivists, who included the graphic designers El Lissitzky and Aleksandr Rodchenko, eschewed fine art and were committed to putting art to the service of the emerging socialist state. In 1920, constructivist ideas strongly influenced the VKhUTEMAS, a newly opened avant-garde design school in Moscow. (Its name is an abbreviation of Higher State Artistic and Technical Workshops.) Like the Bauhaus (see p.19), the school's aim was to train artists for industry. It shared many the characteristics with the German school; indeed, Wassily Kandinsky and El Lissitzky were active in both organizations. One of the teachers at VKhUTEMAS, Aleksandr Rodchenko, designed furniture for the Workers' Club at the 1925 Paris Expo. Textiles produced by his wife Varvara Stepanova (1894–1958) and Lyubov Popova (1889–1924) were also put into production. However, of the many furniture prototypes created by the school, not one became an industrial reality.

Photographic advances

Photography was popularized by the Brownie and the Vest Pocket Autographic Kodak cameras, and, by the 1920s, was an increasingly common hobby. The Leica A went into production in 1924 and was the first widely used 35mm camera, producing good-quality black-and-white shots.

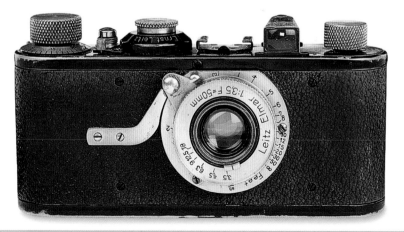

1930–39

Since the beginning of the century, designers had been experimenting with hydro- and aerodynamics. Based on studies of the shape and movement of fish and birds, it was discovered that boats and aircraft could be made more efficient by smoothing and curving the hull or fuselage. In 1933, the Douglas DC1 appeared as a commercial passenger aircraft. Strikingly different from its cumbersome predecessors, it had a streamlined monocoque structure, integrated wings, and a stressed aluminum skin that was strong enough not to need bracing wires. Along with the Boeing 247, it marked the beginning of modern passenger flight. In 1934, Chrysler launched its new streamlined car, the Airflow. Designed by Carl Breer, it was the result of thorough research into aerodynamics. Its curved unitary body, with sloping windshield and extended tail, was so different from previous cars that the public did not take to it and manufacturing stopped after just three years. However, the car was an engineering success and contributed much to the appliance of aerodynamics to car design, paving the way for car designers such as Ferdinand Porsche to create their aerodynamic sports cars.

AMERICAN STREAMLINING

Streamlining suggested speed, efficiency, and, most of all, modernity. Like Art Deco, it had a commercial imperative, for it became obvious that the consumer was attracted, if not to the Airflow, then to other streamlined products. The first sure evidence of this came in 1929 when Raymond Loewy redesigned the Gestetner duplicator (see p.350). Until then, it had been a

City of Salina train
This, the first American streamlined train, was designed in 1935. The torpedo-shaped front and rear ends and the enclosed chassis reduced wind resistance.

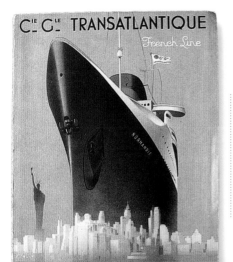

1930s' shipping poster

With transatlantic travel becoming popular, product designers such as Loewy and Teague were influenced by the streamlining of ocean liners, as shown on this poster.

US INDUSTRIAL DESIGN

Raymond Loewy was one of the most successful designers ever to work in the US. Essentially a stylist, he was responsible for redesigning the look of numerous products, including the Coldspot Super Six refrigerator (p.114) — which increased sales by 400 percent — the Lucky Strike cigarette packet (p.428), the Silversides Greyhound bus, and the Shell Oil company logo (p.368).

typical example of industrial machinery — no attempt had been made to make it pleasing to look at or easy to use. Loewy, using a full-size clay model to achieve the desired effect, enclosed all the working parts within a smooth, unifying body. The duplicator was a great commercial success and, in the US, designers began applying streamlining to a whole range of domestic appliances. Although the restyled products suggested improved efficiency, sometimes all that had changed was the housing.

Ergonomic design

Henry Dreyfuss designed for the human form, and in 1937 he collaborated with engineers to develop this telephone, making it supremely practical as well as stylish.

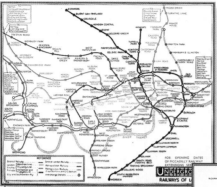

London Underground maps

The original maps showing the routes on the London Underground followed a traditional geographical approach (left). Then, in 1933, Henry Beck persuaded the newly formed London Transport to adopt a diagrammatic map (below). The vertical, horizontal, and 45-degree angles betray Beck's training as an electrical draftsman. Besides being easy to read, the main advantage is that the map permits the crowded central area to be enlarged in relation to the outlying areas. The hugely successful map has been imitated around the world.

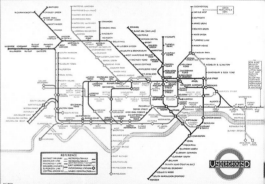

When it came to streamlining, American designers led the way: in addition to Loewy, Norman Bel Geddes, Walter Dorwin Teague, and Henry Dreyfuss all made contributions that influenced design throughout the world. Eventually, Dreyfuss developed a design theory concerned less with styling and more with the relationship between the machine and the operator. He believed that for a machine to be efficient it had to be adapted to people. He developed this theory into a study of ergonomics (how humans relate to objects) and anthropometrics (the study of body size and strength). Dreyfuss' reputation was established with the Bell 300 telephone. He designed it "from the inside out," carrying out detailed tests to ensure it would be easy to operate. It remained the standard American telephone for over 40 years, perhaps largely due to its enlightened approach toward the user.

SWEDISH MODERN

Although Art Deco and American streamlining dominated the 1930s, a separate style evolved in Scandinavia that was to be of increasing international importance during the 1940s and '50s. The term "Swedish Modern" was coined. Key designs during the 1930s were Wilhelm Kåge's ceramics, Kaj Franck's glassware, and the furniture of Alvar Aalto. The look was characterized by a soft, organic, natural feel influenced by traditional Scandinavian design, and a human scale.

BAKELITE AND NEW MATERIALS

In the 1930s, Alvar Aalto and Marcel Breuer both experimented with new forms of machine-processed wood such as plywood. Interest in other new materials was strong and centered on Bakelite. Invented and patented in 1907 by Belgian-born inventor Leo Baekeland, it was one of the first plastics to be used extensively. Its malleable properties were the perfect expression of the smooth, sleek contours of a streamlined product. Initially, it was used as a substitute for wood or ivory and was carved into shape from blocks. As designers began to exploit its own unique properties, it was molded into myriad shapes and used for electrical products. Bakelite was the most successful of the early plastics, and gave freedom to designers to style and restyle artifacts, leading to the boom in plastics after World War II.

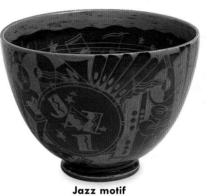

Jazz motif
Victor Schreckengost's 1931 punch bowl is an example of the continuing popularity of jazz.

Bakelite products
Bakelite was used for a wide range of goods. The Radio Nurse (shown left) was designed by the Japanese sculptor Isamu Noguchi in 1937 after the sensational Lindbergh kidnapping in the US. It consists of a microphone in the baby's room and a receiver shaped like a stylized nurse's head. The four-valve mains radio from 1950 (below) was nicknamed "the Toaster."

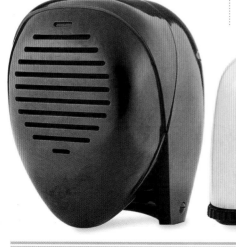

1940–49

World War II had a major impact on product design and manufacturing. Countries involved in the hostilities were quick to restrict the use of raw materials, and factories themselves were frequently turned over to military production. In 1941, Britain introduced a utility program in an attempt to ration the use of scarce resources. The Design Panel, which had Gordon Russell as its chairman, was charged with approving designs for production. The panel followed principles derived from the Arts and Crafts movement, but was also influenced by the European modernists. The furniture was required to be strong and attractive, but not wasteful in the use of materials. The use of some materials, such as silver and aluminum, were completely restricted or not available. Even dyes for textiles had to be approved through the utility program.

AUSTERITY DESIGNS

Of course, it was not only in Britain that government placed controls on manufacturing. In most of Europe, Japan, and the US, government restrictions prevented the unnecessary use of scarce materials. In Germany, under the *Schönheit der Arbeit* ("Beauty in Work") program, designers adopted an Arts and Crafts style, similar to that of Britain, with a particular emphasis on vernacular or rustic designs. In the US and Japan, industries were cut

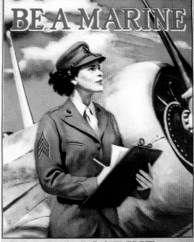

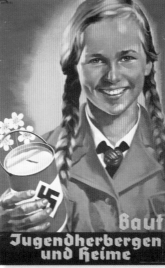

War posters
During wartime, the governments of all the participating countries were quick to commission graphic designers to produce information and propaganda posters. Many encouraged women to work in factories, on farms, or to join the forces.

back and price controls were put in place. Designers were put to work on a range of government commissions and often given an unexpected opportunity to try out new materials. This experimentation paid dividends after the war, as designers applied the new materials to the products they created for the domestic market. The results of these austerity measures were severely pared-down consumer products made from the most basic materials. Although they were low cost and by and large well made, they tended to be drab in appearance and lacked any sense of flair or luxury. In many countries, the regulations lasted long after the end of the war, and consumers soon became impatient with the continuing restrictions.

NEW LOOK FASHION

It was, therefore, hugely refreshing when the French designer Christian Dior showed off his first Paris collection in 1947. Women, desperate to escape from the sensible clothes of the war years, embraced the "New Look" — powerfully feminine, with softly rounded bodices, tight waists, long, very full skirts, and high-heeled shoes. With rationing still in place in many parts of Europe, the yards of fabric required to construct the huge skirts of Dior's designs were mostly unobtainable. Not all women loved the look. Some, who saw it as extravagant and indulgent, picketed the House of Dior, further adding to his reputation. Nevertheless, the more elegant look quickly gained popularity, and manufacturers tried to produce something akin to Dior's vision but using less fabric. For men, too, shapeless wartime suits were replaced with a narrower silhouette.

Dior's "New Look"

After years of rationing and constraint, Dior's "New Look" made a powerful impact. His clothes made women feel feminine again.

Charles Eames' chair
Husband and wife Charles and Ray Eames were famous for their chair designs for the Herman Miller company. Their work featured simple, open designs and the recurrent use of molded wood.

ITALIAN DESIGN
In Italy in 1946, former helicopter designer Corradino d'Ascanio designed the Vespa scooter for Piaggio (see p.305). This exciting, streamlined, modern vehicle became a symbol of postwar *ricostruzione* and attracted worldwide sales. After the war, Italy consolidated its design practice, eventually becoming a world leader. Companies such as Fiat, Olivetti, and Cassina employed avant-garde designers to make products that would hold their own in the world of international commerce.

NEW MATERIALS
Plastics became increasingly important materials after World War II; and their use has significantly changed the way things look. Before then, they had been regarded only as substitutes. But after the war, many designers deliberately chose to exploit the properties of particular plastics for individual projects. The following are just a few examples. Acrylic, such as Plexiglas, had been discovered in the 1930s and was put to use in furniture design and as a lightweight replacement for glass. See-through films, such as PVC, were used to produce waterproof raincoats and umbrellas. Nylon was utilized by the American forces for parachutes. In 1942, Earl Tupper introduced lightweight polyethylene containers with airtight lids. Known as Tupperware, they were available in a range of pastel colors and were both flexible and hardwearing. One of the most exciting developments was in the use

Unconventional vase
Italian designer Paolo Venini combined his bold sense of color and texture with traditional glassmaking techniques to produce the Handkerchief vase. First made in 1946, the design became extremely popular.

of plastics for modern chairs. The pioneers of this work were the American architect Charles Eames, together with his wife, Ray, and Eero Saarinen. During the war, Eames had worked with glass-reinforced polyester to make radar domes for aircraft. By applying the knowledge he had acquired from this work to chair design, he produced a one-piece molded seat shell supported on wire legs, which was known as the DAR chair, in 1948. Unlike the Womb chair produced earlier by Saarinen (see p.62), Eames's chair was left uncovered so the glass-reinforced plastic construction was exposed. Many of Eames's seating designs were put into production by Herman Miller.

RADIO AND TELEVISION

Radio stations had started broadcasting in the early 1920s, and domestic radio became more popular during the following decade. However, it was only with the outbreak of World War II that the various warring governments realized radio's potential for disseminating information and propaganda both to their own civilians and to the enemy. The importance of national broadcasting during the war led to an explosion in the use of the radio.

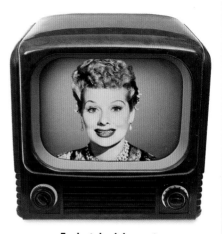

Early television set
This television set by Bush has a Bakelite case molded into a shape reminiscent of the Art Deco radios produced a decade earlier.

After the war, television began to make an impact on domestic life. A television transmitter had been demonstrated by John Logie Baird in 1926, but it was not until the late 1930s that cathode ray tubes were capable of receiving high-definition broadcasts. As with radios and record players, early televisions were housed in traditional cabinets, giving them the appearance of items of furniture, with no indication as to the true purpose. As the technology improved, designers began experimenting with new materials and finding solutions more fitting to the function. Bakelite could be molded, initially to fit the shape of the screen and subsequently to find expressive forms. In Europe, however, it was not until the following decade that the television became commonplace.

1950–59

The inferno that was World War II had given way to the chill of the cold war, played out by the capitalist US and the communist Soviet Union. Competition between the two systems came to be symbolized by the space program: the frantic race between the superpowers to become leaders in space exploration. The Soviets took the initiative: in 1957, they launched Sputnik 1, the first satellite to orbit the earth. Then in 1961, the Soviet cosmonaut Yuri Gagarin became the first man in space. Just eight years later, American Neil Armstrong took his "giant leap for mankind" by walking on the Moon. Science, space travel, and science fiction became an all-consuming obsession. Scientific motifs came to be associated with modernity and appeared everywhere throughout the decade.

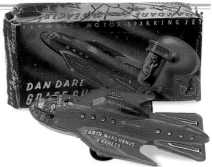

Dan Dare toy
Many manufacturers saw enormous opportunities for product development in the space obsession, and geared product design to this market. A whole new range of toys, for example, featured Dan Dare, hero of the British comic Eagle *(founded 1950).*

Harley Earl's dream machine
Regarded by many as the epitome of 1950s' style, the rocket-styled 1959 pink Cadillac Eldorado convertible is truly a fantasy vehicle.

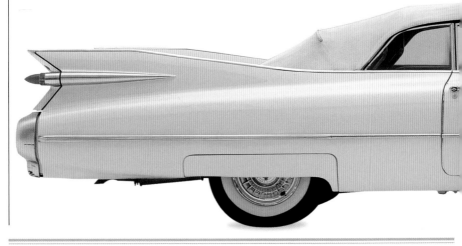

Youth culture

The 1950s marked the emergence of a vibrant new teen culture with its own dress, behavior, music, and language. Singers like Elvis Presley and film stars like James Dean became role models for this affluent consumer group.

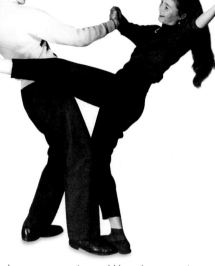

CONSUMERISM

In the 1950s, car design in the US took on a new, extravagant look. Inspired by aircraft and rockets, Harley Earl of General Motors began to alter the shape of cars in a way that expressed the postwar confidence of American society. His cars were wide, low, and very long. They had lavish interiors, imaginative tail fins, loads of chrome, wraparound windshields, and came in striking colors. During this time, the controversial strategy of planned obsolescence emerged in the US. By introducing small stylistic changes, companies could launch new versions of their products each year, thereby appealing to those conscious of social status by making last year's model stylistically obsolete. Of greater concern was the decision to build in physical

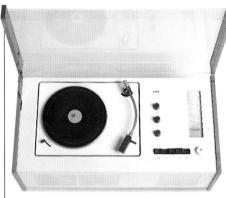

Braun Phonosuper SK55 1956

This stylish piece of minimalist design came just in time for the revolution in music marketing caused by the arrival of rock music. The single unit incorporates both radio and record player. A Plexiglass hood kept the record in view while protecting it from damage.

obsolescence, so that through a lack of actual durability the product only had a limited lifespan. The debatable defense of this huge waste of resources was increased employment.

INTERNATIONAL STYLE

In contrast to the cynicism of planned obsolescence, some companies, most notably Braun in Germany and Saab in Scandinavia, began to design and market goods on the basis of their durability. In 1955, the Swiss industrial designer, sculptor, and painter Max Bill (1908–) co-founded the Hochschule für Gestaltung in Ulm, Germany. Bill had studied at the Bauhaus, and his aim was to continue that school's rationalist approach to design. This revival of the modernist style took the search for a

machine aesthetic further than before; it required design to be forward-looking, reflecting modern life, and embracing technology. This functionalist approach, which is often referred to as the International Style, was most clearly represented in product design by the Ulm school. Financed by commissions, the school had close links with industry. Among its first and most important commissions was a series of radios and phonographs for Braun by Hans Gugelot and Otl Aicher. This helped formalize Braun's reductionist design philosophy, and the continued collaboration between Gugelot and Dieter Rams of Braun brought about the development of the "black box syndrome" in modern design. Anything unnecessary to the function of the product was stripped away. Clean lines, durability, balance, and unification were key requirements. All Braun products are clearly related, often finished in glossy white or black, with the company logo visibly marked on the casing.

TRANSISTORS

One of the most significant developments in the look of electronic equipment was the invention of the transistor in 1947 by Bell Laboratories. Made from silicon and only requiring a low electric current to function,

Molded chair

Arne Jacobsen's 3107 chair is one of many 1950s' furniture designs that incorporated steel rods or steel wire. Ernest Race's Antelope chair (see p.62) and Harry Bertoia's Diamond chair (see p.63) are others. Jacobsen's chair is still much copied today.

these small, robust components were used for items such as radios, televisions, and record players, in which they replaced the cumbersome vacuum tube. The Tokyo Telecommunications Engineering Corporation (later known as Sony) produced the first mass-produced transistorized pocket radio in 1955, and in 1959 developed the

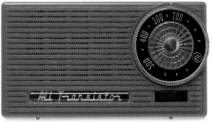

Transistor radio

By replacing radio valves with transistors, which were smaller, more robust, and used less power, radio sets shrank in size. Their low cost and portability made them popular with teenagers, and bright colors were often adopted to add to their appeal. This particular model was made in the US.

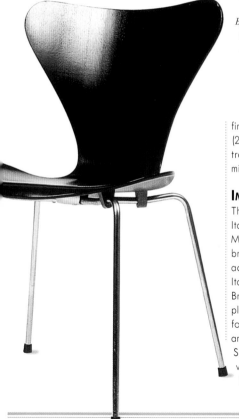

first all-transistorized television with an 8-in (20-cm) screen. The diminutive size of the transistor gave designers the freedom to miniaturize all other electronic appliances.

IMPORTANT COUNTRIES

The 1950s marked a high point in 20th-century Italian design. Designers such as Gio Ponti, Marco Zanuso, Marcello Nizzoli, the Castiglioni brothers, "Pinin" Farina, and Ettore Sottsass achieved great success for themselves and for Italian companies such as Olivetti, Artemide, and Brionvega. Elsewhere, Denmark became a major player on the international design stage, noted for its mass-produced furniture, luxury silverware, and innovative textiles and wallpapers. Denmark's Scandinavian neighbors Finland and Sweden were also enjoying much design success. Finnish glassware became a design leader for years to come.

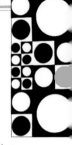

1960–69

During the 1960s, the postwar baby boomers were growing up, and *en masse* they created a powerful new army of consumers. They were coming of age in a period of unparalleled, unrestrained optimism and self-belief: the war, and the postwar austerity, was over; humans were in space and would soon walk on the Moon; the first heart transplant had taken place; and 60 years after the first flight across the English Channel, Concorde would be flying faster than the speed of sound across the Atlantic Ocean. "We live," one commentator said, "in a throwaway society, obsolescence is created by the rapid advances in technology; built-in obsolescence is no longer relevant, so why is the functionalism of the International Style relevant?" So began the rejection of Modernism, which was no longer able to meet the demands of this eager new force of consumers, who wanted change and variety in the place of permanence and uniformity. Most of all, they wanted a look they could call their own, that divorced them from their parents, and that reinforced the gap that had grown between the pre- and postwar generations.

MASS CONSUMERISM

During this period, the power of advertising, particularly on television, led to the birth of mass consumerism. Manufacturers quickly recognized the buying power of the teenage population and began to create products aimed specifically at the youth market.

A combination of new materials, new shapes, new technology, and new colors vied for the attention of these affluent young people. This manifested itself in all areas of design: in the automobile industry, the Mini was born; in fashion, the miniskirt appeared; and in graphics, Wes Wilson produced his barely legible posters. There were myriad radical furniture designs: Danish designer Verner Panton produced his bright red, moulded plastic stacking chair; and Gunner Aagaard Anderson (1919–) of Denmark created his polyurethane Armchair, an extraordinary item that looks like — and, in fact, is — a huge solidified blob of poured liquid plastic.

This period also saw Europe adopting the values that had been prevalent in the United States a decade earlier, those of shortlived products in a throwaway society.

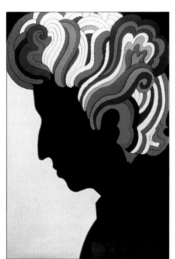

Psychedelic poster for the *Dylan* album

Bob Dylan has himself become an icon of the 1960s. Illustrated here by Milton Glaser in 1966, Dylan's hair is rendered as a pattern of colorful psychedelic swirls.

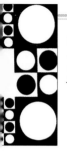

Black-and-white textile
Danish furniture and textile designer Verner Panton designed this Op Art fabric in 1961.

Space-age clothes
In 1969, models displayed the latest Martian wigs by French coiffeur Jean-Louis St. Roch. "Space-age" clothes were made popular by Pierre Cardin and André Courrèges.

1960s FASHION

In the world of fashion, one of the names that stands out above the others is Mary Quant. Rejecting *haute couture*, she aimed her designs at the young, and produced inexpensive and fun clothes. She remains best-remembered as the designer responsible for introducing the miniskirt and hot pants to Britain. The space age continued to influence fashion, and designers created outfits in futuristic materials, typified by Courrèges' "silver-foil" suits.

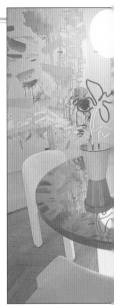

PSYCHEDELIA

Youth movements abounded; each had its own music, its own dress code, and its own visual language. One, Psychedelia, was a shortlived but incandescent revivalist movement that had a far-reaching influence. Psychedelic designers rejected modernism out of hand. Where modernists looked only to the future for inspiration, Psychedelia looked anywhere and everywhere, often through the blur of hallucinogenic drugs. Artists sought inspiration from the early part of the century, incorporating aspects of Art Nouveau and the Vienna Secession into their work; they looked to

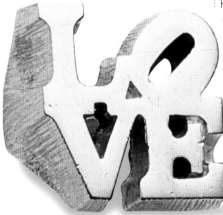

Pop Art jewelry
Pop artist Robert Indiana's LOVE ring was made in gilded metal in about 1966 and became an instant classic.

the East, and as far into the past as ancient Egypt for references; and they looked at their own world, creating a visual drug-inspired language that was aimed at a select audience.

POP ART

Fashion and art have had a huge influence on product design, and no art movement has had a greater impact on commercial design than Pop Art. Pop artists such as Andy Warhol, Jasper Johns (1930–), Roy Lichtenstein (1923–), and Robert Indiana were turning the art world on its head by drawing the everyday into their studios and recycling it as ironic, irreverent art. Andy Warhol openly celebrated American consumerism in his repeat-image paintings of iconic images of popular culture, be it Campbell's soup cans or Elvis Presley. Ironically, manufacturers themselves began to use Pop Art in product design, marketing, and advertising – so much so that it soon became a part of everyday life. For example, Robert Indiana's "LOVE" image appeared on 320 million postage stamps. Other fine art movements, notably Op Art, were also taken up by product and textile designers.

ITALIAN INFLUENCE

In Europe, Italian designers had taken the lead role on the international stage, and many acknowledged the influence of the Pop artists in their work. Joe Colombo, Ettore Sottsass, and

Interior design

This 1960s domestic dining area shows the contemporary fascination with plastics, transparent materials, bright colors, and soft shapes.

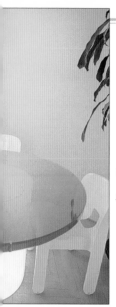

Spherical television

JVC's Videosphere from 1970 has a plastic case and looks like an astronaut's helmet, reflecting public interest in space travel.

plastic Grillo telephone, regardless of its material. Other Italian designers were making a contribution with innovative furniture designs. Two of the most famous are the Sacco chair by Gatti, Paolini, and Teodoro — a structureless, polystyrene-filled bag that is now regarded as the first beanbag chair; and the Blow Armchair by de Pas, d'Urbino, and Lomazzi — an inflatable plastic chair that relied on air for its shape and comfort. These radical Italian designers in turn influenced the post-modernist designers of the following decades.

Marco Zanuso, freed from the constraints of modernism, took on board the playfulness of the age and began to toy with the new themes. Their work, dubbed "Radical" or "Anti-Design," drew on popular taste. Joe Colombo experimented with plastic for his furniture designs, as did Sottsass in such classics as the vividly styled orange-red and yellow Valentine typewriter. The Italian designers more or less rescued plastic from its reputation as cheap and therefore undesirable, an image that had grown from its use in disposable designs such as the Bic Biro. Few could fail to see the beauty and sophistication of Marco Zanuso and Richard Sapper's

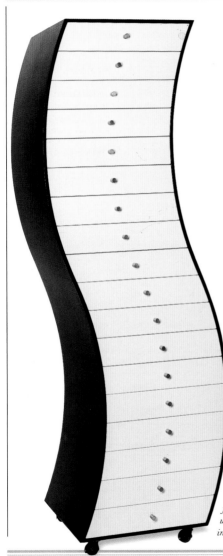

1970–79

Italy continued as a center for design excellence into the 1970s and as a leader in Radical design. Many of its chief designers are linked to the most important design movement of the decade – postmodernism.

POSTMODERNISM

The term can be applied to many aspects of our lives, cultural and social, but has particular relevance in the world of art, architecture, and design. It is essentially a rejection of everything entailed in modernism, which detracters argue is élitist, unintelligible, unattractive, and unappealing. The postmodernist's aim was to popularize the highbrow, and to make the intellectual accessible. Exponents borrowed freely from history, reworking the color, texture, or material, often as a witty parody of the original source. While many of the most important protagonists of postmodernism are Italian, it is a truly international movement. Its leaders include Ettore Sottsass, whose work is typified by the Carlton sideboard (see p.222); the American architect Robert Venturi, who designed the classic postmodernist building Chestnut Hill House in Pennsylvania; and Michele de Lucchi, who created the prototypes shown here. The postmodernists rejected the

Furniture in irregular forms

This wooden chest of drawers is one of the best-known pieces by Shiro Kuramata and was created for Fujiko in 1970 at a time when Japanese design was being recognized as an innovative force on the international stage. It is shaped like an elongated "S."

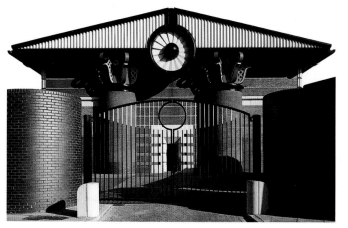

Postmodernist architecture

Architect John Outram's pumping station at Blackwall, Isle of Dogs, London, is a classic example of postmodernist architecture. Many structures described by this term feature elements borrowed from the architecture of older periods, such as classical columns and pediments.

modernist's utopian aims and their search for a universal aesthetic, and instead looked to create a visual language that was made up of signs, visual metaphors, references to the past, and to the work of other designers. As a result, the post-modernists have been accused of continuing the élitism they despise by assuming an understanding of the references made in their work, and for the prevalence of "in-jokes." Another criticism that has been leveled at postmodernism is that it has been manipulated by the forces of commerce, and has produced little more than an incoherent

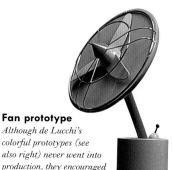

Fan prototype

Although de Lucchi's colorful prototypes (see also right) never went into production, they encouraged more decorative, fun product design.

Toaster prototype

Michele de Lucchi created a series of ten appliance prototypes for Girmi. Made of colored wood, they included a vacuum cleaner, coffee grinder, teapot, and hair dryer, as well as this toaster. They were first shown at the 1979 Milan Triennale.

mishmash of styles. By the 1970s, manufacturing allowed for limited production, and for all types of products to be tailored to accommodate the demands of a small market. This caused a shift in emphasis away from mass production and towards meeting the needs of the individual.

Sports cars

Another important area of Italian design influence in the 1970s is the sports car. The decade saw the birth of the supercar, with Italian manufacturers Lamborghini, Ferrari, and Lancia competing with the likes of Porsche, Triumph, and Jaguar to produce the sleekest, lowest, fastest, most powerful car in the world. Cars such as the Lamborghini Countach were capable of 0–60mph (0–96km/h) in 5.1 seconds, and had a top speed of 187mph (301km/h). However, the spiraling gas prices that resulted from the oil crisis of

1973, made gas-guzzling cars less popular, and so manufacturers began to look at more fuel-economic alternatives.

Japan began to emerge as a main player in car design in the 1970s, and more so in the field of motorcycle design, an area now dominated by the Japanese through the efforts of Yamaha, Honda, Suzuki, and Kawasaki. The Japanese also led the world in the development of new technology. By the 1970s, many of its manufacturing companies, such as Nikon, Olympus, Sony, and Sharp, were growing in commercial stature. Their goods typically featured a "high-tech" look. In graphic design, fashion, and furniture production, too, young Japanese designers were increasingly being recognized as playing an important international role. They were among the first to recognize and exploit the value of computer technology in the design process.

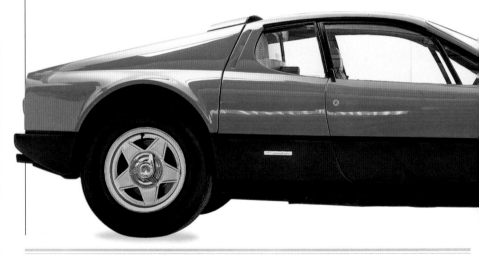

Olivetti Divisumma 18

A leading exponent of Italian design, Mario Bellini has produced many stylish products for Olivetti. This brightly colored calculator is typical of his work, featuring an expressive surface created by the rubber "skin."

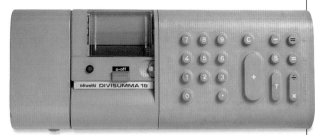

THE MICROCHIP

The theory behind the microchip, one of the most important inventions of the century, was originally devised by an American, Jack Kirby of Texas Instruments. Its development meant that electronic components could be reduced unimaginably in size. By 1970, for example, thousands of components could be printed on top of a single silicon chip measuring only ¼in (5mm) square. Without this invention, a personal computer would take up the space of a living room and a pocket calculator would be the size of a small car. Microchip technology is now commonplace in the household and workplace: in telephones, washing machines, video recorders, and cars. In industry, its use has seen the monotonous tasks of the production-line worker slowly being taken over by robots. A classic example of the application of microchip technology is the Sony Walkman personal stereo (see p.105), which was introduced in 1979. It was originally thought that because it could not record, the product might not be successful; yet it was an instant success and spawned numerous imitators.

Ferrari 365 GT4 Berlinetta Boxer

In production from 1973 to 1976, only 387 Boxers were built. At the time of the launch, it was hyped as one of the fastest GT cars ever built. In fact, it was slower than the Ferrari model it replaced, achieving 170mph (274km/h). During the boom of the mid-1980s, when classic cars were highly sought after, the Boxer was selling for double its original price.

1980–89

Technological advances produced
many changes in the penultimate
decade of the 20th century. The
computer age had definitely arrived,
and designers were increasingly
utilizing sophisticated programs to
carry out many aspects of product
design that had traditionally been
drawn or made by hand. For graphic
designers, too, the new technology
created myriad new possibilities
for manipulating typesetting and
image reproduction.

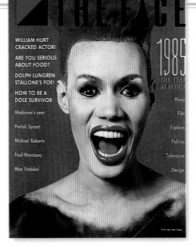

New typefaces
*The new Apple
Macintosh of 1984
enabled designers
to manipulate, and
eventually to invent,
new typefaces. This
design element was
taken to new heights
by Neville Brody,
art director of the
influential British
magazine* The Face.

COMPUTER TECHNOLOGY

Home computing began to slowly take off in the
1980s, accelerating astonishingly into the 1990s.
The first personal computer (PC) had been
developed by IBM in the late 1970s, and
was introduced as the IBM PC
in 1981. However, the real
breakthrough came

**Marketing
phenomenon**
*In less than ten
years the compact
disk has established
itself as the pre-
eminent method
of sound recording
for the home
entertainment market,
despite being more
expensive than the vinyl
recordings that it superceded.*

with the introduction of the Apple Macintosh in
1984 (see p.344). It improved the user-friendliness
of the home computer, and introduced the now
ubiquitous mouse. The compact disk (CD), which
first appeared in 1982, has revolutionized the
music industry. CDs record information digitally
as a series of numbers. This stored information
is read and translated by a laser beam, which
allows the music to be reproduced clearly.
The CD has now all but replaced the vinyl disc
in most homes.

Sound is not the only type of information
that can be recorded on CDs; they are also
able to store text and pictures, and even video
sequences. This ability is utilized in the CD-ROM
player. Invented in 1985 by the Dutch electronics
manufacturing giant, Philips, this innovation was
jointly marketed with Sony. Basically a CD
adapted for use with a computer, a CD-ROM can
store one thousand times as much information as
a floppy disk. The initials ROM stand for "Read-

Only Memory," indicating that the information can only be read, not added to or changed. The CD-ROM did not conquer the domestic market until the 1990s.

THE GLOBAL VILLAGE

The term "global village" began to be used as new technology made possible instant communication with virtually any part of the world. Fax machines became a familiar part of the office, and modems and electronic mail (e-mail) enabled people to communicate cheaply and instantly via computer. Satellites were developed in the US in the 1960s by NASA, the National Aeronautics and Space Administration, and by the 1980s thousands of satellites orbiting the earth were being used for telecommunications and broadcasting. Another invention, the cellular, or portable, telephone, first developed in 1979 by the Swedish company Ericsson, became commonplace during the 1980s.

PUNK AND BRITISH DESIGN

In the late 1970s, Britain saw the appearance of a new, aggressive street style — Punk — that was, in tamer forms, to have an influence on graphics, fashion, and culture in the 1980s. In fashion, Vivienne Westwood's 1981 Pirate collection translated the Punk look into successful main street fashion and marked the revival of British fashion

as an international force. Punk also had a great influence on new-wave graphics, exemplified in Britain by Jamie Reid's controversial record covers for the Sex Pistols, and in Terry Jones's *i-D* magazine. Something of the shock appeal of Punk is also evident in the furniture of Ron Arad (see p.452) and the industrial designs of Daniel Weil (see p.93).

MEMPHIS

Undoubtedly, the most important design group of the decade was Memphis. It was started in Milan by Ettore Sottsass after he left the radical Studio Alchimia in 1980. He surrounded himself with a group of international architects and furniture, fabric, and ceramics designers, including Andrea Branzi, Martine Bedin, George Sowden (1942–), Peter Shire, Michael Graves, Javier Mariscal (1950–), Michele de Lucchi, and Matteo Thun. They first showed their work at the 1981 Milan Furniture Fair, where it was an immediate success, although some critics attacked it for being tasteless. A post-modernist group, Memphis

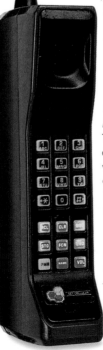

Cellnet mobile telephone

Portable telephones have evolved from large and cumbersome units into sleek, pocket-sized instruments. It has been predicted that their rapidly increasing popularity will one day see the disappearance of fixed-point telephones.

UNIVERSAL DESIGN

In total contrast, the industrial design consultancy Ergonomi Design Gruppen was founded in Sweden in 1969 to specialize in the ergonomic design of everyday tools. A key interest for partners Maria Benktzon (1946–) and Sven-Eric Juhlin (1940–) was design for people with limited physical abilities, and one of the group's best-known designs is a line of cutlery called Eat/Drink, which clearly embodies the design philosophy that "the need and desires of the user shall form the basis of the project." Despite being the focus of increasing concern through the 1980s and '90s, universal design, or design for disability, as it is also known, is still a largely neglected area. Attention is likely to increase as the population balance shifts with more people living into old age. Computer technology is also increasing access and creating opportunities for all people. For example, despite having been "disabled" at the age of 20 by a crippling disease that left him unable to walk, speak, or

Post-modernist ceramics

Peter Shire, who was a member of Ettore Sottsass' Memphis group, is noted for his eccentric ceramic designs. The California Peach Cup, made in 1980, is typical of his work and a good example of post-modernist design.

borrowed from an eclectic variety of sources, including anything from classical architecture to 1950s' kitsch. It made startling and innovative use of bold, often outrageous, coloring, and laid more emphasis on the look and meaning of the object than on its practical usage. What started out as a polemical venture proved to be an enormous commercial success. However, the ideas of the Memphis group, which typified the more excessive aspects of postmodernism, were quickly exhausted.

Eat/Drink cutlery

This functional yet attractive cutlery set was designed in 1980 for people with limited strength. The design of the knife is such that pressure is applied with the arm rather than just the wrist.

write, the eminent British physicist Stephen Hawking has been enabled to work by communicating through a voice synthesizer and computer.

SOCIAL CONSCIENCE

"Design for need" started as an international conference that took place in London in 1976. It pointed to the growing feeling that design should be addressing issues relating to the environment, ecological concerns, and special problems occurring in underdeveloped countries. The problem was that design had for too long been concentrating on production and consumerism. A series of ecological threats in the 1980s provoked designers into focusing more clearly on green issues. One result was a move toward designing products that could be recycled. This began to feed through to affect all areas of design. For example, the French designer Philippe Starck, who

became one of the most celebrated designers of the 1980s, created his Louis 20 stacking chairs (see p.331) with the legs screwed rather than glued to the body, so that the parts could be separated and recycled. Designers began to realize that they had an important role to play in finding solutions to large-scale global problems of the environment and the way that people live.

Modern vase

Philippe Starck's work often gives an appearance of instability that is confounded by its actual sturdiness. This three-legged vase seems precariously balanced on the tapered, slanting feet. However, the sheer weight of the glass makes the structure rigid and stable.

1990–99

On a visit to Africa in the early 1990s, Trevor Baylis, a British inventor, became aware of the importance of radio for sending information to remote communities that lacked an electric power supply. Although many village communities had radios, these were more or less unused, because the batteries were prohibitively expensive. This meant valuable information, particularly relating to health, did not always reach those who needed it most. Baylis' response was to invent a wind-up radio that could generate enough power to be self-sufficient. In collaboration with a manufacturer, he produced a model that is now being successfully used across the world. The wind-up radio highlights two of the most important design imperatives for the 1990s: ecology and communication.

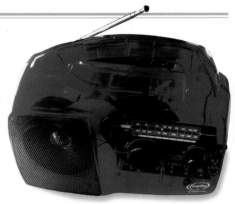

Wind-up Freeplay Radio
Trevor Baylis' wind-up radio was launched in 1995. It shows how knowledge that has been available for generations can be used as effectively as new technology.

ECOLOGICAL CONCERNS

Some designers in the 1990s have been concerned with undoing the damage that humans have inflicted on the planet with the mass industrialization of the 19th and 20th centuries, or at least with trying to stem future damage. In 1985, scientists discovered that there was a dangerously large hole in the ozone layer. They contended that if it was permitted to grow, the temperature of the planet would increase with catastrophic effects. Governments responded with atypical speed, collaborating with the Montreal Protocol — signed in 1987 and reinforced in 1990 — and imposing controls on items such as aerosols and refrigerators that contained potentially harmful chlorofluoro-carbons (better known as CFCs). It had already become clear in the 1970s and '80s that the world's resources were being exhausted at a rate that could not be sustained.

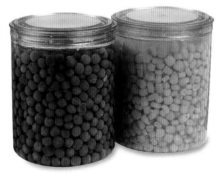

Plastic Can
These plastic cans are made from a new molding technique where the lid and container are made from the same type of plastic. The patented design can be produced in-house alongside the product itself.

Fossil fuels will not last forever, so designers are beginning to explore solutions that may slow down and even stop the depletion of raw materials. For example, alternative sources of energy are being devised: solar cars have been developed in Australia and elsewhere; and the electric car, once an inventor's dream, is now a reality. In response to the rapid depletion of the forests caused by the ever-increasing demand for paper and wood, alternative forms of communication and information storage are being developed, in addition to using more recycled paper. However, the idea of a paperless office, relying solely on electronic storage, is still a long way from being realized.

RECYCLED GOODS

Built-in obsolescence is beginning to be replaced by a more responsible approach to product durability. As well as incorporating more recycled materials in their products, designers are creating more energy-efficient products that can be recycled or repaired. A well-designed car is one that uses little fuel, produces few

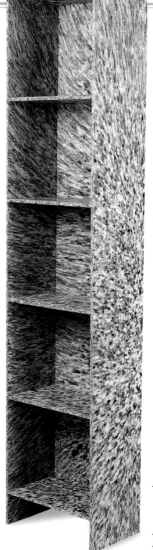

emissions, lasts a long time, can be easily repaired, and at the end of its life can be broken down with the component materials either being recycled or disposed of safely. In the rapidly advancing computer industry, the trend is now to create machines that can be upgraded to keep pace with new developments, rather than having to replace the whole machine.

ADVANCES IN MASS COMMUNICATION

The 1990s have also seen the most astonishing advances in communication. The Internet and the World Wide Web promise to have as much impact on our lives as the invention of the telephone, the television, or the automobile. All you need is a computer and modem to have instant access to information databases around the world. For example, from your own

Recycled storage unit

Jane Atfield's shelving unit, made from plastic recovered from used dish detergent bottles, is an example of the growing trend among designers to produce furniture and other products from recycled materials.

Hot Springs radiators

These efficient tubular radiators are made from a continuous length of steel. Heat output is increased by air being drawn up through the center of the coil.

living room in Paris or Sydney or Munich, you could access the Smithsonian Institute in Washington DC, or tour the Natural History Museum in London. At this relatively early stage in its development, it is impossible to guess just how great its impact will be on the 21st century, just as noone could have guessed in 1900 how great the impact of the telephone would be on our lives.

BUILDING FOR THE FUTURE

There is growing pressure on developers to consider the environment when constructing new houses. Although they still remain in a minority, some architects and designers are taking the idea further by choosing environmentally friendly materials for their buildings. New homes are being made that are energy efficient. Better ventilation systems and improved insulation means less energy is required for cooling and heating. Solar panels are being used to generate electricity or supply hot water. Consumers are also starting to buy "green" products such as low-energy light bulbs and washing machines with economy settings. These not only save money, they also have a long-term benefit for the environment. In the 21st century we may see buildings and products that are ecological, yet still able to deliver the conveniences of a modern home.

THE INFLUENCE OF THE COMPUTER

Microprocessors form an integral part of modern technology. They feature in a huge range of household objects, from refrigerators to video players; but their most spectacular use is in computers. The processing power of computers has grown incredibly since they were first introduced to the public. Most personal computers are able to carry out a wide range of programs and support complex interactive games. The influence of the computer in our working and domestic lives and its use in mass communication has led to a process of digitization in other technologies. Videos are now available in digital format, music on compact discs is recorded digitally, and the digital camera now

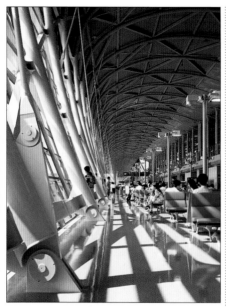

Modern architecture

Kansai International Airport, situated on Osaka Bay, Japan, was designed by Renzo Piano. It has been built on a man-made island and has its own train running the length of its 1 mile- (1.6km-) long terminal.

means that images can be recorded directly onto a computer disk. The image can then be manipulated on the computer screen before being printed out or even sent across the Internet. The influence of computing is also evident in the modern typefaces seen in magazine design, and in the public's increasing acceptance of technology that looks like technology, machines no longer designed to look like articles of furniture.

Traveling the World

Even with all the advances in mass communication people still desire to travel around the world for business or pleasure and, more than ever, our skies are filled with aircraft. To accommodate this growth, new airports are needed. At the same time, older airports are being expanded and local road and rail networks developed to take the extra traffic. The impact of this expansion can be damaging to the surrounding region. New aircraft are being designed to carry more passengers, making them less harmful to the environment. But the damage caused by the infrastructure required to cater for the movement of large numbers of people may be less easy to manage.

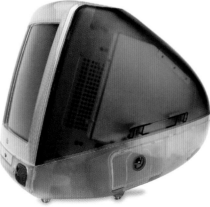

The iMac

The iMac is a general purpose home computer, with a built-in modem, that breaks away from traditional computer design. It is constructed from a strong translucent plastic and comes in a range of colors: strawberry, grape, blueberry, tangerine, and lime.

THE FUTURE

As we look forward most would agree there is a pressing need to protect the world's resources and control the causes of pollution. The arguments for responsible design and manufacture have been well made and our current systems of production and consumption are clearly not sustainable. Yet we in the West seem unwilling to abandon the conveniences of late 20th-century mass production. We have grown accustomed to the advantages of the latest electrical appliances and shopping in stores filled with seductively packaged new goods. In spite of increasing congestion Western drivers insist on traveling even short distances by car.

A BREATH OF FRESH AIR

Our towns and cities are choking from pollution caused by motor vehicles, cars compete for space and public transportation fails to meet the demands of a population that has grown up accustomed to the benefits of private travel. There have been some successes with public transportation: for example the black taxi has become a design icon for London. The latest version of the cab has rounded forms, typical of late 1990s car design. But this particular cab is unique; it is powered by a fuel-cell engine. Until recently, experiments with electric cars failed to provide an acceptable alternative to the internal combustion engine. They still require large heavy batteries and the regular need to recharge them is inconvenient. The fuel-cell engine offers an alternative; it uses hydrogen to generate electricity, removing the reliance on batteries. The result is an almost silent car that emits little more than water vapor.

THE FUTURE

In the final decade of the century, scientific and technological developments are not slowing down; they are increasing with mind-boggling rapidity. The changes that will take place in the next century will be even more marked than those that took place in the last. Although it is impossible to predict exactly what the future will bring, there are some indicators.

The mobile phone

In the 1990s the mobile phone became ubiquitous and manufacturers had to constantly come up with new models in order to market their product. One innovative design was Nokia phones with interchangeable colored covers.

For example, the miniaturization of much technology: machines are being created that are a mere half a millimeter in diameter and that can be injected into the veins to clear blood clots. Probes from the International Space Station visiting Mars, Jupiter, and beyond will increase our knowledge of the solar system. Already the Hubble telescope is sending back photographs that are rewriting our understanding of the universe. This may reawaken interest in space exploration. In the transportation industry, there is now talk of a revolutionary new generation of superjets, superseding Concorde and flying outside the earth's atmosphere. These superjets will make transglobal flights possible in a fraction of the time they currently take.

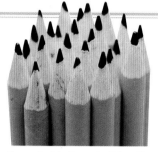

Remarkable Recycled Pencils

These pencils are made from 70 percent recycled polystyrene vending cups. They write and sharpen like traditional pencils, but do not waste natural resources.

between humans and technology, and between our bodies and machines, will clearly be one of the most challenging aspects in the next millennium. It remains to be seen what impact these changes will have upon design. Generally, developments in technology have created new possibilities in design, and the development of increasingly sophisticated materials has freed up designers to experiment with different forms and ultimately change our preconceptions of how an object should look. Sometimes our glimpses of the future can be disturbing; but by studying how designers have found solutions to the problems of the past through the history of design we may look to the future with more optimistic eyes.

THE NEW MILLENNIUM

Scientific and technological developments, then, are speeding up, often at a pace that overwhelms us. The increasing interface

Millennium taxi – TX1

The new London taxi retains its familiar shape and features a host of innovations to improve driver and passenger comfort. The example shown here contains a prototype hydrogen fuel-cell that does not pollute.

THE LIVING ROOM

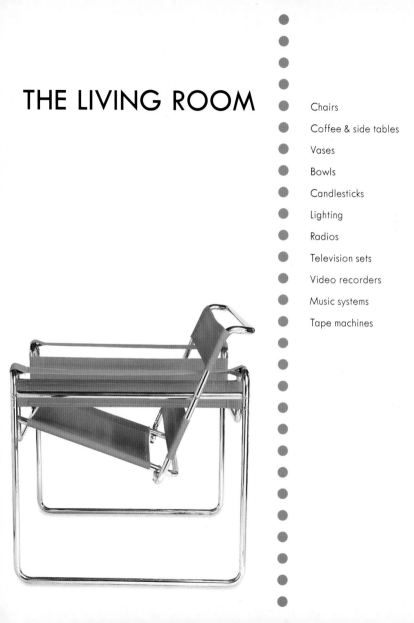

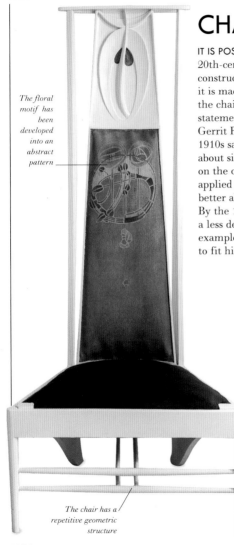

The floral motif has been developed into an abstract pattern

The chair has a repetitive geometric structure

CHAIRS

IT IS POSSIBLE TO TRACE all the major themes of 20th-century furniture design through the look, construction, and materials of the chair. Whether it is made from modern or traditional means, the chair has been used by designers to make statements about their personal design philosophy. Gerrit Rietveld's Red-and-blue chair from the late 1910s says more about spatial harmony than it does about sitting in comfort. Charles and Ray Eames, on the other hand, used advanced technology and applied ergonomic theory to make chairs that were better able to support the human body (see p.64). By the 1960s, furniture designers were exploring a less deterministic approach: the Sacco chair, for example, allows each sitter to shape the chair to fit his or her body (see p.66).

High-backed chair 1902

The beautiful harmony and proportioning of this high-backed chair is typical of Charles Rennie Mackintosh's work. His approach was closer to European Art Nouveau than to the Arts and Crafts movement that was dominant in Britain at that time. The highly stylized floral motif provides surface ornamentation on the top panel of the backrest. It is repeated on the fabric in subdued pastel shades of green and mauve.

Specifications

Country: UK
Materials: Oak and linen upholstery

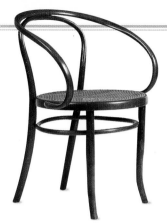

Thonet chair 1902–03

Michael Thonet was an extremely successful mass producer of chairs. His revolutionary manufacturing process, developed in the 19th century, used steam to bend solid wood into ready-made components which could be assembled later. The design, which reduces the chair to a simple structure, is an early example of machine aesthetics.

Specifications
Country: Austria
Material: Bentwood

Cushions were available for the Sitzmaschine, but distracted from its clean lines

Sitzmaschine c.1908

This "Sitting Machine" was designed by Josef Hoffmann for the refurbishment of the Purkersdorf Sanatorium. Constructed from bent beechwood, it is notable for its adjustable backrest. The grid of squares on the backrest and the cut-out vertical lines on the sides follow a strict geometrical pattern that was the hallmark of his design.

Specifications
Country: Austria
Materials:
Beechwood
and brass

The decorative spheres increase the chair's stability at its joints

▶ ▶ ▶

Side chair 1908

Architect and furniture designer Hector Guimard is recognized as one of the leading proponents of Art Nouveau. This chair is a fine example of his style: it has a tall, slender back, elegant legs with out-turned feet, and delicate ornamentation. The long structural supports on either side of the backrest and the open spaces in the headrest give the chair an organic quality.

Specifications
Country: France
Materials: Wood, brass, and leather upholstery

Red-and-blue chair 1917–18

This Gerrit Rietveld design became an icon of the De Stijl movement and is an important example of early modernist chair construction and design, which rationalized the act of sitting and reduced the chair to basic planar shapes. The construction, made up of 15 beechwood supports and two plywood boards, displays Rietveld's interest in the processes of mass production. The lines, shapes, and colors are reminiscent of the work of the artist Piet Mondrian (1872–1944).

Specifications
Country: Netherlands
Materials: Beechwood and plywood

B3 chair 1925

Architect Marcel Breuer decided to
experiment with tubular steel after being
inspired by the construction of a bicycle.
The outcome – later known as the
Wassily chair – is one of the first and
finest examples of modern tubular-steel
furniture. The cubic proportions and the
contrast between the fluidity of the steel
work and the tautness of the canvas
straps find perfect expression in
this structure.

Specifications
Country: Germany
Materials: Tubular steel
and canvas

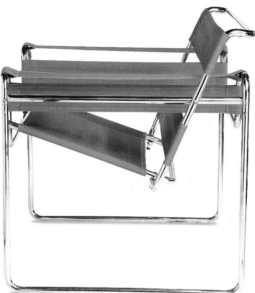

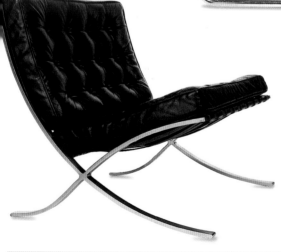

Barcelona chair 1929

Mies van der Rohe's chair was designed
for the King and Queen of Spain for
the opening ceremony of the 1929
International Exhibition in Barcelona.
Its modern appearance retains the sense
of luxury and ceremony associated with
traditional thrones. The frame is made
from two flat, chrome-plated steel bars,
which cross over to provide back and
leg supports.

Specifications
Country: Germany
Materials: Steel and leather

Gentleman's chair 1931

The cane furniture produced by Lloyd Loom was particularly popular in the 1920s and '30s. The company was founded in 1919 by an American, Marshall B. Lloyd, who invented a method of weaving a cane-like material from twisted paper and wire. This chair is part of a suite comprising Gentleman's and Lady's chairs and a sofa.

Specifications
Country: US
Materials: Woven fiber and wood

The woven fiber is attached to the wooden frame with staples

Pressed layers of wood are molded into shape to create the pliancy required for the scrolls

Paimio chair 1932

This armchair was designed by Alvar Aalto for the Tuberculosis Sanatorium at Paimio, Finland. Aalto spent a number of years developing the techniques that would allow his uncompromisingly modern designs to be realized. With the Paimio, he shows that molded plywood has all the properties suited to modern furniture design.

Specifications
Country: Finland
Materials: Laminated birch and birch plywood

Lounge chair 1933–34

A milestone in the evolution of modern furniture design, Gerald Summers' extraordinary chair is made from a single sheet of plywood. It was designed for use in the tropics, where any joints would have been susceptible to the effects of high humidity.

Specifications
Country: UK
Material: Plywood

The fluidity of the curves helps create a sculptural quality

The leather seat is fixed hammock-like to the frame

A lightweight tubular frame provides the chair's structure

Butterfly chair 1938

The much-copied Butterfly chair has a tubular-steel frame with a seat in the form of a canvas and leather sling. It was designed by the Argentinian architects Antonio Bonet, Juan Kurchan, and Jorge Ferrari-Hardoy, inspired by a folding wooden model that dated from the previous century.

Specifications
Country: Argentina
Materials: Tubular steel and leather

▶ ▶ ▶

Womb chair 1947

This iconoclastic item was the first fiberglass chair to be mass-produced. Finnish-born architect Eero Saarinen was eager to produce a modern chair that would accommodate a relaxed sitting posture. He sought to provide the sitter with "psychological comfort," believing that the large, cuplike shell would create a feeling of security.

Specifications
Country: US
Materials: Tubular steel, fiberglass, fabric, and latex foam

The loose latex foam cushions are covered in red fabric

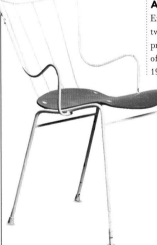

Antelope chair 1950

Ernest Race's Antelope chair was one of two models the British furniture designer produced in 1950 for the outdoor terraces of London's Royal Festival Hall during the 1951 Festival of Britain. It is constructed from enameled metal rods – the designer's trademark material – with a plywood seat. The open structure, biomorphic shape, and splayed legs (ending in ball-like feet on one model) reflected a popular contemporary interest in science and the atomic age. Such motifs continued to appear throughout the 1950s in designs for household items as diverse as clocks and curtains.

Specifications
Country: UK
Materials: Steel and plywood

3107 chair 1952

Arne Jacobsen's hugely popular chair was clearly influenced by the work of Charles Eames (see p.30). The seat and backrest are made from a single sheet of plywood, molded into shape and supported by a bent tubular-steel base. The first version had just three legs and was available only in black, but it was later produced in a range of colors and with four legs.

The pattern of diamonds is lost when the chair is upholstered

Specifications
Country: Denmark
Materials: Tubular
steel and plywood

Diamond chair 1952

Enormously influential in the 1950s and '60s, this chair was designed by the Italian-born sculptor Harry Bertoia. He was concerned with the sculptural qualities of chair design: for him, space, form, and the use of materials were as significant as functional demands. The Diamond chair has two distinct parts: the diamond-shaped seat, with its criss-cross pattern of smaller diamonds, and the steel base on which it sits.

The base is constructed from bent and welded steel rods

Specifications
Country: US
Materials: Steel
and upholstery

Lounge chair and ottoman 1956

This complicated piece of furniture involves three plywood shells padded with upholstery and joined by aluminum supports. Unquestionably placed at the luxury end of the market, the chair was originally designed by Charles and Ray Eames as a birthday gift for film director Billy Wilder.

The chair swivels on its stand, allowing considerable flexibility and comfort

Specifications
Country: US
Materials: Plywood, aluminum, rubber, and leather upholstery

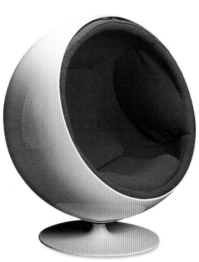

Ball chair 1963–65

Finnish designer Eero Aarnio used state-of-the-art manufacturing processes to produce his space age Ball, or Globe, chair. It is made from a fiberglass ball, cut in section, and swivels on an aluminum base. It was often equipped with speakers or telephone.

Specifications
Country: Finland
Materials: Fiberglass, aluminum, and upholstery

"READY-MADE" STOOLS

Achille and Pier Giacomo Castiglioni's Mezzadro stool is clearly influenced by the "ready-made" sculpture of Marcel Duchamp (1887–1968). The stool consists of a brightly colored, enameled metal tractor seat attached by a wing-nut to a cantilevered bent steel support and with a wooden footrest. The original stools, at first considered too radical to be put into production, did not have holes in the seat and had a dark metal base. This revised version did not appear until the 1970s. The name derives from the Italian mezzadro, *meaning "tenant farmer."*

Mezzadro stool, 1957

Later designers integrated
the leg rest into the overall
design of the chair

First designed in
polyurethane foam,
this stacking chair
was most famously
produced in plastic

Stacking chair 1960–67

The Danish designer Verner Panton
is credited with having created the world's
first single-piece plastic chair. This unusual
cantilevered chair, produced in a range of
vivid colors, has become an icon of the 1960s.
The original versions were produced in 1960,
but it was seven years before technical
problems were resolved and the chair was
put into commercial production. Strong,
comfortable, and with a glossy,
brightly colored finish, the
piece is a tribute to the
unique properties
of plastic.

The flared
base provides
room for the
sitter's feet

Specifications
Country: Denmark
Material: Plastic

Sacco 1968–69

In 1968, Piero Gatti, Cesare Paolini, and Franco Teodoro produced a chair without a fixed form – the first successful beanbag chair. It does not have a frame, but a soft skin filled with polystyrene balls. The idea is that the user should be able to shape the chair to suit his or her body and needs. This reflects a sympathy with the radical anti-design movements prevalent in Italy during the late 1960s.

Specifications

Country: Italy
Materials: Leather or vinyl and polystyrene

Made by Zanotta, the beanbag was available in leather or vinyl

The ornate carved frame is covered in an Impressionist brush-stroke pattern

The pieces of cardboard have been laminated together to form a strong structure

Proust's armchair 1978

Alessandro Mendini was a leading activist for the radical design group Alchimia when he designed this chair. The group rejected modernist design theory in favor of ornament and craftsmanship. For Proust's armchair (Mendini's aim was to create a chair that Proust might have sat in), the designer took a traditional 19th-century chair and hand-painted it all over in the Impressionist style.

Specifications

Country: Italy
Materials: Hand-painted wood and hand-painted upholstery

Little Beaver armchair 1987

Frank Gehry is an American architect and designer whose work includes the Vitra Design Museum in Germany, where some of his own chairs are displayed. This armchair and footrest were designed to form part of a series of low-cost pieces of furniture made from corrugated cardboard. Strength has been achieved by using the edges of the cardboard for the chair's surface.

Specifications
Country: US
Material: Laminated cardboard

'vik-ter chair 1991

This traditionally styled stackable chair by the American designer Dakota Jackson hides some innovative construction features that allow the back to pivot to adjust to different sitters. The wooden seat is wedge-shaped, and the backrest curved to provide greater comfort. The orange-brown seat and backrest are supported by a thin black metal structure. The overall effect is one of elegance combined with strength.

Specifications
Country: US
Materials: Wood and steel tubing

COFFEE & SIDE TABLES

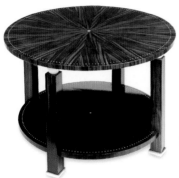

IN THE EARLY PART of the century, the search for pure form found expression in Jacques-Emile Ruhlmann's handcrafted furniture, made to commission using expensive materials. Eileen Gray, also active in France at that time, was allied with the Parisian avant-garde, who were experimenting with new materials and solutions. Donald Deskey's furniture echoes the American aesthetic that was emerging in 1929 and was to peak in the streamlined 1930s. Isamu Noguchi's and Carlo Mollino's strong biomorphic designs of the late 1940s were influenced by the work of Charles Eames. In the 1970s, there was a renaissance of traditional forms, and it was against this backdrop that the radical, antiestablishment Memphis group came together.

Guéridon en palissandre c.1922

Jacques-Emile Ruhlmann was one of the foremost French furniture makers of this century. Specializing in luxury, highly crafted furniture, his classic pieces simplified traditional forms and lent a timelessness to modern design. Ruhlmann was famous for his use of veneers and inlays, and those skills are visible in this beautifully constructed table. Its simplicity is belied by closer inspection of the two table-top surfaces, which reveal a complicated grain effect.

Specifications
Country: France
Height: 19½in (50cm)
Materials: Rosewood and ivory

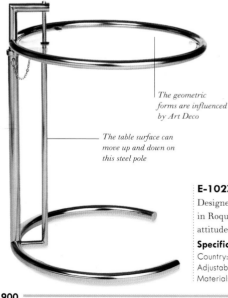

The geometric forms are influenced by Art Deco

The table surface can move up and down on this steel pole

E-1027 adjustable table 1927

Designed by Eileen Gray as part of a commission for a villa in Roquebrune, France, this table demonstrates a progressive attitude to the forms and materials of the machine age.

Specifications
Country: France
Adjustable tabletop height: 30–35in (76–89cm)
Materials: Tubular steel and glass

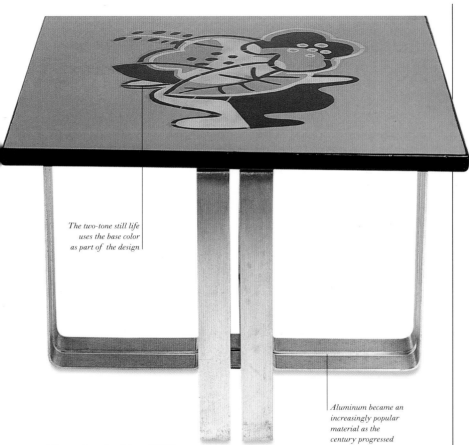

The two-tone still life uses the base color as part of the design

Aluminum became an increasingly popular material as the century progressed

Occasional table c.1929

Produced by Deskey-Vollmer, a partnership formed in 1927 between Donald Deskey and Phillip Vollmer, this table is a good example of Deskey's design. His interest in innovative materials and techniques is exemplified by the aluminum strapwork base. The abstract still life of the enameled top is evidence of his training in fine art.

Specifications
Country: US
Height: 24in (61cm)
Materials: Aluminum, enameled metal, and wood

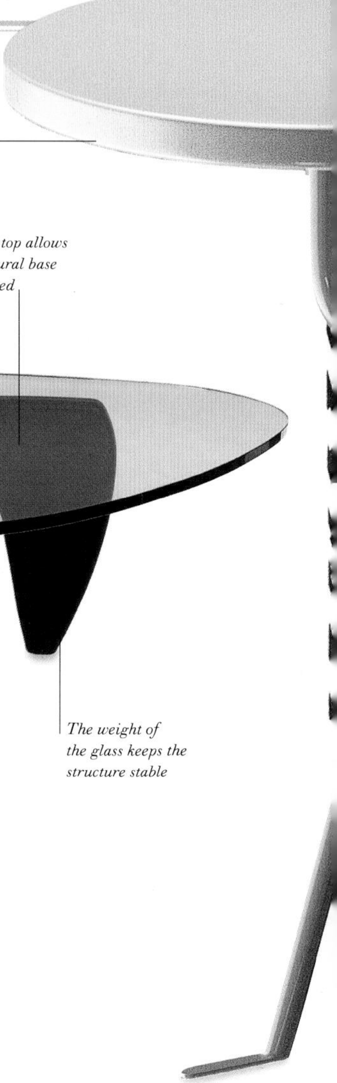

De Lucchi's enthusiastic use of decorated plastic laminate is typical of Memphis designers

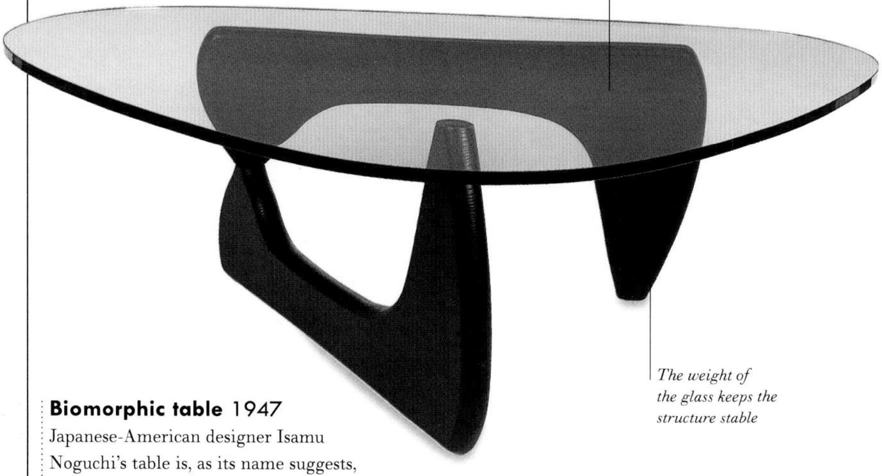

The glass top allows the sculptural base to be viewed

Biomorphic table 1947

Japanese-American designer Isamu
Noguchi's table is, as its name suggests,
organic in form. His grounding in sculpture is
obvious in the structure of the legs: two identically carved
pieces of ebonized birch, one inverted and connected to the
other by means of a socket and pin coupling. The table was
mass-produced by the Herman Miller Furniture Company
from 1947 and is still popular today.

The weight of the glass keeps the structure stable

Specifications

Country: US
Height: 15½in (39.7cm)
Materials: Birch
and glass

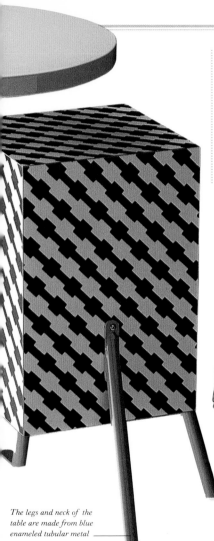

Kristall 1981

Together with his Sofa Lido, Michele de Lucchi's Kristall side table was exhibited in the first Memphis collection in September 1981. Like many of the Memphis designers, de Lucchi created playful pieces with the emphasis on bright colors and asymmetrical form.

Specifications

Country: Italy
Height: 19¾in (50cm)
Materials: Plastic laminate, laquered wood, and metal

Arad's immaculately gleaming steel table is a three-part construction

The legs and neck of the table are made from blue enameled tubular metal

Three Thirds of a Table 1989

Ron Arad's table is made of mirror-polished stainless steel, and like many of his works, it has a distinctly futuristic appeal. Israeli-born Arad made his name as the "Mad Max of design" in the early 1980s, with furniture crafted from salvaged materials. Since the late 1980s his designs have become more sculptural and more expensive.

Specifications

Country: Italy
Height: 20¼in (51.5cm)
Materials: Plywood and glass

VASES

DISPLAYING FRESH FLOWERS in the home brings natural beauty
to an otherwise man-made environment. Whether plainly
understated or flamboyantly decorative, the vessels that
hold flowers are, above all else, designed to enhance the
splendor of their contents. During the 20th century,
vases have provided inspiration for an extraordinary
diversity of designs – from the sculptural, organic forms
crafted by Art Nouveau designer Hector Guimard to the
simplest, most functional pieces typified by Enzo Mari's
double vase (see p.76). While a variety of materials
have been used, from solid silver to the lightest
plastic, the outstanding tradition of the
glassblower's skill is ever present.

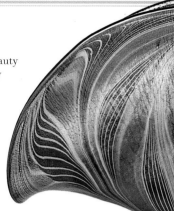

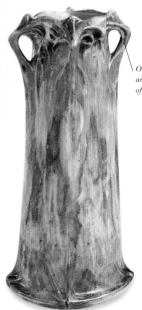

*Organic forms
are characteristic
of Guimard's work*

Peacock vase c.1900

Louis Comfort Tiffany was the outstanding producer
of Art Nouveau glassware. He developed a method of
manipulating color into his blown glass vases to produce
an iridescent effect. These glassworks were known by the
trademark Favrile (French for "handmade"), and were
enormously popular in the US and Europe.

Specifications
Country: US
Material: Favrile glass
Height: 13¼in (33.7cm)

*The brilliant, iridescent
colors and shimmering,
satin finish are associated
with Favrile glassware*

Ceramic vase 1908

When the French porcelain manufacturer Sèvres
undertook to modernize its output, it employed
a number of progressive artists. Among them
was Hector Guimard, a renowned Art Nouveau
designer best-known for his entrances to the
Paris Métro. This was one of a number of
vases Guimard produced for the company.

Specifications
Country: France
Material: Porcelain
Height: 10½in (26.5cm)

Rookwood vase 1909

Founded in Cincinnati in 1880, Rookwood became one of the most successful art potteries in the US. This hand-painted vase, with its muted tones and yellow and brown coloring, is a typical Rookwood piece. The influence of the company's Japanese painter, Kataro Shirayamadani, is clear in the imagery.

Specifications
Country: US
Material: Glazed stoneware
Height: 12¾in (32.5cm)

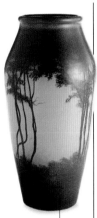

The shape of the vase mimics that of a peacock displaying its tail feathers

Dark tones characterize the Rookwood style

The arabesque pattern of leaves and berries is typical of Pêche's decorative work

Silver vase c.1920

Dagobert Pêche designed this wide-bowled solid silver vase for the Wiener Werkstätte. It stands on a fluted base and has a naturalistic floral motif in relief on the surface. Pêche's work came to represent an alternative to the strictly geometric designs originally produced by Josef Hoffmann and Koloman Moser for the Wiener Werkstätte.

Specifications
Country: Austria
Material: Silver
Height: 9½in [23.9cm)

Ruba Rombic 1928

Reuben Haley's Art Deco vase, produced by the Consolidated Lamp and Glass Company, has a complex multiplane shape influenced by cubism. It is made of green glass that has been blow-molded into shape. The name is derived from *Rubyiay* (meaning "poem") and *Rhomboid* (meaning "irregular shape").

Specifications
Country: US
Material: Molded, cased glass
Height: 15in (38cm)

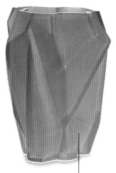

Three layers of glass have been used to produce the subtly changing colors

Rose flute 1926

This extremely refined, blown glass rose flute was produced by the Austrian company Lobmeyr. Its lines are restrained and unadorned, the long, delicate bowl of the vase tapering almost to a point. The design emphasizes the transparent and fragile nature of glass.

Specifications
Country: Austria
Material: Blown glass
Height: 5in (12.7cm)

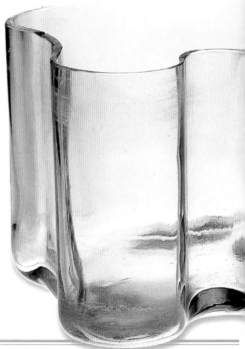

Bronze vase 1930

The work of German designer Margot Kempe, this heavy bronze vase is cone-shaped, with a rounded base. The vessel is supported by two inverted "u"-shaped legs. An important teacher of ceramics after World War II, Kempe arrived in the US via Ecuador in 1947. She taught at the renowned pottery studio Greenwich House, New York, until 1978.

Specifications
Country: Germany
Material: Bronze
Height: 18½in (47cm)

The heavy, dark material and simple design make this an austere piece

Aalto's vase was also produced in brown, green, and azure blue

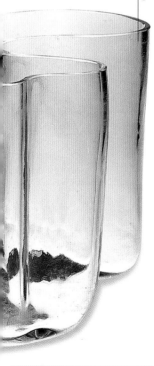

Savoy vase 1936

Designed for the Helsinki Savoy Hotel, and produced by Karhula Glassworks, this vase is by Alvar Aalto, one of the pioneers of a biomorphic style of furniture. The organic shape is inspired by natural forms, and by the work of artists such as Joan Miró (1893–1983). The glass was blow-molded into shape, and the walls vary in thickness.

Specifications
Country: Finland
Material: Blow-molded glass
Height: Not known

Orrefors vase 1940

In the 1930s, the Swedish company Orrefors Glasbruk employed three artists, Simon Gate, Edvard Hald, and Vicke Lindstrand, to work on its ornamental glass production. Their output included this green vase. Made of thick glass, it has a simple, geometric shape that tapers off toward the base. On one of the four sides, there is a flowing figure of a cross-legged woman, who seems to be floating in water.

Specifications
Country: Sweden
Material: Glass with acid-etched decoration
Height: 6½in (16.2cm)

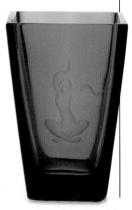

Handkerchief vase 1946

In 1921, Paolo Venini became a partner in a Murano glassmaking
company now known as Venini & Co. Originally, it concentrated
on traditional Venetian forms; but eventually, under Venini's
direction, it adopted more progressive styles. One of the designers,
Fulvio Bianconi, worked with Venini to produce this Handkerchief
vase. It is made from a square of glass, which is shaped into
an irregular form in a manner that inspired its name.

Specifications

Country: Italy
Material: Blown glass
Height: 8¼in (21cm)

*Made from ABS plastic,
the vase is colored a
deep, glossy purple*

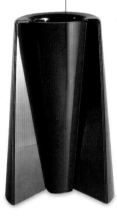

*The irregular
contours of the glass
mimic the folds in
a handkerchief*

Pago Pago 1969

Enzo Mari's Pago Pago
vase is cleverly designed to
hold both small and large
bouquets. It is made from
deeply colored plastic and
has a small, cone-shaped
inner vessel (shown here).
By inverting the vase, the
outer chamber becomes
available for smaller
displays. The cutaway
nature of the design
clearly reveals the
interlocking structure.

Specifications

Country: Italy
Material: Plastic
Height: 11¾in (30cm)

Ruby vase 1989

Czech designer Bořek Šípek used both blown and applied glass in the construction of his Ruby vase. It shows an interesting exploration of textures, colors, and shapes. The clear glass vessel takes on a form reminiscent of an elegant evening dress which is adorned with a belt of red spikes at the waist and a band of red rubies at the neck.

Specifications
Country: Czech Republic
Material: Blown and applied glass
Height: 23½in (60cm)

The "rubies" are crafted in smooth, jewel-shaped forms

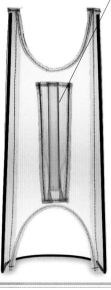

The replaceable glass flower tube is made from a commercial test tube

Flexi vase 1992–93

This vase by Miguel Calvo is notable both for its innovative use of materials and its unusual shape. It is constructed from a bent wire frame onto which a translucent yellow vinyl is sewn. This, in turn, has a sewn-on pocket containing a glass tube for the flowers. The result is a soft, flexible structure that reflects many of the qualities of the flowers it holds.

Specifications
Country: US
Materials: Vinyl, metal, glass, and thread
Height: 14½in (37cm)

BOWLS

A WIDE RANGE OF MATERIALS and a variety of styles have contributed to the wealth of extraordinary and beautiful bowls produced over the past century. Bowls may serve a functional purpose as containers, but they are frequently intended to be purely ornamental. An expression of the designer's artistic philosophy is often discernible in the form and decoration of the product. Josef Hoffmann, for example, used hammered silver to express the hand of the craftsman, while keeping the bowl free of unnecessary ornamentation. In contrast, Lella and Massimo Vignelli used inexpensive synthetic materials to produce household goods that challenged the principles of functionalist design and celebrated the fresh ideas of an emerging pop culture.

Dragonfly c.1900

One of a limited production, this delicate centerpiece is by the Royal Copenhagen Porcelain Factory. Perched on the edges of the rim is a pair of dragonflies, whose outstretched wings form the elegant handles.

Specifications
Country: Denmark
Material: Porcelain
Widest point: 12in (31cm)

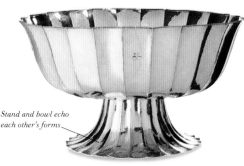

Stand and bowl echo each other's forms

Oval fruit bowl 1917

The architect and craftsman Josef Hoffmann designed this fluted silver bowl for the Wiener Werkstätte. The hammered finish enhances the silver by providing a softly textured surface. The sympathetic use of materials, classical proportions, and lack of ornamentation are typical of the work produced by the Wiener Werkstätte.

Specifications
Country: Austria
Material: Silver
Widest point: 15½in (39cm)

Bowl and stand 1926

Edvard Hald designed this attractive glass bowl for the Orrefors Glasbruk, where he was artistic director from 1924 to 1933. It is engraved with the flat, stylized outlines of four seated women and is typical of Hald's work at this time. He had spent four years in Paris studying under Henri Matisse (1869–1954), whose paintings of nudes clearly influenced this piece.

Specifications
Country: Sweden
Material: Glass
Diameter: 7in (17.8cm)

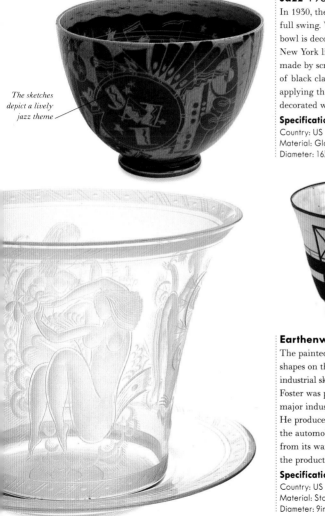

The sketches depict a lively jazz theme

Jazz 1930–31

In 1930, the American Jazz Age was in full swing. Viktor Schreckengost's punch bowl is decorated with stylized images of New York life. The sgraffito designs were made by scratching through a thin layer of black clay over white ground before applying the glaze. The interior is decorated with musical notations.

Specifications
Country: US
Material: Glazed ceramic
Diameter: 16½in (42.2cm)

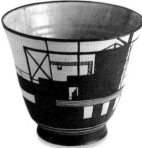

Earthenware bowl 1947

The painted black lines and geometric shapes on this bowl are suggestive of an industrial skyline. Detroit-born artist John Foster was probably inspired by the city's major industrial and commercial status. He produced this piece at a time when the automobile industry was recovering from its wartime concentration on the production of armaments.

Specifications
Country: US
Material: Stoneware
Diameter: 9in (23.2cm)

▶ ▶ ▶

Plastic allows a greater freedom of color and form

The glass is shaped to resemble a shell

Small bowl 1950–60

Flavio Poli was awarded many prizes for his glasswork, including the Compasso d'Oro in 1954. This heavy, hand-blown glass bowl demonstrates Poli's bold use of sharply contrasting colors.

Specifications
Country: Italy
Material: Glass
Widest point: 7½in (19cm)

The cactus stem goes through the glass itself

Fruit bowl 1960–70

Produced by Heller Designs, New York, this compartmentalized fruit bowl was created by Italian design team Lella and Massimo Vignelli. The use of plastic, which could be easily formed in bright and unconventional colors, is typical of Italian design of the 1960s.

Specifications
Country: Italy
Material: Plastic
Diameter: 16in (41cm)

Nevada 1987–88

American-born designer Hilton McConnico created this bowl for the established French glassware manufacturer Daum. In an amusing reference to nature, the stem, made from green *pâte-de-verre*, is shaped in the form of a cactus plant. The bowl itself is made from a thin clear glass, which is actually pierced by the cactus stem.

Specifications
Country: France
Material: Glass
Diameter: 11¾in (30cm)

The striated woodgrain is enhanced with turning

Wooden bowl 1989

Ronald Kent makes his exquisite bowls from Norfolk Island pine. Each bowl is a work of art, individually produced on a lathe and turned until it is extremely thin and translucent. Kent then works on the surface with sealant and fine sandpaper to enhance the natural grain and color of the wood.

Specifications
Country: US
Material: Pine wood
Diameter: 14½in
(37cm)

Basket bowl 1994

Made from a single sheet of hardened silver, this bowl was designed by British artist Rebecca de Quinn. The piece was laser cut according to the artist's pattern, polished, then hand-formed using a specially created jig, and finally gold plated. De Quinn is inspired by creating three-dimensional forms from single pieces of metal.

Specifications
Country: UK
Material: Gold plate on silver
Fullest width: 12in (35cm)

The base silver is "hard-rolled," a specially treated metal that keeps its form

Chamberstick 1905

This brass chamberstick was made by
German designer Paul Haustein, who was
best-known for his enamel work of the
1920s. Intended for use in the bedroom, it
is typical of the handicraft work influenced
by the European Arts and Crafts movement.

Specifications
Country: Germany
Height: 4in (9.6cm)
Material: Brass

*The restrained,
slender stick
exhibits fluid lines*

*The finely
executed brass
was fashioned
with a spinning
technique*

Specifications
Country: Austria
Height: 14in (36cm)
Material: Pewter

CANDLESTICKS

ALTHOUGH THE FIRST commercially viable electric light
bulb, or incandescent bulb, was invented by Thomas
Edison in 1879, for many decades electric lighting
in the home was a luxury beyond the reach of all
but the most wealthy. Instead, kerosene or gas
lamps were used along with candlelight. With
the widespread introduction of affordable electric
lighting, candlesticks were relegated to creating
atmospheric lighting for the dining table or used for
religious and ceremonial purposes. During the last
two decades of the 20th century, however, candlesticks
have once again become fashionable decorative
objects in the home. This has encouraged designers
to invent new forms and to experiment with
different materials to produce objects in a
variety of contemporary and classical styles.

Candelabrum c.1902

Josef Maria Olbrich was a leading member
of the Wiener Werkstätte. This two-armed
pewter piece is typical of his use of curved
organic shapes. Like much of his decorative
work, it illustrates the transition between
the naturalistic forms of Art Nouveau and
the more abstract geometry of Art Deco.

The tiered, geometrical pattern is repeated on each component of the candelabrum

Candelabrum 1928

This candelabrum was produced by silver manufacturers Reed and Barton, which had started to produce pewterware in 1903. One of a pair, the candelabrum's lines are uncompromisingly geometrical and the overall design is functional and devoid of excessive ornamentation.

Specifications
Country: US
Height: 8in (21cm)
Material: Pewter

The symmetrical branches and central post are topped with identical angular candle holders

The polished surface reflects light out into the room

Rectangular-shaped base is typical of Art Deco styling

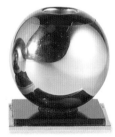

Bubble candlesticks 1930s

During the 1930s, the Chase Brass and Copper Company was the most successful American producer of chrome and nickel domestic utensils and accessories. These Art Deco candlesticks consist of a polished sphere sitting on a deep blue square of glass mounted on a chrome base.

Specifications
Country: US
Height: 2¾in (7cm)
Materials: Chrome-plated metal and glass

▶ ▶ ▶

Candlestick 1959

This amusing candlestick was designed for Boda by Erik Höglund. It is made in thick, clear blown glass with a heavy base. Applied to either side of the body are two short arms with four-fingered hands, which are raised in jubilant fashion.

Specifications
Country: Sweden
Material: Glass
Height: 4¾in (12cm)

The elegant shape is inspired by the graceful arch of the bird's neck

Crane 1988

Matthew Hilton's sensuously curved candlestick is made from polished cast aluminum, although it was also available in bronze. It stands on a flared base, from which it develops into an elongated "S"-shape. The zoomorphic form, in this case derived from the neck of a crane, is carefully controlled and balanced.

Specifications
Country: UK
Material: Cast aluminum
Height: 16½in (42cm)

The polished finish has a pinkish tinge

Cat's eye 1991

This award-winning candle holder, also available in blue, was designed by Laura Handler for Design Ideas. It is made of ten separate units, each made from frosted glass. The overall size and appearance of the finished item is dependent upon the number of units used and how they are interconnected. Here, the units have been formed into a slightly curved triangular shape.

Light passing through the translucent finish illuminates the internal structure

Specifications
Country: US
Material: Cast glass
Height: 2in (4.8cm) each unit

CANDLESTICKS IN THE 1990s

*The final decade of the century
saw a revival of interest in
candlesticks, and shops sold
a dazzling array of candles
and receptacles in which to put
them. These include original
and traditional candlesticks,
sconces, lanterns, floorstanding
candelabra, garden lamps and
pots, chandeliers, and bowls for
floating candles. Some of the most
popular designs are reinterpretations
of Gothic wrought iron and pewter pieces.
Ethnic influences can be seen in many of the
wooden, ceramic, and papier-mâché candlesticks.
From the austere to the whimsical, each style attests
to the enduring charm of the flickering flame.*

**Mirrored wall
sconce**

**Selection of glass
candlesticks**

**Tree-shaped
candelabrum**

**Candlestick with
Napoleonic wreath**

LIGHTING

EARLY SHADES WERE DESIGNED simply to hide the mechanics of the light bulb. However, Louis Comfort Tiffany's stained glass lampshades cast a soft, colorful light in the room and were beautiful objects in their own right. The move toward a machine aesthetic, through Art Deco and later modernism, produced lighting designed with geometric forms. The functional design of George Carwardine's 1933 Anglepoise lamp allowed the user to aim the light directly onto the work area. New materials such as plastic became popular for lighting in the 1950s, and, since then, the use of low-voltage technology has allowed greater flexibility.

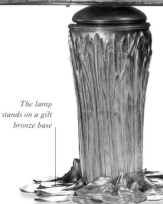

The lamp stands on a gilt bronze base

Dragonfly c.1900–10

Typical of the Art Nouveau work produced by the Tiffany Studios, Clara Driscoll's design employs a theme from nature. A series of dragonflies is positioned around the edge of the shade, and the stem is also inspired by an organic form – waterlilies.

Specifications
Country: US
Materials: Glass, gilt bronze, and lead
Height: 26½in (67.5cm)

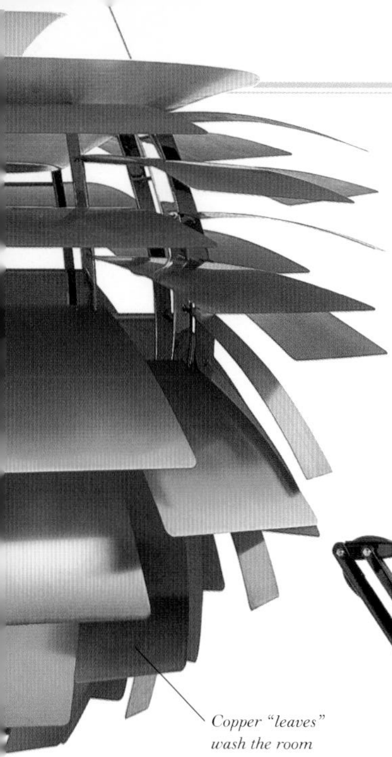

P H Artichoke 1958

Poul Henningsen's lamp is designed
to prevent glare while maximizing
reflected light. Overlapping "leaves"
achieve this by spreading the light
over a large area. Manufactured by
Louis Poulsen & Co., it was originally
designed to hang in public spaces.

Specifications
Country: Denmark
Materials: Copper, steel,
and enameled metal
Height: 27in (69cm)

*Copper "leaves"
wash the room
in a warm light*

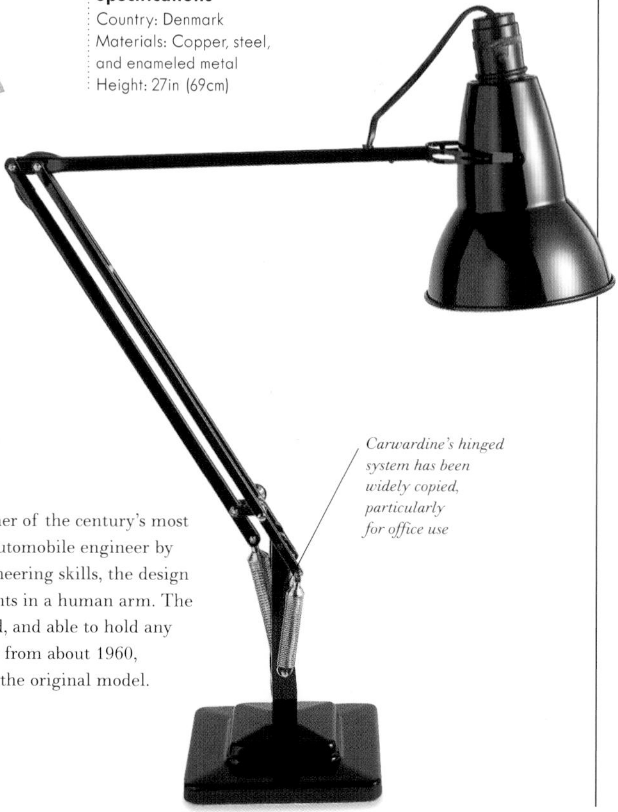

*Carwardine's hinged
system has been
widely copied,
particularly
for office use*

Anglepoise 1933

George Carwardine, the designer of the century's most
successful desk lamp, was an automobile engineer by
profession. Reflecting his engineering skills, the design
uses hinges that mimic the joints in a human arm. The
Anglepoise is flexible, balanced, and able to hold any
position. As this example dates from about 1960,
its design differs slightly from the original model.

Specifications
Country: UK
Materials: Steel,
enamel, and plastic
Height: 35½in (90cm) extended

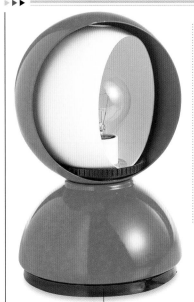

Eclisse 1966

Winner of the Premio Compasso
d'Oro prize at the 1967 Milan
Triennale, Vico Magistretti's
table lamp, manufactured by
Artemide, has an adjustable
light. Its name, Italian for
"eclipse," refers to the
way the light is eclipsed
as it revolves.

Specifications
Country: Italy
Material: Enameled
metal
Height: 7½in
(19cm)

*A low voltage
is conducted
through
the arms*

*The free-standing
lamp may be wall-
mounted by hinges
on its base*

Tizio 1972

Low-voltage lamps started to become popular in the 1970s.
Richard Sapper's high-tech table lamp is a classic example.
A transformer housed in the base greatly reduces the voltage,
which is then conducted through the metal arms to power
the lamp, eliminating the need for internal wiring. The
result is a slender, elegant structure: finely balanced
and, with its heavy transformer, perfectly stable.

Specifications
Country: Italy
Materials: ABS plastic and aluminum
Height: 46½in (118cm) extended

Jazz c.1990

Ferdinand Porsche is from a family of renowned
designers, best-known for its contribution to
the automobile industry. Made by PAF, his
low-voltage halogen table lamp has sensors
that electronically regulate the light.
The switch is luminous.

Specifications

Country: Italy
Material: Plastic
Height: 25in (63.5cm) extended

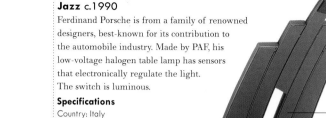

*The adjustable
and movable
arm allows
the lamp to
fold flat*

*Individual spikes
move around,
creating a soft,
diffused light*

Urchin IL36 1991

GoldmanArts describes
its products as "hysterical
architecture." This is
one of several inflatable
lamps designed by Jonathan
Goldman. The gently swaying,
colorful, and playful nylon
structures are intended to resemble
a sea urchin as it moves in the ocean's
current. The lamp's soft shades have no
structural support – a small fan both
inflates the shade and cools the bulb.

Specifications

Country: US
Materials: Ripstop nylon
fabric and metal
Diameter: 25in (64cm)

RADIOS

THE EARLIEST RADIOS, known as crystal sets, had their workings left totally exposed, and the listener was required to wear headphones. It was not until the late 1920s that radios were designed to incorporate all of the components within a single housing. Initially, these resembled items of furniture; but with the introduction of plastics, they began to acquire a visual language of their own. In 1955, Sony launched its first transistor radio, and with it began the journey toward miniaturization. Today, it is possible to make radios only a few millimeters wide.

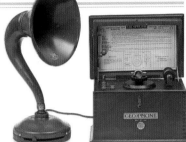

Gecophone c.1925

Using a horn to amplify sound was a huge advance on the early crystal sets, for which headphones were necessary. Apart from the horn, the parts were housed in a plain wooden box, which was better suited to the domestic environment.

Specifications
Country: UK
Height: 6¼in (16cm)
Materials: Wood and metal

Volksempfänger VE 301 1928–33

As with the VW Beetle (see p.314), the design for this radio was endorsed by Adolf Hitler. The model number refers to the date Hitler became Chancellor – January 30, 1933. The Volksempfänger, meaning "people's radio," bears a symbol of the Third Reich under the dial. For propaganda reasons, it was not possible to receive transmissions from abroad on this set.

Specifications
Country: Germany
Height: 15¼in (39cm)
Materials: Bakelite and fabric

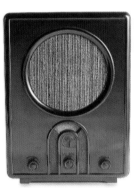

Bakelite control knobs add a modern touch

Pye radio early-1930s

The loudspeaker grille gave designers the opportunity to develop a visual identity for their company. Pye used a stylized sunburst, which was a popular Art Deco motif. The trademark also served as decoration, which increased the radio's aesthetic appeal.

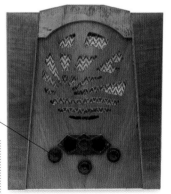

Specifications
Country: UK
Height: 16in (41cm)
Materials: Wood and Bakelite

Ekco Model AD 65 1932–34

Early cabinet wireless sets often had the appearance of pieces of furniture. Breaking with this tradition, the Ekco AD 65, designed by Wells Coates, was made from the new man-made material Bakelite. Its bold circular form, chrome-plated grille, and prominent dials were uncompromisingly modern.

Specifications
Country: UK
Height: 40½in (103cm)
Materials: Bakelite
and fabric

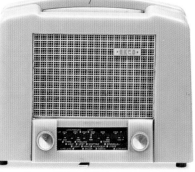

Handles were a distinct feature of the period, meeting the demand for portability

Ekco Type U122 1950s

Plastics radically changed the appearance of radios, which became available in a range of colors and shapes. This process was aided by the miniaturization of the receiver through advances in valve technology.

Specifications
Country: UK
Height: 8½in (22cm)
Material: Bakelite

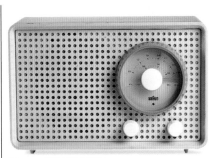

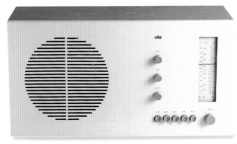

Braun SK 25 1955

In 1954, Fritz Eichler was hired by Artur
Braun to modify the company's product range
by adopting a more functionalist approach.
The basic plastic shell and simple controls of
the SK 25 typify the rationality that has come
to be associated with Braun products.

Specifications

Country: Germany
Height: 6in (15.5cm)
Materials: Plastic and metal

Super RT 20 1961

The range of stereophonic equipment that Dieter
Rams designed for Braun in the 1950s and '60s was all
executed in the same austere, functionalist style. The
Super RT 20 had many of the same characteristics as
his earlier Phonosuper record player (see p.102).

Specifications

Country: Germany
Height: 10in (25.5cm)
Materials: Plastic, metal,
and wood

Brionvega Ls 502 1964

In the 1960s, Richard Sapper and Marco
Zanuso were commissioned by Brionvega
to design a series of radios and televisions.
The Ls 502 folding radio,
an early example of the
application of transistor
technology, was a battery-
powered portable designed
to go anywhere. For easy
transportation, the radio
folded up to form
a small box.

*One side of the
radio housed the
speaker, the other
the receiver*

*The telescopic
antenna could
be pushed into
the cube when
not in use*

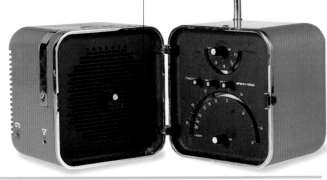

Specifications

Country: Italy
Height: 5in (12.5cm)
Materials: Plastic and metal

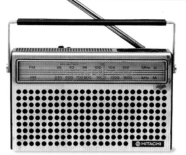

Hitachi KH-434E 1970s

This portable radio is typical of the wide range of electronic consumables produced in Japan. With its competitive prices, Japan now dominates the radio market. This model can be powered either by battery or AC electricity.

Specifications
Country: Japan
Height: 4¼in (11cm)
Material: Plastic

RADICAL RADIO

Daniel Weil's Bag Radio, part of his degree show at the Royal College of Art, London, challenges traditional notions of how a radio should look. Instead of hiding the components within a solid shell, Weil has chosen to display them in a transparent PVC bag. The exposed workings, combined with the splashes of color, provide a quirky, decorative quality.

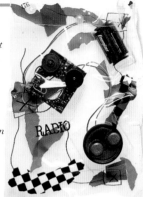

Radio in the Bag, 1981

The heavy plastic casing protects the internal generator and gearbox

Sixty turns of the winding handle give about 30 minutes playing time

Windup Freeplay Radio 1995

Trevor Baylis invented the Windup radio for use in developing countries, where a free and convenient energy source was needed to receive broadcasts. Although very simple in design, the radio incorporates two of the main design concerns of the 1990s: ecology and communication.

Specifications
Country: UK
Height: 7¾in (20cm)
Material: ABS plastic

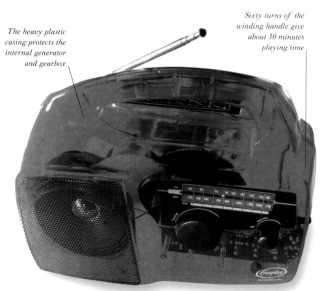

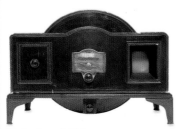

Televisor 1926

The world's first demonstration of television, or "visual wireless," was given by Scottish inventor John Logie Baird (1888–1946) in 1926. However, his mechanical Televisor, with its small screen positioned on the right, could not broadcast sound and pictures together.

Specifications
Country: UK
Materials: Metal and Bakelite
Height: 22in (56cm)

TELEVISION SETS

IN A BROCHURE aimed at its retailers, manufacturer E.K. Cole Ltd. predicted that 1939 would go down in history as "Television Year." In fact, it was the radio that dominated homes as people avidly followed the year's historic international events. Since then, however, the television set has made a greater impact on our domestic lives than almost any other 20th-century invention. In early form, its sheer size made it the dominant item in any room; but the miniaturization of electronic components in the 1950s facilitated its transformation from large, bulky wooden box to the slim, slickly styled consumer desirable we know today.

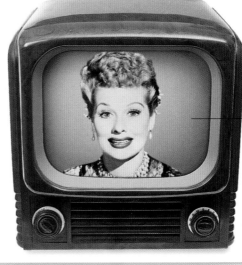

Bush TV12 1949

In the 1930s, mechanical television sets were replaced by electronic models that used cathode ray tubes to project electrons onto the screen. Early sets cost as much as a car; but by 1949 less expensive models, such as this Bakelite television by Bush, were widely available.

Specifications
Country: UK
Material: Bakelite housing
Height: 16½in (42cm)

The hit show I Love Lucy appeared on television screens from 1951

The screen can be both protected and disguised behind cabinet doors

The large, chunky controls typify the uncomplicated styling of the set

Specifications
Country: UK
Material: Wood
Height: 35¼in
(89.3cm)

Mullard 1950s

By the 1950s, the television set was part of the furniture – in some cases, literally so. With its two wooden doors, this Mullard set had the appearance of a cabinet, to be opened when its services were required and disguised when not. Its impressive size indicates the dominant presence that television had established in the home as the century entered its second half.

Sony TV8-301 1959

Original in its design, as well as technically innovative, the TV8-301 was the world's first all-transistor television and established Sony as the world leader in electronics. Sony was able to utilize the miniaturized parts it had developed for its pocket transistor radios to develop this remarkable-looking portable set.

Specifications
Country: Japan
Material: Metal
Dimensions: Not known

The shape and coloring are reminiscent of an astronaut's helmet

JVC Videosphere 1970

In an effort to distance plastic from its disposable associations, designers used it for expensive consumer items like television sets. A radical rethink of the traditional television shape, the Videosphere looks like an astronaut's helmet, reflecting public interest in space travel. In 1969, 600 million people had tuned in to watch men walk on the Moon.

Specifications
Country: Japan
Material: Plastic
Height: 11in (28cm)

Sony KV-32 FD 1 1998

Millions of dollars are now spent by electronics companies in an effort to produce the highest-quality television set with the most desirable appearance and price. There has been a vast range of technological innovations in the 1980s and '90s, including the development of flat- and wide-screen televisions, exemplified by this sleek, angular Sony Trinitron® flat-screen model.

Specifications
Country: Japan
Material: Plastic
Height: 27in (68.5cm), Width: 35½in (90cm)

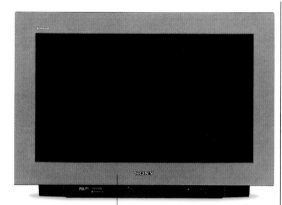

Minimalist designs dominated the late 1990s

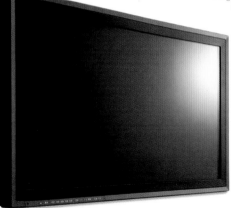

With a depth of less than 6in (15cm), the screen can be positioned flat against a wall

Sony PFM500A1WU 1999

These large, flat-panel, plasma display screens opened a new world of viewing possibilities. They offer dramatic home theater images with clear, crisp detail and high-quality color purity. This model includes features such as adjustable picture size, picture zoom, picture still function, on-screen display in five languages, self-diagnostic function, and a built-in audio amplifier.

Specifications
Country: Japan
Material: Plastic
Height: 25in (63.5cm)
Width: 40¾in (103.5cm)

VIDEO RECORDERS

THE FIRST VIDEO RECORDER was developed by John Mullin and Wayne Johnson in California in 1952. Early models, such as the Ampex VR-1000 and the BBC VERA — enormous machines that used more than 10 miles (16km) of tape per hour — were never intended for use in the home. The first domestic video recorder, the Sony CV-2000, was developed in 1965. Video cassette recorders were introduced by Philips in 1971, and soon became as commonplace in the home as a television. Integrated television and video recorders were introduced in the mid-1990s.

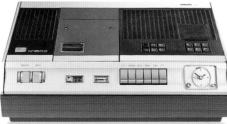

Philips N-1500 1971

Although a monochrome video recorder was developed in 1956 and a color recorder in 1959, the Philips N-1500, with its mechanical clock, was the first commercially successful video recorder.

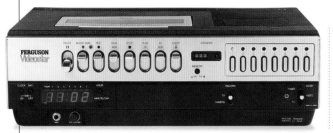

Ferguson Videostar 1980

After the 1970s' "video war" between Sony and Matsushita (the latter's VHS format won the day), video recorders, like the Videostar, became technically more sophisticated. However, they remained bulky appliances.

Panasonic NV-HD645 1999

Highly-styled slender video machines dominated the 1990s. Features included remote control, multi-program operations, long play facilities, and bar-code programming. This Panasonic model also features 60-second jet rewind, a power saving function, and an owner identification code for security.

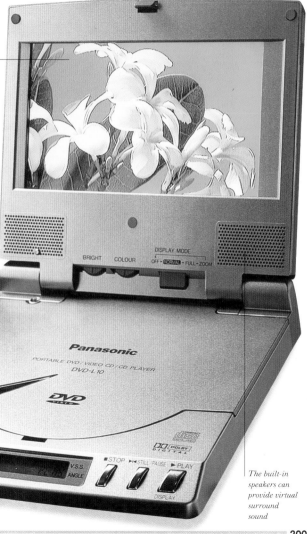

The compact design of this palm-top unit includes an LCD screen

Panasonic
DVD-L10 1998

In the late 1990s, the DVD (Digital Versatile Disc) format revolutionized home entertainment. In addition to excellent audio and video performance, DVD players offer viewing features that include widescreen format and multiple camera angles. This model was the world's first portable DVD player.

Specifications

Country: US
Height: 1⅝in (4.3cm)
Width: 6¼in (16cm)

The built-in speakers can provide virtual surround sound

MUSIC SYSTEMS

MECHANICAL, WIND-UP disc players were introduced in 1886 by Emile Berliner, who coined the term "gramophone." Their sound quality was better than the cylinder versions they replaced and the discs could be mass-produced. The huge amplifying horns meant that these first machines were uncased; but designers soon reduced the size of the motor and developed the internal horn, so the whole unit could be housed in a single cabinet. In 1956, Braun transformed the look of the radio-record player with the Phonosuper SK4. With its clear plastic lid and detached speakers, it became the industry standard. Bang & Olufsen's 1972 Beogram 4000 was one of the most sophisticated turntables ever produced, only to be superseded in the 1980s by the compact disc player. Today, digital technology threatens the vinyl disc with obsolescence.

Sound travels up through the body of the horn

Graphophone c.1900

The cylinder phonograph was developed by Thomas Edison in 1878. Initially it was sold for dictation, but companies soon turned to the more profitable line of music. The Graphophone worked by picking up vibrations from a cylinder through a stylus, which was connected to an amplifying horn. With this system it was possible to make home recordings, but the sound quality was poor.

Specifications

Country: US/UK
Length of stand: 11½in (29cm)

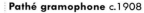
Pathé gramophone c.1908

This gramophone was designed as a piece of furniture
– something that would be given center stage in
the home. A clockwork motor is housed beneath
the turntable in a wooden box, which has a carved
decorative edging. The influence of Art Nouveau
can be seen both in the carving and the attractive,
flower-shaped horn. This style of horn was known
as "Morning Glory" after the flower.

Specifications
Country: France
Height: 26½in (67cm)

Selecta portable 1920s

Portable gramophones
changed little in style from
the 1920s to the 1950s. This
example, housed in its own
carrying case, is wound by a
spring and has an internal
horn. Records can be stored
in a pocket under the lid.

Specifications
Country: UK
Height: Not known

Bermuda Dansette 1950s

By the 1950s, popular music had
become a major industry. With the
advent of rock 'n' roll, teenage
culture was taking off and new
commercial opportunities were
beginning to emerge. The
Dansette, with its colorful,
modern styling, was aimed
at this youthful market.

Specifications
Country: UK
Height: 23½in (60cm)

*The large horn
is shaped to
resemble the
petals of a flower*

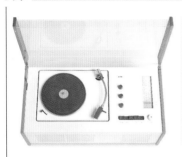

Braun Phonosuper SK55 1956

Also known as "Snow White's Coffin," the SK55 was exhibited at the XI Triennale in Milan in 1957, when Braun was awarded the grand prize. Designed by Dieter Rams and Hans Gugelot, it is a fabulous piece of minimalist design. The clear Plexiglass lid was an innovative concept that was widely copied in the hi-fi industry.

Specifications
Country: Germany
Height: 9½in (24cm)

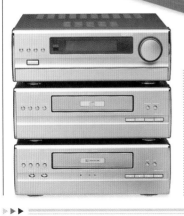

The flat, minimalist design still seems contemporary

Beogram 4000 1972

Aimed at the top end of the market, Jakob Jensen's Beogram 4000 turntable for Bang & Olufsen was designed using the most sophisticated electronics and precision engineering. It was the first record player to have an electronically operated tangential arm, which gives superior sound quality.

Specifications
Country: Denmark
Height: 4in (10cm)

Denon Stacking System D-90 1995

The compact disc has become so popular that in the 1990s most music systems do not include a record player. Integrated stacking systems, like this D-90 by the British company Denon, are the most common. This system includes receiver, CD player, and cassette tape deck, each styled in the sleek silver gray that characterizes Denon products.

Specifications
Country: UK
Height: 11¾in (30cm)

CD TECHNOLOGY

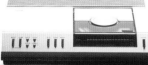

Philips compact disc player, 1983

In a joint venture in 1979, Philips and Sony developed the compact disc. Sound is recorded onto an aluminum plate in millions of tiny micro-cells, known as "pits." It is then reproduced by a laser beam scanning across the surface of the disc as it spins, and sending a signal back to the player for decoding. The first compact disc player was launched in Japan in 1982, and in Europe in 1983. This Philips CD 200 was one of the earliest models available.

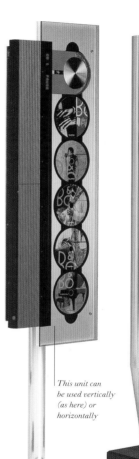

The loudspeakers are made of aluminum and mounted on a solid cast-iron base

This unit can be used vertically (as here) or horizontally

Beosound 9000 1999

This audio system by Bang & Olufsen can play six CDs one after another without a pause. An arm that plays the CDs moves up and down the row of discs. The unit can be displayed vertically, laid on its side, or face up. Amplifiers are housed in the loudspeakers, one has treble, the other bass.

Specifications

Country: UK
Main unit (without stand):
35½ x 12in (90 x 30cm)

TAPE MACHINES

LATE 19TH-CENTURY EXPERIMENTS with tape recording included Danish engineer Valdemar Poulsen's Telegraphone, the first magnetic sound recorder. However, it was not until the 1930s and the invention of plastic magnetic tape that tape-playing machinery became a practical proposition. The appearance of the machine itself has changed and adapted as technology has advanced. Early reel-to-reel tape machines looked plain, utilitarian, and prohibitively bulky. However, since the launch of Philips' Compact Cassette in 1963, machines have became more portable, more streamlined, and more inventive in design.

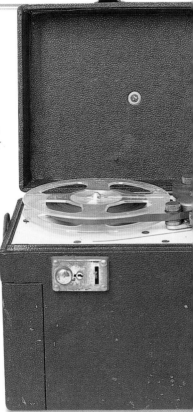

Reel-to-reel tape machine 1950

Traditional reel-to-reel, or open-reel, tape machines like this 1950 model had their origins in a system called the Magnetophon, produced by AEG Telefunken in 1935. The design determined the shape of tape recorders into the 1960s and '70s, with the flat, top-loading system challenged only by the introduction of the front-loading rack systems.

Specifications
Country: Not known
Material: Not known
Width: 14¼in (36.2cm)

The carrying case suggests this model was aimed at reporters

Philips EL3300 1964

In 1963, Philips introduced the world's first compact tape cassette, measuring just 4in (10cm), it could play both stereo and mono recordings. It was launched with the first compact cassette recorder.

Specifications
Country: Netherlands
Material: Polystyrene housing
Width: 4½in (11.5cm)

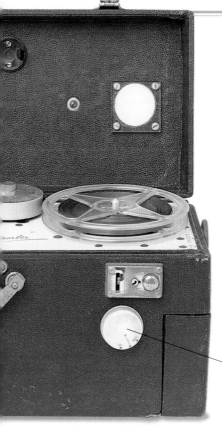

Yamaha **TC800D** 1975

In the mid-1970s, Yamaha commissioned Mario Bellini to design a new cassette recorder. The result was this innovative wedge-shaped "Natural Sound Stereo Cassette Deck." The recorder has a pitch control that can vary the tape speed, and a Dolby noise reduction system.

Specifications
Country: Japan
Material: ABS plastic housing
Width: 12in (30.5cm)

*The recording
button is on
the outside
of the casing*

Sony **Walkman** 1979

The world's first personal stereo, the Walkman, was launched by
Sony in 1979, pioneering a major new product in the audio industry.
The Walkman uses advanced micro-electronics to produce high
quality, unwavering sound from the smallest possible unit.

Specifications
Country: Japan
Material: Aluminum & plastic housing
Width: Not known

Panasonic ghetto blaster 1980s

"Ghetto blaster" is a generic term derived from the young urban population that was attracted to a particular type of large, portable music system. Produced in hard-edged black or, like this Panasonic model, brightly colored, these rectangular boxes often have detachable speakers. Even though they are battery-operated, they produce a powerful sound.

Specifications
Country: Japan
Material: Plastic housing
Width: 21¾in (55cm)

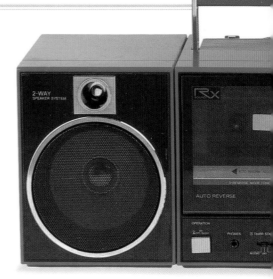

Philips DCC170 1995

In 1992, Philips introduced the Digital Compact Cassette system, an innovation in digital sound recording. The technological sophistication is reflected in the hardworking design of the housing, with its numerous function buttons.

Specifications
Country: Netherlands
Material: Plastic housing
Width: 4¼in (11cm)

Matsui STR323 1996

The 1990s have witnessed the return of softer styling in tape machinery, with rounded forms and pastel colors recalling 1930s streamlining and the car designs of Harley Earl. As the Matsui STR323 shows, the hi-tech features that were given center stage on models like the Yamaha TC800D have been hidden in favor of retro styling.

Specifications
Country: Japan
Material: Plastic housing
Width: 16¾in (42.5cm)

The rounded speaker casing recalls 1930s styling

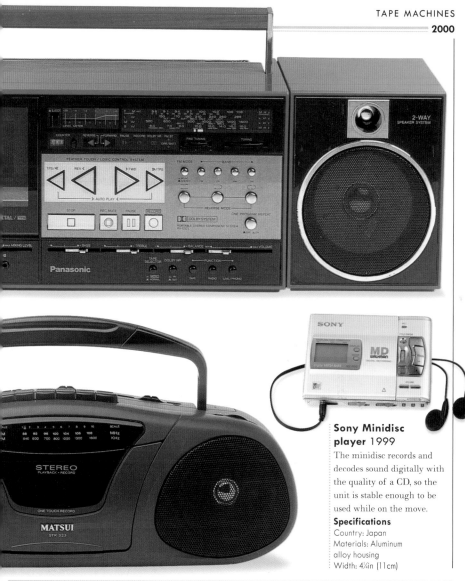

Panasonic

2-WAY SPEAKER SYSTEM

MATSUI
STR 323

STEREO
PLAYBACK · RECORD

ONE TOUCH RECORD

SONY

MD WALKMAN
DIGITAL RECORDING

Sony Minidisc player 1999

The minidisc records and decodes sound digitally with the quality of a CD, so the unit is stable enough to be used while on the move.

Specifications
Country: Japan
Materials: Aluminum alloy housing
Width: 4⅓in (11cm)

KITCHEN & DINING ROOM

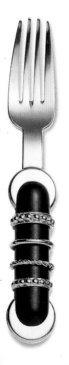
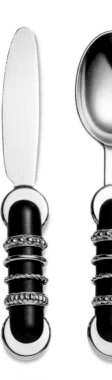
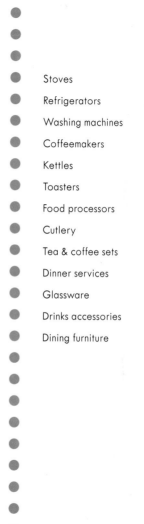

Stoves

Refrigerators

Washing machines

Coffeemakers

Kettles

Toasters

Food processors

Cutlery

Tea & coffee sets

Dinner services

Glassware

Drinks accessories

Dining furniture

The Metropolitan c.1910

By the 1900s, many urban households had access to a gas supply. This gas stove, constructed from cast iron, is typical of early kitchen appliances. It has a crude, industrial appearance and would have been difficult to operate. Later, enamel replaced the rust-prone cast-iron finish.

Specifications

Country: UK
Height: 33in (84cm)

Gas was turned on by means of these simple levers

STOVES

EARLY GAS STOVES resembled the heavy cast-iron ranges of the 19th century. Later, they were raised on slender legs – a feature that emphasized the lighter mechanics of the gas appliance. Designs for electric stoves, introduced in the 1920s, tended to emulate their gas counterparts; and by the end of the 1930s, a standard type had been established that was to endure in popularity for decades. This compact, flat-topped stove formed a continuous surface with the kitchen worktop. Today, technical advances make it possible to combine electric oven and gas stove or vice versa, an innovation that coincides with a flexible new kitchen aesthetic catering to the individual's taste.

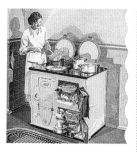

Aga 1929

Gustaf Dalen, a Swedish Nobel Prize winner, invented the Aga stove in 1922. It was licensed for production in the UK in 1929 and, after several redesigns, it is now available in a range of colors, in addition to the traditional cream enamel finish. The Aga burns fuel constantly, retaining heat for cooking – used through several ovens and the hotplates – in its cast-iron shell.

Specifications
Country: UK
Height: 33½in (85cm)

The simmering and boiling plates have elegant, chromed insulating lids

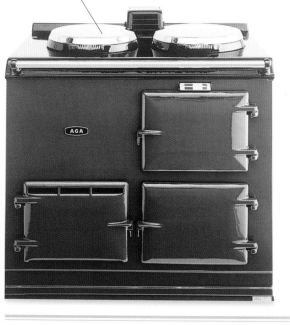

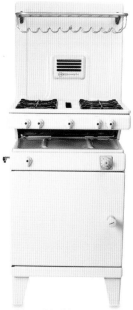

New World stove 1950s

Designed for the modern home, this cream enameled stove is representative of the standard type established in the late 1930s – a flat-topped box that fitted into the continuous horizontal work surface of the custom kitchen. It has four hotplates, a grill, a plate rack, and a thermostatically controlled oven.

Specifications
Country: UK
Height: 56in (142cm)

▶ ▶ ▶

FAST FOOD

The idea of microwave cooking was developed by Percy LeBaron Spencer, an engineer at a radar equipment company in the US. The microwave oven was patented in 1946, but the first models were bulky, expensive, and restricted to industrial use. In the 1960s, domestic models became available.

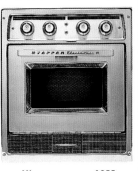

Microwave oven, 1955

This mesh tray can be used to store vegetables or cooking pots

Kitchen Tree 1984

Designed by Stefan Wewerka for Tecta, the Kitchen Tree is the ultimate in space economy, comprising a sink, three electric hotplates, a work surface, storage basket, and hanging facility – all extending from a central column. Wewerka's asymmetrical design breaks with convention, challenging the traditional kitchen.

The fan-shaped stove maximizes use of space around the tree

COMPACT KITCHEN

Designed for the Italian manufacturer Boffi by Joe Colombo, this self-contained mobile mini kitchen consists of a two-ring electric stove, refrigerator, cupboard, and drawer space – all housed within an area of approximately one cubic meter (35 cubic feet).

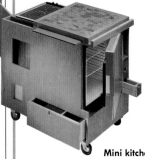

Mini kitchen, 1963

Specifications
Country: Germany
Height: 77in (196cm)

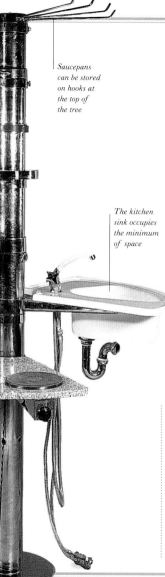

Saucepans can be stored on hooks at the top of the tree

The kitchen sink occupies the minimum of space

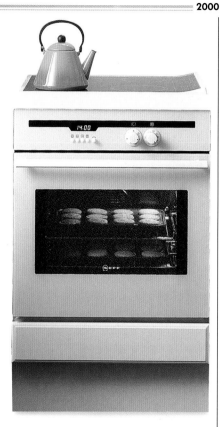

Neff B1441 oven and stove 1996

The integral oven and stove unit is no longer the standard in cooker design. The two parts can be bought separately and the kitchen layout manipulated to suit the consumer's requirements. Top-of-the-range built-in ovens offer a range of user-friendly features, including a heat-reflective glass oven door, slender bar handle, pushaway control knobs, and illuminated dials.

Specifications
Country: Germany
Height: 23in (58.9cm)

REFRIGERATORS

AT THE TURN OF THE CENTURY, for those lucky enough to have one, refrigerators were simply wooden cabinets housing ice boxes. The first domestic refrigerators appeared in 1913. These were cumbersome and had relatively small storage spaces. Some had the cooling mechanism mounted outside the appliance, above the food compartment, earning them the nickname "the beehive." The use of sheet metal led to the traditional metal box shape. For a long time, Europeans considered refrigerators to be an unnecessary luxury. In the US, refrigerators were far more popular with consumers (sixty percent of the population owned one by 1941) and, as a result, many design features originated there. Since the 1950s, refrigerators and freezers have been available in a much wider range of styles, colors, and configurations.

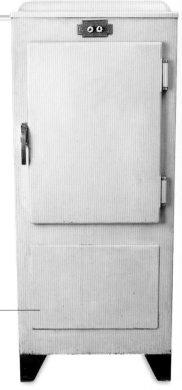

The lower half of the refrigerator houses a heavy motor

STREAMLINING

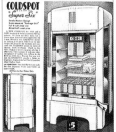

Coldspot Super Six, c.1934

This refrigerator was designed by Raymond Loewy for the US mail order firm Sears Roebuck. Its streamlined, pressed-steel styling resembles the bodywork of a car. The rounded corners and gleaming white finish created a new "hygienic" look that was widely copied by other manufacturers.

Small-capacity fridge 1930s

Made by The British Thomson-Houston Company, this refrigerator is typical of early models. Although it is large and heavy, the cold storage area is small, with the motor occupying considerable space. The two dials at the top of the fridge operate the on/off mechanism and the temperature control.

Specifications

Country: UK
Height: 52in (132cm)

Prestcold fridge late-1950s

This Prestcold refrigerator is clearly influenced by Raymond Loewy's Coldspot Super Six. Its shape demonstrates many of the characteristics of the automobile industry's products. The gently curving lines, the handle, and the logo in the right-hand corner are all reminiscent of car styling.

Specifications
Country: UK
Height: 47in (119cm)

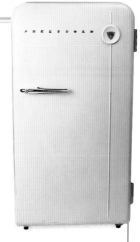

This handle pulls down to reveal a large freezer section

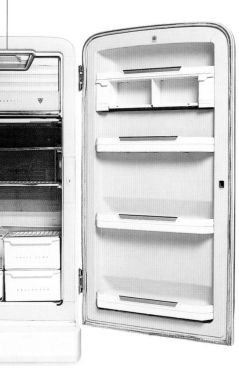

Prestcold fridge 1950s

This Prestcold refrigerator demonstrates a move away from the functional, hygienic-looking white or cream finish that had become standard. The inside is light blue, which, along with pink, was particularly popular. The spacious interior is compartmentalized to separate different food types. A small freezer section is for frozen foods, which had started to become readily available after World War II. The exterior's rounded corners, refined graphics, and square handle give it a modern look.

Specifications
Country: UK
Height: Not known

▶ ▶ ▶

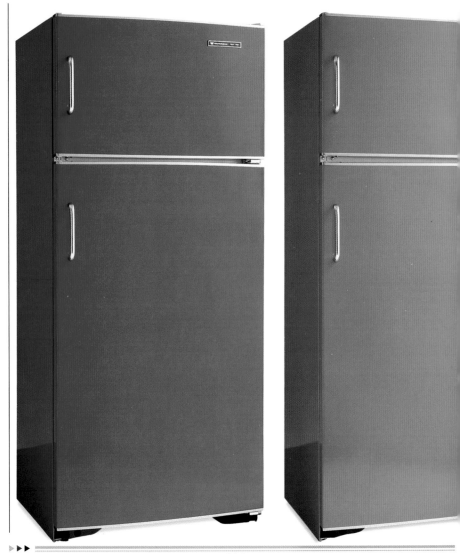

Smeg SP16 1995

During the 1980s the vogue was for refrigerators to be invisible, hidden behind panels in custom kitchens. The Italian manufacturer Smeg is one of a number of companies that challenged this in the 1990s: its large-capacity fridges and freezers are produced in bold primary colors. The overall shape maintains a simple geometry with clean lines.

Specifications
Country: Italy
Height: 64¼in (164cm)

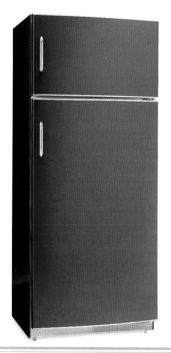

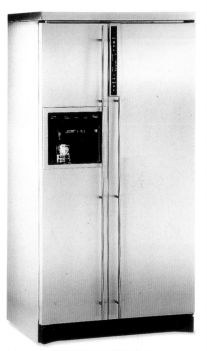

Amana SRDE520TBW 1999

Traditionally, the US market has favored larger capacity refrigerators than have been standard in Europe. However, large models are steadily gaining popularity with Europeans, like this side-by-side Amana unit, which measures 35⅞in (91cm) wide. The left-hand door opens onto a freezer cabinet, while the right houses a normal refrigerator. This model includes an external cold water and ice dispenser and aluminum cladding.

Specifications
Country: US
Height: 68½in (174cm)

WASHING MACHINES

WASHING MACHINES HAVE BEEN AVAILABLE in one form or another for over 200 years. Before the widespread use of electricity, they were aimed at the industrial market and those who could afford to send their clothes to public laundries. Early tubs had to be filled manually with preheated water, and then turned by hand. Until the introduction of the twin-tub, with its separate drum for spinning, saturated clothes were passed through a mangle or wringer. Twin-tubs, such as the Rolls Duo-Matic (see pp.120–21), remained in common use until as recently as the 1980s, as acceptance of the less labor-intensive front-loading machine was surprisingly slow. As discreet in styling as they are powerful in performance, front-loaders now dominate the market. The latest models minimize environmental impact, attesting to the eco-conscious attitudes of the 1990s consumer.

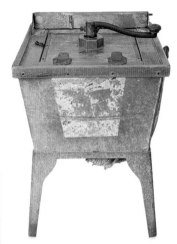

Early washtub 1920s

Before electricity became widely available, washtubs were hand-operated. There were numerous ways of agitating the wash, including pounding, squeezing, and rocking, which were all very labor intensive. This machine is driven by a handle linked to a central paddle that churns the laundry.

Early wringer 1920s

From the beginning of the century, most households would have been equipped with a wringer. This was used to squeeze water out of wet laundry and to smooth linen. There were many different styles of wringer, both freestanding and table-mounted. This one is attached to a hinged roller-frame, which folds downward to convert into a table.

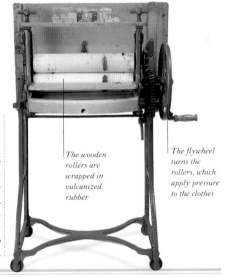

The wooden rollers are wrapped in vulcanized rubber

The flywheel turns the rollers, which apply pressure to the clothes

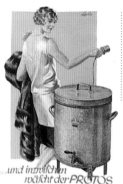

...und inzwischen wäscht der PROTOS

Protos washtub c.1930

Throughout the century, advertisements for domestic appliances have tended to exaggerate their laborsaving properties. This advertisement for the Protos electric washtub implies that the machine will relieve the drudgery of laundry day, giving the housewife freedom to pursue other interests.

When not in use, the wringer can be folded into the machine

The detachable handle enables the wringer to fold into the machine

Simple in design, the square lid has two slots to aid its placement

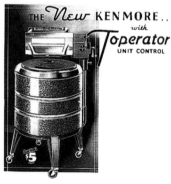

Kenmore Toperator 1933

Designed by Henry Dreyfuss and sold through the Sears catalog, the Toperator shows the growing importance of styling in domestic appliances. Finished in mottled green enamel with chrome trim, the sleek, streamlined body conceals the mechanics.

Hoover Model 0307 1948

This freestanding washtub with hand wringer was the first product manufactured by the UK branch of Hoover. Capable of handling a full family wash, the semi-automatic machine could heat the water electrically to maintain a steady temperature. The wash was agitated by a pulsator attached to the side of the tub.

▶ ▶ ▶

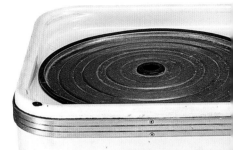

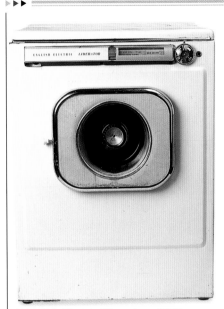

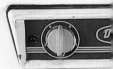

English Electric Liberator c.1950

Relatively expensive front-loaders were
introduced in the 1940s, revolutionary
for combining fully automatic washing
and spinning in a single drum.

Rolls Duo-Matic 1963

The twin-tub has separate drums for
washing and spinning. It did not require
plumbing, but included hoses for water
input and waste. The machine can be
wheeled to the sink for water.

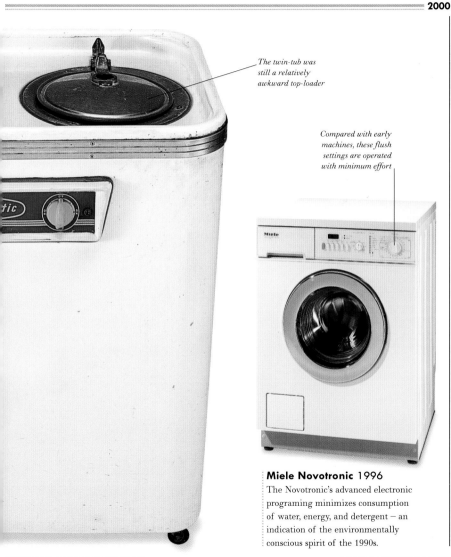

The twin-tub was still a relatively awkward top-loader

Compared with early machines, these flush settings are operated with minimum effort

Miele Novotronic 1996

The Novotronic's advanced electronic programing minimizes consumption of water, energy, and detergent – an indication of the environmentally conscious spirit of the 1990s.

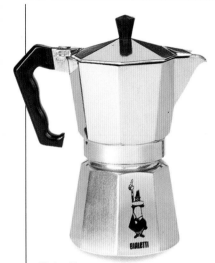

COFFEEMAKERS

MOST COFFEE CONNOISSEURS have their own preferred – and usually very precise – techniques for preparing their favorite beverage. This is reflected in the rich assortment of coffee machines available, which includes percolators, drippots, vacuum pots, cafetières, and cappuccino makers. One of the most popular is Alfonso Bialetti's Moka Express, still favored by Italians for its excellent, strong espresso. Among the modern pots, the elegant Filumena 2 by Sabattini best embodies the simple, formal aesthetics that perfectly suit the ritualistic nature of coffee-making.

Moka Express 1933

The enduringly popular Moka Express coffee-maker was first designed and manufactured in the 1930s by Alfonso Bialetti. This octagonal-shaped percolator is cast in aluminum and has a plastic handle. It continues to be manufactured today by Alberto Bialetti, grandson of Alfonso.

Specifications
Country: Italy
Materials: Aluminum
and Bakelite
Height: 8in (20.2cm)

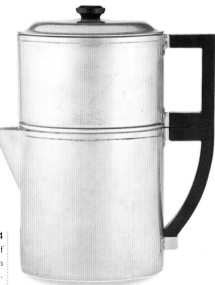

Wear-Ever coffee pot 1934
Lurelle Guild was employed by a number of companies in the 1930s to design aluminum kitchen utensils. The form of this well-proportioned cylindrical coffee pot clearly expresses function. Designed by Guild for easy production, the pot is made from aluminum, with the handles molded in Bakelite.

Specifications
Country: US
Materials: Aluminum and Bakelite
Height: 11in (28cm)

"CONA" coffeemaker 1957

This attractive, hourglass-shaped coffeemaker is by British industrial and graphic designer Abram Games. The heat-resistant glass bowls are suspended from a plastic arm, which is mounted on a polished metal base.

Specifications

Country: UK
Materials: Glass and plastic
Height: 11½in (29.6cm)

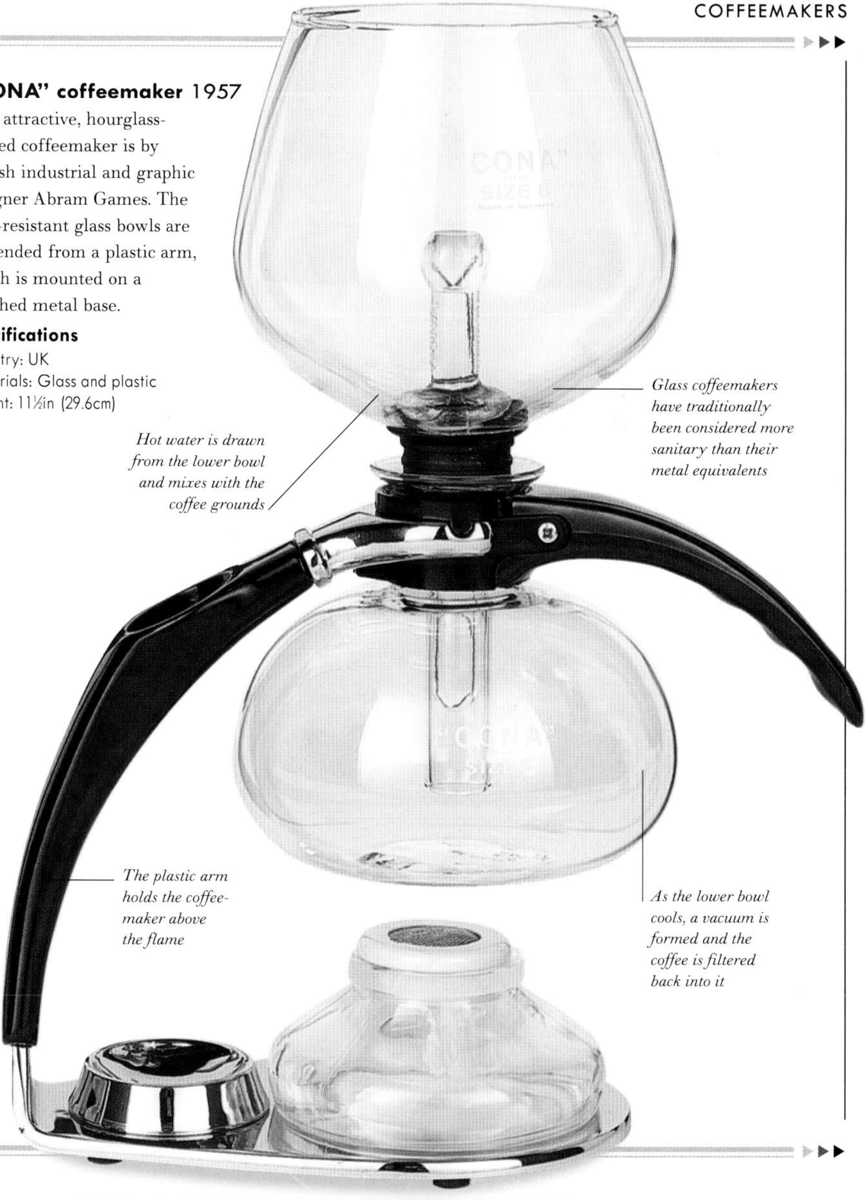

Hot water is drawn from the lower bowl and mixes with the coffee grounds

Glass coffeemakers have traditionally been considered more sanitary than their metal equivalents

The plastic arm holds the coffee-maker above the flame

As the lower bowl cools, a vacuum is formed and the coffee is filtered back into it

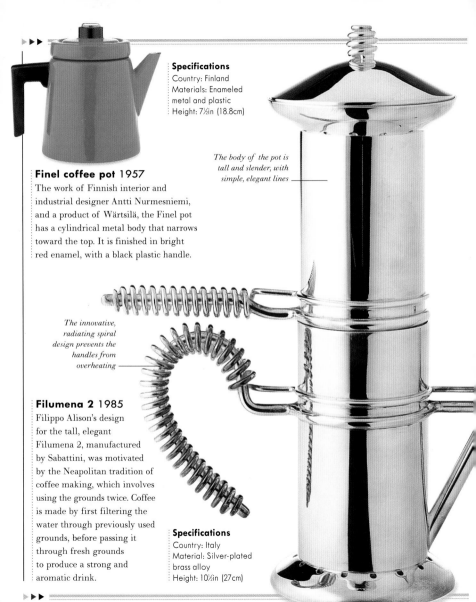

Specifications
Country: Finland
Materials: Enameled
metal and plastic
Height: 7½in (18.8cm)

The body of the pot is tall and slender, with simple, elegant lines

Finel coffee pot 1957

The work of Finnish interior and industrial designer Antti Nurmesniemi, and a product of Wärtsilä, the Finel pot has a cylindrical metal body that narrows toward the top. It is finished in bright red enamel, with a black plastic handle.

The innovative, radiating spiral design prevents the handles from overheating

Filumena 2 1985

Filippo Alison's design for the tall, elegant Filumena 2, manufactured by Sabattini, was motivated by the Neapolitan tradition of coffee making, which involves using the grounds twice. Coffee is made by first filtering the water through previously used grounds, before passing it through fresh grounds to produce a strong and aromatic drink.

Specifications
Country: Italy
Material: Silver-plated
brass alloy
Height: 10⅝in (27cm)

Cafetière 1986

Aldo Rossi began working with Alessi in the early 1980s. His method of working is to present the technicians with outline sketches, rather than finished plans. From these, some of Alessi's most successful coffeemakers have been created. This cafetière shows Rossi's passion for architecture – the lines and proportions of the machine have clearly been inspired by classical columns.

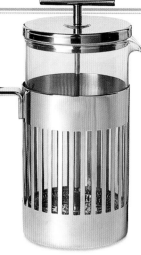

Specifications
Country: Italy
Materials: Stainless steel and glass
Height: 8½in (22cm)

GAGGIA

Although the first espresso machine was patented in 1902 by Italian Luigi Bezzera, the process of forcing hot water through a filter of ground coffee beans was popularized by Achille Gaggia in the late 1940s. His domestic espresso machine, with its piston and lever system, was introduced in 1948 and became an essential ingredient in the 1950s' cult of the coffee bar.

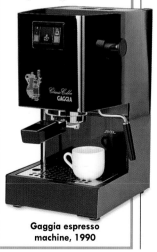

Gaggia espresso machine, 1990

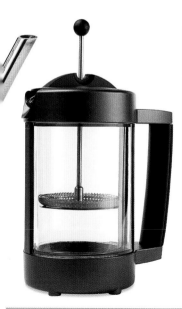

Hot Cafetière 1998

This innovative design consists of a glass jug inside plastic outer walls. The unique twin-walled system keeps the coffee warm for up to 90 minutes, while the outside of the cafetière remains cool to the touch. Although insulated models had been produced for catering use, this was the first see-through design, thus maintaining the look of the traditional cafetière while adding new features.

Specifications
Country: UK
Materials: Glass, plastic, and stainless steel
Height: 9in (22.7cm)

Copper kettle 1909

One of the most successful and influential projects by the pioneering German designer Peter Behrens was the line of kettles he introduced in the early years of the century. There were three basic body shapes: octagon, cylinder, and half-oval; three different colors: brass, copper, and nickel; three types of finish: hammered, dragged, and plain; two lid designs; two handle shapes; and two plinth styles. They were all interchangeable, so that 81 different kettle combinations were possible, though only 30 were marketed.

Specifications
Country: Germany
Materials: Plated, hammered
copper and wicker

KETTLES

EARLY ELECTRIC KETTLES were hazardous appliances: the metal heating element was not waterproof and therefore had to be configured beneath the base of the kettle. Immersable elements first appeared in 1921 – some 30 years after the first kettle had been produced by the US company Carpenter Electric Co. However, the electric version never completely replaced the traditional hob kettle, which enjoyed a new lease of life in the 1980s when the Italian company Alessi produced its "Kettle with a Bird-shaped Whistle" (see pp.128–29). The company has since sold more than 100,000 of these a year.

Silver kettle 1920s

When Danish silversmith Georg Jensen died in 1935, the *New York Daily Herald* called him "the greatest craftsman in silver of the last three hundred years." This hot water pot from the 1920s is a fine example of his craft. Although the solid silver pot could be lifted from the base to be filled, to pour water it was pivoted forward on its two side arms. The stand included an integral oil lamp that heated the water.

Specifications
Country: Denmark
Materials: Silver and ebony

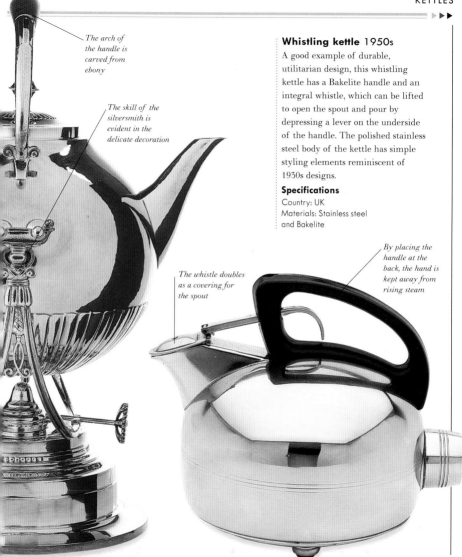

The arch of the handle is carved from ebony

The skill of the silversmith is evident in the delicate decoration

Whistling kettle 1950s

A good example of durable, utilitarian design, this whistling kettle has a Bakelite handle and an integral whistle, which can be lifted to open the spout and pour by depressing a lever on the underside of the handle. The polished stainless steel body of the kettle has simple styling elements reminiscent of 1930s designs.

Specifications
Country: UK
Materials: Stainless steel and Bakelite

By placing the handle at the back, the hand is kept away from rising steam

The whistle doubles as a covering for the spout

AUTOMATIC TEA MAKERS

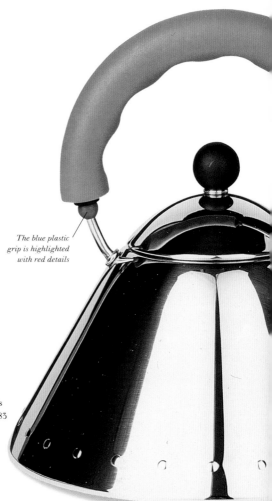

Goblin Teasmade, 1950s

*Goblin introduced its legendary
Teasmade automatic tea maker
in 1937. With its curvaceous cream
styling, this plastic 1950s model
was handsome in appearance,
but not without technical
drawbacks. In theory, the kettle
would heat the water to boiling
point as the user slept; but, in
practice, it did so with such clatter
that only the heaviest sleeper
would fail to wake up. Tea was
produced when the boiling water
was drawn up the metal pipe to
the teapot, where it dribbled
onto the tea leaves.*

*The blue plastic
grip is highlighted
with red details*

Alessi kettle 1983

The architect Michael Graves designed this
"Kettle with a Bird-shaped Whistle" in 1983
for Alessi. With its ornamental detail and
playful imagery, it is a highly successful
and typical piece of postmodernist design.

Specifications

Country: Italy
Materials: Stainless steel
and polyamide

Rowenta Express 1983

The development of plastics able to withstand high temperatures revolutionized kettle design and paved the way for the jug kettle. Exemplified in this 1983 model by Rowenta, jug kettles are able to hold more water than traditional kettles. Some have a coolwall feature that makes them safer than metal kettles, and all have a gauge to indicate how much water there is in the jug.

Specifications
Country: Germany
Material: Plastic

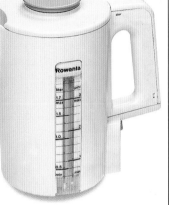

The whistle is shaped like a bird in flight

Russell Hobbs Millennium kettle 1999

This kettle has an OPTEC heating element constructed by screen printing conductive ink onto a stainless steel substrate. It has a low thermal mass so that energy is rapidly transferred to water. The kettle's flat OPTEC element produces rapid boiling and reduced energy consumption.

Specifications
Country: UK
Material: Plastic

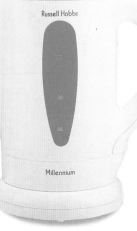

TOASTERS

THE AUTOMATIC POP-UP TOASTER was the invention of American mechanic Charles Strite. His pioneering appliance had a spring device that was operated by thermocontact and ejected the toast at a set time. There were earlier electric toasters, but these were not thermostatically controlled and had to be watched to avoid burning. Today, burnt toast is a thing of the past, with electronic timing control enabling toasters to be set to suit any taste.

The grilling plates were lowered by pressing the heat-resistant wooden buttons

Universal 1920

Designed as a centerpiece for the dining room table, the Universal toaster was more advanced than earlier machines. Although it could only toast one side at a time, it turned the bread to toast the second side. A decorative front plate held the bread against a heated metal element.

Specifications
Country: US
Materials: Metal and wood

Toast-O-Lator mid-1930s

An innovative solution to toasting both sides of the bread at once was the Toast-O-Lator – the bread was grilled as it traveled from one side of the machine to the other on a mini conveyor belt. The lower section of this model features Bakelite styling.

Early toasters were a hazard as the exposed heating element glowed red-hot during use

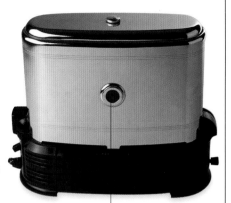

Specifications
Country: US
Materials: Chrome and Bakelite

A quirky feature was the peephole that allowed progress to be monitored

The detailing is typical of Art Deco design

Sunbeam Model T-9 1937

The "Sunbeam silent automatic toaster," created by George Scharfenberg, was patented as an "ornamental" toaster, revealing its dual purpose as a practical household appliance and status symbol. Pop-up toasters were available in the US long before they appeared in Europe.

Decorative features indicate that the toaster was a dining room "ornament" rather than a kitchen appliance

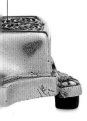

Specifications
Country: US
Materials: Chrome and Bakelite

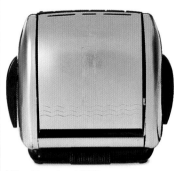

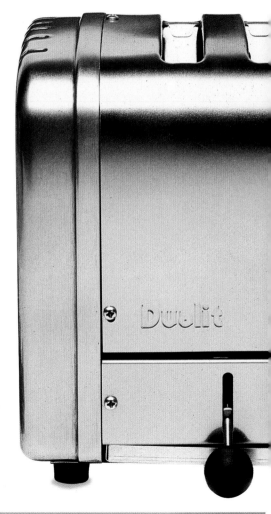

Pye Toaster 1950

Created by Hawkins, this toaster has a Bakelite base and handle designed to protect the user from the heat. The aerodynamic design shows the American passion for streamlining. Drop-side toasters of this type were superseded in the 1950s by an American invention, the pop-up toaster.

Specifications
Country: UK
Materials: Chrome and Bakelite

Dualit 1950s

This classic stainless steel toaster is still available today in two-, four-, and six-slice versions. It was originally intended for use in the catering trade, but is now a sought-after domestic design icon. It has not changed since its invention in the 1950s, a tribute to its timeless design.

Specifications
Country: UK
Material: Stainless steel

Breville Sandwich Toaster 1980–90

Kitchen gadgets, such as sandwich toasters and waffle irons, became popular in the 1970s. The Breville toasts, cuts, and seals the sandwich. The plain white exterior reflects the idea that modern kitchen appliances should be both hygienic and functional.

Specifications
Country: UK
Material: Plastic

Kenwood Coolwall 1990

So-named because even during use the sides do not get hot, the Coolwall toaster offers a range of novel features, including electronic timing control. Housed in a sleek, white shell, the Coolwall is the epitome of rationalized styling for domestic appliances, an approach pioneered by Braun in the 1950s.

Specifications
Country: UK
Material: Plastic

FOOD PROCESSORS

EARLY FOOD MIXERS tended to be scaled-down versions of industrial appliances from the commercial kitchen. They were reliable, but difficult to operate as they were not designed for domestic use. This industrial form continued until the 1950s, when the mixers began to show stylistic references to motor cars, regarded then as symbols of modernity. At the end of the century, small, versatile, robust, easy-to-use machines with a vast array of functions are the norm and are better suited to the modern kitchen.

The unadorned, industrial styling of this early mixer gives it the look of a machine tool

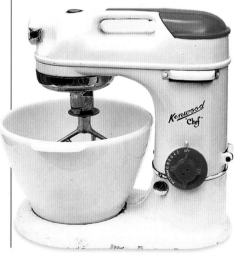

Domestic mixer 1918

Typical of early domestic mixers, this model has a simple, functional design, free from ornamentation. The frame is hinged to allow the mixer to be turned horizontally. It is a smaller, less complex version of an industrial machine, designed purely to mix.

Specifications
Country: France
Material: Metal

Kenwood Chef 1948

The first Kenwood Chef model retains the industrial features associated with early food mixers. Its metal casing has a rounded form, giving the appliance a solid, heavy appearance, which was criticized for identifying housework with work.

Specifications
Country: UK
Materials: Metal, Bakelite, and porcelain

Sunbeam
Mixmaster c.1955

This ingenious design has a detachable mixer unit, which combines the convenience of a hand-held mixer with the versatility of a food processor. It has a space-age appearance and uses motifs from the car industry. A wide range of attachments was available.

Specifications

Country: US
Materials: Chrome-plated metal, plastic, and glass

The detachable pull-out beaters are designed to fit the sides and bottom of the bowl

Kenwood Chef 1960

Kenneth Grange's redesign of the Kenwood Chef represents a
trend in the late 1950s away from industrial styling and toward
a more user-friendly domestic aesthetic. As kitchen appliances
became more commonplace, designers began to create a new
look for the domestic machine. Grange believed that the design
of a product should be incorporated in its manufacture, with
the designer as innovator as well as stylist. The lines are
crisper than the 1948 model, with a single plastic molding
to house the machinery.

Specifications

Country: UK
Material: Plastic

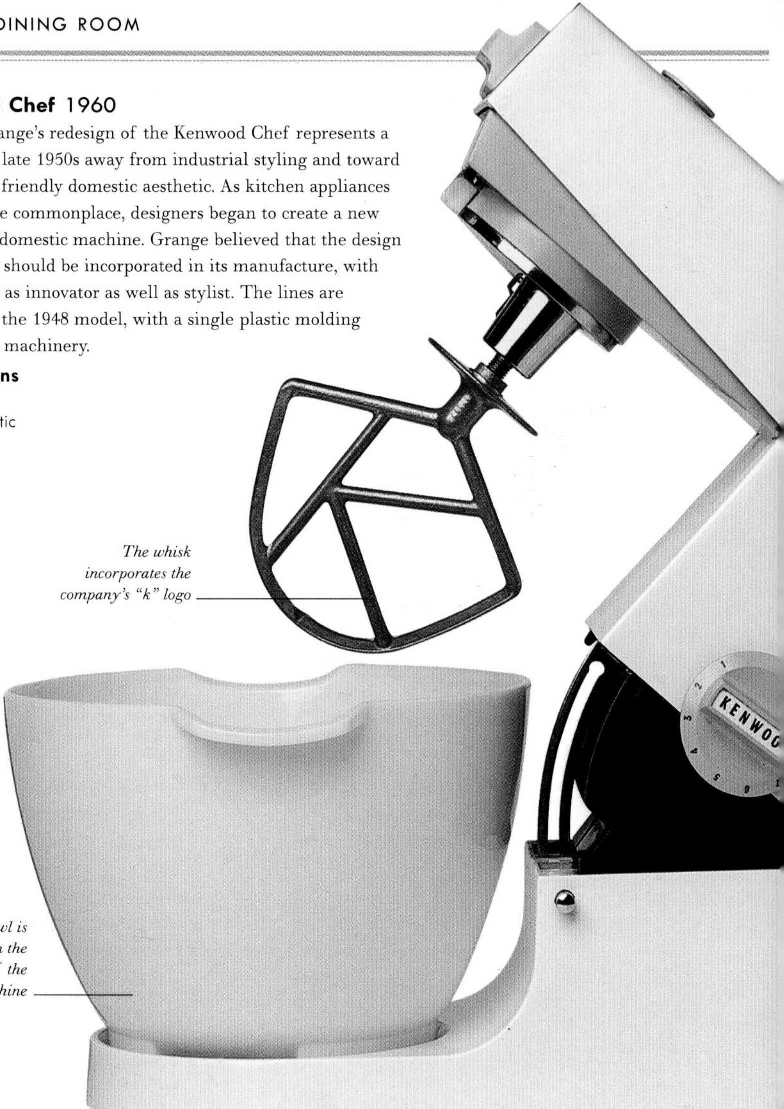

*The whisk
incorporates the
company's "k" logo*

*The bowl is
detachable from the
main body of the
machine*

The redesigned Kenwood Chef has harder edges and sharper lines than the original

Magimix c.1978

The compact Magimix marked a radical departure in food processor design. Devised to carry out a wide range of functions without having to change attachments, it replaces previous mixers with just one bowl and four blades. It takes up little space in the kitchen as the bowl is housed above the stand. The bowl is made of hard-wearing lexan, the same material used for the windows of aircraft, making it dishwasher-safe and impossible to shatter.

Specifications
Country: France
Materials: Plastic and shatterproof lexan

Soft colors and elegant lines typify Braun's skillful styling of domestic appliances

Braun Multipractic 1983

In the 1950s, the bowl and stand arrangement of Braun's electric kitchen machine was similar to that of the Kenwood Chef. In 1983, Braun introduced a new look with the Multipractic. Its design is closer to that of the Magimix than previous mixers. The sleek machine has a covered bowl that slots into grooves in the stand.

Specifications
Country: Germany
Material: Plastic

CUTLERY

BESIDES ITS OBVIOUS UTILITARIAN purpose, cutlery – or flatware as it is sometimes known – also plays an aesthetic role in 20th-century living. The look of a dining room or restaurant table can be greatly enhanced by the cutlery settings. The production of metal utensils has a long tradition, particularly in England, reflected here in David Mellor's Pride service from the late 1950s. Since World War II, there has been an increase in the use of plastics in cutlery, particularly in the design of disposable items. The postmodernist designers of the 1980s and '90s have reintroduced ornament into cutlery: Matteo Thun's decorative Hommage à Madonna (see p.140) elevates knives, forks, and spoons from mere utensils to objects of contemplation.

Silver cutlery c.1908
Charles Rennie Mackintosh designed this cutlery for Miss Cranston's Ingram Street Tearooms in Glasgow. The set is simply decorated with a flared floral motif at the end of each piece; otherwise, a clean, gently elongated line is maintained.

Specifications
Country: UK
Material: Silver plate
Length of knife: 8¼in (21cm)

American Modern 1950
This service was designed by Russel Wright to complement his enormously successful American Modern dinnerware (see p.151). Characterized by disproportionately long handles (in contrast to the abbreviated fork prongs), each piece has been stamped from a single sheet of stainless steel.

Specifications
Country: US
Material: Stainless steel
Length of knife: 8¾in (22cm)

Long handles give greater leverage, compensating for the short fork prongs and spoon bowl

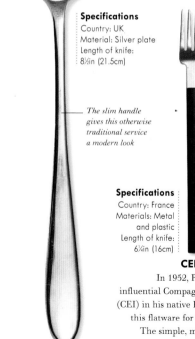

Pride 1957

David Mellor comes from Sheffield, the center of the British steel industry and a city renowned for its flatware. This was his first endeavor at cutlery design for the manufacturers Walker and Hall. Although the style is restrained, the light, slender pieces are without decoration. The set was also produced with contrasting celluloid handles. Pride's success was confirmed in 1957, when it received one of the first British Design Council awards.

Specifications
Country: UK
Material: Silver plate
Length of knife:
8½in (21.5cm)

The slim handle gives this otherwise traditional service a modern look

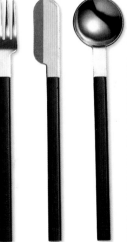

Specifications
Country: France
Materials: Metal and plastic
Length of knife:
6¼in (16cm)

CEI airline cutlery c.1978

In 1952, Raymond Loewy founded the influential Compagnie d'Esthetique Industrielle (CEI) in his native Paris. The company designed this flatware for Air France in the late-1970s. The simple, matching geometry creates an elegant, yet functional, set.

DISPOSABLE PLASTIC CUTLERY

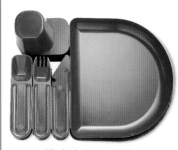

Plack picnic set, 1979

Made from polystyrene, this ingenious disposable picnic set was created by the French designer Jean-Pierre Vitrac in 1979. Plastic has been used as an alternative to wood, metal, and glass since the 19th century, but it has only been with the development of new plastics, such as PVC (polyvinyl chloride), polystyrene, and Plexiglass that we have seen its full potential. Manufactured by Diam, this bright red, lightweight set is easy to stack and store. The knife, fork, spoon, cup, and plate are joined together – so nothing can be lost in transit – and are then separated by the user.

Hommage à Madonna c.1985

Since the 1980s, postmodern designers have been responsible for putting symbolism and metaphor back into design. In his Hommage à Madonna service, made by WMF, Austrian ceramicist and designer Matteo Thun applies luxurious decoration to everyday objects, making reference in the process to the famous performer's flamboyant style.

Specifications

Country: Germany
Materials: Gilded brass and PVC plastic
Length of knife: 7in (18cm)

Brass rings refer to Madonna's ornate personal style

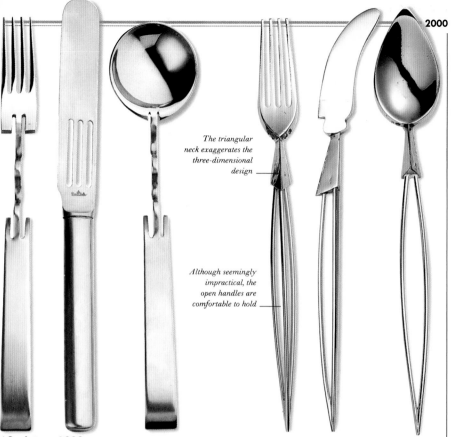

The triangular neck exaggerates the three-dimensional design

Although seemingly impractical, the open handles are comfortable to hold

Sculptura 1989

This extravagant cutlery set was produced for Rosenthal by the Italian designer Lino Sabattini. The strange, curved stems break the line of the conventional cutlery form and show the influence of deconstructivism.

Specifications

Country: Germany
Material: Stainless steel
Length of knife: 10in (25cm)

Open-handle cutlery 1991

Instead of the solid form normally favored for flatware, Czech designer Bořek Šípek has left the handles of this cutlery set open, each piece gently bowing in the middle and finishing in a point.

Specifications

Country: Czech Republic
Materials: Stainless steel and gold plate
Length of knife: 8in (20.5cm)

TEA & COFFEE SETS

The handle of the tea kettle is coated in rattan

THROUGHOUT THE WORLD, tea drinking is an opportunity for ceremony and ritual. Perhaps it is for this reason that so much attention has been paid to the production of tea and coffee sets, with contributions made by some of the world's best-known designers. Diverse materials have been used, from traditional earthenware to silver, iron, copper, and glass. One of the most celebrated sets, Jan Eisenloeffel's fine Arts and Crafts service, is made from brass. Some designers have applied their artistic concepts to product design; although, as Malevich's half cup demonstrates (see p.145), these are not always practical. In terms of popularity, it is often the traditional designs, such as Royal Doulton's best-selling Old Country Roses (see p.146), that prove the most enduring.

Brass tea set 1900–03

Dutch designer Jan Eisenloeffel trained as a goldsmith and silversmith, and later went on to study under Fabergé (1846–1920) in St. Petersburg. His work expresses control and harmony: this brass tea set is beautifully made in the Arts and Crafts tradition, with decoration kept to a minimum. A similar set was exhibited to acclaim at the first International Arts and Crafts Exhibition, held in Turin in 1902.

Specifications

Country: Holland
Materials: Brass, rattan, and ebony
Height of tea kettle: 8¾in (22.5cm)

Each item has broad, plain surfaces

Specifications

Country: Soviet Union
Materials: Porcelain
with enameled
decoration
Height of sugar bowl:
4¼in (10.6cm)

*The details of
craftsmanship
are left exposed
to view*

Russian sugar bowl and cream pitcher 1920–25

These two items by Zinaida Kobylestskaya have all the
hallmarks of Russian avant-garde design of the early 1920s.
The fragmented, semi-abstract images of agricultural and
industrial scenes, together with the hammer and sickle, had a
powerful symbolic resonance for the post-revolutionary citizens
of Soviet Russia. Fragments of cogs, which were used as the
State Porcelain Factory trademark, can be seen on both lids.

*Decoration is limited
to a simple pattern
of three engraved
parallel lines*

*Strong, geometric
silhouettes typify
Eisenloeffel's work*

The bold stripes are both structural and decorative

Silver tea service 1928

Jean Puiforcat's tea services from the 1920s and '30s are characterized by their simple geometry. He was interested in a mathematical principle known as the Golden Section, which provided a system of proportion for his work.

Specifications

Country: France
Materials: Silver and walnut
Height of teapot: 4½in (11.4cm)

The geometric design is repeated in slightly different form on the separate pieces

Japanese teapot and sugar bowl c.1930s

Nowhere is the serving of tea more ritualized than in Japan, where the tea ceremony has been raised to an art form. This teapot and sugar bowl were produced for export to the West. The decoration and geometric styling show the influence of Art Deco. By the 1930s, distinct design styles had become truly international, leading to the creation of products that could be marketed on a global scale.

Specifications

Country: Japan
Material: Ceramic
Height of teapot:
6¼in (16.1cm)

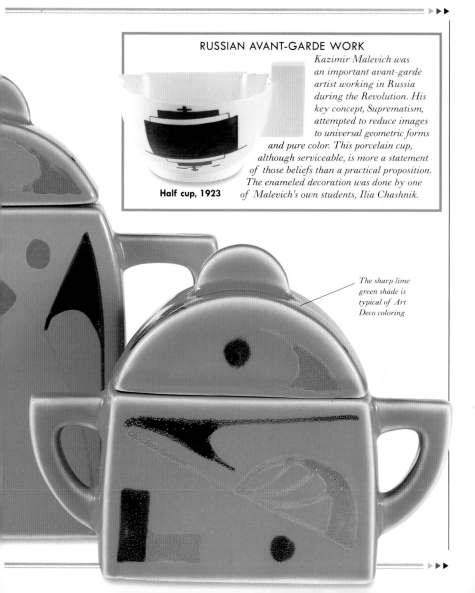

RUSSIAN AVANT-GARDE WORK

Kazimir Malevich was an important avant-garde artist working in Russia during the Revolution. His key concept, Suprematism, attempted to reduce images to universal geometric forms and pure color. This porcelain cup, although serviceable, is more a statement of those beliefs than a practical proposition. The enameled decoration was done by one of Malevich's own students, Ilia Chashnik.

Half cup, 1923

The sharp lime green shade is typical of Art Deco coloring

Royal Doulton Old Country Roses tea set 1962

With estimated sales of well over 100 million pieces since its launch, Old Country Roses is indisputably the world's best-selling tableware design. It was created by Harold Holdcroft, who found inspiration in the typical English country garden with roses in full bloom. This traditional tea set is made of the finest china and has a delicate, ornate line taken to its full effect in the elegant handles. Although tableware constitutes the core of the Old Country Roses collection, a vast range of associated items also bear the distinctive floral imagery, including photograph frames, trinket boxes, and stationery.

Specifications

Country: UK
Material: Bone china
Height of teapot: 7¼in (18.5cm)

These pieces have deceptively generous volumes

The form of each piece is emphasized by the mixture of gloss and matt finishes

TAC 1 tea set 1969

In 1945, Walter Gropius founded The Architects Collaborative (TAC). A former director of the Bauhaus, Gropius is one of this century's most influential architect/designers. Gropius, Louis McMillen, and Katherine de Souza designed this sophisticated two-tone tea set for Rosenthal. Its clear lines and lack of ornamentation demonstrate the designers' concern for harmony and clarity.

Specifications

Country: Germany
Material: Porcelain
Height of teapot: 5in (12.5cm)

Drop tea set 1971

This inventive, streamlined tea set by Luigi Colani is produced here in white porcelain, but was also available in black or gold. It was commissioned by Rosenthal for its Studio Line. The flowing forms have an organic quality, particularly evident in the teapot and milk jug, which together seem to relate like an adult and child.

Specifications

Country: Germany
Material: Porcelain
Height of teapot: 4¼in (10.7cm)

The choice of black glaze — more often associated with coffee drinking — is an unusual one

Alessi tea set 1983

In the 1980s, Alessi commissioned a series of
tea services that elevated functional objects
to high art. Oscar Tusquets' silver set
cleverly combines the flowing
forms of the handles with
angular, cutaway spouts.

Specifications

Country: Italy
Material: Silver
Height of teapot: 7½in (19cm)

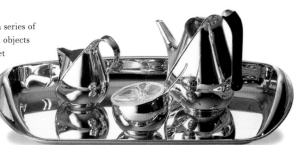

VENTURI'S VILLAGE

*American architect and designer
Robert Venturi is a leading
proponent of postmodernism.
His theories are played out in
this 1986 tea set for Swid Powell.
References to classical and
vernacular architecture can be
seen, together with colors and
shapes that might have been
derived from theme parks
and carnivals.*

Village tea set, 1986

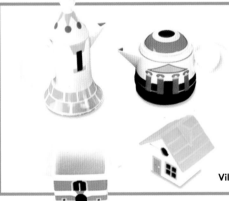

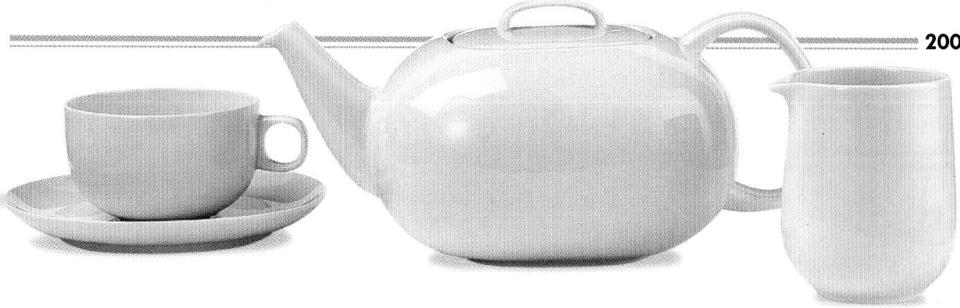

Moon tea set 1997

This beautifully simple design was created by British designer Jasper Morrison for Rosenthal. Morrison's work is a fine example of purism, a minimalist concept of design that abandons ornament and unnecessary shaping in favor of purity of line and form. The 1990s saw a move toward minimalism in many areas of design.

Specifications
Country: Germany
Material: Porcelain
Height of teapot:
4½in (11.5cm)

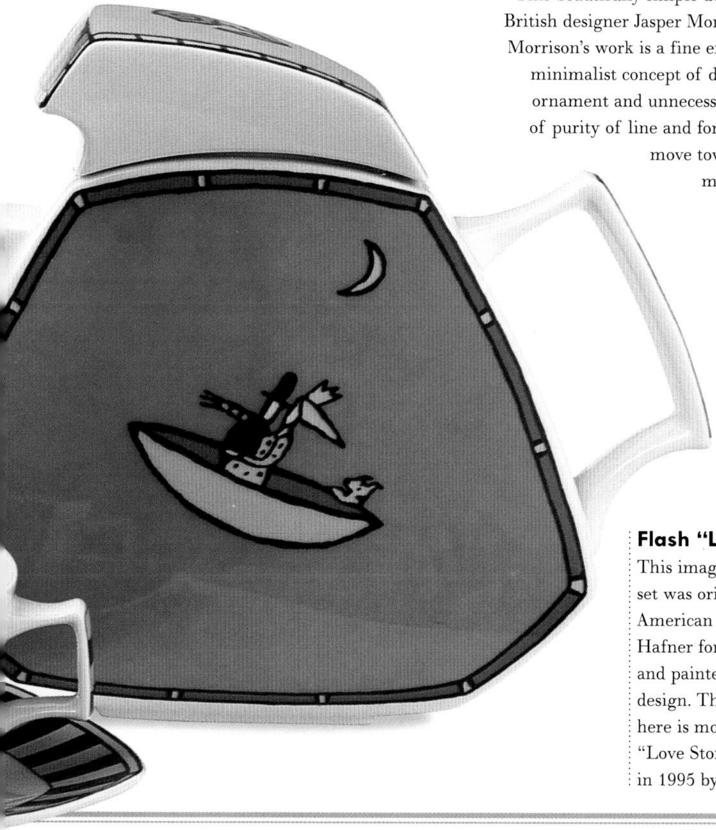

Specifications
Country: Germany
Material: Ceramic
Height of teapot:
7½in (19cm)

Flash "Love Story" 1987

This imaginatively shaped tea set was originally designed by American ceramicist Dorothy Hafner for Rosenthal in 1987, and painted with an abstract design. The decoration shown here is more recent. Entitled "Love Story," it was created in 1995 by Kitti Kahane.

DINNER SERVICES

THE 20TH CENTURY HAS SEEN the introduction of a profusion of interesting dinner service designs alongside traditional, high quality porcelain sets. During the 1920s, many designers, including Clarice Cliff in the UK, chose earthenware over porcelain. At the end of the 1930s, Russel Wright's name became famous for his American Modern service, which was revolutionary for its "mix and match" colored glazes and organic shapes. Eva Zeisel was another leading contemporary ceramic designer at work in the US; and she too embraced new, more organic shapes. Other designers have retained a formal geometry, and, in the hands of Postmodern designers like Aldo Rossi, dinnerware has taken on humorous architectural motifs.

Frank Lloyd Wright c.1920

Between 1915 and 1922, Frank Lloyd Wright was working in Tokyo on a commission to design the Imperial Hotel and its interior furniture and decor. This seven-piece dinner service was designed in about 1920, but not produced for the mass market by Noritake until about 1962. It is made from hand-painted white porcelain and has a pattern of red, green, and yellow circles.

Asymmetrical geometric motifs were hand-painted onto the porcelain

Specifications
Country: Japan
Material: Porcelain
Diameter of plate:
6½in (17cm)

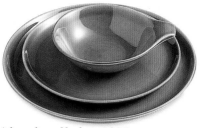

Specifications
Country: US
Material: Glazed earthenware
Diameter of plate: 10in (25.2cm)

Shown here in Seafoam Blue, each piece came in a choice of six colors

American Modern 1937

Although Russel Wright's unusually shaped dinner service was thought to be daring when it was first introduced in 1939 by Steubenville Pottery, it sold a phenomenal 80 million pieces over 20 years. The soft curves and the use of muted colors that could be mixed and matched, created an informal quality.

Museum 1942–45

This dinner service was the first modern porcelain set to be produced in the US. It was designed by Hungarian ceramicist Eva Zeisel, following a recommendation from the Museum of Modern Art, New York, and was produced by the Shenango Company for Castleton China, Inc.

Specifications
Country: US
Material: Porcelain
Diameter of saucer: 6½in (17cm)

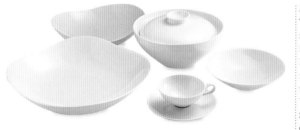

Homemaker 1955

Designed by Enid Seeney for Ridgeway Potteries, this informal and self-conscious dinner service was clearly aimed at young consumers. The shape of the set remains traditional compared, for example, with Russel Wright's American Modern, but its quirky drawings of modern furniture are typical of the 1950s.

Specifications
Country: UK
Material: Glazed ceramic
Diameter of plate: 10in (25.5cm)

The lively illustrations feature a variety of household items

▶ ▶ ▶

Idillio Bokara 1985

British designer Tricia Guild (1947–)
is well-known for her radiant color
compositions. She was commissioned
by Rosenthal to provide the
decoration on the elegant Idillio
service, designed by Paul
Wunderlich (1927–). In
Bokara she has produced
a dazzling pattern of
colors in bold reds
and yellows.

Specifications

Country: Germany
Material: Porcelain
Diameter of plate:
10½in (27cm)

*Rich colors
dominate
this striking
modern service* —

*The elegant
form of the
service is
complemented
by the vibrant
colors* —

Cupola Strada 1990

The white Cupola dinner service was designed by Mario Bellini and introduced in 1988 as part of the German company Rosenthal's Studio Line. This particular version, featuring black and gray decoration by Yang, appeared in 1990. By adopting a geometric approach, Bellini has produced a well-balanced and extremely attractive service.

Specifications
Country: Germany
Material: Porcelain
Diameter of plate:
10¼in (26cm)

The unusual banded handles are a recurring element in the design

Specifications
Country: Germany
Material: Porcelain and glass
Diameter of plate: 12¼in (31cm)

Il Faro Finestra 1994

Architect and designer Aldo Rossi produced this dinner service for Rosenthal. In it he incorporates architectural shapes to humorous effect, making coffee pots as lighthouses, sugar bowls as beach huts, and salt-cellars as obelisks. The decoration on this Finestra variation was created by the Indonesian artist Yang (1953–).

Decoration is provided by a pattern of circles and squares

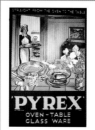

Early poster

PYREX
Invented by scientists working for the American Corning Glass Company, these heat-resistant, low-expansion oven dishes were first available for baking and roasting in 1915. Early Pyrex examples used thick glass and were without handles. However, they were easy to clean and were suitable as oven-to-tableware.

GLASSWARE

THE VENETIAN ISLAND OF MURANO, Orrefors in Sweden, Iittala in Finland, and Corning in the US are four outstanding centers of excellence in a long history of glassware design and production. The variety of techniques and finishes developed over the centuries has allowed designers to experiment freely with style and decoration. Glass design in the 20th century began with the memorable work of the Art Nouveau designers — most innovatively in the form of Louis Comfort Tiffany's high-quality Favrile glassware (see pp.72–73). Since then, other glass designers have perfected the arts of pressing, layering, engraving, and staining.

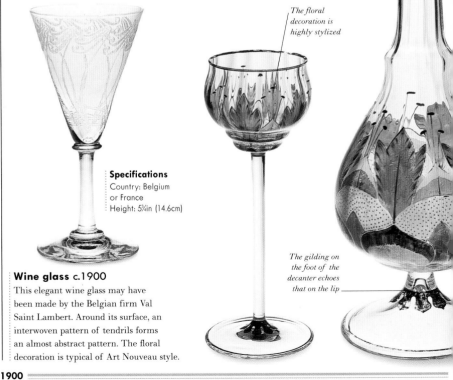

The floral decoration is highly stylized

Specifications
Country: Belgium or France
Height: 5¾in (14.6cm)

The gilding on the foot of the decanter echoes that on the lip

Wine glass c.1900

This elegant wine glass may have been made by the Belgian firm Val Saint Lambert. Around its surface, an interwoven pattern of tendrils forms an almost abstract pattern. The floral decoration is typical of Art Nouveau style.

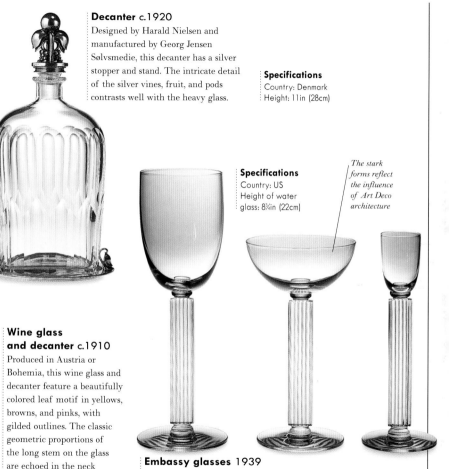

Decanter c.1920

Designed by Harald Nielsen and manufactured by Georg Jensen Sølvsmedie, this decanter has a silver stopper and stand. The intricate detail of the silver vines, fruit, and pods contrasts well with the heavy glass.

Specifications
Country: Denmark
Height: 11in (28cm)

Specifications
Country: US
Height of water glass: 8¾in (22cm)

The stark forms reflect the influence of Art Deco architecture

Wine glass and decanter c.1910

Produced in Austria or Bohemia, this wine glass and decanter feature a beautifully colored leaf motif in yellows, browns, and pinks, with gilded outlines. The classic geometric proportions of the long stem on the glass are echoed in the neck of the decanter.

Specifications
Country: Austria
Height of decanter: 12¾in (32.5cm)

Embassy glasses 1939

These glasses – for water, champagne, and cordial – were designed by Edwin Fuerst and Walter Dorwin Teague for the 1939 New York World's Fair, and made by Libbey Glass Co. The stem resembles a classical column, remaining the same height for each of the glasses.

Theme Formal goblets 1950s

While Russel Wright's products were typically informal and inexpensive, they always displayed an innovative use of material and form. His Theme Formal goblets are decorated with bands of blue and orange.

Specifications

Country: US
Height of large
goblet: 8½in (22cm)

Wright's simple, streamlined styling makes the goblets comfortable to hold

Decanter and glass 1953–59

This highly textured olive green decanter and glass set was produced by the Swedish company Boda. The designer, glassmaker, and metalworker Erik Höglund, adopted a mold-blown technique to create a relief pattern featuring human figures on the surface of the glass.

Specifications
Country: Sweden
Height of decanter: 5¾in (14.4cm)

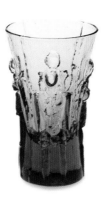

Maaru glasses 1980

Tapio Wirkkala's glassware is renowned for its organic form and fine surface decoration. This set was made at the Iittala glassworks in Finland.

Specifications
Country: Finland
Height of large glass: 6in (15cm)

Calici Natale goblet 1990

For centuries, the tiny Venetian island of Murano has been famous for its glassmaking. This elegant goblet was produced there by the Carlo Moretti Studio. Its long, deep bowl has a finely textured surface and rests on a blue base.

Specifications
Country: Italy
Height: 9½in (24cm)

DRINKS ACCESSORIES

IT IS NOT UNCOMMON for predominant design movements to influence the look of the most humble of items, and drinks accessories are no exception. Craftsmen inspired by Art Nouveau expressed themselves through elaborate floral patterns and curvilinear forms, while Art Deco afforded a sleek, luxurious quality to items that might previously have been given only a perfunctory treatment. In the Soviet Union, constructivism and, later, social realism, intended to reflect the endeavors of the masses to build a new society. For the modernists, it was new materials that generated particular enthusiasm.

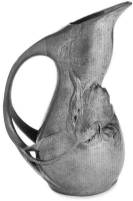

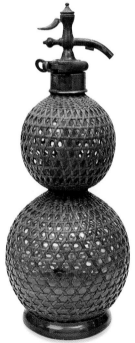

Pitcher 1895–1909

Designed in the Cologne studio of Engelberg Kayser, this pitcher is influenced by French Art Nouveau. The handle divides and extends to either side of the jug, where it develops into a flower head.

Specifications
Country: Germany
Material: Pewter
Height: 8in (20.6cm)

Soda siphon
c.1910

A wicker casing creates a decorative geometric pattern on this hourglass-shaped clear glass siphon. The use of wicker is reminiscent of the styling of Chianti wine bottles.

Specifications
Country: France
Materials: Glass, wicker, and metal
Height: 19¾in (50cm)

The gleaming chromed surface contrasts strikingly with the solid black of the plastic

Vacuum pitcher 1930

Designed by Nowland and Schladermundt for the manufacturing company American Thermos, this vacuum pitcher was sold in the 1930s. Its black spherical stopper echoes the rounded form of the body.

Specifications
Country: US
Materials: Chromium and plastic
Height: Not known

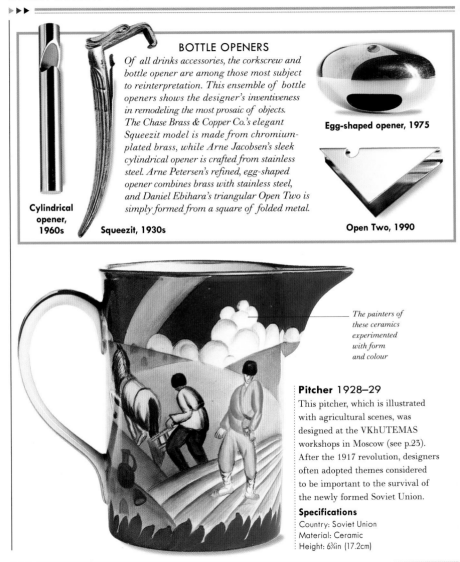

BOTTLE OPENERS

Of all drinks accessories, the corkscrew and bottle opener are among those most subject to reinterpretation. This ensemble of bottle openers shows the designer's inventiveness in remodeling the most prosaic of objects. The Chase Brass & Copper Co.'s elegant Squeezit model is made from chromium-plated brass, while Arne Jacobsen's sleek cylindrical opener is crafted from stainless steel. Arne Petersen's refined, egg-shaped opener combines brass with stainless steel, and Daniel Ebihara's triangular Open Two is simply formed from a square of folded metal.

Egg-shaped opener, 1975

Cylindrical opener, 1960s

Squeezit, 1930s

Open Two, 1990

The painters of these ceramics experimented with form and colour

Pitcher 1928–29

This pitcher, which is illustrated with agricultural scenes, was designed at the VKhUTEMAS workshops in Moscow (see p.23). After the 1917 revolution, designers often adopted themes considered to be important to the survival of the newly formed Soviet Union.

Specifications

Country: Soviet Union
Material: Ceramic
Height: 6¾in (17.2cm)

Cocktail shaker c.1930

Cocktail wares were at the peak of their popularity during the 1930s. Manufactured by Napier, this amusing penguin cocktail shaker exhibits all the hallmarks of Art Deco styling.

Specifications
Country: US
Material: Silver
Height: 12¼in (31.1cm)

The polished, streamlined body is adorned with penguin features

The chromium body transforms a functional object into a stylish article

Soda siphon c.1930s

The gently curved body of this popular soda siphon demonstrates the industrial designer Norman Bel Geddes' application of streamlining to household objects.

Specifications
Country: US
Materials: Chromium and enamel
Height: 10¼in (26cm)

Ice bucket 1960

Danish modernists, such as Jens Quistgaard, eschewed the quest for new materials and used traditional ones, in this case teak, to produce beautifully sculpted forms.

Specifications
Country: Denmark
Material: Teak
Height: 15½in (39.4cm)

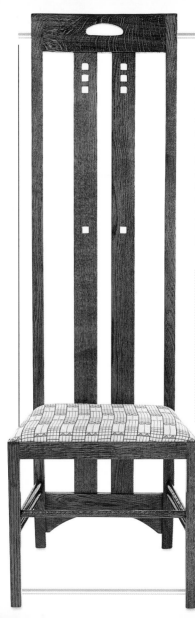

DINING FURNITURE

TRADITIONAL WOODEN DINING TABLES and chairs have maintained a popularity throughout the century, even though wood is expensive and easily damaged. Designers like Josef Hoffmann and Charles Rennie Mackintosh produced boldly modern furniture while retaining the distinctive qualities of wood. Carlo Mollino is one of a number of designers who used machine manufacturing techniques and manipulated plywood to produce original dining furniture (see p.164). Other designers used new materials, particularly plastic, to find alternative solutions.

High-backed chair c.1900

The enduring popularity of dining furniture by Charles Rennie Mackintosh is demonstrated in this modern reproduction of a chair designed for the Ingram Street Tearooms, Glasgow. Mackintosh often incorporated the curvilinear motifs of continental Art Nouveau into his rectilinear designs; but here a strictly geometric style is used.

Specifications
Country: UK
Material: Stained oak

Purkersdorf chair 1905

Spheres, rectangles, and squares are characteristic motifs in Josef Hoffmann's work. This limited edition chair was manufactured by Thonet Brothers for the dining room of the Purkersdorf Sanatorium in Vienna. The chair has an austere rectilinear form, with a high back for firm support.

Specifications
Country: Austria
Materials: Bent beechwood and leather

The carved sphere reinforces the joint and repeats the ornamental motif

Dining table with stacking chairs 1949

Designed by Hans Wegner for Fritz Hansen, this dining furniture was constructed using traditional carpentry methods. Although some items are machine made, quality craftsmanship is evident in the finish and joints. The arrangement of the chair legs gives the diner greater freedom of movement and facilitates stacking.

Specifications

Country: Denmark
Materials: Beech and plywood

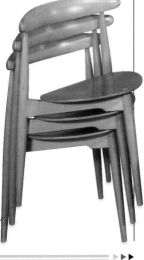

The chair is designed to stack easily

Bentwood chair 1952

One of two versions, this molded plywood
chair was designed by Carlo Mollino for the
Casa Cataneo-Agra in Varese, Italy. It has a
strong sculptural quality expressed in the
flowing organic lines. Like much of Mollino's
work, this piece was made by Apelli & Varesio.

Specifications
Country: Italy
Materials:
Bentwood and
laminated ash

Tulip Group 1956

The Pedestal, or Tulip Group as
it became known, was designed by
Eero Saarinen for Knoll. Saarinen's
aim was to form the entire chair in
plastic. But the stem, lacking the
strength to bear the shell, had to
be cast in aluminum. The single
pedestal was Saarinen's solution
to the "slum of legs."

Specifications
Country: France
Materials: Plastic-coated
aluminum and fiberglass

The molded plastic chair back provides flexibility

The supporting single stem offers diners maximum leg room

Tesi, Quinta 1986

In his high-tech Tesi table and Quinta chair, Mario Botta made use of perforated sheet iron and steel to create a defined silhouette.

Specifications
Country: Italy
Materials: Steel, sheet metal, and glass

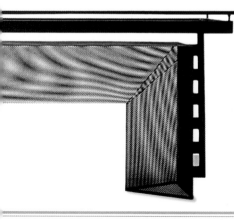

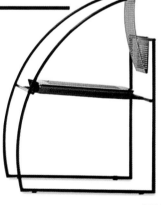

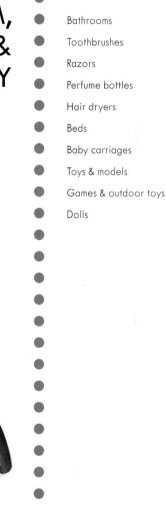

BATHROOM, BEDROOM, & NURSERY

BATHROOMS

THE EARLIEST BATHROOMS were a luxury afforded only by the wealthy, but improved plumbing and an increased concern for hygiene led to their inclusion in most homes by the 1920s. Wood gave way to shiny, white nonporous materials, such as ceramic tile and enameled cast iron. By the 1930s, suite ensembles appeared in various colors, enthusiastically adopted in plastic form in the 1950s. Later, shower units were installed and matching accessories became available.

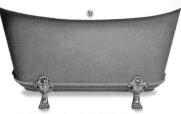

Flush toilet 1902

This high-level flush toilet was manufactured by the Scottish company Shanks. The decorative, hand-painted, floral transfer print is a British county council pattern, used for public conveniences only. The cast iron cistern rests on two sunflower brackets.

Specifications
Country: UK
Height with cistern: 89½in (228cm)
Materials: Porcelain, cast iron, nickel, and mahogany

Chariot bath 1900–05

This double-ended French Empire bath would have been filled from central, wall-mounted faucets, leaving both ends free for bathers. It is considerably shorter and deeper than the City bath. Originally, it would have been produced in white.

Specifications
Country: France
Height: 31½in (80cm)
Material: Cast iron

City or Times bath 1903–15

This freestanding, roll-top bath represents a departure from the heavily wood-paneled fittings of the typical Victorian bathroom. It is Art Nouveau in style, with polished metal ball-and-claw feet and built-in, fan-shaped soap dishes.

Specifications
Country: UK
Height: 24in (61cm)
Material: Cast iron

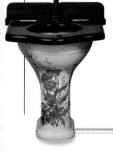

Art Nouveau basin 1903–15

Even households without adequate plumbing could have used this wash basin. It was designed to be freestanding, and therefore without faucets, drain pipe, or bathroom plumbing. Its elaborate stand has been crafted from scrolled wrought iron, with the circular bowl made from nickel or porcelain.

Specifications
Country: France
Height: 53in (135cm)
Materials: Wrought
iron and porcelain

Edwardian basin 1905

The easy-to-clean shrouded faucets of this wash stand reflect the growing concern for hygiene at the turn of the century. The basin may have been used with a splashback against the wall.

Specifications
Country: UK
Height: 36in (91cm)
Materials: Mahogany, marble, and porcelain

The decorative stand is crafted from polished wrought iron

Art Deco basin 1920s

This typically Art Deco octagonal basin, made by Jacob Delphon, is still in production today. Unusually for the time, its basin-mounted faucets are color coded to indicate hot and cold.

Specifications
Country: France
Height: 32in (81cm)
Material: Porcelain

Pampas suite 1970s

The 1970s witnessed a proliferation of colored bathroom suites. This pedestal basin by Armitage Shanks is equipped with gold-plated faucets and plastic dome heads, while the matching toilet has the flushing mechanism completely enclosed.

Specifications
Height of both basin and toilet: 30¾in (78cm)
Materials: Porcelain and plastic

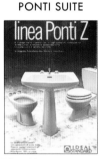

PONTI SUITE

linea Ponti Z

IDEAL STANDARD

Advertising poster, 1953

Gio Ponti was one of Italy's foremost modern designers, influenced both by classicism and the products of the Wiener Werkstätte. In 1953, he designed this bathroom suite for Ideal-Standard, each item carefully shaped and refined to express its function. The hand basin is particularly successful: the stand tapers toward the curve of the sink to give it perfect support and balance; and the sink itself has a flat surround on which toiletries can be placed.

Matching plastic toilet seats and lids were common in the 1970s

Belvedere Suite 1996

This stylish streamlined suite has a sculptural, futuristic quality, which fits discreetly into the bathroom. It is finished in a hardwearing white glaze, which is easy to clean. The elegant toilet conceals the tank and pan in one body, while the basin has a false pedestal, concealing the pipework, so that it can be mounted at any level.

Specifications
Height of basin: 24½in (62cm), height of toilet: 30¾in (78cm), height of bath: 26¾in (68cm)
Materials: Vitreous china and reinforced acrylic

STARCK SUITE

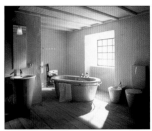

Philippe Starck bathroom, 1990s

This bathroom suite was inspired by the most basic functional objects — buckets, tubs, and handpumps. The basin has a pearwood surround, and the bath a built-in towel rail.

Amea Twin Jacuzzi 1995

The first fully integrated whirlpool bath was invented by Roy Jacuzzi in 1968. Since then, Jacuzzis have accommodated changing lifestyles by incorporating time- and space-saving shower units into whirlpool baths.

Specifications

Country: Italy/US
Height: 85in (216cm)
Materials: Acrylic, fiberglass, tempered glass, and steel

The waterfall-style faucets are gold-plated

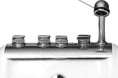

The monocontrol valve regulates the water temperature

The gleaming white finish enhances the sculptural quality of the bathtub

Globe faucet, c.1900

Crapper faucet, c.1900

Lever faucet, c.1910

Art Deco faucet, c.1920

Early 20th-century faucets

Early 20th-century faucets were often made from brass or nickel. Spouts varied in shape and size: the Globe faucet has a short, downward-pointing spout most suitable for baths, whereas the Crapper faucet has a long-reach spout. Four finial heads were most common, until the lever type was introduced for easier use.

Specifications
Country: UK
Materials: Nickel and brass

Water pressure creates small jets directed into the center of the frame

Needle shower c.1910

This luxurious early shower earns its name from the six perforated, horizontal bars from which water is sprayed with force. Designed predominantly for male use, this large, cage-like shower was referred to as the "morning bracer."

Specifications
Country: UK
Height: 87½in (222cm)
Material: Brass

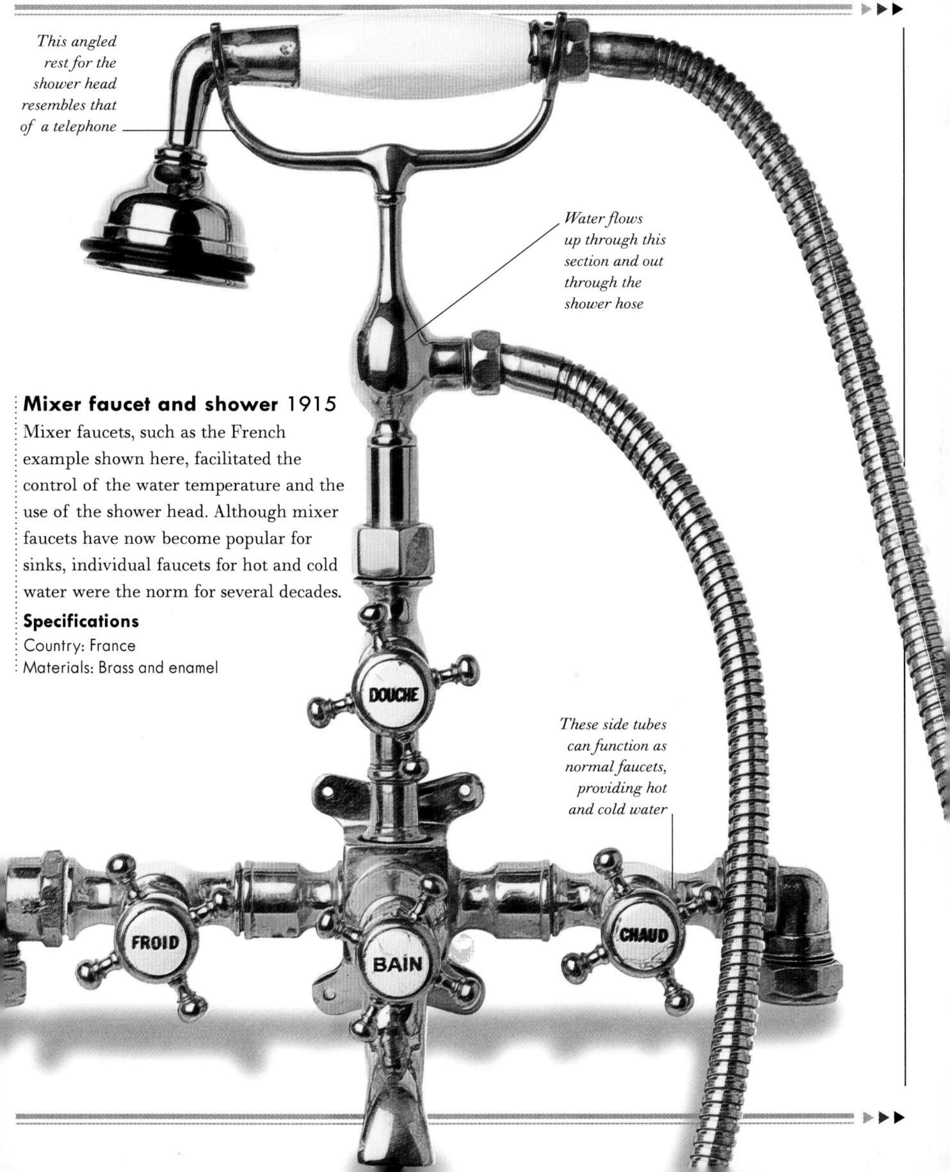

This angled rest for the shower head resembles that of a telephone

Water flows up through this section and out through the shower hose

Mixer faucet and shower 1915

Mixer faucets, such as the French example shown here, facilitated the control of the water temperature and the use of the shower head. Although mixer faucets have now become popular for sinks, individual faucets for hot and cold water were the norm for several decades.

Specifications

Country: France
Materials: Brass and enamel

These side tubes can function as normal faucets, providing hot and cold water

DOUCHE

FROID

BAIN

CHAUD

Shower 1980s

In the 1980s, British manufacturer Aqualisa produced a range of "power showers" that were designed to massage and invigorate the body. The shower includes two body jets, with adjustable water force.

Specifications
Country: UK
Height: 17¼in (44cm)
Materials: ABS plastic and chrome-plated brass

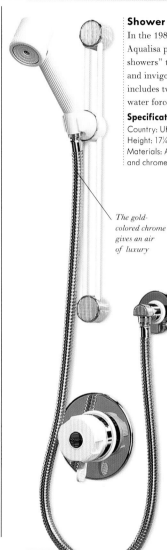

The gold-colored chrome gives an air of luxury

Class shower 1990s

This shower kit was designed by Mario Bellini for Ideal Standard. Its head is attached to a vertical bar, allowing it to be adjusted to a suitable height. Its solid bars are softened with rounded edges.

Specifications
Country: Italy
Height: 24in (61cm)
Material: Chromium-plated metal

The plug mechanism becomes an integral part of the faucet design

The faucet takes just a quarter turn

Late 20th-century faucets

Designed by Marco Bellini as part of the Class range for Ideal Standard, the single-lever mixer (left) has appeared in museum exhibitions. It utilizes ceramic disc technology to allow full pressure water with minimum lever movement. Similarly efficient, the Dallas basin mixer (above) can be fully activated in just a quarter turn. The dome faucet (below) is more conventional.

The ridged acrylic faucet head provides a firm grip

Ceramic discs inside the faucet control the flow of water

TOOTHBRUSHES

FOR THE MODERN CONSUMER, selecting a toothbrush is no easy matter. There is a bewildering range to choose from: "designer" brushes, such as Philippe Starck's Fluocaril; brushes with flexible heads; brushes with multi-angled or multicolored bristles; electric brushes; and brushes in any color combination. Before 1953 it was simpler; for that was the year in which plastic-handled, nylon-bristled toothbrushes were first mass-produced. In 1900, the choice was even easier: comparatively expensive, ivory-handled brushes could be afforded only by the well-to-do.

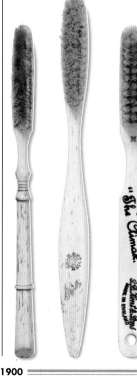

The coarse bristles were made to last, and now seem rather unhygienic

Durable bone handles were the norm

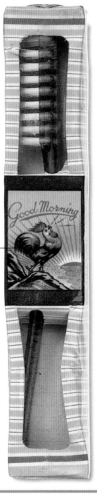

Both brushes and packaging became increasingly colorful

Early toothbrushes c.1900s

Although toothbrushes had been used for several centuries, by the beginning of the 20th century they remained expensive items made of bone and bristle, expected to last for a long time. The shape of the handle was much the same as the standard one used today, but the bristle heads were about twice as long as modern versions.

with pure natural bristles

Wisdom

Plastic toothbrushes 1930s–'40s

The first plastic toothbrushes were made in the 1930s, but on a small scale. These brushes retained the long heads of their forerunners. Nylon bristles began to replace natural bristles in the late 1940s, but it was not until the plastic handle and nylon bristles were married in 1953 that the toothbrush as we know it was born. Natural bristles continued to be used, marketed as "pure," and therefore healthy, but nylon was cheaper, longer-lasting, and available in various thicknesses – and so prevailed.

The wide expanse of nylon bristles brushes top and bottom teeth at once

This 1940s brush is similar to current designs

The large central thumb plate repeats the shape of the brush head

The broad contours of the handle allow the fingers a strong grip

Radius 1984

Designed in the US by Kevin Foley and James O'Halloran, the plastic Radius brush is a successful attempt to rethink established toothbrush design. In three sections, with its large head echoed in the middle thumb plate and wide, rounded handle, the Radius is ergonomically designed to allow the user to apply firm pressure to the teeth while brushing. The size of the head allows pressure to be distributed over a larger area than is conventionally possible.

RADIUS

▶ ▶ ▶

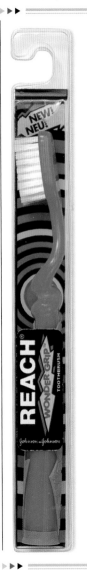

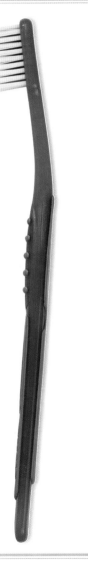

Modern toothbrushes
1980s –'90s

While plastic has enabled designers to mold handles into any shape, there is little difference between the basic design of these brushes and that of 1950s' plastic models. Designers now compete over the details: the most eye-catching colors, the most comfortable grip, the optimum angle and reach, and the best bristle combination.

Although a popular design feature, flexible heads have little functional value

Fluocaril 1989

Available in a range of subtle, translucent colors, the plastic handle of Philippe Starck's gorgeous Fluocaril toothbrush is sculpted in his trademark flame motif. Bearing Starck's signature on its neck, the item has become known as the ultimate "designer" toothbrush. Starck's intention seems to have been to create something beautiful out of an existing functional design; even so, the handle is remarkably comfortable and well-balanced.

TRAVEL TOOTHBRUSHES

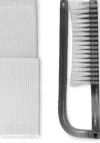

Early travel brush

The handle of this early plastic travel toothbrush formed a zigzag shape when it was opened, making it difficult to use for cleaning any but the inside front teeth. Today, travel toothbrushes tend to be constructed in separate sections, with the thick hollow handle often doubling up as the casing for the head and neck.

The beautifully proportioned brush measures 7½in (19.3cm) in length

Electric toothbrush 1990

The most radical innovation in 20th-century toothbrush design is the electric model, first seen in the early 1940s and widely used in the 1950s and '60s. Pressure can be applied in effective degrees to all teeth, without the necessity to "brush" manually.

INTERPLAK ®

RAZORS

ALTHOUGH, BY MODERN STANDARDS, the "safety razors" available at the beginning of the century did not live up to their name, they were, in fact, a considerable improvement on the "cut-throat" razors that they replaced. Since then, however, the development of wet-shave blades has gone from strength to strength, with manufacturers competing to produce a closer, safer, more comfortable shave. New features have been launched regularly over the last three decades: the first twin-bladed razor in 1971; swivel heads and disposables in 1975; lubricating strips in 1986; and protective bars in 1992. Radical progress has also been made with the electric razor. Experiments with mechanized shaving began in the early years of the century, but it was Colonel Jacob Schick who, in 1928, patented the first electric razor to be widely accepted. Today, there is a plethora of sleekly styled and multi-functional models for both men and women.

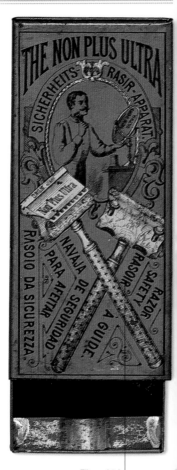

The multiple languages used on the box show that this was a truly international product

PHILIPS ELECTRIC RAZORS

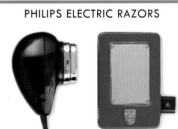

Philips Philishave, c.1950

Philips razors differ from the standard system of most electric razors, which have a rotating foil head. The battery-operated Philishave has two or three bladed discs, which spin, catch, and cut the beard.

Non Plus Ultra 1910

The safety razor was a remarkable invention: it had a disposable double-edged blade that did not need stropping; and, since only a small sliver of the blade was exposed, serious cuts were impossible. The first safety razor was patented in 1895 by King Camp Gillette, who set up the Gillette Safety Razor Company in 1900. By 1910, Gillette had many rivals, including the ornate Non Plus Ultra.

Specifications

Country: Not known
Material: Metal
Length: 4in (10cm)

The razor blade is clamped between two metal plates

The ornate handle gives improved grip

Braun products were described as examples of "order, harmony, and simplicity"

The lined grooves on the Bakelite casing give an improved grip

Braun S50 c.1950

Max Braun first developed the S50 electric razor in 1938, but World War II delayed production until 1951. The streamlined body, which tapers elegantly to the electric cord, suggests efficiency and fits comfortably in the hand. The cream coloring is highly unusual; men's razors are produced almost exclusively in black, gray, or silver.

Specifications

Country: Germany
Materials: Bakelite and metal
Length: 4½in (11.3cm)

Creazioni Cavari c.1987

The sleek, modern Creazioni
Cavari range of "designer"
razors was created by Ernesto
Spicciolato and Dante Donegani.
All three razors – from left to
right, Sauro, Spazio, and Samurai –
are produced in matt black. The
solid brass handles of the Sauro
and Samurai have a pleasing
weightiness, while the Spazio,
made from coated aluminum,
is as light in weight as
it is slender in form.

Specifications

Country: Italy
Material: Anodized metal
Length: Sauro 6¾in (17cm); Spazio
7in (18cm); Samurai 6in (15.5cm)

*The functions
are indicated
with discreet
pictograms*

*The Sauro
razor has a
postmodern
profile*

Philips Ladyshave Aqua 1990s

The key difference between this electric
razor and a men's model is the styling.
Very few women's razors are made in
black, whereas the vast majority of
men's are black or a similarly somber,
"masculine" color. Women's razors are
invariably colored pastel or white –
here a marbled green has been used.
The curvaceous shape is also
intended to be feminine.

Specifications

Country: Netherlands
Material: Plastic
Length: 5¾in (14.7cm)

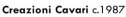

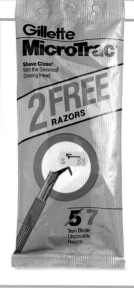

DISPOSABLE RAZORS

Plastic, which first appeared in the US in the 1930s, made possible the mass-production of a huge array of items, and began a craze for cheap, disposable artifacts. In 1953, Baron Bich introduced the first disposable ballpoint pen, the Bic (see p.338). Its phenomenal success encouraged him to turn his attention to razors. He cut the existing blade in half and used the funds saved in manufacturing to produce a cheap plastic handle. The result was the world's first disposable razor, launched in 1975. All the major manufacturers, including Gillette, quickly introduced their own versions. Environmental concern in the 1990s resulted in a move away from disposable products, and the trend for reusable razors for both men and women was favored once more.

Gillette disposable razor

The recharging unit is color-coordinated for further feminine appeal

Wilkinson Sword Protector Razor 1992

British designer Kenneth Grange's Protector Razor for Wilkinson Sword combined all previous razor features – swivel head, lubricating strip, and twin blades. However, its chief advertised features were the wire bars that stopped the blades from nicking the skin. Just as inventive was the biomorphic handle, designed to fit snugly in the hand.

Specifications
Country: UK
Material: Plastic
Length: 5in (12.5cm)

The scrolled ends meet in the center to create an inverted heart shape

PERFUME BOTTLES

NOWHERE IS PACKAGING more important than in the perfume industry. When Baron Bich, encouraged by the successes of his disposable pens, razors, and lighters, developed a cheaply packaged scent, it failed miserably. The public wanted glamour, sophistication, and expense – a combination never better evoked than when Marilyn Monroe, asked what she wore in bed, replied, "Chanel N° 5," and sent sales of the perfume rocketing. Despite the ultimately decisive power held by the advertisers, a great deal of energy is expended both in the concoction of the scent itself and in the design of the bottle. This can range from the nostalgic, floral excesses of Zenobia to the clean, simple angularity of classic Chanel.

The unadorned design reflects Chanel's simple fashion style

Chanel N° 5 1921

The Chanel N° 5 bottle has changed 15 times since it was introduced by Coco Chanel in 1921, but remains the essence of simplicity. It is square, with a plain wedge stopper, and a minimal white label. There are nine stages involved in sealing the fragrance in its bottle, including the placement of the wax-drawn "CC" at the neck.

L'heure bleue 1912

In 1912, Pierre Guerlain created L'heure bleue, a blend of roses, irises, vanilla, and musk that was typical of the romantic perfumes produced by this famous parfumier. The Baccarat glass bottle reflects this romanticism. With its inverted heart-shaped stopper, Art Nouveau swirls at the shoulders of the bottle, and delicately drawn label, the design suggests sensuality.

Zenobia pre-1925

The design of this bottle is resonant of nostalgia for the 19th century. Every element is intended to suggest a sweet, natural, floral fragrance, from the rather syrupy name, Sweet Pea Blossom, to the combination of pastel colors used on the label and the pink bow tied around the neck of the bottle.

The pink petal motifs suggest the name of the scent

SCHIAPARELLI'S SCENTS

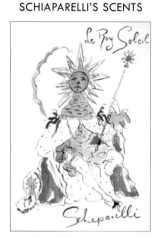

Poster for Le Roy Soleil

Elsa Schiaparelli rivaled Coco Chanel as the most famous couturier in Paris in the 1930s. She launched her own perfumes – Shocking, in 1938, and Le Roy Soleil in 1945. The bottle for Le Roy Soleil was designed by Salvador Dalí, with whom Schiaparelli collaborated on several occasions. This poster, which advertises the fragrance, was the work of Marcel Vertes.

Jabot 1939

Created by Peter Fink, director of design for couturier Lucien Lelong in Paris, this bottle for the fragrance Jabot is a wonderful flight of fancy. The stopper is finished in the shape of a knotted bow and the base of the bottle resembles the skirts of a petticoat fanned out across the floor.

The delicate folds reflect a trend in 1930s' fashion for drapes

The bottle is stored in a container styled like a soup can

Jean-Paul Gaultier 1993

Jean-Paul Gaultier's perfume bottle is molded in the shape of a woman's torso, pinched and pushed into shape by a corset. Various versions of the bottle are available, including one with a metal corset. Gaultier was not the first to model a perfume bottle on a woman's body; more than 50 years earlier, Elsa Schiaparelli's Shocking was made to the exact proportions of the actress Mae West's figure.

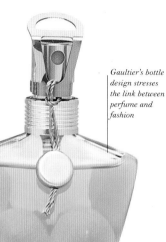

Gaultier's bottle design stresses the link between perfume and fashion

The bottle tapers at the center in emulation of the female waist

DNA 1993

Just as 1950s' design was influenced by public interest in space travel and science fiction, so the name and bottle design of this perfume reflect 1990s interest in genetics. The bottle is shaped like the double helix form of DNA.

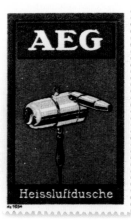
Heissluftdusche

HAIR DRYERS

THE EARLY PART OF THE CENTURY witnessed the introduction of three revolutionary elements in hairstyling: synthetic hair coloring, developed in 1909 by chemist Eugene Schueller, who later founded the L'Oreal company; "the perm," a method of giving hair a lasting curl; and the electric hair dryer. The latter was first designed and manufactured in Wisconsin in 1920, and became one of the most desirable electrical gadgets of the following decades. Early models, including the first hand-held dryers of 1925, were made of aluminum, stainless steel, or chromium. Modern versions, with their proliferation of attachments and sophisticated controls, are invariably produced in plastic.

AEG 1927

The chromium-plated dryer pictured on this AEG stamp exemplifies Peter Behrens' view that good products should be practical and elegant. This characterizes all of his work at AEG, including the pioneering corporate identity program (see p.369).

The dryer is constructed of two identical pieces screwed together

Edir 1936–38

This compact, bright red hair dryer was redesigned in 1936 by Herbert Marloth for Siemens-Schuckertwerke AG. The casing is made from the tough, glossy plastic melamine. It has a simple cylindrical shape, with an expanded area to house the electric motor. The case is held together by six screws, which can be removed for maintenance.

Specifications
Country: Germany
Height: Not known
Material: Melamine

Supreme 1938

Bakelite offered the manufacturers of
electrical goods some excellent advantages.
It was relatively cheap to produce, could
easily be molded into shape, and acted as
an efficient heat insulator. The Supreme
hair dryer, produced by L.G. Hawkins & Co.
Ltd., is a fine example of Bakelite design.
The pistol-shaped casing is held together by
screws, allowing access for maintenance, and
the handle can be unscrewed for storage.

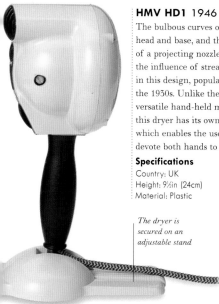

HMV HD1 1946

The bulbous curves of the
head and base, and the lack
of a projecting nozzle, show
the influence of streamlining
in this design, popular since
the 1930s. Unlike the more
versatile hand-held models,
this dryer has its own stand,
which enables the user to
devote both hands to styling.

Specifications
Country: UK
Height: 9⅖in (24cm)
Material: Plastic

*The dryer is
secured on an
adjustable stand*

*Bakelite was
often produced in
this wood effect*

Specifications
Country: UK
Height: 8¾in (22cm)
Material: Bakelite

MEN'S STYLING

For many years, hairstyling for men relied either on the skilled scissor control of the barber or on the use of manually operated clippers. When electric clippers were introduced, they ensured a close, precise haircut. This "Air Clip," a simple, functional design by Henry Dreyfuss, includes a hose to draw the cut hair away.

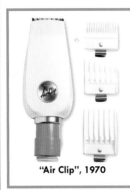

"Air Clip", 1970

Braun AG HLD231 1964

As the travel industry started to grow in the 1960s, manufacturers responded with a range of portable appliances. Reinhold Weiss' portable hair dryer has the minimalist styling associated with Braun's personal care products. The case is made from light gray plastic with a white switch. The only color is a single dot of orange to indicate the "on" position.

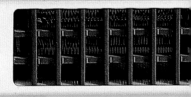

The diffuser has a high-tech, professional appearance

The basic nozzle can be swiftly detached and replaced

Sassoon's name features prominently on the dryer in his trademark gold lettering

Vidal Sassoon **VS-500UK** 1995

Vidal Sassoon is one of the world's best-known hairdressers. He made his name during the 1950s and '60s with his radically geometric hairstyles, and has since expanded into product development. This powerful turbo hair dryer has a 6in- (15cm-) long spiked attachment called a diffuser, or "volumizer," which diffuses air in the hair to give the style maximum body. The black and gold styling successfully suggests luxury.

Specifications
Country: UK
Height: 7½in (19.2cm)
Material: Plastic

Specifications
Country: Germany
Height: 3½in (9cm)
Materials: Plastic and metal

The handle widens at its base to offer the user a comfortable grip

BEDS

DESIGNERS HAVE RARELY GIVEN the same degree of attention to the design of beds as they have to other items of furniture, yet the bed usually sets the style and tone for the whole room. This is especially true of the elaborate Art Nouveau and Art Deco pieces, represented here by beds designed by Frenchmen Louis Majorelle and Louis Sognot. These imposing forms must have dominated the rooms in which they were placed. The latter's pale green Art Deco bed recalls the first-class cabins of the great ocean liners. A more modest and functional approach to bedroom furniture is evident in the designs of Kho Liang Ie and Carlo Mollino. More recently, Toni Cordero's striking Sospir recalls the long tradition of four-poster beds.

The extravagant floral motifs are typical of Art Nouveau styling

Majorelle's design uses the grain of the wood to emphasize the curves

MACKINTOSH BEDROOM

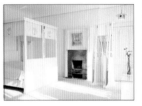

Bedroom at Mackintosh house, c.1906

Charles Rennie Mackintosh designed entire interiors for a small number of homes. This bedroom in one of his own Glasgow houses features his characteristic painted white furniture with Celtic-inspired motifs. Mackintosh used his decoration as part of the structure of the design.

Nenuphar bed 1905–09

Louis Majorelle was a key exponent of the Ecole de Nancy Art Nouveau style. Unlike their Parisian counterparts, who tended toward abstraction, these designers favored a literal interpretation of nature. Majorelle's double bed, produced in his factory, displays the flowing lines and elegant carving that earned him such critical acclaim.

Specifications
Country: France
Dimensions: Not known
Materials: Mahogany and gilt bronze

Specifications
Country: France
Height: 43½in (110cm)
Width: 128in (325cm)
Length: 86in (218cm)
Materials: Chromium and glass

Double bed 1930
Louis Sognot designed the bedroom furniture for the Maharajah of Indore's palace, which was built and decorated by German architect Eckart Muthesius. The materials, symmetry, proportion, and restricted ornamentation of the bed are typical of Art Deco styling.

The ormolu (gilt bronze) mounts are inspired by floral images

Bunk bed c.1954

Carlo Mollino's simple wooden bunk bed has no decoration aside from the brass fittings. However, two wooden coat hangers have been attached, and there is a small laminated table on the lower bunk.

Specifications
Country: Italy
Height: 84in (213cm)
Width: 34in (85.5cm)
Length: 77in (195cm)
Materials: Oak, brass, and laminated plastic

Dense slats provide screening for the head of the bed

The spearlike rods topped with mythical symbols guard the bed

The side table is the one hint of luxury in an otherwise practical design

Single bed unit 1970

In this unit, created by Kho Liang Ie, the bed is enclosed by an "L"-shaped surround of painted cupboards and shelves. A light is included in the design.

Specifications
Country: Holland
Width: 65in (165cm)
Length: 78in (198cm)
Materials: Marble, wood, stainless steel, and acrylic

▶ ▶ ▶

UTILITY FURNITURE

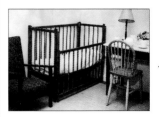

Utility cot, 1942

In Britain, World War II brought about harsh restrictions in the use of raw materials. In response, the Board of Trade established a Design Panel under the chairmanship of Gordon Russell. Its solution to the problem was Utility furniture. Although it aspired to be inexpensive, yet well designed and of a high quality, in reality the furniture was often drab — largely because of the lack of materials. The design of the furniture owed much to the Arts and Crafts movement. The Utility style was to have an influence on British design that would last until the 1960s.

Sospir 1992

Toni Cordero designed the Sospir double bed for the Italian furniture company Sawaya & Moroni. It has a metal and wooden structure with twin headrests, but its most dramatic features are the four corner lances. Made from bamboo, these come with a variety of decorative finials.

Specifications

Country: Italy
Height: 83in (210cm)
Width: 68½in (174cm)
Length: 92½in (235cm)
Materials: Metal, wood, and bamboo

Art Nouveau molding

BABY CARRIAGES

THE STORY OF BABY carriage design in the 20th century is one of remarkably little change during the first 60 years, followed by a radical redesign later to adapt to women's changing lifestyles. During the first period, babies and toddlers were usually transported by heavy, bulky perambulators, while smaller-wheeled strollers were used for older children. Everything changed with the introduction of the Maclaren buggy (see p.199), patented in 1965. This lightweight, collapsible stroller allowed parents to transport children much more easily and could even fit into a car trunk or the hold of an aircraft.

Dunkley 1919
The design of the molding on this khaki carriage is clearly inspired by Art Nouveau. The coloring of the large hood complements that of the body, while the two different wheel sizes resemble those of contemporary bicycles. The suspension is a spring type and there is no braking system.

Specifications
Country: UK
Wheel diameters: 19in (48cm);
25½in (65cm)

Sol Dainty 1928
The styling of this carriage is very simple, with the nuts, bolts, and screws undisguised. The subtle two-tone color might go unnoticed, were it not for the bright red lines that echo the dark panels. When the hood is down, the carriage's shape changes dramatically.

Specifications
Country: UK
Wheel diameter: 12in (30cm)

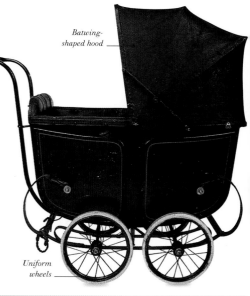

Batwing-shaped hood

Uniform wheels

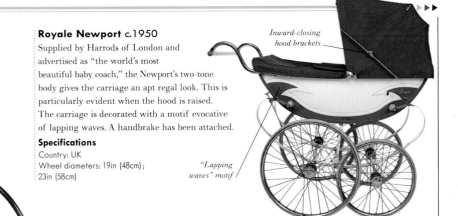

Royale Newport c.1950

Supplied by Harrods of London and
advertised as "the world's most
beautiful baby coach," the Newport's two-tone
body gives the carriage an apt regal look. This is
particularly evident when the hood is raised.
The carriage is decorated with a motif evocative
of lapping waves. A handbrake has been attached.

Specifications
Country: UK
Wheel diameters: 19in (48cm);
23in (58cm)

Inward-closing hood brackets

"Lapping waves" motif

Hisa Gloria De Luxe 1962

Because of its small wheels
and lack of an elaborate
suspension system, the body
of this unique carriage is set
low to the ground and the
wheels are equipped with
thick rubber tires. A longer
handle gives a feel of
something more akin to
a lawnmower than a
carriage. It is, how-
ever, supposedly
fashioned after the
classic Mini car
design (see p.317)
and is equipped
with a front
bumper, trunk, and sun
visor. The hood gives the
carriage the look of a
"convertible" car.

Specifications
Country: Switzerland
Wheel diameter:
9in (23cm)

Bassinet on chassis
1980s

This detachable bassinet can be lifted from the metal frame and put on another surface, while the chassis itself, which is made from a combination of aluminum and plastics, folds flat. The bassinet follows the form of earlier prams and shares many features. The product is clearly an attempt to provide a traditional-looking carrier at a lower price.

Specifications
Country: UK
Dimensions: Unknown

The long handle enables the parent to run while pushing the buggy

In later models this frame would simply push down to form the buggy

The lower tray provides space for shopping or for childcare accessories

Convertible stroller c.1990

Although heavier and less compact when folded than an E-type buggy, the convertible stroller offers a convenient means of responding to the changing needs of a growing child. Newborn babies can travel in safety in the bassinet attachment, and this can be replaced with the bucket seat for a baby able to support its own head.

Specifications
Country: UK
Dimensions: Unknown

BUGGY INNOVATIONS

Owen Finlay Maclaren, a retired aeronautical engineer, sold his first lightweight, small-wheeled, aluminum buggy in 1967. His revolutionary design incorporated two "X"-shaped hinges, which, when folded, made the buggy flatter and narrower. The stroller had many improvements and could be folded with just one hand and one foot. It was a huge commercial success.

Maclaren E-type buggy, 1994

The canvas seat provides a more flexible ride than more rigid materials

Jogging Buggy 1996

The Jogging Buggy is an all-terrain vehicle – the idea being that the parent can take the child with them over rough terrain, while hiking, or even running. It represents a return to more simple but strengthened forms after the complex construction of the Maclaren buggy.

THE ZIPPER

Specifications
Country: US
Height: 38½in (98cm)
Length: 45in (114cm)

Magic lantern c.1900

Projection devices have been
available since the 17th century.
This lantern was made by Ernst
Plank at the turn of
the century. Although
intended for children,
its oil-powered lamp
gave little concession
to safety.

Specifications
Country: Germany
Height: 6½in (17cm)
Material: Tin

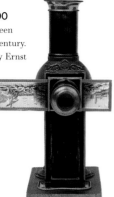

TOYS & MODELS

ALTHOUGH BY THEIR VERY NATURE toys and
models belong in the nursery, many have
also become collector's items for adults,
particularly teddy bears, train sets, and
model vehicles. The last are ingenious
designs and by no means mere copies of
the original full-scale items. Constructional
toys were popularized early in the century
by Frank Hornby, whose Meccano kits were
later rivaled by Lego (from the Danish *leg
godt*, meaning "play well").

Noah's Ark c.1900

Noah's Ark, complete with wooden
animals, was considered a respectable
toy for children to play with on Sundays,
because of its biblical connections.
The ark continues to inspire toy
designers today.

Specifications
Country: Germany
Height: 21¼in (54cm)
Material: Wood

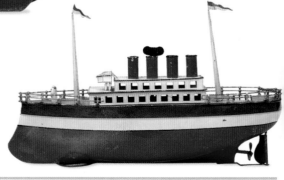

Clockwork ship 1904

Produced by Bing, this delightful clockwork ship is propelled by winding it up
through one of the smokestacks. It has
an adjustable rudder, and a support
bracket that allows it to be displayed.

Specifications
Country: Germany
Height: 8½in (21.5cm)
Material: Tin

Steiff teddy bear c.1905

The teddy bear gained its name following President Theodore (Teddy) Roosevelt's refusal to shoot a bear on a 1902 hunting expedition, prompting a New York toy shop to display a stuffed bear labeled "Teddy's Bear." The cinnamon-colored bear shown here was made by the Felt Toy Company, which in 1906 became the famous Steiff.

Specifications
Country: Germany
Height: 28in (70cm)
Materials: Mohair plush
and wood-wool stuffing

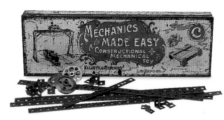

Meccano 1910

Frank Hornby's Meccano is one of the century's great success stories. An infinite variety of vehicles and objects could be built using fully interchangeable components. In 1926, colored parts became available, and electric motors were introduced later.

Specifications
Country: UK
Height: Not applicable
Material: Nickel-plated
metal

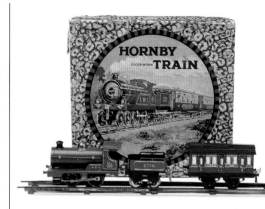

Hornby train set 1920s

By the 1920s, clockwork trains had been in existence for over 30 years. But popularity increased when Meccano models were widely promoted in toy shops and in *Meccano Magazine*. This model is made from pressed tin, and runs on purpose-built tracks.

Specifications
Country: UK
Height: 3½in (9cm)
Material: Tin

Dinky cars 1930s

Meccano began to produce small, die-cast model cars in 1933. They were christened "Dinky" after the Scottish slang word meaning "small and neat." An enormous number of vehicles were produced until the company closed in 1980.

Specifications
Country: UK
Length: 3½in (9cm)
Material: Die-cast metal

Scalextric 1950s

Designed by Fred Francis, the first Scalextric cars were clockwork. Later, electric motors and handheld controls allowed the cars to be raced at furious speeds. This track was produced in 1968 by Tri-ang.

Specifications
Country: UK
Length of car: 4¾in (12cm)
Material: Plastic

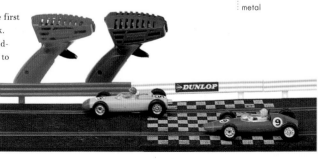

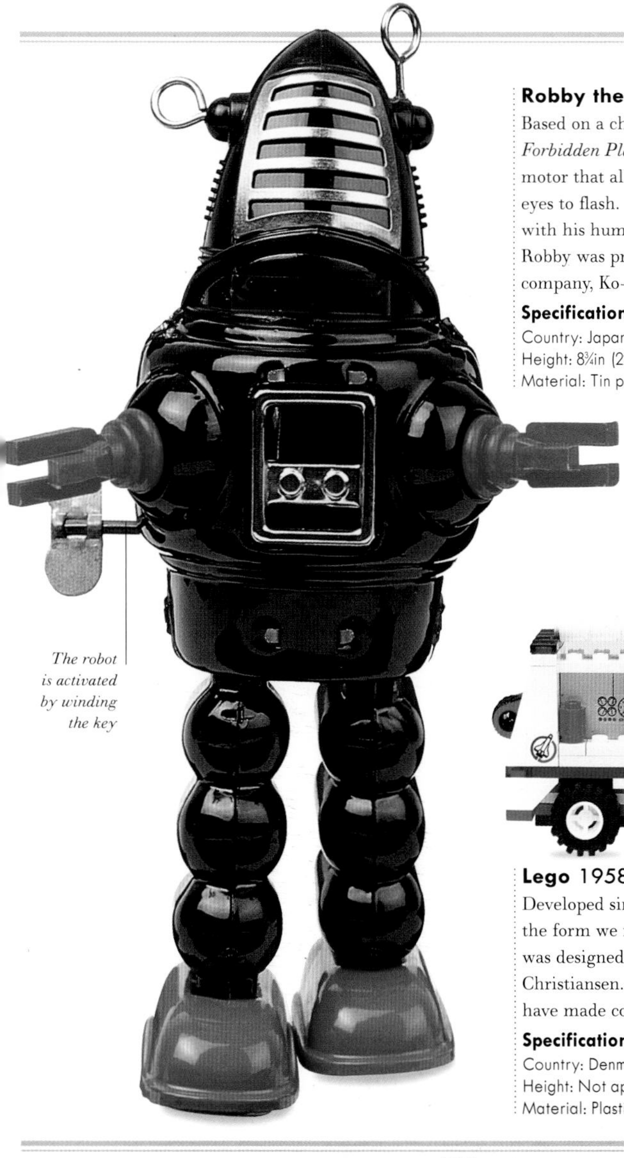

Robby the Robot 1956

Based on a character from the film
Forbidden Planet, Robby has a clockwork
motor that allows him to walk, and his
eyes to flash. A typical 1950s' robot,
with his humanoid appearance,
Robby was produced by the Japanese
company, Ko-Yoshiya.

Specifications
Country: Japan
Height: 8¾in (22.5cm)
Material: Tin plate

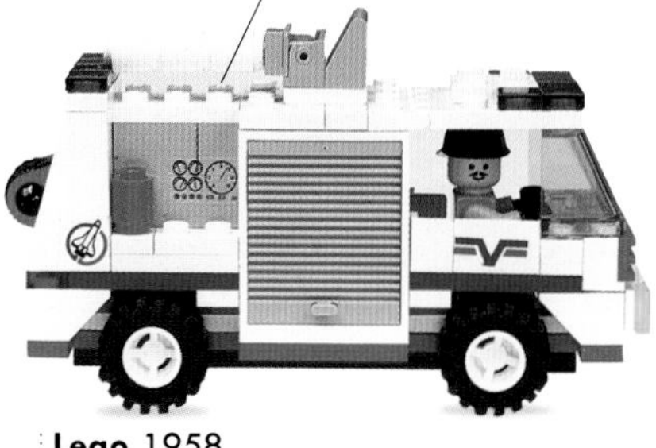

*The studs that
enable the bricks to
be coupled together
were the innovation of
Godtfred Christiansen*

*The robot
is activated
by winding
the key*

Lego 1958

Developed since the 1930s and born in 1958 in
the form we recognize today, the Lego brick
was designed by Ole and Godtfred Kirk
Christiansen. Increasingly specialized pieces
have made construction possibilities endless.

Specifications
Country: Denmark
Height: Not applicable
Material: Plastic

▶ ▶ ▶

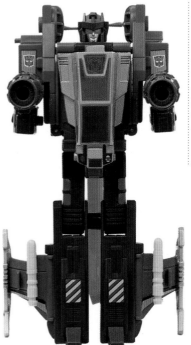

Transformer robot 1980s

These multi-jointed, armored warriors by Hasbro transform from robots into destructive vehicles. With its seven missiles, the Turbomaster, shown here, reflects the popularity of aggressive, sci-fi inspired toys.

Specifications
Country: UK
Height: 7in (18cm)
Material: Plastic

Tamagotchi 1996

The "lovable egg," brainchild of Japanese housewife Aki Maita, derives its name from a rough translation of the Japanese *tamago tchi*. The handheld "pet" consists of an ovoid electronic device with LCD display depicting a bird. Owners must care for it by giving food, discipline, and love.

Specifications
Country: Japan
Height: 2in (5.3cm)
Material: Plastic

After hatching from its virtual egg, with care, a cyberchick can live for up to a month

Playmobil 1 2 3 1990s

Playmobil 1 2 3 provides a wide variety of brightly colored, safety-conscious toys for infants, which feature figures, animals, and vehicles. More challenging versions are designed for older children.

Specifications
Country: Germany
Height: Not applicable
Material: Plastic

TV SPIN-OFFS

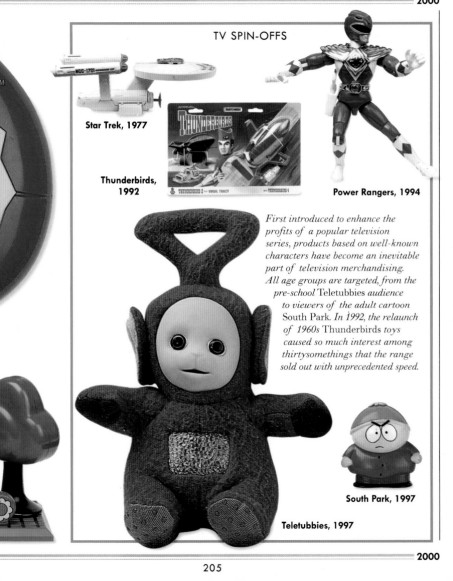

Star Trek, 1977

Thunderbirds, 1992

Power Rangers, 1994

First introduced to enhance the profits of a popular television series, products based on well-known characters have become an inevitable part of television merchandising. All age groups are targeted, from the pre-school Teletubbies *audience to viewers of the adult cartoon* South Park. *In 1992, the relaunch of 1960s* Thunderbirds *toys caused so much interest among thirtysomethings that the range sold out with unprecedented speed.*

South Park, 1997

Teletubbies, 1997

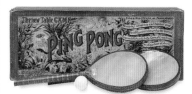

Ping Pong 1905

This game was launched in 1905 by Jacques and Hamley Bros., the name deriving from the sound of the paddle hitting the ball. The paddles are crafted using two sheets of vellum, with the long handles shaped more like lawn tennis rackets than the abbreviated modern table tennis paddles we now use. The illustrated box promises "immense excitement and healthy exercise."

Specifications
Country: UK
Length of paddle head: 19in (48cm)
Materials: Net, vellum, and wood

Specifications
Country: UK
Length of board: 29in (74cm)
Materials: Cardboard and metal

Peter Rabbit's Race Game 1910

An early example of merchandising a popular children's character, this game is based on Beatrix Potter's well-loved animal creations. Produced by F. Warne and Co., the board is printed with exquisite illustrations.

The body of the car is made of scrap steel

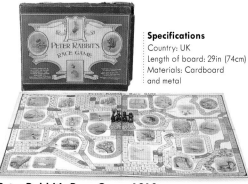

GAMES & OUTDOOR TOYS

THERE IS OFTEN LITTLE to distinguish between adults' and children's games. Board games in particular have long been established as favorites with all age groups; most recently, Trivial Pursuit was designed to test and expand knowledge in an enjoyable format. Other games have been conceived with the purpose of promoting physical exercise and good sportsmanship, the most notable being Ping Pong, now a recognized competitive sport. Perhaps the most significant change in toy design, and the cause of the greatest upheaval in children's play, has been the arrival of computer games. First seen in the 1970s, and now showcases for highly complex computer graphics, these stimulate sharp hand-eye coordination, but have been criticized for encouraging a sedentary lifestyle.

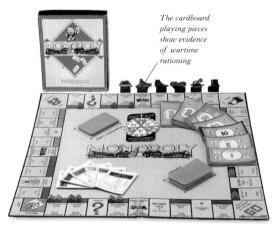

The cardboard playing pieces show evidence of wartime rationing

Monopoly 1934

Invented by Charles B. Darrow, Monopoly was based on the street names of Atlantic City, N.J. It was successfully marketed by switching the location to any major world city, and is now the world's best-selling copyrighted board game. This British example, produced by Waddingtons, dates from the 1940s.

Specifications
Country: US
Length of board: 19in (49cm)
Materials: Cardboard, metal, and plastic

Pathfinder pedal car 1949

Austin produced this child's racing car at its Welsh factory, which was a nonprofit outlet set up to employ former miners. Constructed using scrap steel, the car is propelled by the use of pedals. Although expensive playthings, toy vehicles have remained popular in many shapes and forms.

Specifications
Country: UK
Length: 63in (160cm)
Materials: Steel and rubber

Thick rubber wheels emulate the look of real racing car tires

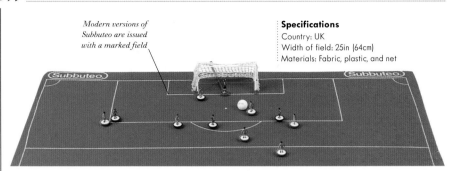

Modern versions of Subbuteo are issued with a marked field

Specifications
Country: UK
Width of field: 25in (64cm)
Materials: Fabric, plastic, and net

Subbuteo 1947

Invented by Peter Adolph, the first game of table football was introduced in Britain in 1947 during severe postwar rationing, and included a piece of chalk and instructions to mark a field on an old blanket. Cardboard players were available in 24 team colors, allowing every child to own his favorite team. Since then, millions of fans have formed special leagues, and even organized a Subbuteo World Cup. This British example by Waddingtons dates from 1995.

Space Hopper 1950

The much-loved Space Hopper was introduced at a time when space exploration was becoming a realistic possibility, and science fiction films were drawing large audiences. The cylindrical ears serve as handles for the child, who sits astride the inflated body and bounces.

Specifications
Country: France
Height: Variable
Material: Rubber

Cluedo 1949

Devised by Anthony Pratt and designed by his wife in 1944, Cluedo was launched in 1949. The design of this world-famous board game differs between countries, although the current British version remains the same as the original. This German set dates from 1993.

Specifications
Country: UK
Length of board: 19¼in (49cm)
Materials: Metal, cardboard, and plastic

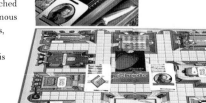

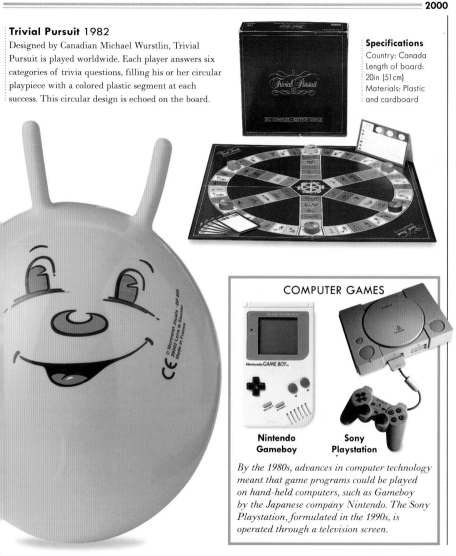

Trivial Pursuit 1982

Designed by Canadian Michael Wurstlin, Trivial
Pursuit is played worldwide. Each player answers six
categories of trivia questions, filling his or her circular
playpiece with a colored plastic segment at each
success. This circular design is echoed on the board.

Specifications
Country: Canada
Length of board:
20in (51cm)
Materials: Plastic
and cardboard

COMPUTER GAMES

**Nintendo
Gameboy**

**Sony
Playstation**

*By the 1980s, advances in computer technology
meant that game programs could be played
on hand-held computers, such as Gameboy
by the Japanese compány Nintendo. The Sony
Playstation, formulated in the 1990s, is
operated through a television screen.*

DOLLS

UNTIL THE 20TH CENTURY, dolls were typically modeled on adults, often with elaborate wigs, glass eyes, and eyelashes made from human hair. "Baby" dolls were simply smaller versions, and even after the turn of the century very few dolls were made to resemble real babies – the best-known being George Borgfeldt's Kewpie doll. It was in the 1930s that doll design really took off, with more and more models being mass produced. Baby dolls were fashioned to look increasingly realistic, and to sound and even function like real babies; by the 1960s, dolls could cry and wet their diapers. Adult dolls did not fall out of favor. Barbie and G.I. Joe, first popular in the 1960s, have since been redesigned to appeal to new generations of children.

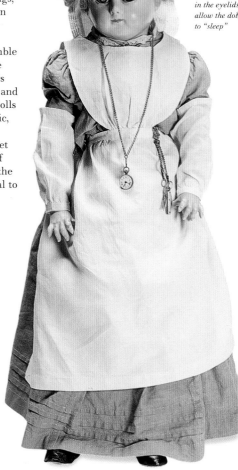

Lead weights in the eyelids allow the doll to "sleep"

Schilling doll c.1900

Relatively large at 23½in (60cm), Stephan Schilling's adult doll is dressed as an English nanny. Parts of the body are made from composition (pulped wood or a paper-based mixture), with upper arms, legs, and mid-torso made from cloth stuffed with straw to allow greater movement. More expensive dolls of the time had a softer stuffing, such as animal hair.

Specifications

Country: Germany
Materials: Composition
with straw-stuffed fabric

The Kewpie trademark is printed on a prominent paper label

Kewpie c.1913

Designed by Joseph Kallus and made in the US by George Borgfeldt, this doll was based on the illustrations of Rose O'Neill featured in the *Ladies Home Journal*. The body and head were cast from liquid clay in a single piece, with arms added afterward. The definition of this rudimentary design was achieved by the painted finish.

Specifications

Country: US
Material: Bisque

Tyrolean dolls early-1950s

Designed by Käthe Kruse, this pair of dolls was manufactured by the famous German Rheinische Gummi- und Celluloid-Fabrik and both bear the trademark turtle label. The factory also made celluloid heads for export to the UK and US, which would be used on composition or stuffed bodies. Celluloid was cheap, easy to use, and lightweight. Its drawbacks were its flammability, its crushability, and its tendency to fade in light.

My Dream Baby mid-1920s

Manufactured in bisque and composition, Armand Marseille's design is clearly intended to look like a real baby, with chubby legs and a button nose. The arms and legs are moved by means of elasticated string joints, and the large head is painted to give the impression of soft baby hair. Because the facial features were hand-painted, each doll was a unique item.

Specifications

Country: Germany
Materials: Bisque head with composition body and limbs

Specifications

Country: Germany
Material: Celluloid

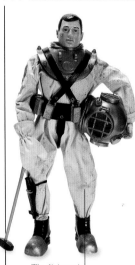

The diving suit is made from unbleached calico

G.I. Joe 1964

First produced in 1964 in response to the realization that boys also enjoy playing with dolls, G.I. Joe was multijointed to allow him to be manipulated in all kinds of action positions. The doll was later restyled as a "global adventurer," and was most recently updated and relaunched by Hasbro in 1993.

Specifications
Country: US
Material: Plastic

Cabbage Patch Kid 1983

Between 1983, when they first caught the public imagination, and 1996, when Mattel updated and relaunched them for a new generation, more than 77 million Cabbage Patch Kids were "adopted" by children across the world. Created by Xavier Roberts of the Original Appalachian Artworks, Inc. in Cleveland, Georgia, each doll has individual physical details that make it unique and comes with its own birth certificate and adoption papers.

Specifications
Country: US
Materials: Vinyl and polyester

Baby Born 1991

Designed by Victor M. Pracas and manufactured by Zapf Creation, Baby Born has proved to be one of the most successful dolls of the 1990s, with over three million sold before 1996. Its lifelike appeal rests in the multitude of "bodily functions," which include eating, crying, and soiling its diaper. Joints at the hips, shoulders, and neck allow realistic flexibilty and movement.

At 17in (43cm) in height, Baby Born is created to resemble a real baby

Specifications
Country: Germany
Material: Plastic

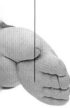

The soft-sculptured form makes the doll very comfortable to cuddle

THE CHANGING STYLE OF BARBIE

Probably the most famous of all dolls, Barbie started life in the 1950s as Lilli, after a risqué German newspaper cartoon character. She first appeared as Barbie in 1959. US manufacturer Mattel's designers have been kept busy ever since as Barbie has metamorphosed through fashion changes of the past 40 years. While the early Barbies were highly coiffed, heavily made-up ladies, the modern doll is a younger, wholesome, all-American girl, with open face, wide eyes, and smiling lips. Nearly 12 inches (30cm) tall and made from molded plastic with nylon hair rooted into the head, Barbie has hard bent arms and rigid legs. However, flexibility is offered in the jointed hips and swivel waist. Barbie's passion for clothes has ensured a variety of outfits and accessories to fill her pink wardrobe, each reflecting her ever-changing lifestyle.

"Airline Stewardess" Barbie, 1963

"Happy Holidays" Barbie, 1990s

AROUND THE HOME

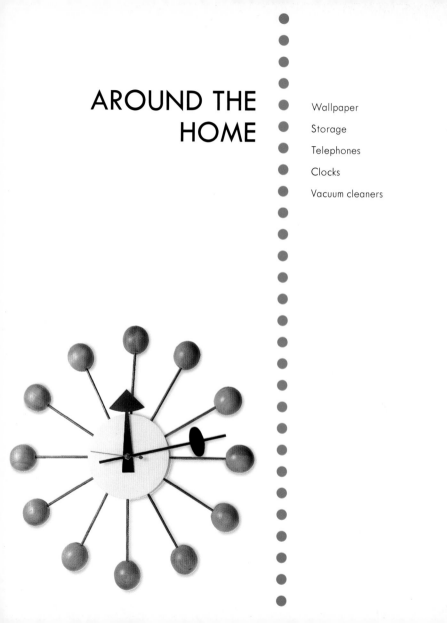

WALLPAPER

SINCE WORLD WAR II, wallpaper producers have found increasing competition from the paint industry, which has offered consumers a wide and inexpensive selection of colors in a variety of finishes. In response, new types of wallpapers have been developed, including self-adhesive paper and, in the 1950s, vinyl paper. To breathe more life into the craft of wallpaper design, manufacturers have frequently commissioned highly respected artists to create compositions for them: these include exuberant floral patterning, science-inspired imagery, and abstract designs.

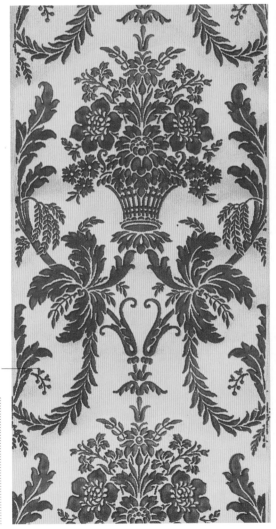

This sumptuous paper is typical of the elaborate brocades of late Victorian and Edwardian furnishings

Block-printed and flocked wallpaper c.1900

Flock wallpaper, with its richly textured finish and appearance of velvet, has been produced since the 17th century. In this early 20th-century example from Züber et Cie, the designer has used a symmetrical floral pattern of red flock over a gold ground.

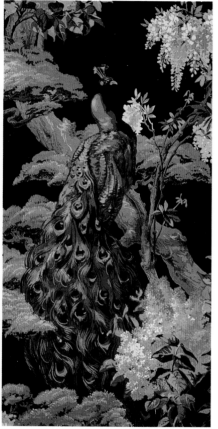

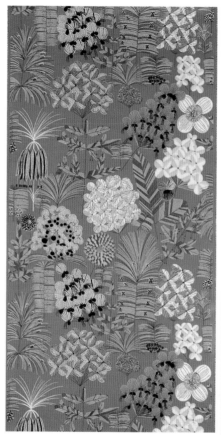

The Cedar Tree c.1910

This flamboyant design by Louis Stahl was created for British wallpaper manufacturer Sanderson's. The combination of rich colors, fine detail, and solid black ground is a striking one. Hand-printed from carved woodblocks, the paper was still in production in 1957.

Blossom Garden c.1930

Particularly admired for her textile and ceramic designs, Felice Rix was a member of the Wiener Werkstätte and studied under Josef Hoffmann. Her Blossom Garden wallpaper design features a fine pattern of grasses and flowers, machine-printed on a beige ground.

The design mixes both figurative and abstract elements, reflecting public interest in patterns and motifs drawn from chemistry, physics, and medicine

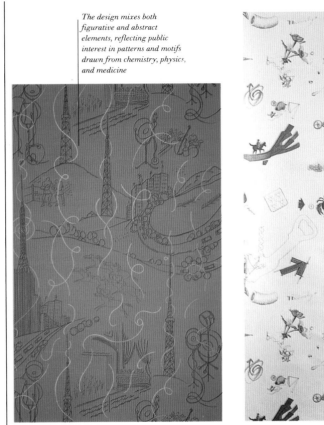

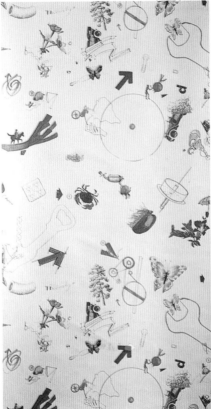

Television 1951

By the 1950s, television ownership was rapidly growing, with over 19 million sets bought in the US by 1952. This screen-printed wallpaper from 1951 represents an enthusiastic response to the new medium. The designer, Mildred Coughlin McNutt, created an image evocative of the many faces of television – sport, theater, music, and urban life.

Vive la Liberté 1972

This composition by the Swiss artist Jean Tinguely (1925–) for the German company Marburger shows freedom from typical imagery in the use of an unexpected sampling of objects found in modern life. Ranging from flowers and butterflies to spanners and bottle openers, the images have been overlaid onto a metallic surface.

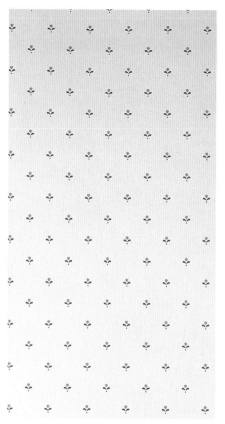

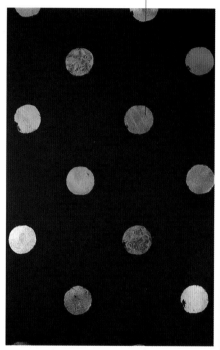

Discs of metallic leaf are individually brushed, rubbed, and burnished, and then applied to hand-painted rice paper

Laura Ashley wallpaper 1980

This restrained pattern for the Laura Ashley company consists of a small floral motif printed in several shades of blue on a crisp white background. The internationally successful company was founded by Laura Ashley in the 1950s, and has become famous for its range of products that evoke English country life.

Trip the Light Fantastic (TLF4) 1998

This richly-textured design, which changes with the light, was created by Anya Larkin for Donghia. Larkin is influenced by ancient European and Asian cultures and uses strict architectural proportions to order her designs. Her work has been acquired by the Arts Décoratifs archives at the Louvre in Paris.

STORAGE

PROVIDING SPACE and protecting items in storage are the key priorities for designers of sideboards, shelving units, and wardrobes. However, many of these functional pieces have become objects of desire in their own right. Changes in design ethos can be traced through the century, from Gustave Serrurier-Bovy's wooden cabinet, which communicates the craftsmanship of Art Nouveau, through the tongue-in-cheek exercises of Memphis, to Jane Atfield's Made of Waste shelving, which expresses the environmental concerns of the 1990s.

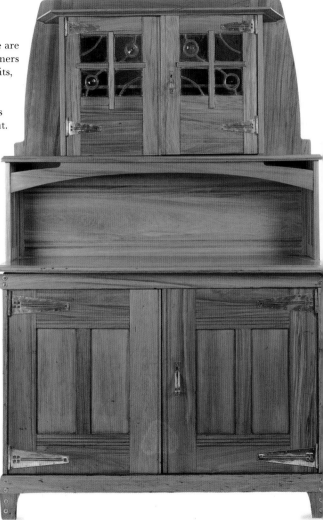

Fruitwood dining cupboard c.1900–10

A classic example of Art Nouveau designer Serrurier-Bovy's work, this cupboard stores its contents behind geometrically styled wooden doors with brass fittings.

Specifications

Country: Belgium
Materials: Fruitwood and brass
Height: 80in (203cm)

"MOBILE INFINITO"

Studio Alchimia was founded in Milan in 1976 by Alessandro Mendini and Ettore Sottsass, among others. This wardrobe is part of a major project known as "Mobile Infinito," for which over 30 artists created individual pieces of furniture. Mendini's wardrobe has feet designed by Denis Santachiara (1950–), handles by Ugo la Pietra (1938–), and flags by Kazuko Sato. The decoration, which can be placed anywhere on the magnetic body, was designed by several artists, including Sandro Chia and Francesco Clemente.

Mobile Infinito wardrobe, 1980s

Edelstahl container 1927

Designed by Marcel Breuer in 1927, simplicity is the essence of these "precious steel" drawers. With the ideals of the Bauhaus behind its design, it achieves a compatibility between art and mass production.

Specifications

Country: Germany
Material: Steel
Height: 39½in (100cm)

PROGRESSIVE STYLE

The Czech designer Bořek Šipek created this unique "wardrobe" for Vitra. A playful combination of colors and materials, it is capped with halogen lighting. Šipek has said of design: "Tradition is the law of progressiveness; progressive design does not destroy that which was, but rather places it in another dimension."

Wardrobe, 1989–91

Twelve-drawer sideboard 1950s

This sideboard is an example of American designer Florence Knoll's work from her most influential period, after World War II. Utilizing new techniques and structures, pieces of furniture such as this classically austere twelve-drawer sideboard were widely imitated. It was manufactured by Knoll Associates, a design group founded by Florence and husband Hans in 1938.

Specifications

Country: US
Materials: Steel, wood, and marble
Height: 24⅜in (62cm)

The angles of the supporting structures create storage spaces of varying volume ⸻

Carlton sideboard 1981

Ettore Sottsass showed his "programmatic" shelving unit-cum-room divider in the first exhibition by his furniture design group Memphis in Milan in 1981. The show created a stir, and this piece has come to be regarded as an icon of postmodernist design. This substantial unit is covered with brightly colored plastic laminate.

Specifications

Country: Italy
Material: Plastic laminate
Height: 77¼in (196cm)

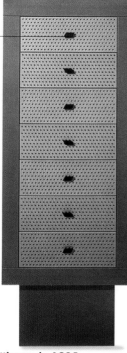

Handles follow the same direction as the metal meshing on each drawer

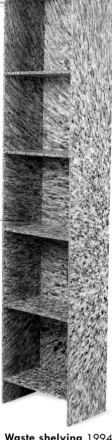

The colors of the shelving are determined by the selection of waste bottles used

Settimanale 1985

This steel cabinet is the work of Matteo Thun, a founding member of Memphis. Its industrial appearance is typical of "micro architecture," a style characterized by its references to architectural concepts. The diamond-shaped holes are punched out in a geometric pattern.

Specifications

Country: Italy
Material: Pressed steel
Height: 63in (160cm)

Made of Waste shelving 1994

British designer Jane Atfield set up the Made of Waste partnership in 1992. She uses recycled plastic bottles to produce furniture in a wild mixture of colors.

Specifications

Country: UK
Material: Plastic
Height: 72½in (184cm)

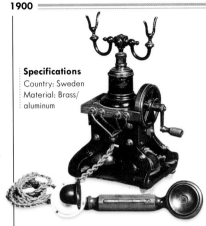

THE TELEPHONE, INVENTED by Alexander Graham Bell in 1876, is now a common feature in households around the world. Early models were often designed to be wall-mounted, and tended to be cumbersome and oversensitive. The candlestick was the first successful compact desk telephone; but it was not until the Ericofon of the 1940s that all the components were unified in a single-element instrument. Since then, the use of plastics has given us cheap, light-weight telephones — including the pocket-sized cordless models of the 1990s — in a range of vivid colors.

Specifications
Country: Sweden
Material: Brass/aluminum

Skeleton c.1900

The hugely successful Skeleton model was first produced in the late 19th century by L.M. Ericsson. This elegant telephone was often finished in high-quality black lacquer and decorated with gold transfers. The ingenious design utilizes the four curved legs to form the magnets of the generator. The working parts are exposed, as are the bells.

Candlestick c.1910

The familiar, classic shape of the Candlestick telephone derives from the practical necessity of keeping the transmitter upright. However, the apparent simplicity of the design is misleading, for the telephone requires a separate bellset — containing induction coil, capacitor, and ringer — in order to operate.

Specifications
Country: US
Material: Enameled brass

Desk telephone 1937

Inspired by the modern plastic telephone designed by painter Jean Heiberg in 1930, Henry Dreyfuss created this self-contained metal model for American Telephone and Telegraph. It was later produced in Bakelite or similar plastic.

Specifications
Country: US
Material: Die-cast metal

Neophone 1929

Siemens' Neophone, originally
made of black Bakelite, was the
first completely molded plastic
telephone ever produced. Until its
introduction, it was still common
for telephones to be made from
wood or metal.

Specifications

Country: UK
Material: Bakelite

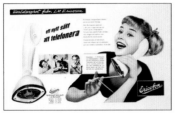

Single-element telephone 1950s

The first single-element (one-piece)
telephone was the Ericofon, designed by
Ralf Lysell and Hugo Blomberg in the
1940s. The design of this single element
model combines sensuality of
form with the function of
technology: the earpiece
and transmitter are
contained in a unified
plastic body, and the
dial is on the base.

Specifications

Country: Sweden
Materials: Plastic,
rubber, and nylon

*The dial and
circuitry are in the
base of the phone*

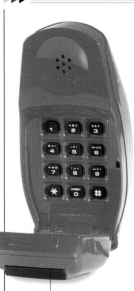

Grillo 1965

The smart, modern-looking Grillo telephone was designed by Richard Sapper and Marco Zanuso in the 1960s; this model dates from the 1980s. It is made from brightly colored plastic, with either push-button keys or a traditional dial. The mouthpiece and main body are hinged so that the unit can be folded away when not in use.

Specifications
Country: Italy
Material: Plastic

The Grillo was half the size of previous telephones

Mickey Mouse typifies modern pop imagery

Mickey Mouse telephone 1980

The 1970s and '80s witnessed a departure from the restrictive conventions of the past, and a variety of inexpensive plastic telephones were produced. This Mickey Mouse telephone by the British company Plessey is lighthearted and fun; and as an item of modern technology, it functions perfectly well.

Specifications
Country: UK
Material: Plastic

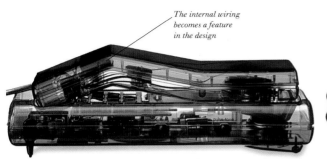

*The internal wiring
becomes a feature
in the design*

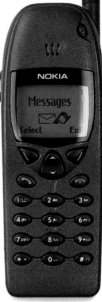

Swatch Twinphone 1994

This telephone, which can be used by
two people at the same time, has a
simple shape, but decoration is provided
in the form of the internal wiring and
electronics. This is in contrast with
the original manufacturers of plastic
telephones and suggests how we are
increasingly at ease with technology.

Specifications
Country: Switzerland
Material: Plastic

Nokia 6110 1998

The 1990s have seen a giant
leap in the quality of mobile
phones, and their use has accelerated
dramatically. This compact piece
of modern design can send text
messages and faxes, as well as
offering games, functioning as a
calculator, and of course as a phone.

Specifications
Country: Finland
Material: Plastic housing

VIDEOPHONE TECHNOLOGY

*The 1980s and '90s saw the adoption of further
technological advances in the production of telephones,
first with cordless models, and then with videophones.
Color video pictures are transmitted with sound,
enabling callers to see each other during
conversations. Although early users experienced
a delay of up to half a second between the
reception of video and voice signals, newer
models make the two simultaneous when
used on a high-speed digital network.
Standard calls can also be made to
telephones without the video facility.*

BT videophone, 1990s

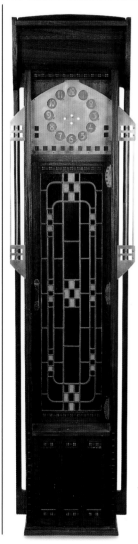

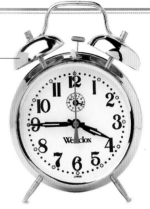

The two earlike bells are linked by a slim, curved handle

Grandfather clock 1900

Gustave Serrurier-Bovy was one of Belgium's leading Art Nouveau designers. Inspired in his youth by William Morris, his later work showed a German influence. Key hallmarks evident in this partially restored piece include architectural form, geometric decoration, and subtle use of brass fittings.

Specifications
Country: Belgium
Height: 91¾in (233cm)

Double bell alarm clock 1920s

This modern version of the traditional double bell alarm clock, with earlike bells, luminous hands, and slender legs, has a common mechanism. It offers the user the option of waking up to a single ring or a repeat ring every few seconds. Many models also feature a small seconds dial.

Specifications
Country: US
Height: 6in (15cm)

CLOCKS

ALTHOUGH A FORM of electric clock had been invented by 1900, the majority of clocks were still mechanical, generally encased in wood or metal. Electric models of increased accuracy became popular in the 1920s; but it was not until 1928, with the design of the first quartz clock, that near total accuracy was possible – the maximum error being one second every ten years. Smaller movements, together with the development of plastic housings, have since given designers greater freedom for innovation.

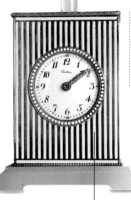

Strongly vertical designs were favored in the 1920s

Cartier clock c.1920

French jewelers Cartier also produced a vast array of clocks. One of the most famous is the Art Deco mantel clock, renowned for its invisible movement. This tiny, exquisite clock is decorated with stripes of gold and white enamel, and has diamond-studded hands.

Specifications
Country: France
Height: 3¼in (8cm)

Zephyr c.1930

Kem Weber was a proponent of the streamline aesthetic, which characterized much American design during the 1930s. He applied that principle in the design of this elegant digital clock for Lawson Time Inc. "Zephyr" is both the Greek god of the west wind and the name of the streamlined trains that appeared in 1934.

Specifications
Country: US
Length: 8in (20.6cm)

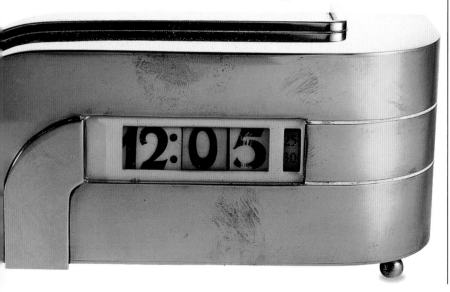

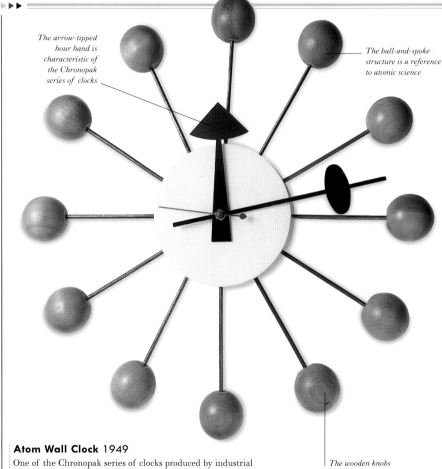

The arrow-tipped hour hand is characteristic of the Chronopak series of clocks

The ball-and-spoke structure is a reference to atomic science

The wooden knobs were often painted

Atom Wall Clock 1949

One of the Chronopak series of clocks produced by industrial designer George Nelson for the Howard Miller Clock Company, the Atom Clock uses shapes borrowed from atomic science. Designed in 1949, the clock prefigures the impact that scientific imagery was to have on art and design in the 1950s – culminating in the construction of the Atomium, a large-scale exhibition sculpture for the Brussels Expo of 1958.

Specifications
Country: US
Diameter: 13¼in (34cm)

Optic 1968

Reissued by Alessi in 1988, the Optic alarm clock was
originally manufactured by Ritz-Italora to a design by
Joe Colombo. Colombo's functional design approach
is evident in the extended case, which shields the dial
from reflection, and in the luminous digits that make
it easy to read in the dark.

Specifications
Country: Italy
Height: 3¼in (8.3cm)

*The numerals form
a minimal part
of the design*

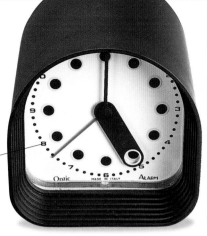

Helix 1979

In designing the Helix clock, Steve Diskin reviewed
the traditional hands or digital approach to displaying
time. The hours, minutes, and seconds are displayed
in a straight line.

Specifications
Country: US
Length: 23¼in (59.3cm)

*The playful
primary colors
are typical of
postmodernist
design*

Vercingetorige 1994

British designer Julian Brown created
the Vercingetorige alarm clock for the
Italian company Rexite. Brown drew
inspiration for the conical body of the
clock from a warrior's helmet. His use
of materials is innovative, combining
Rynite – composed of recycled
photographic plates – transparent,
milky polycarbonate, and brightly
colored acrylic.

Specifications
Country: Italy
Diameter: 3½in (9cm)

VACUUM CLEANERS

THE BEGINNING OF THE CENTURY saw the demise of the domestic servant, and many middle-class families were responsible for their own cleaning for the first time. This coincided with growing paranoia about the dangers of inhaling the germs in household dust – in 1907, one French doctor wrote: "Dry sweeping and dusting are homicidal practices." Soon, the hand- or foot-operated bellows vacuum cleaners that had been available since the 1890s became essential household items. These were rapidly replaced by electric-powered suction cleaners, developed in 1908 by the American Murray Spangler and financed by William Hoover. For many years, Hoover has dominated the market. Only recently have traditional cleaners been challenged by new technology.

Baby Daisy c.1908

One of many introduced in the 1900s, the Baby Daisy was a hand-operated bellows vacuum cleaner. Although it was cumbersome and difficult to use – one hand pumped the bellows while the other guided the hose – it was an improvement on sweeping. Within a decade, hand-operated machines were replaced by power-driven vacuum pumps.

Specifications

Country: UK
Height: 39in (100cm)

Baby Daisy was easier to operate if an assistant pumped the bellows

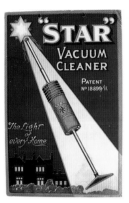

Advertising the Star

The relatively expensive Star cleaner was designed to be lightweight and easy to use: "The Light of Every Home," proclaimed the advertising.

Star 1911

Although easier to use than the unwieldy Baby Daisy, the Star had to be hand-pumped and was without rotating brushes. Its utilitarian design – no attempt has been made to hide the wing nuts or rivets – suggests that it was to be kept out of sight when not in use.

The bellows produced sufficient suction to draw up the dust

Specifications
Country: UK
Height: 51in (130cm)

Hoover 700 1920

In 1916, the American Hoover Suction Sweeper Company introduced an upright vacuum cleaner that became the standard for the next two decades. The cleaner has a canvas bag housing a disposable paper sack in which the dust was collected. Rotating brushes loosened the dust as the cleaner sucked. The angle of the handle to the head could be adjusted; it was connected on swing hinges.

Specifications
Country: US
Height: 47in (120cm)

Brushes, fan, and motor are housed in a single casing

Electrolux 1920

Despite the prevalence of the upright vacuum cleaner,
the cylinder type continues to challenge its popularity.
Manufactured by Electrolux, the original design of 1915
had a horizontal cylinder with cleaning brushes attached
to a flexible hose. This enabled the user to clean curtains,
upholstery, and fabrics at any height.

Specifications
Country: Sweden
Height: Not known

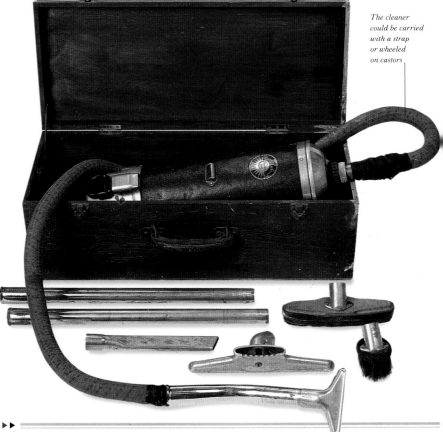

*The cleaner
could be carried
with a strap
or wheeled
on castors*

HAND-HELD CLEANERS

Hoover Dustette

The Hoover Dustette is one of many hand-held cleaners designed specifically to dispose of crumbs or pet hairs. Light, portable, and cordless, these appliances are far more convenient than full-size vacuum cleaners for small-scale, precise work. Hand-held vacuum cleaners first gained popularity in the 1960s and '70s as a convenient way to clean car interiors, and were powered by the car's battery via the cigarette lighter socket. Such models are now marketed for general use.

The sleek, cylindrical body gives the cleaner a high-tech, futuristic appearance

Dyson Dual Cyclone 1986

Not since the introduction of the original Hoover has there been so revolutionary a development in upright cleaner design as the Cyclone. The dust bag has been eliminated; instead, dirt is collected in the cylindrical body, using G-force technology. Dyson claims 100 percent suction, even when the cleaner is almost full, because centrifugal spin keeps the airstream clear.

The yellow and gray styling recalls 1950s space-age designs

Specifications
Country: UK
Height: 42in (107cm)

CLOTHING & ACCESSORIES

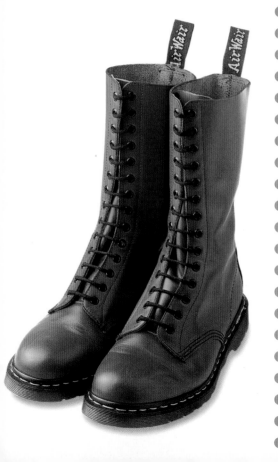

Childrenswear

Womenswear

Menswear

Shoes

Watches

Fountain pens

Makeup

Jewelry

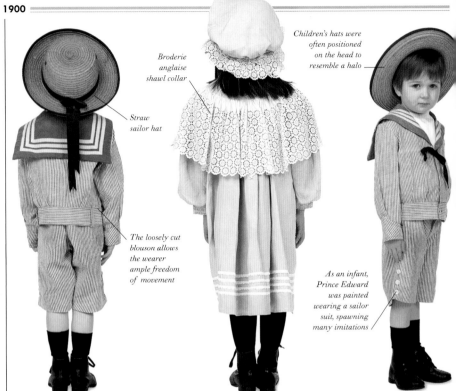

*Broderie
anglaise
shawl collar*

*Straw
sailor hat*

*Children's hats were
often positioned
on the head to
resemble a halo*

*The loosely cut
blouson allows
the wearer
ample freedom
of movement*

*As an infant,
Prince Edward
was painted
wearing a sailor
suit, spawning
many imitations*

CHILDRENSWEAR

ALTHOUGH THE CLOTHING REFORMS of the late 19th century prompted a relaxation in public attitudes toward children's dress, it was World War I that witnessed the first significant upheavals. Children were taken out of their heavy, formal outfits — invariably scaled-down versions of their parents' — and dressed in lighter, plainer, less restrictive garments. When, in the 1950s, an array of new man-made fibers, easy-care fabrics, and simpler fasteners emerged, the industry was galvanized anew. The revolution was finally complete with the advent of mass production, when traditional hand-tailored clothes were universally replaced by ready-to-wear outfits.

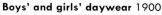

Boys' and girls' daywear 1900

Although children's sailor suits had been available for decades, they came into their own at the turn of the century, when changes in education meant that clothing had to be suitable for the recently introduced gymnastics and outdoor games that formed part of the revised school curriculum. Looser clothing for girls, like this linen coat-dress, began to gain popularity. Even so, it was still customary to wear heavy, lace-up boots and black cashmere stockings.

The linen suit is trimmed with blue smocking

Straw Panama

Button-through coat-dress

Lace-up boots and stockings were worn until after World War I

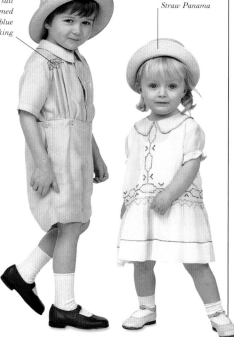

Boys' and girls' daywear 1920s

It was after World War I that children's clothes changed most dramatically and universally. This transformation echoed the radical changes taking place in adult fashion. Lighter, less elaborate garments, including soft collars, jerseys, and socks instead of stockings, were adopted, in contrast to the formal styles of the first decades of the century. Girls wore simple dresses with dropped waists, and boys wore updated versions of the skeleton suit — brief shorts buttoned onto a shirt top.

Outdoor clothing 1930s

Matching coat and leggings outfits were popular outdoor wear for young children throughout the 1930s and '40s. They were immensely practical because the leggings were loose enough for dresses to be tucked into them, and they could be zipped or buttoned tightly over the shoes for extra warmth.

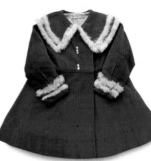

Knitted Fair Isle pullover

Boys' and girls' daywear 1940s

With the outbreak of World War II children's clothing took on a more practical aspect than previously. Clothes were designed to be comfortable and hard-wearing. Outfits like this double-breasted suit, worn with a knitted sweater, were common. American styles — including snow suits, knee breeches, and checked shirts — which were to flourish in the postwar years, began to filter into Europe with the packages of clothes sent from the US to aid war-stricken countries.

Easy-care fabrics like this Tobralco dress were ideal for children's clothes

Ankle-strap shoes were worn with ankle socks

The open-textured cotton fabric Aertex dates from the 1880s

Floral prints and brightly colored fabric were popular in the 1950s

Sandals were popular for both boys and girls

Boys' and girls' daywear 1950s

The postwar baby boom emphasized the potential market for children's clothing. Outfits for very young children were influenced by adult styles; but subtle changes did start to appear, and slowly their dress began to follow teenage rather than adult fashions. Teenagers were an important market force in the 1950s. They used their newfound income to show off their independence, purchasing the clothes, records, and accessories associated with the new pop culture.

CHILD STAR

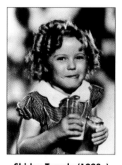

Shirley Temple (1928–)

In the 1930s, film played a major role in influencing fashion. Nobody had more impact on children's clothes than Shirley Temple, one of the most successful child stars in the history of film. After her debut at the age of three, she was for a decade one of the biggest stars in the US. She acted in films such as Dimples, Curly Top, Poor Little Rich Girl, *and* Baby Take a Bow. *During the Great Depression, Temple was celebrated by an adoring public, and the dresses she wore – with puffed sleeves and Peter Pan collars – became very popular. She retired from Hollywood in the late 1940s and went on to enjoy a successful career with the United Nations.*

▶ ▶ ▶

BABYGRO

In the 1950s, Viennese business-man Walter Artzt designed and patented a one-piece outfit for babies, made from a stretch fabric that he invented. The suit was designed for the dual purposes of comfort and practicality, and has been steadily improved over the decades. It is now internationally known and sold as the Babygro.

The clear PVC coat is decorated with a geometric pattern inspired by Op Art

Boys' and girls' daywear 1960s

It was not until 1965 that hemlines rose above the knee and the daring, provocative styles of the 1960s flourished. From 1965 to 1968 brief, simple clothes were mass produced in bright, inexpensive styles, which were ideally suited to the children's market. In the late 1960s, the hippie movement emerged. Developing the experimental nature of the decade, hippies encouraged the adoption of ethnic clothing, flowing robes in natural materials, exotic beads, and long hair.

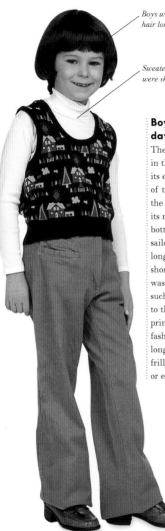

Boys wore their hair longer

The headscarf completes the rural appearance

Sweaters and shirts were skin-tight

Boys' and girls' daywear 1970s

The style of dress that had evolved in the late 1960s was developed to its extreme in the 1970s. The cut of trousers altered, flaring from the knee to the hem, known in its most exaggerated form as bell-bottoms (a revival of the style of sailors' outfits). Boys now wore long trousers or jeans, rather than shorts, from an early age. There was a revival of interest in crafts, such as patchwork, which led to the production of patchwork-printed textiles. Following adult fashions, girls' skirts became longer, and were often worn with frilly blouses inspired by historical or ethnic costume.

Imitation patchwork dress

Platform shoes were popular in the 1970s

The baseball cap is an icon of US street style

Boys' daywear 1980s

The influence of television and video on childrenswear intensified throughout the 1980s. One effect of this was the spread of American styles to Europe; baseball caps and sneakers becoming enormously popular. Denim jeans, standard casual wear for the young since the 1960s, returned to a straight-legged shape after the demise of flares.

Hooded jacket

Loose-fitting denim jeans

The popularity of branded sports shoes began in the 1980s

Quick-release Velcro fastenings are ideal for children's shoes

LADYBIRD

The history of the Pasold family and its transformation from domestic weavers in the remote village of Fleissen, Bohemia, to mass-producers and brand leaders of children's clothing spans 300 years. Two important landmarks in this history were the acquisition of its British plant in 1932, when the company began to shift production from ladies' to children's garments; and the purchase of the Ladybird trademark in 1938. Today, Ladybird clothes are sold throughout the world – its name is used everywhere except in the US and Spain, but the "bug" motif is universal and instantly recognizable.

Boys' and girls' daywear 1990s

There is no one style that definitively characterizes the 1990s. The number of manufacturers designing especially for children has multiplied and the number of looks available is vast. Many styles or materials have endured or been rediscovered with regular 1950s, '60s, and even '70s revivals. One children's fashion item that has made a dramatic impact is the sneaker, which has become a billion-dollar industry as companies such as Nike and Adidas (see p.279) vie to persuade the young that their product is coolest.

Primary colors are perennially popular for childrenswear

The sturdy, practical shoe design is enlivened by the decorative trim

WOMENSWEAR

THE CHANGING VALUES AND ATTITUDES of the century
are clearly reflected in the way women dress: the role
of women, the permissive society, and the growth of
the youth market have all had an impact. In daywear,
restrictive full-length dresses, with a multitude of
petticoats, were replaced by clothing better suited to
modern lifestyles. New looks were created through
a combination of aesthetic judgment, new materials,
and the challenging of past conventions.

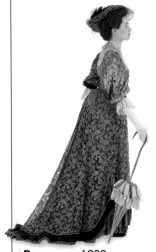

Daywear 1920s

In the decade of the
tubular silhouette,
dresses were shorter,
light, and elegant,
in silk or crêpe-
de-chine, often
revealing the
arms and back.
Beige stockings
were worn to
suggest bare
legs, and
rayon provided
an affordable
alternative
to silk.

Daywear c.1900

Although less restrictive than
the multilayered, late 19th-
century style, women's dress at
the turn of the century was still
uncomfortable. The "S"-shaped
silhouette was molded by
a corset, pushing the bust
forward and the hips back.

Daywear 1910s

In 1914, Mary Phelps Jacobs
designed the brassière – two
handkerchiefs with ribbon
straps, intended to flatten the
bust. World War I brought
more women into the workplace,
increasing the demand for
less restrictive clothing.

Daywear 1930s

The Depression influenced fashion in the 1930s. Women's clothes became more sober and the hemline dropped once again. The overall silhouette was more curvaceous. Elegant suits in soft fabrics were popular, often worn with fox fur.

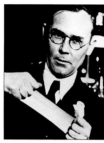

NYLON

First produced by the Du Pont laboratories in 1938, nylon was named after the cities where it was hoped it would sell, New York and London. This fine, strong, elastic, synthetic fiber was an ideal substitute for rayon or silk. Research was led by Wallace H. Carothers; after his death the patent was awarded to Du Pont.

Carothers testing nylon

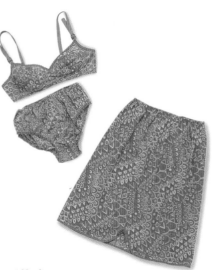

Underwear

New, easy-to-care-for underwear perfectly suited the carefree lifestyles of women during the 1960s. Matching sets of nylon bra, briefs, and half-slips appeared in bold, bright prints.

Daywear 1940s

Cloth became scarce during World War II, and clothes were plainer and used less fabric than previously. A utility scheme was set up in Britain to ration clothes. Nylons were introduced in America in 1940, but were very difficult to obtain in Europe.

Daywear 1950s

Christian Dior's "New Look," introduced in 1947, had a huge impact on everyday fashion. The tight-fitting bodice, narrow waist, and full skirt gave a curving silhouette. The brassière was padded and wired to enhance the bust.

Daywear 1960s

Although the decade witnessed a multitude of styles, the 1960s will be forever associated with the miniskirt. It was no longer possible to wear traditional stockings, so designers experimented with fine-quality colored and patterned tights.

Daywear 1970s

In the 1970s, fashion designers drew inspiration from a variety of sources: feminism, the hippie movement, and civil rights. Continuing trends set in the 1960s, easy-care synthetic fibers and psychedelic and patchwork patterns were popular.

Daywear 1980s

Clothes in the 1980s were a mix of glamour, body consciousness, and the casual, multilayered look. Lycra, invented in 1958 in the US and previously used only for underwear, gave rise to the body-hugging designs that went with the 1980s' fitness craze.

Daywear 1990s

Unlike previous decades, the 1990s are not epitomized by any single "look;" individualism is the key. There has been a shift in emphasis away from the high achievement that influenced the look of the 1980s and toward a more casual, comfortable style.

MENSWEAR

COMPARED TO THE RADICAL changes in women's dress during the 20th century, menswear has appeared more constant in character. The suit, worn at the turn of the century, has undergone changes in material and cut, but remains similar in form to its modern derivative. However, the fashionable male silhouette like its female counterpart, has been molded to suit changing social values and advances in technology. Heavy Edwardian suits and starched collars have given way to separates in lightweight and synthetic fabrics; waistcoats and hats, once essential components of daywear, are now optional extras. The biggest change in men's dress occurred in the 1960s, when young men adopted colorful, casual clothes that challenged strict gender definitions.

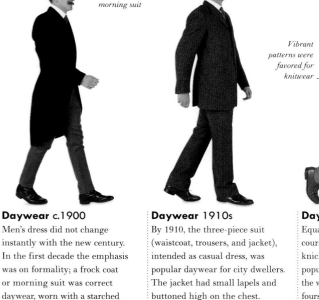

The formal top hat was worn with the morning suit

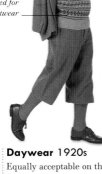

Vibrant patterns were favored for knitwear

Daywear c.1900

Men's dress did not change instantly with the new century. In the first decade the emphasis was on formality; a frock coat or morning suit was correct daywear, worn with a starched shirt collar that averaged 4in (10cm) in height.

Daywear 1910s

By 1910, the three-piece suit (waistcoat, trousers, and jacket), intended as casual dress, was popular daywear for city dwellers. The jacket had small lapels and buttoned high on the chest. It was worn with narrow trousers and a bowler hat.

Daywear 1920s

Equally acceptable on the golf course or as informal daywear, knickers became extremely popular in the 1920s. In the UK the wide trousers were called "plus-fours" because they fell 4 in (10cm) below the knee. They were usually made from tweed.

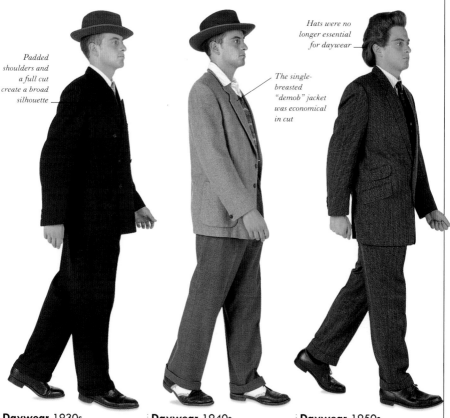

Padded shoulders and a full cut create a broad silhouette

Hats were no longer essential for daywear

The single-breasted "demob" jacket was economical in cut

Daywear 1930s

The ideal male silhouette in the 1930s had broad shoulders and narrow hips. These features were accentuated in the cut of the double-breasted suit, which had padded shoulders and wide lapels. Trouser legs were cut wide with cuffs at the hem.

Daywear 1940s

It is difficult to identify any definitive style during the postwar period because the lack of raw materials and, in some countries, rationing meant that many clothes were recycled, a concept that would have been unheard of before the war.

Daywear 1950s

The 1950s saw a steady paring down of the male silhouette. A narrower cut was adopted for suits, with slimmer trousers and a long single-breasted jacket. Known as the drape suit, it was worn in an extreme form by the "Teddy boys" in Britain.

POP CULTURE INFLUENCE

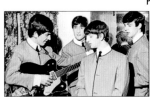

The Beatles, early-1960s

Owing to the immense popularity that followed their first hit records in the early 1960s, the Beatles had an enormous impact on menswear. The collarless jacket shown here, designed by Pierre Cardin, was particularly associated with the group. As Beatlemania swept across the world, fans began to mimic the group's style. Although it seems unremarkable now, the "mop-top" haircut, with its thick bangs was considered shockingly long at the time.

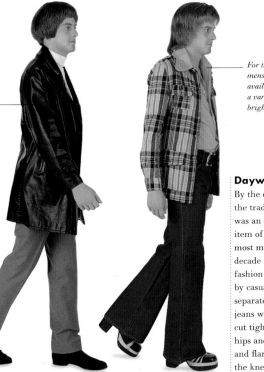

Formerly exotic fabrics such as leather became commonplace

For the first time, menswear became available in a variety of bright colors

Daywear 1960s

The male wardrobe underwent a radical transformation in the 1960s. Cheap, colorful clothes were produced for young men and sold in the new boutiques. "Swinging" London, particularly Carnaby Street, was the center of an emerging pop culture.

Daywear 1970s

By the early 1970s, the traditional suit was an occasional item of dress for most men. The decade in men's fashion was typified by casual wear and separates. Hipster jeans were popular, cut tight over the hips and thighs and flaring from the knee.

THE T-SHIRT

**James Dean,
1955**

In 1942, the US Navy introduced a knitted cotton undershirt with short sleeves and a round collar. It was known as the T-Type because it formed a "T" shape when laid flat. Worn initially by soldiers and marines, it was later popularized by James Dean, who wore one in Rebel Without a Cause, *1955.*

The Nehru collar on this Armani outfit is inspired by Chinese costume

Padded shoulders mimic 1930s styling

Daywear 1980s

Menswear took a new direction in the 1980s when specialized men's clothing store chains developed a significant presence. An economic boom led to the creation of a new type of young city gent with a distinctly corporate image.

Daywear 1990s

The mood swung again in the 1990s, with a rejection of the professional look that characterized the 1980s. Soft, natural fabrics, such as linen and silk, were favored. Shirts were often worn untucked in a loose, layered style.

SHOES

REFLECTING AND COMPLEMENTING new styles of clothing, shoe design has always been an important branch of the fashion industry. Italian designer Salvatore Ferragamo was one of the first to put new synthetic materials to use, combining cork platform soles with plastic uppers in the 1930s. Another notable Italian innovation, the stiletto, appeared in the 1950s and has played a controversial role in women's fashion ever since. Elsewhere in footwear, the distinction between men's and women's styles lessened noticeably toward the end of the century.

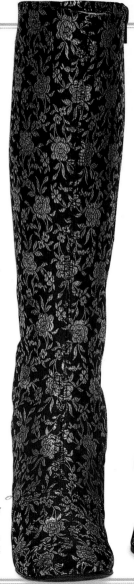

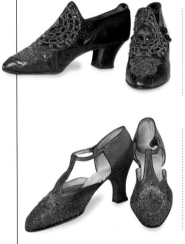

Bead shoes c.1900
These ornate shoes from early in the century combine a high upper with the slightly waisted heel of a court shoe. The pattern cut into the leather is enhanced by an arrangement of tiny steel beads.

T-bar shoes 1920s
These elegant, high-heeled shoes are made from embroidered purple fabric. The bar shoe is the definitive women's style of the 1920s, the T-bar shown here being a variant of the style below.

Skin shoes 1920s
Reptile skin has been exceptionally popular in women's shoe design for much of the century. Recently, synthetic copies have developed in response to concerns for wildlife.

SALVATORE FERRAGAMO

The work of the greatest Italian shoe designer of the century, this "invisible shoe" with nylon toe straps was launched in 1947. It followed the legendary cork wedge heel, patented in 1936 and imitated throughout the world.

Invisible shoe, 1947

Correspondent shoes 1920s

The two-tone correspondent, or spectator, shoe was popular during the Jazz era. Primarily a fashion for men, these black or brown and white shoes enjoyed a revival in the 1940s.

Crepe sole shoe 1950s

Emerging with the cult of the teenager, crepe soles became popular in the 1950s. These shoes were colloquially known as "brothel creepers," because of their thick, rubbery soles and soft suede uppers.

The stiletto 1950s

Since it was introduced in Italy in 1953, the stiletto has varied significantly in shape. Although originally 2in (5cm) thick and gently tapered, the heel has changed over time to become increasingly tall and pointed.

Knee boots 1960s

Although boots were originally made to protect the ankles and calves, by the 1960s they had become more of a fashion statement. Produced in leather or synthetic material, they varied in length from ankle to thigh.

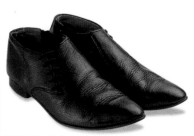

Winklepickers 1960s

Introduced in the late 1950s, the winkle-pickers' pointed toes show design influences from as long ago as the 14th century. The name refers to the sharp pin used to pick periwinkles (mollusks) out of their shells.

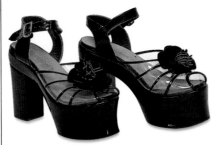

Ladies' platform shoes 1970s

The celebrated platform soles of the 1970s are a radical version of the 1940s' wedge. Revived as a fashionable, slightly offbeat shoe, they were made from an affordable combination of leather and plastic.

The design has retro Art Deco styling

Men's platform shoes 1970

In the 1970s, platform shoes were worn by both men and women. Some soles, as with these men's lace-ups, reached such heights that they posed the danger of broken ankles.

RED OR DEAD

Red or Dead was founded in 1982 by Wayne and Gerardine Hemingway. It began as a market stall in London, growing into a chain of international shops. The label's innovative fashions often demonstrate a futuristic, space-age influence.

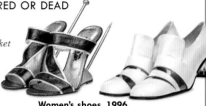

Women's shoes, 1996

Dr. Martens 1960–90

Dr. Maertens and Dr. Funck pioneered air-cushioned soles in 1945, as a comfortable solution to shodding Maertens' injured foot. They were an instant success. The 1960s' "1460," shown here, was the first Dr. Martens boot and has remained a firm favorite.

The molded toe and heel is stitched to a soft leather upper

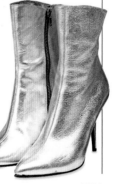

Silver boots 1990s

These calf-length boots have a central seam running to a pointed toe. The inside zipper is a practical fastening that creates a slimline silhouette, emphasized by the stiletto heels.

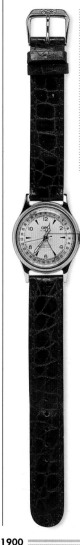

Oris Big Crown
1910s
Named for its oversized winder, the Big Crown was designed to allow World War I aviators to wind it without removing their gloves. It is still produced today.

Specifications
Country: Switzerland
Materials: Stainless steel and leather

The Big Crown also has a hand showing the month of the year

Waltham 1920s
The bulbous case design of this early lady's wristwatch is little removed from the pocket fob. The miniaturization of movements for small women's watches added to their expense.

Specifications
Country: US
Materials: White gold and leather

WATCHES

THE FIRST WRISTWATCHES were manufactured in the 1890s and closely resembled the traditional pocket watch. The idea of strapping a watch to the wrist was not initially favored, and considered more suitable for women than men. When World War I officers found them more efficient than fumbling in their pockets, this feminine image was dispelled. In the 1960s, electronic advances resulted in the digital watch, with its easy-to-read display and highly accurate timekeeping.

Cocktail watch 1930s
Ornate cocktail watches were prestigious accessories for evening wear during the 1930s. This Art Deco example houses a Swiss movement in a diamond-encrusted case.

Specifications
Country: Switzerland
Materials: Platinum and diamonds

Fixed lugs hold the strap in place

The square edges are typical of Art Deco styling

Bracelets were made of white gold or platinum

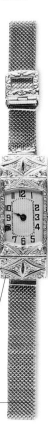

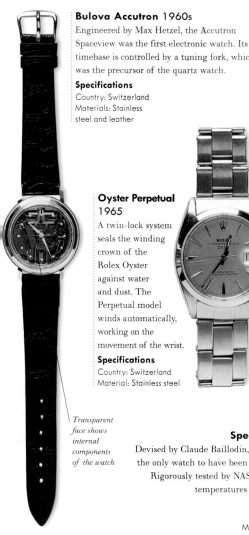

Bulova Accutron 1960s

Engineered by Max Hetzel, the Accutron
Spaceview was the first electronic watch. Its
timebase is controlled by a tuning fork, which
was the precursor of the quartz watch.

Specifications
Country: Switzerland
Materials: Stainless
steel and leather

*A calendar is
incorporated
into the
watch face*

Oyster Perpetual
1965

A twin-lock system
seals the winding
crown of the
Rolex Oyster
against water
and dust. The
Perpetual model
winds automatically,
working on the
movement of the wrist.

Specifications
Country: Switzerland
Material: Stainless steel

*Transparent
face shows
internal
components
of the watch*

Speedmaster 1969

Devised by Claude Baillodin, the Speedmaster is
the only watch to have been worn on the Moon.
Rigorously tested by NASA, it can withstand
temperatures up to 199°F (93°C).

Specifications
Country: Switzerland
Material: Stainless steel

▶ ▶ ▶

Lasser digital 1970s

Forerunner to the electronic digital, this mechanical version was more common for some time. Its space-age references epitomize the 1970s' vogue for futuristic styling.

Specifications
Country: Switzerland
Material: Stainless steel

The shimmering bracelet strap is substantially wider than the watch face

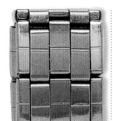

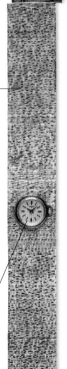

At just ½in (1.2cm) wide, the watch face is a discreet element of the design

The watch is set on an expandable bracelet

DIVER'S WATCH

Omega Seamaster, 1995

The Swiss-made Sea-master is one of a new breed of professional diver's watches. This stainless steel model has a self-winding chronometer movement showing hours, minutes, seconds, and the date. It has a power reserve of 42 hours, an anti-reflective, scratch-resistant sapphire crystal face, and is waterproof to a depth of up to 1,000ft (300m).

Gold watch 1970s

From the most affordable to the most exclusive examples, women's watches in the 1970s commonly resembled jewelry. This wide bracelet and small watch face are typical.

Specifications
Country: Not known
Material: Gold

SWATCH

Developed by Ernst Thonke, Jacques Müller, and Elmer Mock in 1983, the Swatch was the first integrated watch, in which the action was not a separate component from the case. The introductory Swatch model, marketed in 1983, was the Delirium, a modest example compared to the 1990s' Alumo, with its brightly patterned strap and face. Swatch has frequently employed artists to create exclusive watches, such as photographer Annie Leibovitz (who made a contribution to mark the 1996 Atlanta Olympic Games) and Vivienne Westwood.

Delirium, 1983

Alumo, 1996

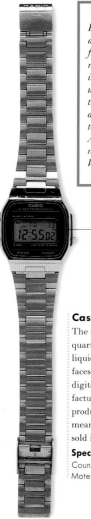

The digital face includes alarm, calendar, and stopwatch

Casio digital 1990s

The combination of quartz powering and liquid crystal display faces revolutionized digital watch manufacturing. Low production costs mean they can be sold inexpensively.

Specifications

Country: Japan
Material: Stainless steel

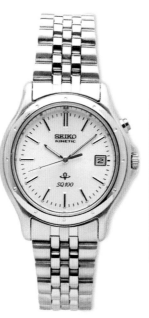

Seiko Kinetic 1990s

An improvement of the Automatic Generating System, introduced in 1988, the Kinetic is one of the most reliable self-winding watches. The need for batteries is eliminated.

Specifications

Country: Japan
Materials: Stainless steel and gold

FOUNTAIN PENS

THROUGHOUT THE 19TH CENTURY, designers experimented with ways to improve dip-pens, until then the standard writing instruments. By 1900, the main principles for a successful fountain pen had been established: a reservoir for ink, a filling system, and a method of supplying ink to the tip. Finding the most successful combination has provided a constant challenge, with three American companies – Parker, Waterman, and Sheaffer – dominating the market. The design of the fountain pen has not relied solely on the demands of engineering; aesthetics have also played an important role. The look of a pen, its size, weight, color, and the materials used in its construction all contribute to its success. Despite the ascendency of the cartridge pen and ballpoint pen, the nostalgic tastes of the late 20th century ensure the continued desirability of the fountain pen both as collectable item and functional tool.

The successful Lucky Curve tip was also used on other Parker models

The Lucky Curve was produced in a range of sizes, including baby, short, and standard

An eyedropper was commonly used to fill the reservoir

Waterman Eyedropper c.1903

Fountain pen pioneer Lewis E. Waterman began his successful company by patenting an improved feed design involving fine grooves under the tip. This was incorporated in this early Eyedropper pen.

Specifications
Country: US
Length: 5in (13cm)
Materials: Hard rubber with gold trim

Parker Lucky Curve c.1916–23

To prevent fountain pens from blobbing ink onto the paper if left lying horizontally, Parker developed a feed that channeled the ink back into the reservoir. This was used for pens such as the Lucky Curve.

Specifications
Country: US
Length: 4½in (11.5cm)
Materials: Hard rubber with gold trim

Conklin Crescent Filler c.1923

Conklin's crescent filler system, patented in 1901, was copied by all the major pen manufacturers in the world. Air is expelled when the crescent is pressed, and ink drawn into the sack when it is released.

Specifications
Country: US
Length: 5⅛in (14cm)
Material: Hard rubber

This ring locks the crescent and prevents the pressure bar inside from pushing against the ink sack

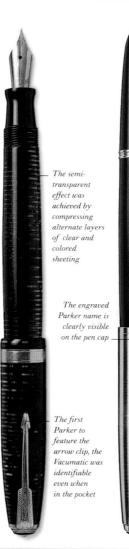

The hooded tip was the most distinctive feature of the Parker 51

The semi-transparent effect was achieved by compressing alternate layers of clear and colored sheeting

The engraved Parker name is clearly visible on the pen cap

Parker Pearly Vacumatic c.1935

As famous for its fine appearance as its technological innovation, Parker's Vacumatic design introduced a rubber diaphragm to replace the traditional sack, as well as new mechanisms to suck up the ink.

Specifications
Country: US
Length: 4¾in (12cm)
Material: Plastic

The first Parker to feature the arrow clip, the Vacumatic was identifiable even when in the pocket

Parker 51 c.1948

Marking the 51st anniversary of the company's foundation, the Parker 51 inspired a fashion for slim, elegant pens with hooded tips. None emulated the commercial success of this original, which was still in production in the 1960s.

Specifications
Country: US
Length: 4¼in (11cm)
Materials: Plastic with silver trim

▶ ▶ ▶

*The tip of
the Parker 61
was protected
from damage*

*The pen can be
filled without
the need to
submerge the
tip in the ink*

*This model was
available with
black, gray, red,
or turquoise
plastic barrel*

PARKER PEN COMPANY

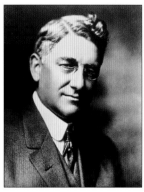

*Born in the US in 1863, George S.
Parker worked as a school teacher,
selling fountain pens to his students
to supplement his income. As the
school pen repairman, he mastered
the inner workings of the pens
and decided to put his knowledge
to commercial use. His first major
success arrived in 1892, when he
designed the Lucky Curve pen.
Subsequent coups have included
the mass-produced Vacumatics.
As the century draws to a close,
there is a growing nostalgia for
old-fashioned writing tools, and pre-
1920s' Parkers are among the most
valuable of collectable fountain pens.*

Parker 61 1956

Although similar in
appearance to the Parker 51,
the 61 model incorporates
an unusual filling system
using a new ink called Super
Quink. The ink cell, not the
tip, is immersed in ink,
which is drawn into the
cell by capillary action.

Specifications
Country: US
Length: 4¼in (11cm)
Materials: Plastic
with gold trim

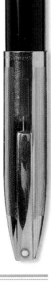

Sheaffer Pen
for Men 1960

Walter A. Sheaffer's 1907
lever filler — widely used
for the next 40 years —
established him as a leading
figure in pen design.
The Pen for Men uses the
Snorkel system for filling
pens, introduced in the 1940s.

Specifications
Country: US
Length: 4¼in (11cm)
Material: Plastic

The white star represents the snow-capped mountain Mont Blanc

The twin-headed tip produces both thick and thin lines

Montblanc 149 Masterpiece c.1970

The Masterpiece pen dates from 1924, with this 149 model introduced in the 1970s. The figure 4,810 engraved on the tip refers to the mountain's height and symbolizes the company's high standards of craftsmanship.

Specifications
Country: Germany
Length: 5¼in (13.25cm)
Materials: Plastic with gold trim

At 5¼in (13.25cm) long and with a wide barrel, the Montblanc is a solid, weighty pen

Parker 180 c.1980

This pen is called the 180 because, by turning it 180 degrees, the user can achieve a fine line with one side of the tip, and a thicker one with the other. The pen originally had a 14k gold tip and often a lacquer-coated barrel with gold trim.

Specifications
Country: US
Length: 4¼in (11cm)
Materials: Gold-plated stainless steel

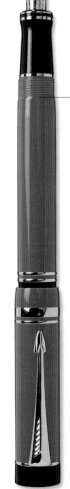

The glossy red color recalls the lacquered color of the original Duofold

This Duofold from 1929 features the early pocket clip

Parker Duofold 1929; 1994

In keeping with 1990s' tastes for retrospective styling, Parker has relaunched its 1920s' Duofold. The original could be converted from pocket pen to desk pen by replacing the blind end cap with an extension to the barrel.

Specifications
Country: US
Length: 5½in (14cm)
Material: Rippled rubber/acrylic

MAKEUP

"AT TIMES THE URGE to improve one's appearance, even if only temporary, becomes too strong to resist" (*Vogue*). Through the ages, both men and women have searched for ways to enhance their appearance using artificial aids. The first decade of the 20th century is regarded as the heyday of the beauty palor. After World War I, women's looks attained a more classless appearance, and before long they studiously copied the hair and makeup styles of glamorous film stars. The 1950s heralded a new era for the cosmetics industry, which turned its attention to a younger clientele, seducing them with novel packaging and seasonal lines.

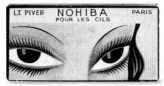

Eye makeup c.1930
Diaghilev's Ballets Russes, which arrived in Paris in 1909, had a lasting effect on cosmetics. The dancers' exotic eye makeup created a vogue for colored eyeshadows and heavy use of mascara.

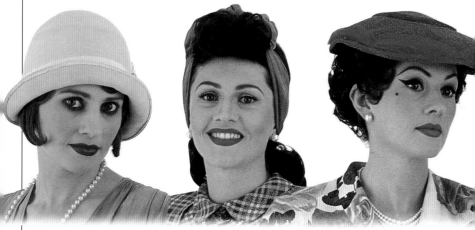

The Jazz Age 1920s
Lipstick made its debut in the 1920s, in vivid shades that were designed to shock. The look to aim for was cropped, smooth, bobbed hair; kohl around the eyes; severely plucked and penciled eyebrows; and a white complexion.

Wartime cosmetics 1940s
During World War II, makeup was in short supply. Cosmetics were good for feminine morale, and many women used homemade substitutes. Deep red lipstick, available on the black market, was worn with matching nail polish.

Hollywood glamour 1950s
There was a return to a more feminine look after the war. The eyes were emphasized by shorter hairstyles and by the exaggerated use of black eyeliner on the upper lids. A variety of new products aimed at a younger market was launched.

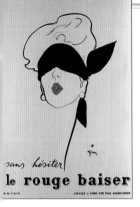

sans hésiter

le rouge baiser

Red Lips 1949

This provocative poster, by René Gruau reads "the red kiss." Color is confined to the lips, which when contrasted with the monochrome illustration has a stunning impact.

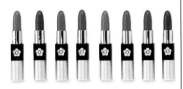

Mary Quant 1970

To complement her fashion collection, Mary Quant launched a range of cosmetics in 1966. They were strikingly packaged in black and silver, with the famous daisy logo. These 1990s lipsticks indicate the enduring popularity of Quant's products.

The cult of youth 1960s

During the 1960s, cosmetics were aimed at the teenage consumer. Girls used pale lipstick and heavy eye makeup. Cosmetics that were easy to use were favored, such as powder compacts and mascara in tube form.

Career woman 1980s

A new type of young, urban career woman emerged during the 1980s. Cosmetics adopted a more assertive look with bold definition of facial features, and the longevity of cosmetics was stressed to appeal to busy women.

The natural look 1990s

Subtlety was the key to applying makeup in the 1990s. The names of cosmetics hinted at the clinically tested ingredients and indicated a move away from the glamour of the early 20th century toward a purer aesthetic.

JEWELRY

JEWELRY CAN BE DIVIDED into three basic groups: classic pieces in high-value metals or stones; paste and metal imitations, originally produced for security reasons and later known as costume jewelry; and art jewelry, a category in which innovation takes precedence over value. The first two are as popular today as they have ever been, with designers using their skills to create subtly modern variations on classic themes. As attitudes to women's fashions have relaxed, so limitations on jewelry design have been discarded, to the point where a necklace of beaten nails may be as celebrated as a string of pearls.

Used in jewelry since the late 1700s, marcasite became fashionable again in the 1920s as a cheap substitute for diamonds

Buckle 1904

The Danish silversmith Georg Jensen was well-known for the quality of his craftsmanship, and his impeccable standards are evident in this fine buckle. It is centered on a large piece of agate, which is surrounded by smaller, symmetrically positioned amber and peridot stones.

Specifications

Country: Denmark
Materials: Silver, green agate, amber, and peridot

Art Deco brooch c.1925

This enameled piece demonstrates a key hallmark of Art Deco jewelry: geometric combinations of circular and angular blocks of solid color. The influences of cubism and fauvism are evident in the bold use of color and geometry.

Specifications

Country: The Netherlands
Materials: Brass and enamel

A type of feldspar, moonstone has a pearly appearance

Decorative Bakelite pendants were attached to the chain links

Bakelite necklace 1936

Lightweight, mass-produced jewelry flourished in the 1930s as designers began to exploit the decorative qualities of Bakelite. The subject matter for such costume jewelry was often inspired by topical events. This necklace was made to commemorate the coronation of King George VI of England.

Specifications
Country: UK
Materials: Bakelite and metal

Specifications
Country: US
Material: Silver

Bakelite was favored in the production of cheap souvenirs

Art Deco necklace c.1930

The success of this stunning Art Deco necklace lies in the subtle color combination of dulled silver and pale blue moonstones. Marcasite and semiprecious stones are used to create an inexpensive piece that would have been highly popular in the 1930s.

Specifications
Country: Germany
Materials: Silver, moonstones, and marcasite

Dancer brooch 1947

Ed Wiener modeled this brooch on a photograph of Martha Graham taken in 1941. She was a champion of the modern dance movement and viewed dance as an organic structure. A biomorphic shape cut from sheet silver defines the body, dress, and right arm; one wire suggests the dancer's head and left arm, and another the skirt frill.

The silver is molded to follow the natural contour of the neck

The hook acts as a clasp and the anchor from which the pendant is suspended

Silver and quartz neckring 1959

Designed by Vivianna Torun Bülow-Hübe in 1959 and made in 1967, this neckring typifies the simplicity of the Scandinavian approach to jewelry design. Its attraction lies in its simplicity: an undecorated silver band that supports a large quartz droplet.

Specifications
Country: Denmark
Materials: Silver and quartz

LOVE ring c.1966

The Pop artist Robert Indiana's ring is about as close as you can get to summing up the 1960s' "Love and Peace" movement in one artifact. Indiana's LOVE motif, first shown in his one-man exhibition in 1962, was also used in a best-selling poster, and has appeared on 320 million US postage stamps.

Specifications
Country: US
Material: Gilded metal

The petals diminish in size as they spiral inward

Necklace of nails 1982

At first glance, this extraordinary necklace by Oslo-born Tone Vigeland seems to be made of feathers; it is actually made of hammered steel nails. The nails have been used in such a way that their simplicity is retained while completely disguising their form.

Specifications
Country: Norway
Materials: Steel, silver, gold, and mother-of-pearl

Steel bindings beneath the gold decoration hold the nails together

The hammered nails resemble feathers

Dahlia necklace 1984

Dutch sculptor and designer Gijs Bakker describes his experimental jewelry as "wearable art." In this piece, he has preserved dahlia petals in a flat ring of laminated plastic. His use of ephemeral materials represents a new approach to jewelry design – exploiting nature's intrinsic aesthetic qualities.

Specifications
Country: The Netherlands
Materials: Plastic and flower petals

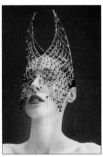

Beaded silver headpiece, 1997

SCULPTURAL FORMS

One of Britain's best-known jewelry designers, Scott Wilson works with unusual materials such as Plexiglass, stainless steel, and leather to create sculptural forms with a contemporary feel. Influenced more by architecture than fashion, Wilson's bold designs follow the contours of the body and keep decoration to a minimum. The framework of this horned headpiece is embellished with silver chains and fragments of jet crystal.

LEISURE

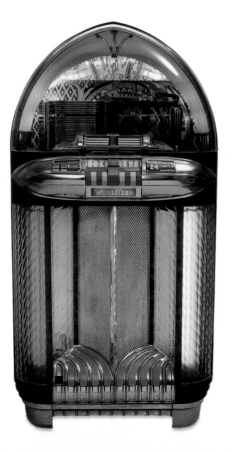

SWIMWEAR

EARLY BATHING SUITS were highly proper garments, with women's ensembles much like regular daywear. However, the adoption of elasticated and synthetic fabrics led to a succession of modifications, and swimsuits became progressively less restrictive – and more revealing. For men, the original one-piece suit was soon abbreviated to shorts. For women, the key innovation was the two-piece, launched in the 1940s as a result of US fabric rationing and christened the "bikini."

The swimsuit was fastened at the shoulder

Men's one-piece 1909
One-piece suits were the only option for male swimmers early in the century, before the introduction of elasticated fabrics. This example is made of cotton stockinet; not an ideal material, as it grew heavy when saturated. As pale-colored suits were transparent when wet, dark colors were preferred.

FABRICS
Early in the century, impractical fabrics, such as serge, worsted, and flannel, were still used for bathing costumes. This loose-fitting cotton suit, for example, would have become heavy and uncomfortable when wet. Progress arrived in the form of a light, knitted jersey, which was superseded, in turn, by a new generation of elasticated and synthetic fabrics.

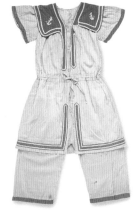

Bathing suit, 1902

Women's one-piece 1920s
This suit is made from clinging wool jersey, a material popularized by Coco Chanel during the 1920s and a chief contribution to the relaxation of women's clothing styles. But for its skirt, the suit is almost identical in design to the men's suit. Extra fabric has been sewn into the skirt to exaggerate the curve of the hips.

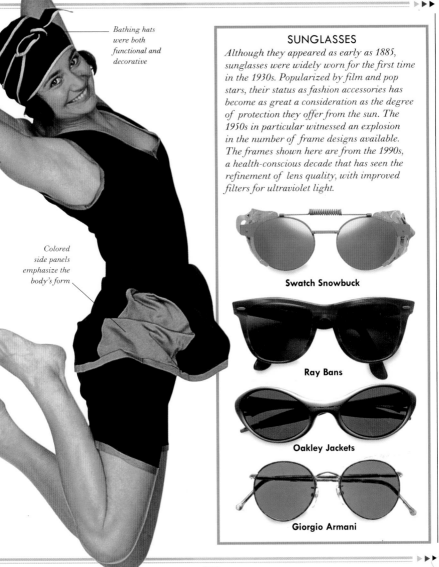

Bathing hats were both functional and decorative

Colored side panels emphasize the body's form

SUNGLASSES

Although they appeared as early as 1885, sunglasses were widely worn for the first time in the 1930s. Popularized by film and pop stars, their status as fashion accessories has become as great a consideration as the degree of protection they offer from the sun. The 1950s in particular witnessed an explosion in the number of frame designs available. The frames shown here are from the 1990s, a health-conscious decade that has seen the refinement of lens quality, with improved filters for ultraviolet light.

Swatch Snowbuck

Ray Bans

Oakley Jackets

Giorgio Armani

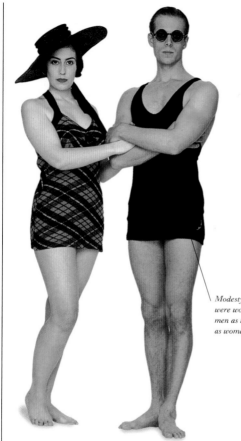

The bodice is highly structured

Modesty skirts were worn by men as well as women

Lightweight materials were used for swimsuits

Women's and men's one-pieces 1930s

By the 1930s, women's suits had become less substantial, with halterneck, bare-back designs a popular choice. The waist and bust were slightly more defined, although the inclusion of modesty skirts helped create a tubular look. Men continued to wear one-piece swimsuits until the mid-1930s.

Women's one-piece 1950s

With its boned bodice, this suit enhances the wearer's form, emphasizing the bust and reducing the waist. A departure from the tubular style, the influence of Dior's "New Look" is unmistakable (see p.248).

▶▶▶

Trunks 1970s

Introduced in the 1930s,
swimming trunks allowed
men to display a bare torso.
By the 1970s, tight-fitting,
square-legged trunks such
as these showcased new,
brightly colored, drip-dry
synthetic fabrics.

*The briefly
cut bikini is a
favorite for
sunbathing*

*High-cut, one-
piece styles
typify women's
swimwear in
the 1990s*

Bikini 1960s

Pioneered by French couturiers
Jacques Heim and Louis Reard in 1946,
the bikini was named after the Bikini
Atoll, where the Americans were
conducting atomic tests. It reached
its peak in popularity in the 1960s.

Women's one-piece 1990s

Lycra has made a valuable contribution to the revival of the one-
piece swimsuit in the 1990s. Closely
sculpted to the shape of the body,
modern suits are able to retain their
shape perfectly even when wet.

SPORTS EQUIPMENT

THE MAJORITY OF THE SPORTS that we enjoy today have existed for centuries. "Real" tennis and soccer date from the Middle Ages, and football was first played in the 19th century. In the 20th century professionalism has brought a demand for lighter, stronger, and more flexible sports equipment. Today's professional sportsmen and women are now afforded greater precision, control, and protection from injury than ever before, with the combination of sophisticated materials and advanced engineering resulting in masterpieces of sports technology.

Fishtail tennis racket c.1900
In the early years of the century, with lawn tennis established as a popular sport, tennis racket frames less resembled the loosely-strung, pear-shaped real tennis racket and now had a symmetrical head. To improve the grip, handles were grooved. Fishtail ends such as this were very trendy.

Early metal racket 1920
Although most racket frames were made from a solid piece of ash, experiments began in the 1920s with aluminum racket heads that were strung with piano wire. This long-handled grip is made of bare wood, but others at this time were bound in leather to improve the grip.

Classic wooden racket 1950
By the 1950s, the wooden racket had reached a design peak, remaining largely unchanged for the next 20 years. The lightweight frame had reinforced shoulders and was laminated in various woods for extra durability. It was not until the 1970s that wood was seriously challenged by metal.

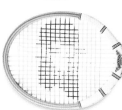

Graphite racket 1980
The lightweight metal rackets widely favored by professionals in the 1970s were soon rendered extinct by molded frames made from a combination of materials that included carbon graphite and fiberglass.

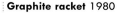

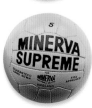

Soccer shoes c.1900
Early in the century, the "toe-poke" technique of kicking the ball with the toe of the boot was favored by players. As a result, their leather ankle boots had steel toes to protect the feet.

Toe reinforced with steel plate

Soccer balls 1930s & 1990
Early leather balls (top) were heavier and less waterproof than their modern counterparts (above) and had to be laced. Stiff, strong, and durable, modern balls are made from 18 panels of waterproof leather.

Soccer boots 1950
By the 1950s, soccer shoes were lighter at 1lb (500g) each and were more streamlined in style, with decorative stitching on the leather uppers. Shin pads were now worn inside rather than outside the socks.

Soccer shoes 1970
These vivid blue and yellow shoes, designed by Adidas for the 1970 World Cup in Mexico, are streamlined, supple, and light. They were the first soccer shoes with injected nylon soles, and feature removable screw-in studs.

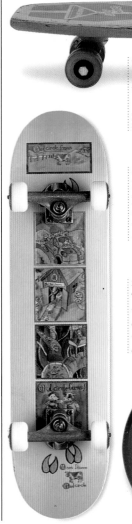

Goofy Foot skateboard 1950

Although skateboarding became hugely popular in the 1970s, the activity was invented in California in the 1950s as a kind of "street surfing." Then, it was a much gentler pastime, with clay-wheeled, flat wooden boards, like this one by Nash Manufacturing Inc., ridden like scooters.

Mad Circle skateboard 1995

Modern skateboards curve upward at each end and feature coarse plastic grips on the upper surface to aid the spectacular leaps and stunts performed by many devotees. Made from Canadian maple with polyurethane wheels, this Mad Circle board is painted on the underside with a colorful cartoon strip.

Snowboard late-1990s

The late-1990s saw increased popularity in dangerous sports, where risk to life and limb is an essential part of the experience. Snowboarding is surfing on snow, a more daredevil version of skiing. A wider surface means that snowboards can be used on more uneven snow surfaces than skis.

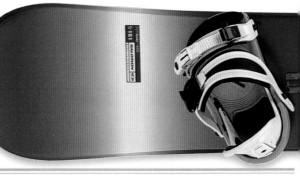

Rollerblades 1996

Those who have rolled around the park on heavy, leather-strapped, metal roller skates would barely relate the high-tech modern in-line skates to those traditional "quads." In-line skates, like these by the US manufacturer Rollerblade, are closer in design to ice skates than roller skates. Rollerblades have excellent ankle support, shock-absorbing heel brakes, and "micro-closure" straps to ensure a snug fit. The outer boot and frame are molded from high-quality, light-weight polyurethane.

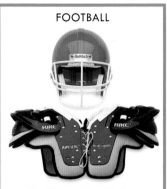

FOOTBALL

Shoulders pads and helmet

The enormous amount of protective padding worn head-to-toe by football players is essential in this most physical of sports. In 1905, before the introduction of stringent clothing rules, 18 college players were killed playing with inadequate protection. Those early boiled leather helmets have now been replaced by helmets of the toughest plastic, with built-in shock absorbers.

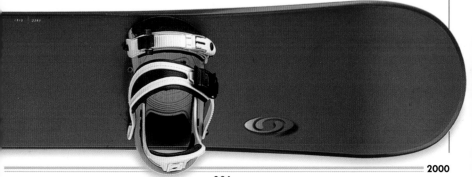

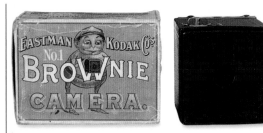

The Brownie 1900

In an attempt to sell more film, Eastman Kodak commissioned Frank Brownell to design a truly low-cost camera. The result was the hugely successful Brownie, a box camera made from the cheapest materials — cardboard and wood.

Specifications
Country: US
Width: 3¼in (8.2cm)

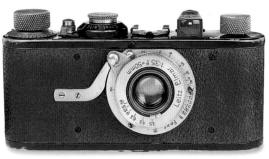

Leica 1A 1929

The Leica, designed by Oskar Barnack in 1913, was the first commercially successful 35mm camera. The Leica 1A, based on the earlier model, was put into production in the mid-1920s. The camera format has become the industry standard.

Specifications
Country: Germany
Width: 5¼in (13.4cm)

CAMERAS

THE EASTMAN KODAK box camera of 1888, with its ready-loaded roll film and widely advertised developing and printing service, opened up photography to the amateur. "You press the button, we do the rest" stated the advertisement. Various designs for small, hand cameras existed from the early days of photography, but the Leica, introduced by Leitz optical works in Germany in 1924, had an enormous and lasting impact on camera design and 35mm photographic technique. The 35mm single lens reflex (SLR) camera was developed throughout the 1940s and '50s, attaining true popularity with the Nikon F in 1959. Modern cameras have integral light meters, auto-focus, and use highly sensitive film — making the Kodak adage seem truer than ever.

Film is advanced using this lever

No. 2 Beau Brownie 1930

In 1926, Walter Dorwin Teague set up an industrial design consultancy. For Eastman Kodak, his first major client, he redesigned the Brownie, transforming it from a simple box into a sophisticated camera. He restyled the camera exterior with themes associated with Art Deco.

Specifications
Country: US
Width: 4in (10.5cm)

The casing has a geometric Art Deco design

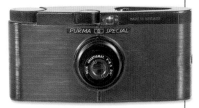

Purma Special 1937

Designed by Raymond Loewy and produced by R.F. Hunter Ltd., the Purma Special was made from black Bakelite and had a unique Plexiglass lens. This was cheaper than the usual glass lens so the camera could be retailed at a lower cost.

Specifications
Country: UK
Width: 6in (15.5cm)

▶▶▶

Aluminum fixtures make for a light, portable machine

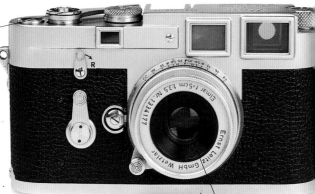

Leica M3 1954

First of a new generation of rangefinder cameras, the Leica M3 had a bayonet lens mount, which facilitated a faster lens change. Although production of this model ceased in 1966, a phenomenal 250,000 cameras had been made since 1954.

Specifications
Country: Germany
Width: 5½in (14cm)

An arrangement of internal mirrors allows the viewer to look through the actual lens

The lens is detachable

Nikon F 1960s

SLR 35mm cameras, like the Nikon F, were developed as early as 1935. The SLR design is popular because it allows the user to view the image through the lens. The Nikon F, introduced in 1959 by the Japanese firm Nippon Kogaku, is a classic design which spearheaded Japanese dominance in the industry.

Specifications
Country: Japan
Width: 6in (15cm)

Rolleiflex 2.8F 1965

The twin-lens Rolleiflex is a bulky device, with a mirror housing and viewing panel mounted above a roll-film box camera. It was favored by professionals because it could take medium-format film, giving high-quality results.

Specifications
Country: Germany
Width: 4⅝in (11.5cm)

The cover shields the photographer's eye from the glare of lighting

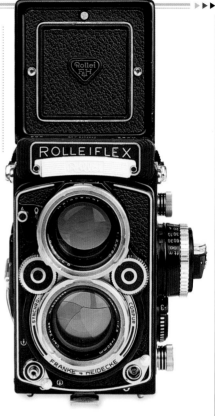

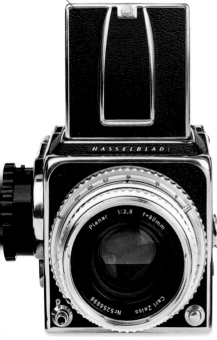

Hasselblad 500 1972

This roll-film SLR camera was produced by a firm set up by Victor Hasselblad in 1941 to make aerial cameras. Based on an earlier model, designed by Sixten Sason, it is a celebrated professional camera.

Specifications
Country: Sweden
Width: 4in (10.5cm)

▶ ▶ ▶

The camera body folds down into a compact shape

A simple dial gives options for different light

Polaroid SX-70 1972

Edwin Land invented the Polaroid camera in 1947. The processing took place in the camera body, producing a print within a minute of exposure. In 1972, Polaroid launched the SX-70, the first SLR Polaroid camera.

Specifications
Country: US
Width: 4in (10cm)

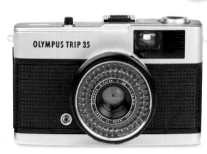

Olympus Trip 35 1968

Grandfather of the compact instamatic, the Olympus Trip 35 is a small, user-friendly camera. It was the first notable departure from the bulky forms of earlier 35mm SLR cameras.

Specifications
Country: Japan
Width: 4¾in (12cm)

The automatic flash pops up from the main camera body

Olympus µ[mju:] Zoom 1993

Designed to slip into a jacket pocket, the stylish µ[mju:] has won many awards. When the sliding lens is closed, the camera is fully protected by its ultra-compact body.

Specifications
Country: Japan
Width: 4¾in (12cm)

VIDEO CAMERAS

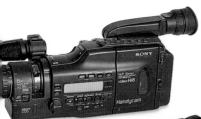

Before the development of the camcorder – a video camera and recorder combined in a portable unit – the recording of moving images involved a 16mm camera or, later, the smaller, more versatile 8mm camera. Although early camcorders were large and unwieldy, they did enable the user to play back recordings immediately through the viewfinder and to edit recordings simply and instantly. The palmcorders are the smallest and lightest of the camcorders and use 8mm or VHS cassettes. The simplest "point-and-shoot" versions rely on automated functions. More expensive machines incorporate sophisticated additional facilities and allow for greater manual control of key functions.

Sony Handycam, late-1980s

Sony palmcorder, 1992

Sony MVC-FD7 digital camera 1999

The digital camera does not use conventional film, but instead records the image – which can be viewed on a small screen – onto a computer floppy disk. The disks can be used over and again, thus cutting out the cost and hassle of developing film.

Specifications
Country: Japan
Width: 5in (13cm)

Images are recorded onto a floppy disk, and can then be manipulated on a computer

Previous images can be viewed on this small screen

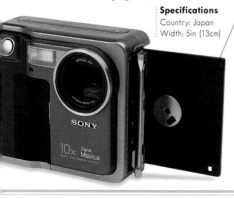

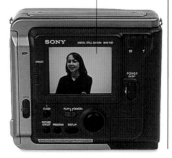

Gibson Style O 1908

The Gibson Mandolin-Guitar Manufacturing Co. was formed in Michigan in 1902 by Orville Gibson. It quickly became one of the leading names in guitar design and manufacture. Early Gibson acoustic models had arched tops, including the handsome Style O. It features an unusual scroll decoration – which recalls the design of Gibson's mandolins – an oval-shaped soundhole and a trapeze tailpiece. This version dates from 1916.

The flat cutaway was an unusual feature so early in the century

The body is decorated with a sandblasted Hawaiian landscape

The oval-shaped soundhole is typical of early Gibsons

A perforated plate covers the resonator

GUITARS

ALTHOUGH THE CLASSIC ACOUSTIC version is still widely strummed, it is the electric guitar that has stolen the limelight and determined the evolution of the instrument's shape and sound this century. Introduced in the 1930s, the first electric guitars merely electrically amplified the acoustic guitar sound. But by the 1940s, solid-bodied guitars with a bright new sound were being designed. In 1950, the pioneering Leo Fender released the first mass-produced solid-body – the Broadcaster, following up its success with the legendary Stratocaster. Today, guitars are produced in innovative shapes and constructed of new materials, although these rarely improve the sound.

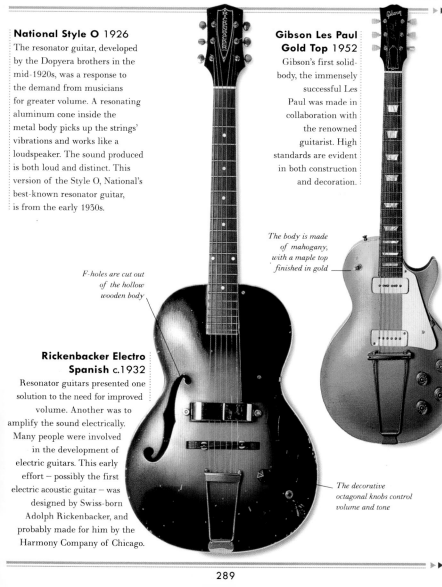

National Style O 1926

The resonator guitar, developed by the Dopyera brothers in the mid-1920s, was a response to the demand from musicians for greater volume. A resonating aluminum cone inside the metal body picks up the strings' vibrations and works like a loudspeaker. The sound produced is both loud and distinct. This version of the Style O, National's best-known resonator guitar, is from the early 1930s.

Gibson Les Paul Gold Top 1952

Gibson's first solid-body, the immensely successful Les Paul was made in collaboration with the renowned guitarist. High standards are evident in both construction and decoration.

The body is made of mahogany, with a maple top finished in gold

F-holes are cut out of the hollow wooden body

Rickenbacker Electro Spanish c.1932

Resonator guitars presented one solution to the need for improved volume. Another was to amplify the sound electrically. Many people were involved in the development of electric guitars. This early effort – possibly the first electric acoustic guitar – was designed by Swiss-born Adolph Rickenbacker, and probably made for him by the Harmony Company of Chicago.

The decorative octagonal knobs control volume and tone

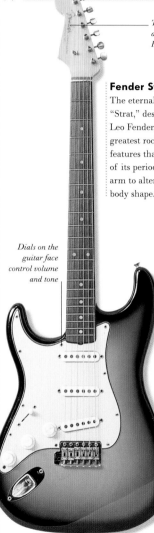

The headstock displays the original Fender logo

Fender Stratocaster 1954

The eternally popular and much copied "Strat," designed by the California-based Leo Fender, has been played by some of the greatest rock and pop stars. Among the features that set it apart from other guitars of its period are three pickups, a "tremolo" arm to alter pitch, and a distinct, contoured body shape. This model dates from 1957.

Dials on the guitar face control volume and tone

Gibson Double-12 late-1950s

This early Gibson twin-neck combined 6- and 12-string necks, and was produced until 1962. However, due to the fact that they were only built to order, there are very few examples still surviving. This twin-neck has a maple body, carved spruce top, and mahogany necks.

There are separate controls for each neck

*The guitar has
no headstock*

Steinberger Bass 1982

This headless bass guitar, made of molded fiber-reinforced epoxy resin, resulted from industrial engineer Ned Steinberger's attempt at producing a bass guitar with a clean tone. The choice of materials and abbreviated body and neck shapes make it, at 8lb (3.6kg), lighter than traditional bass guitars. This version dates from 1983.

*The ebony
fingerboard
is a sign
of quality*

*The 24-fret fingerboard
is made of phenolic fiber*

*The anchor
plate pivots to
allow the bass
to be held in
any position*

Ibanez 1990

Japanese production began in the 1960s with relatively low-quality copies of US models. From the mid-1970s, however, the quality of Japanese guitar design improved dramatically with original designs. This Japanese Ibanez model comes in a metallic finish particularly popular in the early-1990s.

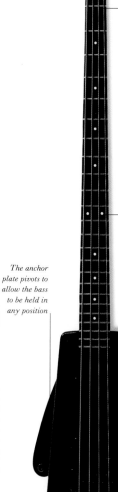

*The bright
metallic finish
is typical of
Ibanez's six-
string guitars*

JUKEBOXES

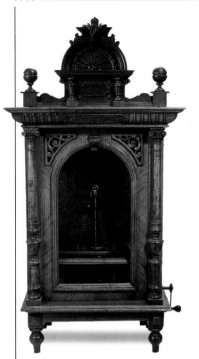

COIN-IN-THE-SLOT music machines were already well established by the time the golden age of the jukebox dawned in the 1940s. While designers of this era, such as Paul Fuller, are particularly revered, design aficionados are beginning to pay closer attention to the two decades that followed. The machines of the rock 'n' roll era – with which the jukebox has become synonymous – scream teenage rebellion with their blatant use of flashy automobile looks. The bold, bright colors of these classics are probably the first thing to cross most people's minds on hearing the word "jukebox."

Polyphon c.1900

This wooden, turn-of-the-century coin-in-the-slot machine does not play records – because they did not exist at the time it was made – but plays large metal discs with "pins". The pins pluck the tuned teeth of a comb-like metal plate, as in a music box. This clockwork machine must be fully wound before it will play.

Specifications

Country: Germany
Height: 51in (130cm)
Number of selections: 1

Wurlitzer 1100 1948

Paul Fuller is generally considered to be the "genius" of jukebox design, and the incredible Wurlitzer 1100 was his last jukebox model. It plays from a selection of 78rpm records – seven-inch 45s were still two years away – although the revolving selection display shows only eight at any one time.

Specifications

Country: US
Height: 57in (145cm)
Number of selections: 24

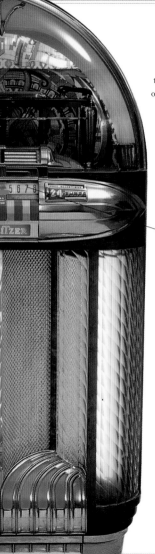

Wurlitzer **1800** 1955

At first glance, the design of this jukebox may seem rather muted. However, the colors, the lights, and the generous use of chromium combine to make this machine aesthetically pleasing. In addition, the user has a far greater choice of music than before.

Specifications
Country: US
Height: 53in (135cm)
Number of selections: 104

Clean and functional controls lie flush with the machine's front

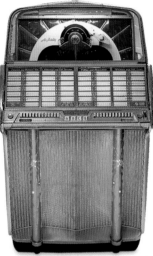

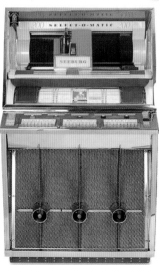

Seeburg **KD200** 1957

One quirk of Seeburg jukeboxes is that they play records vertically; this requires only one motor instead of three. The distinctive fins on the front are based on the tail fins and lights of 1950s' American cars. The KD200 plays seven-inch vinyl records.

Specifications
Country: US
Height: 58in (147cm)
Number of selections: 200

▶ ▶ ▶

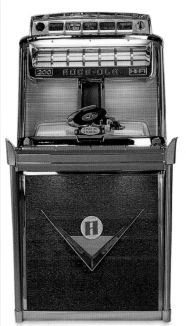

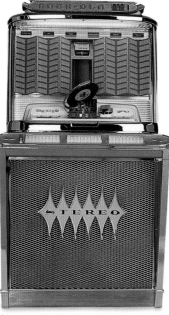

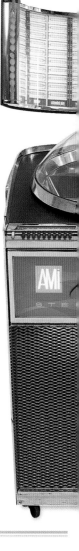

Rock-Ola Tempo 1475 1959

Many jukeboxes of this era were based on the rear ends of US cars, and the very rare Rock-Ola Tempo is no exception. Tailfins make another appearance, though far more subtly than in the case of the Seeburg KD200. Even the V-shaped logo on the front of the machine is similar in essence to many automobile emblems. Note the revolving-drum selection display at the top of the machine.

Specifications
Country: US
Height: 59in (150cm)
Number of selections: 200

Rock-Ola Regis 1495 1961

Stereo jukeboxes first appeared in 1959, and one of the most instantly striking design features about the Rock-Ola Regis is the rather bold emblazoning of the word "stereo" across its front, ensuring that everyone is well aware of this fact. Another point of interest is the use of pastel colors in its pink-and-blue color scheme. All 200 selections are visible at the same time.

Specifications
Country: US
Height: 59in (150cm)
Number of selections: 200

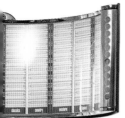

AMi Continental 2 1961

This 200-selection stereo machine by AMi (Automatic Musical Instruments) is of particular interest because of its domed glass top. AMi was one of only two jukebox manufacturers ever to do this – the other was UK-based Chantal – because it was very expensive to produce. The design also makes extensive use of the word "stereo." Sharp-eyed viewers of the 1990 Patrick Swayze movie *Ghost* may recognize this machine.

Specifications
Country: US
Height: 64in (162cm)
Number of selections: 200

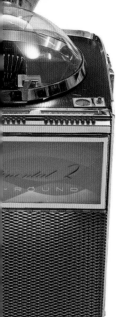

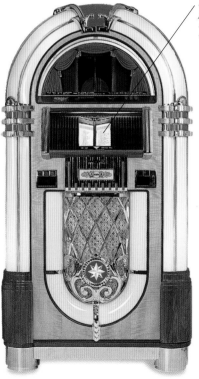

Just 50 of this jukebox's 2,500 selections can be viewed at a time

NSM Nostalgia Gold 1995

This machine's design is based on Paul Fuller's 1946 Wurlitzer 1015, the most popular jukebox ever: during 1946 and 1947 Wurlitzer built 56,000 of them. The original would have held twelve 78rpm records, but this replica can accommodate up to 100 compact discs. It would actually be possible to listen to this jukebox for more than five days and nights without hearing the same track twice.

Specifications
Country: Germany
Height: 61in (155cm)
Number of selections: Up to 2,500 (approx.)

TRANSPORTATION

BICYCLES

SINCE THE APPEARANCE of the first safety bicycles in the 1870s, a remarkable – and enormously popular – form of transportation has emerged. The modern machine is not only lightweight, strong, and fast, but also easy to ride and comfortable. Various models have been designed to meet specific market demands: for instance, in the 1900s, versions without high top tubes were introduced to suit women riders; and aerodynamic models have been developed for the highly competitive sport of cycle racing. At the end of the century, lighter, more durable materials, such as titanium and carbon fiber, are frequently favored over traditional materials like steel.

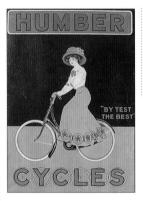

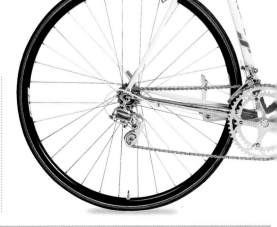

Ladies' Humber 1905

By the time the Ladies' Humber was introduced, the key features of the modern bicycle were well established. Instead of the diamond-shaped frame of men's bicycles, the ladies' had an open frame. This catered for the long dresses worn at the time, as illustrated in this poster.

Battaglin 1980s

The development of racing bikes, such as this Italian model, saw the introduction of drop handlebars, which reduced body-created wind resistance. The "aero-tuck" body position was further exaggerated by the saddle, which is favored by racers.

Specifications
Country: Italy
Wheel diameter: Not known
Material: High-tensile steel

Teamline 1100s 1980s

Racing bike manufacturers like Peugeot vie to produce increasingly lightweight bicycle frames. In the 1970s, versatile, lightweight alloy steels were developed, followed by aluminum tubing in the 1980s.

Specifications

Country: France
Wheel diameter: 26in (66cm)
Material: Carbon fiber

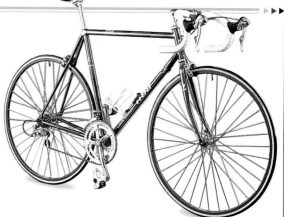

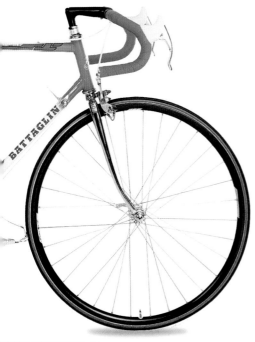

COLLAPSIBLE BICYCLES

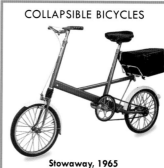

Stowaway, 1965

For their portability and ease of storage, foldaway bicycles are often favored. Alex Moulton, who worked on the suspension of the Mini in the 1950s (see p.317), went on to design this compact, collapsible bicycle. The innovative rubber suspension on both front and back wheels made the bike easy to handle and comfortable to ride.

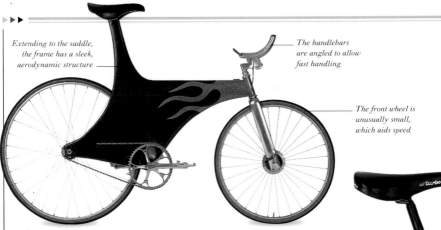

Extending to the saddle, the frame has a sleek, aerodynamic structure

The handlebars are angled to allow fast handling

The front wheel is unusually small, which aids speed

Windcheetah Monocoque c.1986

The essence of this racing bike's prodigious speed is in its streamlined monocoque frame. A single-fork front wheel blade, together with the small front wheel and gull-wing handlebars, make it unusually aerodynamic. The one-piece frame meant that the Windcheetah was originally disqualified from official races by the sport's governing body, a ban that was enforced for five years. Built by Mike Burrows, the bike is constructed of carbon fiber, a material as stiff as steel.

Specifications
Country: UK
Front wheel diameter: 24in (61cm)
Material: Carbon fiber

Fat Chance "Yo Eddy" off-road racer 1989

Developed in California by Charlie Kelly and Gary Fisher during the 1970s, mountain bikes have opened up a new experience for cyclists. This model has been refined from the early prototypes, which weighed 26lb (12kg).

Specifications
Country: US
Wheel diameter: 26in (66cm)
Material: High-tensile steel

Sociable Tandem 1992

This motor-assisted, three-wheeled recumbent bicycle can accommodate two riders. Using pedals alone, it can reach up to 19mph (30km/h). But with assistance from the electric motor, it can travel over twice as fast.

Specifications

Country: Switzerland
Front wheel diameter: 20in (51cm)
Materials: Fiberglass and aluminum

The body shell is made of glass fiber

Sturdy frame designed for all-terrain riding

The triple chainring allows up to 30 gears, which are essential for steep inclines

At 2½in (6.3cm) wide, these tires provide good grip even in difficult conditions

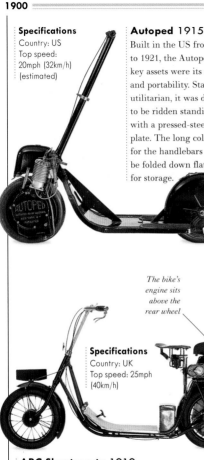

Specifications
Country: US
Top speed:
20mph (32km/h)
(estimated)

Autoped 1915
Built in the US from 1915 to 1921, the Autoped's key assets were its size and portability. Starkly utilitarian, it was designed to be ridden standing up, with a pressed-steel foot-plate. The long column for the handlebars can be folded down flat for storage.

The bike's engine sits above the rear wheel

Specifications
Country: UK
Top speed: 25mph (40km/h)

ABC Skootamota 1919
Much in demand after World War I, the British-designed ABC Skootamota had one great advantage over the Autoped: a seat. Designed by Granville Bradshaw, the machine featured the step-through frame that has defined the look of the scooter ever since.

SCOOTERS

YOUNG ITALIANS dodging traffic through the backstreets of Rome or 1960s' "Mods" driving in gangs to British coastal resorts: scooters are synonymous with street style and youth culture. The machines traditionally favored by both groups are the Italian classics Vespa and Lambretta. These elegant, streamlined machines are notable for their rounded body panels, as opposed to the largely angular bodywork of non-European scooters, such as those built by the American company Cushman. Scooters have been popular since the 1920s, when they bore little difference to a child's push-along toy vehicle. Since then, there have been a bewildering array of these cheap, lightweight, easy-to-ride motorcycles.

Specifications
Country: US
Top speed: 30mph (48km/h) (estimated)

SCOOTERS AND STREET STYLE

Although originally popularized as a cheap and convenient form of transport in the postwar era, by the 1960s, the scooter had been adopted by young people as a fashion accessory. Members of the British "Mod" cult dressed in tailored, often Italian, clothes and large "parka" coats rode customized Vespas or Lambrettas en masse to coastal resorts. Here they invariably clashed with rival "Rocker" gangs, who themselves favored heavier, more powerful motorcycles.

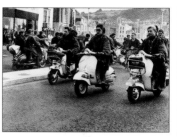

"Mods" at Hastings, England, mid-1960s

Cushman Auto-Glide 1937

Cushman produced a remarkable range of outlandish scooters in the middle decades of the century. While its European counterparts were characterized by their curves, Cushman favored angularity. The Auto-Glide is the epitome of simplicity in vehicle design.

Specifications
Country: US
Top speed: Not known

Cushman 32 Auto-Glide 1945

This model 32 first appeared in 1945. Unlike its predecessor, the Auto-Glide (see left), it had lights as standard, "Floating Drive" suspension, and an automatic clutch and transmission system. The engine capacity on this model was increased to 14.88 cu. inches (244cc). Designed with convenience in mind, it had a large storage compartment behind the seat for baggage.

Specifications
Country: US
Top speed: 35mph
(56km/h) (estimated)

Specifications
Country: Italy
Top speed: 50mph
(80.5km/h)

Indian Papoose 1948

The famous American motorcycle manufacturer Indian gave its name to a small British scooter originally designed as a folding bike for paratroopers in World War II. The Papoose included a retracting saddle column, which enabled the handlebars to be folded down flat.

Lambretta LD150 1957

Lambretta was the main challenger to Vespa in the 1950s and '60s, and the Lambretta LD150 sold in enormous quantities. It had easily removable engine and gearbox covers, two separate seats, and carried a spare wheel. Like the Vespa, it was rounded in styling, compared with its angular American cousins. The first Lambrettas were built in 1947, and production stopped in Italy in the 1970s.

Simplex Scooter 1958

Although it never challenged market leader Cushman, Simplex took advantage of the 1950s' scooter boom by introducing this version of its Servi-Cycle. The characteristic clean, straight lines of the American scooter are typified by the simple, tubular steel frame.

Specifications
Country: US
Top speed: 45mph
(72km/h)

Fuel tank

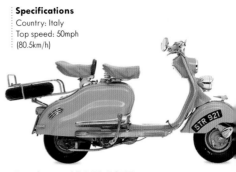

Vespa Grand Sport 160 1963

The Vespa (Italian for "wasp" and so-named for its buzzing
exhaust noise) is the most famous of all scooters. It was
designed in 1946 by Corradino d'Ascanio, whose
previous involvement in aircraft design is clearly
evident. It has a waisted rear and a rounded
pressed-steel monocoque chassis. One of the most
attractive scooters built was the Vespa Grand
Sport (GS) 160 Mark 1, considered by many
aficionados to be the best Vespa ever designed.

Specifications
Country: Italy
Top speed: 62mph
(100km/h)

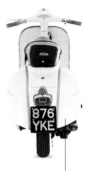

*The GS featured
a distinctive
waisted rear*

*Individual
elements are
incorporated into
the overall shape
of the machine*

Vespa ET2 1996

The new Vespas combine references to
earlier models with a modern, ergonomic
shape. Marketed as "a real Time
Machine on two wheels," they have
been a real success, coinciding
with a revival in mid-1960s'
styling. The latest machines
feature fuel-saving capacities
of up to 30 percent, reflecting
the environmentally conscious
consumer of the late 1990s.

Specifications
Country: Italy
Top speed: Not known

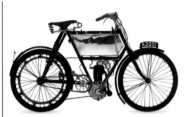

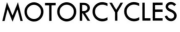

MOTORCYCLES

THE FIRST MOTORCYCLES WERE INTRODUCED toward the end of the 19th century. With chassis based on the newly developed safety bicycles (see pp.298–99), they lacked power, were difficult to ride, and had inadequate lights and brakes. It was not until the Werner brothers produced their motorcycle of 1901, with its advanced braking system and electric ignition, that practical motorcycling became possible. Thirty-five years later, Harley-Davidson produced the 61E, a motorcycle that demonstrated just how rapidly technology, performance, and style had evolved. Throughout the century, there were a remarkable array of weird and wonderful designs. Designers continue to exploit the latest materials and technology to enhance performance and provide a safe ride.

Werner 1901
In 1897, the French Werner brothers made the first motorcycle to be sold in significant numbers. The 1901 Werner was one of the first bikes to move from a "bicycle-plus-engine" design to a more integrated look: in some ways, the first "real" motorcycle.

Specifications
Country: France
Top speed: 20mph (32km/h)
Weight: Not known

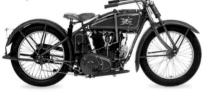

Excelsior 20R 1912
Until it collapsed in 1931, Excelsior was one of the big three American manufacturers with Harley-Davidson and Indian. The first bike to break the 100mph (161km/h) barrier, the 20R had a 61 cubic inch engine (1,000cc). It featured the long, upright handlebars that were prevalent in the US until the 1920s.

Specifications
Country: US
Top speed: 100mph (161km/h)
Weight: 500lb (227kg)

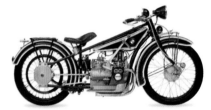

BMW R32 1923
Created by aircraft designer Max Friz, the first BMW was an astonishing leap forward in motorbike design: its 500cc engine was fitted into the frame so that the cylinders were cooled by the air.

Specifications
Country: Germany
Top speed: 53mph (85km/h)
Weight: 269lb (122kg)

The main stand is mounted on the rear of the frame

Megola Racing Model 1923

The Megola was one of the most unconventional motorcycles ever built. Designer Fritz Cockerell's five-cylinder side-valve radial engine was mounted within the front wheel; as the wheel turned forward once, the engine turned six times in the opposite direction.

Specifications
Country: Germany
Top speed: Not known
Weight: Not known

Harley-Davidson Knucklehead 61EL 1936

In 1936, Harley-Davidson broke its own design tradition and introduced a machine with an overhead-valve construction. It was the most important Harley ever built and established the look for all those that followed. Its performance completely outstripped that of rival Indian motorbikes.

The distinctive "knuckle" appearance is formed by the rocker covers

Specifications
Country: US
Top speed: 100mph (161km/h)
Weight: 515lb (234kg)

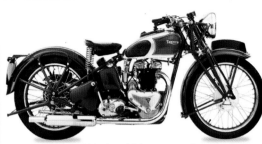

Vincent Black Shadow Series C 1949

In 1949, when the first Vincent C-series Black Shadow was introduced, it was the fastest and the classiest bike in the world. The black bodywork continued in the baked-on black 998cc engine, and the mudguards were made of stainless steel, with stainless steel and chrome engine details and exhaust pipes. The Shadow had an oversized speedometer, emphasizing its impressive top speed of 125mph (201km/h).

Triumph Speed Twin 1939

Designed by Edward Turner with speed in mind, the Speed Twin's lines are elegant from any angle. The model formed the basis of Triumph's big bike range for the next 40 years. Turner was also responsible for adapting Triumphs for the American market in the 1950s.

Specifications
Country: UK
Top speed: 93mph (150km/h)
Weight: 378lb (171kg)

Specifications
Country: UK
Top speed: 125mph (201km/h)
Weight: 458lb (208kg)

Indian Chief 1947

Built for comfort not speed, the Chiefs were stylish machines that reached their peak with this 1947 design. Valanced mudguards and elegant girder forks combined with the sprung leather saddle and chrome-plated details to give an air of streamlined luxury.

Specifications
Country: US
Top speed: 85mph (137km/h)
Weight: 550lb (249kg)

Honda 50 Super Cub 1958

Originally designed as a basic, cheap
form of transportation, the ubiquitous
Cub is the most successful bike ever made,
with sales in excess of 21 million. It
was among the first machines to make
extensive use of plastic, in the form
of the front mudguard, the side panels,
and the leg shields.

Specifications

Country: Japan
Top speed: 43mph (69km/h)
Weight: 143lb (65kg)

*Philip Vincent bought
the rights to the HRD
name to give credibility
to his new company*

*Tools are stored in
a drawer positioned
under the seat*

*Where possible,
Vincent preferred
to use steel rather
than chrome*

Honda CB750 1969

The CB750 launched the era of the superbike, combining in one powerful machine disc brakes, five-speed gearbox, electric starter, four-cylinder engine, and 124mph (200km/h) performance.

Specifications

Country: Japan
Top speed: 124mph (200km/h)
Weight: 485lb (220kg)

Honda's CB750 was the first bike to be equipped with a front disc brake

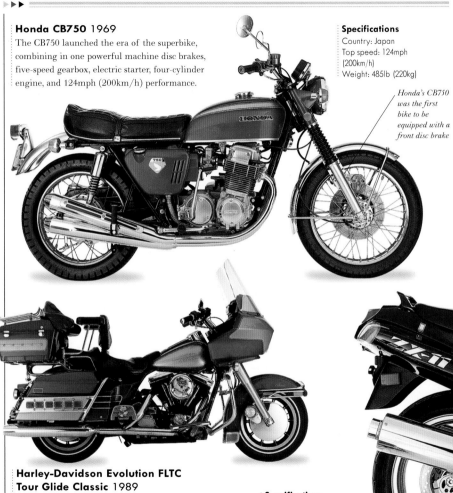

Harley-Davidson Evolution FLTC Tour Glide Classic 1989

In direct competition with Honda's massive Goldwing, the Tour Glide rejected the retro styling of previous Glides. Comfort was the prime design objective, with footboards for the rider and armrests and backrests for the passenger.

Specifications

Country: US
Top speed: 110mph (177km/h) (estimated)
Weight: 732lb (332kg)

MOTOCROSS

Light, strong bikes with good suspension are required for the grueling sport of motocross, which began as "scrambling" in 1920s' Britain. It gained in popularity after World War II, and the first World Championship was held in 1957. Excellent suspension makes the Husqvarna a popular off-road choice.

Husqvarna TC610, 1992

Kawasaki ZZ-R1100 1990

Everything about the ZZ-R is big, from its top speed of 175mph (282km/h) to its enormous twin front-brake discs. Aerodynamic styling (the tank is sculpted to fit the rider's legs snugly) and superb power delivery made the ZZ-R the fastest bike of its day.
This model is from 1994.

Specifications
Country: Japan
Top speed: 175mph (282km/h)
Weight: 513lb (233kg)

CARS

FEW THINGS MAP the development of design in this century better than the car. In 1900, cars were just beginning to shed their "horseless cart" look, yet by 1915, all of the basic design features of the modern car were already in place. All that remained was for cars to get bigger, smaller, safer, more beautiful, more bizarre, and, of course, faster. At the end of the century, there are nearly one billion cars on the road, including some lovingly restored early models. But overtaking these vintage vehicles are a vast array of cars: sports cars such as Jaguar's E-type (see p.319); city cars such as the Fiat 500 (see p.316); outlandish cars such as the 199 Cadillac (see pp.316–17); and supercars like the Lamborghini Miura (see p.319).

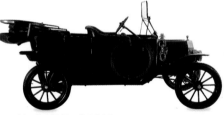

The Ghost has a low-slung "slipper" body

The driver was largely exposed to the elements

De Dion-Bouton Model Q 1903
The key to the Model Q's success was its powerful 846cc gas engine. De Dion's revolutionary engine design was used in over 100 makes of car from 1898 to 1908, and helped launch companies such as Renault.
Specifications
Country: France
Top speed: Not known

Model T Ford 1908
This was the first car to be mass produced, with over 15 million made. The car's minimal design, the use of standardized parts, and new production techniques kept costs down. By the 1920s, every second car on the world's roads was a Model T Ford.
Specifications
Country: US
Top speed: 42mph (68km/h)

*The Ghost features
a six-cylinder engine
with a full pressure
lubrication system*

Rolls Royce 40/50 1907

In 1907, when Rolls Royce launched the 40/50, or "Silver Ghost"
as it became known, it described the model as "the best car in the
world." Emphasis was placed on mechanical precision and
craftsmanship rather than innovation. The winged figurehead,
known as the "spirit of ecstasy," was modeled by Charles Sykes
and first graced the top of a Rolls-Royce radiator in 1911.

Specifications
Country: UK
Top speed: 55mph
(88km/h)

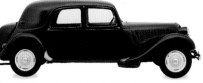

Citroën Traction Avant 1934

A revolutionary cocktail of innovations, André
Citroën's Traction Avant featured front-wheel drive,
monocoque construction, overhead-valve engine,
hydraulic brakes, and long wheel base, allowing
more passenger space.

Specifications
Country: France
Top speed: 70mph (113km/h)

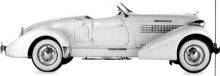

Auburn 851 Speedster 1935

The body of this luxury car is boat-shaped, with
the tail ending in a point. The curvaceous wings
are drawn back, echoing the body shape. Details
such as the "V"-shaped radiator and the headlights
help give the car a feeling of forward movement.

Specifications
Country: US
Top speed: 103mph (166km/h)

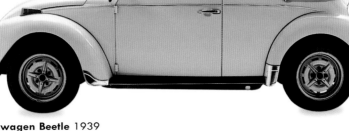

Volkswagen Beetle 1939

In 1973, the Beetle became the best-selling car ever produced. The work of Ferdinand Porsche, it originated in Germany and attracted the attention of Adolf Hitler. Since the Beetle went into full production in 1945, there have been over 78,000 minor design modifications. The Karmann Cabriolet, shown here, is one of the most sought-after models.

Specifications
Country: Germany
Top speed: 82mph
(132km/h)

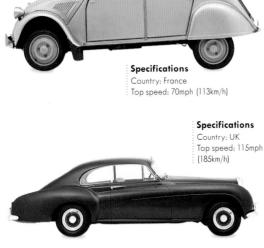

Specifications
Country: France
Top speed: 70mph (113km/h)

Citroën 2CV 1948

Flaminio Bertone is responsible for the appearance of some of Citroën's most successful cars: the Traction Avant (see p.313), the DS (see p.318), and the 2CV or *Deux Chevaux* ("Two Horses"). Built in part as a response to the Volkswagen Beetle, the 2CV uses a simple construction and simple manufacturing techniques to fulfill a practical need — a cheap and reliable means of transporting people and goods.

Specifications
Country: UK
Top speed: 115mph
(185km/h)

Bentley R-type Continental 1952

Launched in 1952, Bentley's R-type Continental was the fastest production car in the world. Only 208 were made, and many revered it as the greatest car of all time. Described as "a modern magic carpet," the wind-tunnel inspired lightweight aluminum housing enabled the car to reach 60mph (97km/h) in 14 seconds.

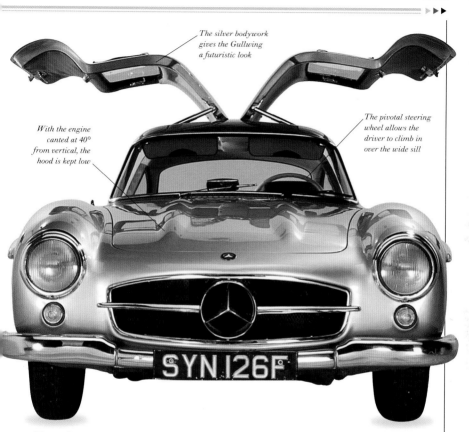

The silver bodywork gives the Gullwing a futuristic look

With the engine canted at 40° from vertical, the hood is kept low

The pivotal steering wheel allows the driver to climb in over the wide sill

SYN 126F

Mercedes-Benz 300SL 1954

When its top-hinged doors were both fully open, the Mercedes 300SL was said to resemble a seagull in flight, hence it became known as the "Gullwing." With a top speed of 135–165mph (217–265km/h), depending on gearing, and acceleration of 0–60mph (0–97km/h) in eight and a half seconds, it practically *could* fly. Far and away the world's fastest production car at the time, the Gullwing was the forebear of the modern supercar. One of its key claims to fame was that it utilized the first ever application of fuel-injection in a production car.

Specifications
Country: Germany
Top speed: 165mph
(265km/h)

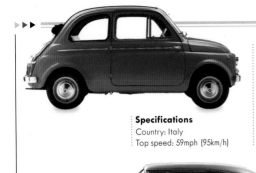

Fiat 500 1957

You could practically fit the Fiat 500 into the trunk of the Cadillac, so opposite are the two cars in philosophy. This charming car's gently rounded body is molded into shape by unitary construction, and has come to symbolize Italy's postwar *ricostruzione*. It appeared two years before the British Mini and was 3¼in (8cm) shorter.

Specifications
Country: Italy
Top speed: 59mph (95km/h)

Specifications
Country: US
Top speed: 112mph (180km/h)

Buick Roadmaster 1957

The massive Buick Roadmaster was all about power. At 18ft (5.5m) long and 6ft (1.8m) wide, it needed its V8 engine to propel its mighty bulk to 60mph (96km/h) from standing in just 10.5 seconds. The giant chrome bumpers were just one statement of the car's might. In the 1950s, aircraft design was a major influence on car design, evident here in the wraparound windshields and the tail fins.

The tail fins rise over 3 feet (1 meter) above the ground

At 20ft (6.1m) in length and two tons in weight, the Cadillac was unchallenged in size and power

AUSTIN MINI COOPER

The classic British rally car of the 1960s, the Austin Mini Cooper was a high performance version of Alec Issigonis' 1959 Morris Mini Minor. These box-shaped vehicles set the standard for small cars and, along with the miniskirt, became British icons of modernity in the 1960s. The suspension was designed by Alex Moulton, who also created the collapsible bicycle.

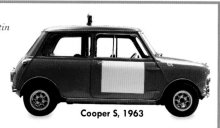

Cooper S, 1963

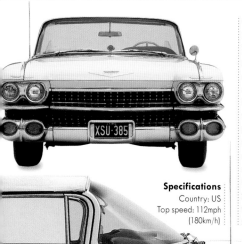

Specifications
Country: US
Top speed: 112mph
(180km/h)

Cadillac Eldorado Convertible 1959

Nothing sums up the optimism of the 1950s better than the 1959 Cadillac Convertible. The most flamboyant and extravagant of mass-produced cars, this beautiful, brash machine was the creation of coach builder and stylist Harley Earl. He was influenced by Clarence Johnson, the designer of the Lockheed P38 airplane, which was certainly a source of inspiration. Earl used clay to model the shape of his cars, giving him the freedom to experiment with form. The outcome was a series of cars that owe as much to science fiction and a fascination with space flight as they do to empirical research. For America in the 1950s, the style of these cars represented more than just an enthusiasm for modernity, they embodied a dream.

Chevrolet Impala 1960

In 1959, Bill Mitchell succeeded Harley Earl as Director of Styling at General Motors, but Earl's obsession with all things space age clearly rubbed off on his protegé: there was even an emblem of a speeding rocket on the rear door of his Chevrolet Impala. Everything about the Impala expresses speed, from the contoured tail fins to the stylish paintwork stripes on the chassis.

Specifications
Country: US
Top speed: 112mph (180km/h)

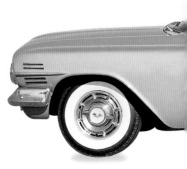

Citroën DS 1960

The technically and stylistically daring Citroën DS was an immediate success on its launch in 1960: 80,000 were sold in the first week. The impressive and aerodynamic body shape, the wide area of glass, the spacious interior, and the space-age instrument panel set this car apart from all others.

Specifications
Country: France
Top speed: 116mph (187km/h)

The body shape of the Citroën DS earned it the nickname, "The Shark"

The aerodynamic design of the chassis enabled the car to reach high speeds

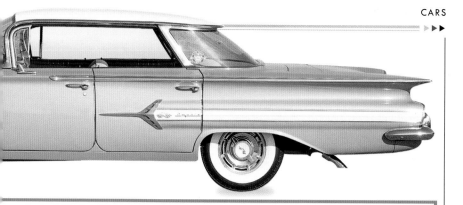

THE LEGEND OF LAMBORGHINI

When tractor magnate Ferrucio Lamborghini had problems with his Ferrari, he went straight to the top with his complaints. Enzo Ferrari refused him an audience and Lamborghini vowed to build a better car carrying his own name – and so the Lamborghini legend was born. The Miura was capable of 175mph (282km/h), a top speed that was matched by its racy looks – all futuristic, low lines, and swooping curves. When it was launched at the 1966 Geneva Motor Show, it created the motoring sensation of the decade.

Lamborghini Miura, 1966

Specifications
Country: UK
Top speed: 150mph
(241km/h)

E-Type Jaguar 1961

At its launch in 1961, the E-type caused a sensation. This beautiful sports car's looks, with its distinctive elongated hood, were only part of the attraction, for it was capable of 150mph (241km/h) and cost half the price of its main competitors. Designer Malcolm Sayer (1916–) claimed that the E-type was the first car to be "mathematically" designed.

▶ ▶ ▶

Volvo P1800 1961

From a manufacturer renowned for safe, strong, reliable cars, the stunningly styled P1800 seems a fluke. But closer inspection reveals a car as robust as any other Volvo, mechanically based on the Amazon Saloon and therefore not especially fast. It will forever be known as the car driven by Roger Moore in the hit television series *The Saint*.

Specifications
Country: Sweden
Top speed: 105mph (169km/h)

Porsche 911 1963

Launched at the Paris Motor Show in 1963, the 911 is the most enduring of the Porsche sports cars and is an outstanding piece of design; to many, it is *the* classic road car of all time. The work of Ferdinand "Butzi" Porsche, it is a direct descendant of Ferdinand Porsche's Type 356. Echoes of the VW Beetle from the 1930s (see p.314) are also evident in the lines of the 911. Countless incarnations have appeared over the decades, including the 911 Turbo, which in 1984 was recorded as the fastest accelerating production sports car in the world. The rear-mounted, air-cooled engine, with its vast reserves of power, has contributed to over 20,000 senior race wins.

Specifications
Country: Germany
Top speed: 150mph (241km/h)

The bumpers typify the car's black and red styling

The bodywork is constructed of thin-gauge steel panels

Specifications
Country: US
Top speed: 117mph
(188km/h)

Ford Mustang 1964

To most Europeans, the Ford Mustang is
a big American car. In fact, when the Mustang was introduced it was
a mold-breaking "compact," conceived as a sports car for the masses.
After the excesses of the 1950s, its low-key styling was something of
a relief. However, a vast range of options was offered. In 1965, the
average buyer spent $1,000 on options, almost half the car's price.

*The 911 was
the first car to
have matt black
window borders*

*Echoes of Ferdinand
Porsche's Type 356 are
clear in the body shape*

*All 911s have rear-
mounted, air-cooled
six-cylinder engines*

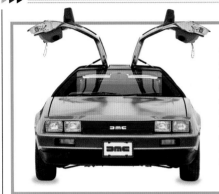

A GLIMPSE OF THE FUTURE

Despite £65 million of British government backing and a starring role in the Hollywood film Back to the Future, *the DeLorean DMC12 was a spectacular failure. With its stainless steel body and gull-wing doors, the Giorgio Giugiaro design was intended to be a glimpse of the future. In reality, it was dated before it even reached production. A total of 8,583 DeLoreans were manufactured between 1981 and 1983; those still in existence are considered to be collector's items.*

DeLorean DMC12, 1979

Pontiac GTO 1964

Taking a step back in time toward the big American cars of the 1950s, the innovative division of General Motors, Pontiac, put the biggest possible engine into a medium-sized body and came up with the GTO. Designed by John DeLorean (1925–), it was a powerful car, with an agility that earned it the nickname "The Goat." The first full-sized car to offer sports car performance and handling, it found an eager audience in the US, particularly among younger drivers. After various modifications, the car was relaunched in 1970 with a new design.

Ferrari Dino 246GT 1969

The beautiful, sweeping lines of the Ferrari Dino are unmistakable: it is the archetypal Italian sports car. Invariably red in color (this metallic brown model was rare), it was aimed at the Porsche 911 market and made an immediate impact. The Dino was named after Enzo Ferrari's son, Alfredino, who died at 24 of kidney disease.

Specifications
Country: Italy
Top speed: 148mph
(238km/h)

Mazda RX7 1978

Almost half a million RX7s were sold in seven years of production – 75 percent in the US – making it the most successful rotary-engined car of all time. Pop-up headlights added glamour and reduced wind resistance. Indeed, the car was styled to slice through the air; its shape was so well conceived that only minor changes were ever made to its design.

Specifications
Country: Japan
Top speed: 125mph (201km/h)

Specifications
Country: US
Top speed: 135mph (217km/h)

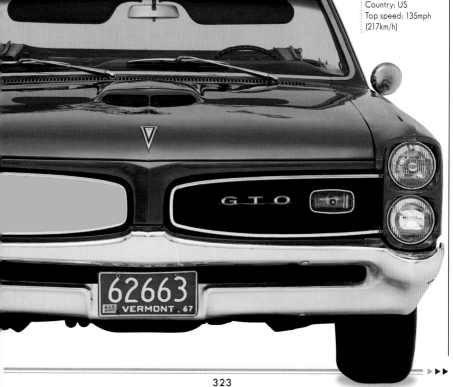

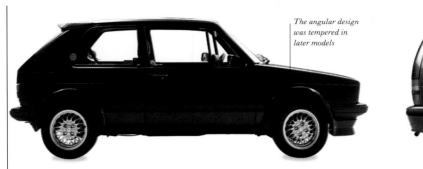

The angular design was tempered in later models

Volkswagen Golf GTi 1976

The car that launched a thousand imitations, the Golf was single-handedly responsible for the craze for hatchbacks that swept the world in the 1970s and '80s. It boasts an appealing combination of good performance and handling, practical design, and great reliability: the engine was easily capable of 150,000 miles (241,400km).

Specifications
Country: Germany
Top speed: 111mph
(179km/h)

Compact, with sleek lines, the Ka is only available in a 3-door model

Audi Quattro Sport 1983

The first four-wheel drive road car with impressive all-around performance, Audi's most expensive car, the Quattro Sport, can travel fast in mixed conditions. In looks, it is boxy with an unremarkable interior. However, the excellent handling and safety-conscious design ensure that it appeals to a wide range of users, from families to long distance drivers.

Specifications
Country: Germany
Top speed: 155mph (250km/h)

Renault Espace 1984

When it first appeared, the Renault Espace sparked a brand new philosophy in car design. Its so-called "one-box" construction offers maximum interior versatility, with space for seating and storage utilized according to the number of travelers and the type of trip. It is possible, for instance, to swivel seats or convert seating into a table top.

Specifications
Country: France
Top speed: 118mph
(190km/h)

Ford Ka 1999

The new, small cars of the late 1990s offer functionality, safety, security, style, and innovation – essential features for driving in the new millennium. The Ka epitomizes Ford's aim of making cars more compact and recyclable, quieter, safer, cleaner, more efficient, and less intensive in their use of materials. Designed to be fun and exciting to drive, the Ka also offers the styling, sophistication, and features associated with a larger car.

The futuristic design makes for a very distinctive profile

Specifications
Country: UK
Top speed: 96mph
(163km/h)

T957 AYY

THE OFFICE

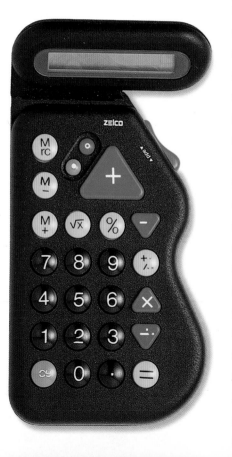

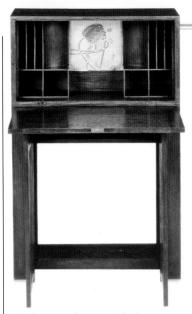

DESKS & CHAIRS

AT THE BEGINNING OF THE CENTURY, desks and chairs were considerable pieces of furniture: they were made of wood, made by hand, and made to last. However, the development of new materials and the introduction of computers made them chief targets for innovation. The traditional solid desk, with its high back and numerous drawers, has gradually been transformed into a simple work surface. Chairs, the items of office furniture most vital to workers' comfort and efficiency, now include unexpectedly comfortable high-tech structures and ergonomic masterpieces. An office planner's choice of both desk and chair is fundamental to the establishment of the company's image, and is often an indication within the office of company hierarchy.

The spindles were individually turned

Mahogany bureau 1920s
This solid mahogany bureau by Charles Rennie Mackintosh is one of the designer's numerous furniture designs for the study. The formality of the elongated lines is enlivened by a decorative panel.

Specifications
Country: UK
Material: Mahogany

Swivel chair 1930s
This carved and bentwood swivel chair is an attractive combination of sturdiness and elegance, with its solid oak base and slender turned spindles. Originally developed to suit the movements of the user, the chair's height is adjustable. The leather seat covers a web of criss-crossed canvas that provides surprising comfort.

Specifications
Country: UK
Materials: Oak and leather upholstery

1900

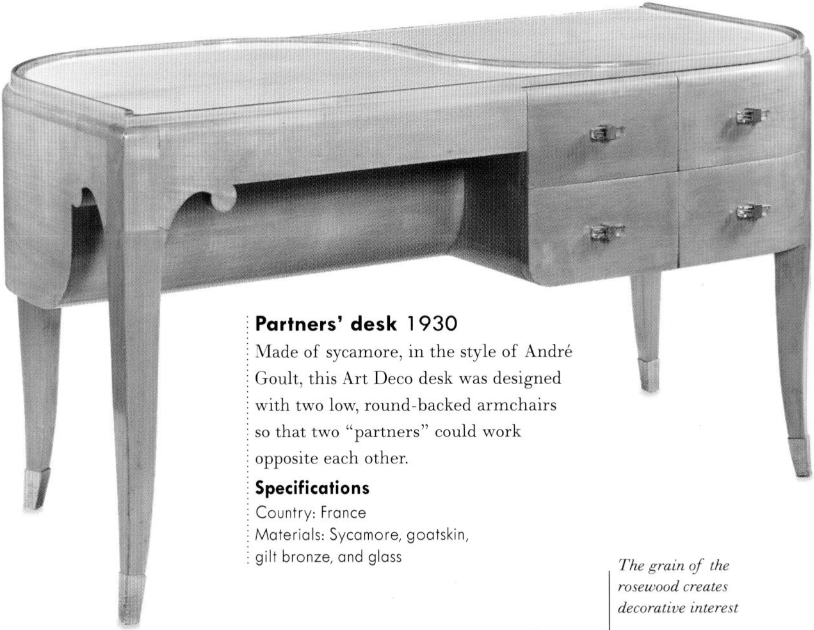

Partners' desk 1930

Made of sycamore, in the style of André
Goult, this Art Deco desk was designed
with two low, round-backed armchairs
so that two "partners" could work
opposite each other.

Specifications

Country: France
Materials: Sycamore, goatskin,
gilt bronze, and glass

*The grain of the
rosewood creates
decorative interest*

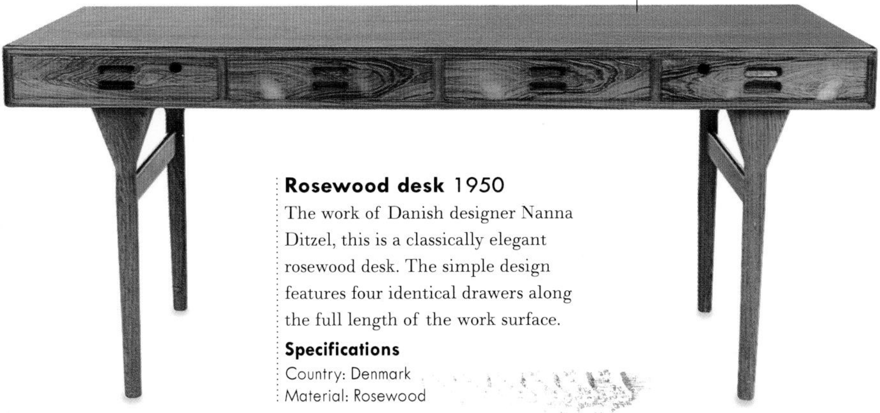

Rosewood desk 1950

The work of Danish designer Nanna
Ditzel, this is a classically elegant
rosewood desk. The simple design
features four identical drawers along
the full length of the work surface.

Specifications

Country: Denmark
Material: Rosewood

▶ ▶ ▶

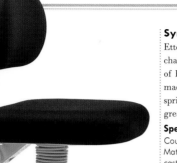

Synthesis 45 office chair 1972

Ettore Sottsass's chunky secretary chair for Olivetti shows the influence of Pop Art. Its back and supports are made of bright plastic, and even the spring cover has been styled with great exaggeration.

Specifications

Country: Italy
Materials: Lacquered
cast-aluminum,
plastic, and fabric upholstery

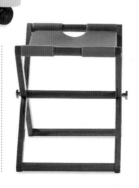

Pippa folding desk and chair 1985

Rena Dumas and Peter Coles, designers of the impeccably finished Pippa furniture collection for Hermès, claimed that the complexity of the designs demanded "perfect materials."

Specifications

Country: France
Materials: Pearwood, leather, and brass

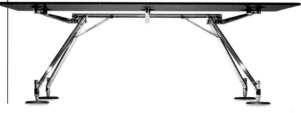

Nomos desk 1987

Norman Foster's range of "Nomos" furniture was designed for Tecno. This glass-topped steel desk has a strikingly high-tech appearance.

Specifications

Country: Italy
Materials: Chromium-plated steel and glɑ

Balans chair 1990s

A product of the Norwegian firm Stokke, the Balans chair represents a complete rethink of the structure of the office chair. The aim is to reduce stress on the sitter's spine caused by working all day at a desk. This was achieved by redistributing the upper body weight: the typist perches on the sloping seat, with his or her knees bearing much of the weight as they rest on a cushioned "knee seat."

Specifications
Country: Norway
Materials: Pine and fabric upholstery

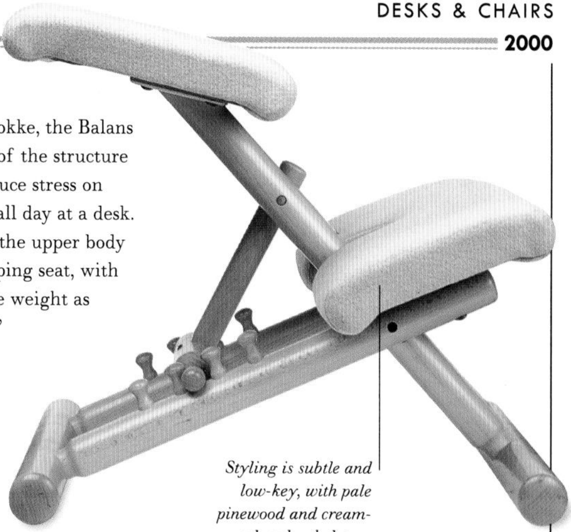

*Aluminum
armrests are
screwed to
the body of
the chair*

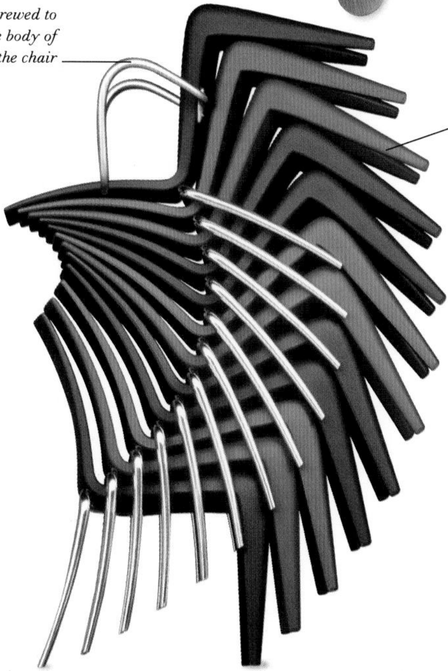

*Styling is subtle and
low-key, with pale
pinewood and cream-
colored upholstery*

*Weight is distributed
between plastic and
aluminum legs*

Louis 20 chair 1995

The back, seat, and front legs of Philippe Starck's Louis 20 chair are made from a single piece of molded plastic, with the rear legs formed by a bridge of tubular aluminum. These are screwed rather than glued to the body for ease of separating and recycling the different pieces. The chair is available with or without armrests, also constructed of tubular aluminum. Several chairs can be stacked together, as seen here.

Specifications
Country: France
Materials: Polypropylene and aluminum

OFFICE EQUIPMENT

BEFORE WORLD WAR II, the office was
a distinctly impersonal place, with the
stark, industrial appearance of a factory
environment. Office equipment was
purely functional; machines such as
typewriters and photocopiers had
their inner workings exposed, and
the use of dictation machines,
commonplace by the 1930s,
depersonalized office life further.
Decades passed before any link
was acknowledged between
productivity and environment.
It was only as recently as the
1950s that designers began to
place the aesthetics of office
equipment on a par with
performance. It was still later
that this became the norm.

AEG fan 1911
Cofounder of the Deutscher Werkbund
in 1907, a group of manufacturers,
retailers, architects, and designers, Peter
Behrens was as concerned as any designer
of his time with the function of the
machinery he designed. However,
Behrens' refined sensibilities meant that
his designs stole a march on those of his
rivals. This pioneering electric desk fan
for AEG is a fine example of Behrens
tailoring the design of the item
to emphasize its function.

Specifications
Country: Germany
Material: Cast iron
and brass

*The solid base
resembles the
form of an
early telephone*

Edison Protechnic Ediphone
early 20th century

With only three months of formal education, Thomas Alva Edison was responsible for over 1,200 patents and was one of America's greatest inventors. His inventions included the light bulb, the origins of moving pictures, and the phonograph. Before Edison saw the potential of the phonograph for home entertainment, it was used in business to record dictation, the sound recorded on a wax cylinder. The cabinets of this large, early machine were unwieldy, but represented one of the few areas of office furniture design where consideration was actually given to aesthetics.

Specifications
Country: UK
Material: Metal

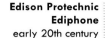

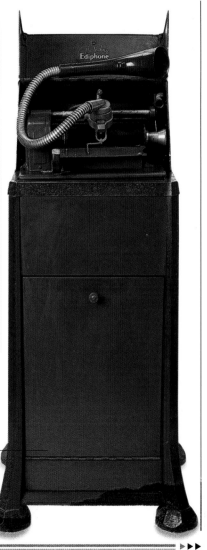

The bars of the guard resemble ribbons fluttering in a breeze

The cabinet doors have the smooth finish of a piece of domestic furniture

Bandolero desk fan 1930s

The streamlined Bakelite Bandolero fan was produced by Diehl, the electrical division of Singer, for the American mail order company Sears. The design dispenses with metal blades, using in their place crosshatched fabric blades, which were safer. This removed the need for a protective cage and contributed to the fan's sharp, modern image. The fabric blades were later replaced with rubber versions.

Specifications
Country: US
Materials: Bakelite and fabric

This sleek design looks back to modernist styling

The fabric blades exemplify the safety-conscious design of the fan

Edison Voicewriter 1953

Manufactured by the Ediphone Division of Thomas A. Edison, Inc., this compact magnetic tape recorder was produced 22 years after Edison's death, but his influential name appears four times on the machine. Designed by Carl Otto, the Voicewriter was revolutionary for its portability.

Stability is created by the broad base

Specifications
Country: US
Material: Metal

Pocket Memo 1993

The development of cassette tapes, and now microcassettes, has meant that dictaphones have become smaller and more sleekly styled over the years. The diminutive Pocket Memo Executive 396 dictaphone manufactured by Philips Dictation Systems, was designed by Austrian Konrad Ellermeier.

Specifications
Country: Austria
Material: Plastic

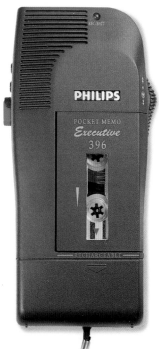

Swing-out drawers provide a number of storage compartments

Boby trolley 1970

The ingenious Boby trolley was designed by Joe Colombo for the Italian company Kartell in 1970, and is now produced by Bieffeplast. Made of ABS plastic, its structure is an excellent example of how designers mastered the storage potential of plastics in the 1960s and '70s. It is light enough to be moved around an office on its large castors.

Specifications
Country: Italy
Material: Plastic

DESK ACCESSORIES

MOST OFFICE DESKS are littered with items that are, in their way, design classics. The humble paperclip, invented in 1899 by Norwegian Johann Vaaler, has hardly changed. The pencil sharpener, developed in Germany in 1908 by the TPX Bias company, still remains an essential office item. The Rolodex, which first appeared in 1950, has survived the age of electronically stored information as a simple and efficient means of storing addresses. Even the disposable ball-point has a fascinating history.

Juwel Elastic Stapler c.1930

The French Juwel Elastic stapler operates, as its name suggests, by means of an elastic band rather than the spring used in modern staplers. The beautiful, Deco-inspired geometric enameling in black and white ensures that the Juwel lives up to its name.

Specifications
Country: France
Materials: Metal and enamel

Rolodex 1952

Arnold Neudstadter's 1952 design of the Rolodex card file was so successful that the company claimed that "there's a Rolodex file on almost every desk in America." The Rolodex is deceptively simple; made of heavy steel, it rotates "Tuff Fiber" index cards and will stop in any position, thanks to an ingenious ball-bearing clutch mechanism known as the "Rolomatic."

Specifications
Country: US
Materials: Metal, plastic, and paper

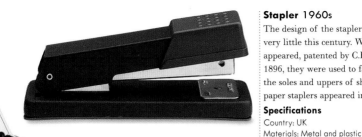

Stapler 1960s

The design of the stapler has changed very little this century. When they first appeared, patented by C.H. Gould in 1896, they were used to fasten together the soles and uppers of shoes. The first paper staplers appeared in the late 1890s.

Specifications
Country: UK
Materials: Metal and plastic

Index cards are divided alphabetically and rotated to view

Folle stapler 1980s

Resigned to the fact that little can be done to improve the stapler's function, designers toy with its looks. This round-headed model is available in a range of bright colors. It was designed by Henning Andreasen for Folle APS of Denmark.

Specifications
Country: Denmark
Material: Steel

The tubular metal frame supports more than 500 index cards

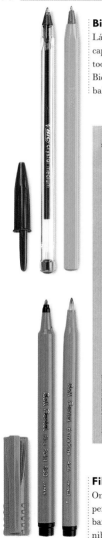

Bic pens 1938

László Biró first developed a pen that utilized quick-drying ink, capillary action, and a ball point in his 1938 "Biro." Marcel Bich took over the patent in 1958 and created a disposable version, the Bic. It is now so ubiquitous that it has become synonymous with the ballpoint pen. In the 1990s, three billion Bics are sold each year.

Specifications
Country: France
Material: Plastic

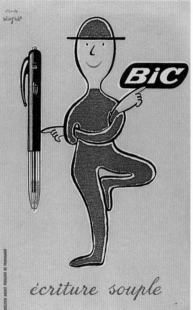

écriture souple

Blotting paper c.1955

In the 1950s, collecting printed blotting paper was popular in many European countries and in the US. The widespread introduction of the Bic biro killed off the fad in the 1960s. This advertisement was designed by French illustrator Savignac.

Specifications
Country: France
Material: Paper

Magnifying lens

Stapler

Fiber-tip pens 1963

One of the few advances on the ballpoint, the first fiber-tipped pens, developed in Japan in 1963 by Pentel, used a bamboo inner barrel. This was superseded by a fiber tube that fed ink to the nib by capillary action. This system is still used.

Specifications
Country: Japan
Material: Plastic

23 OCT MON

Everlasting calendar 1967

Enzo Mari designed his stylish calendar for Danese in 1967. The innovative design uses PVC cards in three lengths indicating the day, date, and month. The cards were printed in English, Italian, German, and French.

Specifications
Country: Italy
Material: ABS plastic and PVC

Lamy pens 1982

Walter Fabian's pen designs for the German company Lamy were an enormous success, elevating them to "classic" status immediately. The pens were popular for their styling rather than for any new technical advances.

Specifications
Country: Germany
Material: Plastic

Staple remover

◄ REMOVER

MEASURE ►

◄ LENS

Tape measure

Factory™ PLUS

Factory F2 desk tool 1986

Developed by brothers Yoshihisa and Kohji Imaizumi for Plus Coporation, this compact desk accessory is in the style of a Swiss army knife. It has a stapler, magnifying glass, tape measure, hole punch, staple remover, pin case, scissors, and tape dispenser.

Specifications
Country: Japan
Materials: Plastic and metal

Mouse mat 1998

With a computer on every desk, the mouse mat has become commonplace in the office. Mats are often decorated with bright advertising logos, while this example has an unusual, irregular shape.

Specifications
Country: UK
Material: Plastic

TYPEWRITERS

THE FIRST TYPEWRITERS, made in 1873, had a QWERTY layout, from the word spelled by the first six letters on the top row of keys. This system was developed to slow the fingers down on complicated manual typewriters. However, because it became an industry standard, it is still used today. Early typewriters had an industrial appearance; but by the 1930s, portables had been introduced and electric machines developed. By 1961, when IBM launched the "Golfball," electric models had largely replaced manuals. The use of personal computers in the 1990s delivered the final death blow to the traditional typewriter.

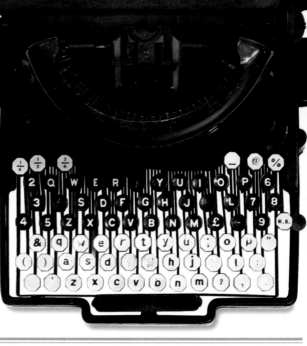

Royal Bar-Lock
c.1910

This typewriter has a double keyboard. Without a shift key, which had been developed by Remington in 1878, it was necessary to have two keyboards, one for the upper case and one for the lower. The position of the typebars would have made it very difficult for the typist to see what was being printed. The open body gives the typewriter an industrial look, which would not have appealed to the domestic market.

Specifications

Country: US

Width: 15¾in (40cm)

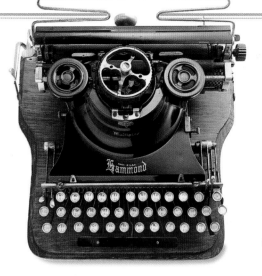

Multiplex 1919

Hammond produced many innovative typewriters. The Multiplex had a system of interchangeable type shuttles that carried different fonts. The typewriter bears the legend "For All Nations and Tongues," which implies that the various fonts might be used for foreign languages. Most shuttles carried the fonts in three rows; but for specialized shuttles that had four, a second shift key was required.

Specifications
Country: US
Height: 9in (23cm)
Width: 14½in (37cm)

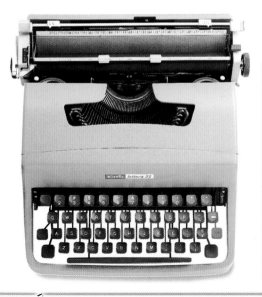

Lettera 32 c.1960

Marcello Nizzoli was Olivetti's first and most influential product designer. In the 1940s and '50s, he created office appliances, including adding machines (see p.354) and typewriters, which have achieved classic status. The Lettera 32 is based on his portable typewriter of 1950, the Lettera 22. The hallmark of Nizzoli's designs was his keen attention to form and applied graphics.

Specifications
Country: Italy
Height: 3in (8cm)
Width: 12in (31cm)

Valentine 1969

The Valentine is the ultimate portable typewriter, comprising two simple elements. The machine and handle form one element and the matching carrying case the other. It was designed for Olivetti by Ettore Sottsass and Perry A. King, who wanted to create a typewriter that would be light enough to carry anywhere and that would not be associated with the work environment. It is made from bright orange-red molded plastic, with yellow caps on the ribbon spools "like the two eyes of a robot," as Sottsass himself described them. It represents a radical departure from traditional office equipment.

Specifications
Country: Italy
Height: 4in (10.3cm)
Width: 13in (33cm)

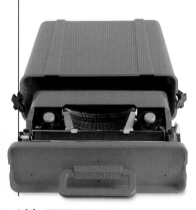

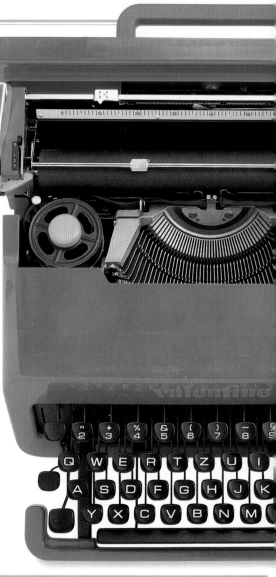

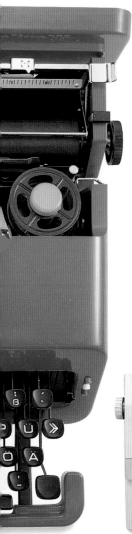

THE "GOLFBALL"

Eliot Noyes designed the innovative Selectric or "Golfball" typewriter for IBM in 1961. It was a revolutionary design because the typebars were replaced by a small spherical typing head shaped like a golfball. This head carried the usual 88 characters, but it moved while the carriage remained stationary. Heads were interchangeable, allowing for a greater selection of typefaces. The Selectric was part of Noyes' program to create a corporate identity for IBM, and its style owes a great deal to Marcello Nizzoli, who was so instrumental in reshaping Olivetti's post-1945 product range.

IBM Selectric, 1961

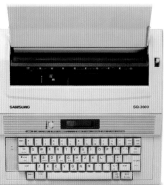

Samsung SQ-3000 1990s

This Samsung is an example of a crossbreed of typewriter that combined a compact electronic machine with a memory facility. The small screen allowed the user to view a line of text before it was printed. Such models were popular from the mid-1980s, until the development of the personal computer rendered their features obsolete.

Specifications
Country: South Korea
Height: 4½in (11.3cm)
Width: 15¼in (39cm)

COMPUTERS

THE BOOK THAT YOU ARE READING was written on a computer small enough to fit in a briefcase, and designed and edited on versatile desktop computers. Yet the first electronic computer, the ENIAC (Electronic Numerical Integrator And Calculator), developed in 1946, weighed 30 tons and occupied a surface area of $1,722 \text{ft}^2$ (160m^2). The invention of the transistor in 1947 and its successor, the integrated circuit, in 1959, facilitated the reduced size and greater power that characterize computers today. As more schoolchildren are taught to use computers, they are becoming as common-place in the Western home as televisions.

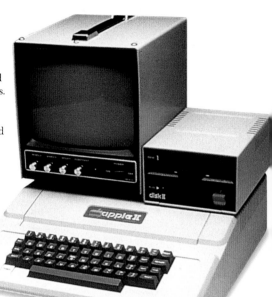

THE APPLE MAC

The Macintosh, designed by frogdesign for Apple Computer and unveiled in 1984, was by far the most original personal computer of its day. With its high-definition screen, graphic icons, and mouse pointing device, it proved exceptionally user-friendly. The disk drive and monitor were built into a single unit, giving the Apple Mac a more streamlined, compact look than its rivals. But it was the sophistication and speed of the machine's graphics that made it popular in desktop publishing and revolutionized printed media in the late 1980s.

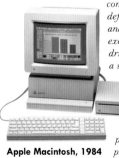

Apple Macintosh, 1984

Apple II 1977

The success of the Apple II, shown here with the Disk II disk drive introduced in 1978, lay in its user-friendliness. Developed by Steve Jobs and Steve Wozniak, it was the first commercial personal computer.

Specifications
Country: US
Dimensions: Not known

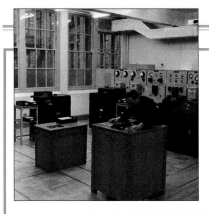

EARLY COMPUTERS

Many early computers were developed for defense purposes, such as the electronic codebreaker developed at Bletchley Park, England during World War II, or the "Whirlwind," the first real-time computer, built for the US air defense system in 1951. The first electronic computer contained 19,000 electronic tubes, enabling it to compute 5,000 additions, and about 300 multiplications per second. It was child's play, though, compared to the capabilities of modern computers such as the Cray Y-MP (1988), which can perform more than two billion computations per second.

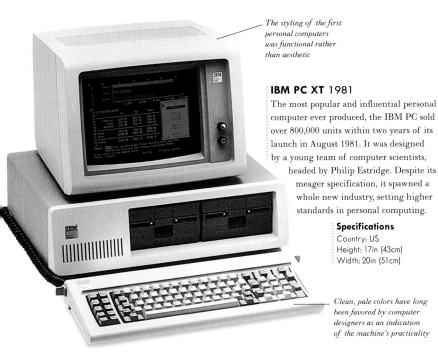

The styling of the first personal computers was functional rather than aesthetic

IBM PC XT 1981

The most popular and influential personal computer ever produced, the IBM PC sold over 800,000 units within two years of its launch in August 1981. It was designed by a young team of computer scientists, headed by Philip Estridge. Despite its meager specification, it spawned a whole new industry, setting higher standards in personal computing.

Specifications

Country: US
Height: 17in (43cm)
Width: 20in (51cm)

Clean, pale colors have long been favored by computer designers as an indication of the machine's practicality

Amstrad **PC1512** 1986

The British company Amstrad, established by entrepreneur Alan Sugar, launched the hugely successful PC1512 in 1986. Compatible with IBM's PC, it was, however, easier to use, twice as fast, and substantially lower in price. It made IBM standard computing, previously restricted to the US market, accessible to the European home-user for the first time.

Specifications
Country: UK
Dimensions: Not known

The monitor has an 80-column display and a palette of 16 colors

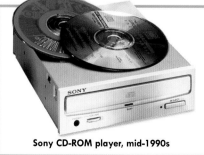

Sony CD-ROM player, mid-1990s

CD-ROM

Invented by Philips, and promoted internationally in collaboration with Sony, the CD-ROM is a laser-read disc that can be used to produce images on a computer screen. The ROM stands for "read only memory," meaning the disc can be recorded on only once. It holds a large amount of information, which is displayed either in the form of text and images or as narrated animated sequences. Until the 1990s the main market for CD-ROMs was professional, but they are now available to the home audience.

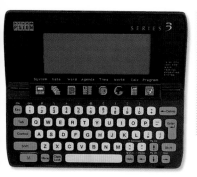

Psion Series 3 1992

The miniaturization made possible by the microchip is epitomized in this palmtop computer, which incorporates a personal organizer and word-processor. It has more power than the computers aboard the Apollo spacecraft.

Specifications

Country: UK
Height: 2in (5cm) open
Width: 6½in (16.5cm)

The holes that keep the machine cool are featured as part of the design

Acer Aspire 1996

In the marketing of computers, the emphasis has generally been on function rather than form. Previously, computer use was largely restricted to offices, but the 1990s saw the emergence of the home office. Companies like Acer recognized this change in the market and offered something more attractive than the ubiquitous beige box. With its decorative surface, sculpted shape, and ultramodern appearance, the Aspire is an attractive item of domestic furniture as well as a powerful computer.

Specifications

Country: Taiwan
Height: 19¼in (49cm)
Width: 15½in (39.5cm)

The extended keyboard provides a rest for the wrist, thus preventing Repetitive Strain Injury

Veridata laptop mid-1990s

As the decade progressed, the laptop became more and more essential for the busy executive. Indeed, the majority of the text for this book was written on just such a machine. Further reduction in the size of the computer is restricted by the size of the keyboard, which becomes unusable if reduced any further. However the depth of the latest machines shrinks with every new model.

Specifications
Country: Taiwan
Length: 11in (28cm)
Width: 10in (25cm)
Depth: 2in (5cm)

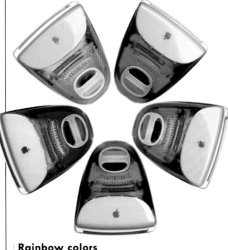

iMac 1998

Launched in late 1998, the iMac quickly became a design icon, influencing the design of other products as diverse as cars and desk accessories. The compact unit, with hard disk and modem included, enabled Apple to notch up sales of 800,000 in five months, doubling company profits and stealing a lead on the PC market. The iMac has quickly become the most admired and celebrated computer design ever.

Specifications
Country: US
Height: 15.8in (39.5cm), Width 15in (38cm),
Depth: 17¼in (44cm)

Rainbow colors

A few months after the initial launch of the iMac (right), new colored casings were introduced. Despite its generous technical capacity, the machine has become equally influential for its looks.

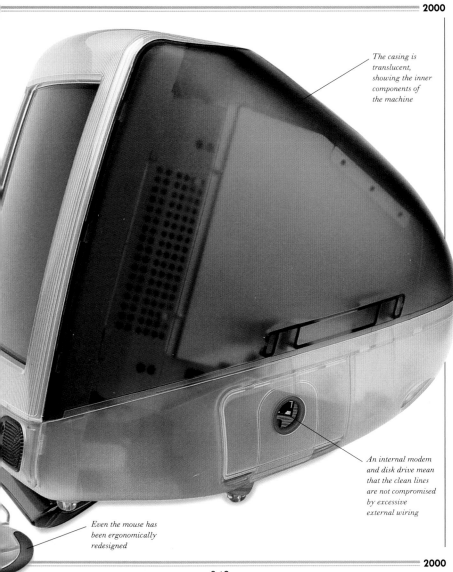

The casing is translucent, showing the inner components of the machine

An internal modem and disk drive mean that the clean lines are not compromised by excessive external wiring

Even the mouse has been ergonomically redesigned

PHOTOCOPIERS & FAX MACHINES

THE PRINCIPLES for duplicating and transmitting documents have existed since the beginning of the century. However, it is only with the development of an integrated telephone system and advances in electronics that photocopiers and facsimile machines have come to play such crucial roles in the office. Originally forbidding-looking, the first copiers were transformed as early as the 1930s, thanks to Raymond Loewy's "face-lift" of a Gestetner duplicating machine. Fax machines were developed much later, emerging in Japan and the US simultaneously in 1968, when it took six minutes to transmit a single-page document. Today, communication by fax is an instantaneous and indispensable process.

Gestetner duplicating machine 1929

Gestetner commissioned Raymond Loewy to restyle the exterior of its duplicating machine in the late 1920s. In contrast to the overtly utilitarian appearance of the original machine, Loewy's simplified version is sleek and refined, with the mechanism concealed in a casing. He used a full-scale clay model to achieve the desired sculptural qualities – a working method that was subsequently adopted by designers in the car industry.

Specifications
Country: UK
Materials: Wood and metal
Dimensions: Not known

THE FIRST COMMERCIAL COPIER

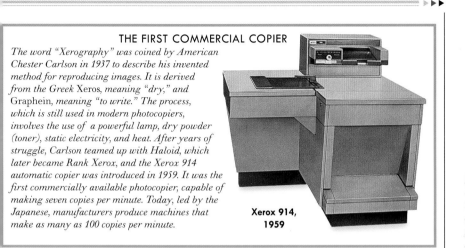

The word "Xerography" was coined by American Chester Carlson in 1937 to describe his invented method for reproducing images. It is derived from the Greek Xeros, meaning "dry," and Graphein, meaning "to write." The process, which is still used in modern photocopiers, involves the use of a powerful lamp, dry powder (toner), static electricity, and heat. After years of struggle, Carlson teamed up with Haloid, which later became Rank Xerox, and the Xerox 914 automatic copier was introduced in 1959. It was the first commercially available photocopier, capable of making seven copies per minute. Today, led by the Japanese, manufacturers produce machines that make as many as 100 copies per minute.

Xerox 914, 1959

Qwip 1200 1970s

By the 1970s, fax machines were starting to become a familiar feature in modern office environments. By offering companies the very latest technology in a new, compact form, the Qwip 1200 series revolutionized the market. The machine was designed in two sections: the main sender/receiver and the acoustic housing for the telephone headset. It required special paper to receive documents; but otherwise it was simple to use, taking about four minutes to transmit or receive a document.

Specifications
Country: US
Material: Plastic
Height: 6¼in (16cm)
Width: 22in (56cm)

▶ ▶ ▶

Brother Fax-160 1980s

Compact and unobtrusive, this integrated telephone/fax machine could serve either in the office or the home. The light gray plastic housing conceals the working apparatus. It has push-button keys and a memory facility, which allows high-speed dialing to a choice of 50 programed numbers. Sixteen shades of gray help ensure accuracy of reproduction.

Specifications
Country: UK
Material: Plastic
Height: 4⅗in (11.6cm)
Width: 16¾in (42.4cm)

Paper for incoming transmissions is stored inside the machine

Canon PC-3 portable copier 1993

This portable desktop copier by Canon was designed to meet the growing need for a photocopier suitable for infrequent use. It works in the same way as a conventional office photocopier, but is restricted to the most basic operations. It is unable to enlarge or reduce documents, and is without a paper stack.

Specifications
Country: Japan
Material: Plastic
Height: 5¾in (14.6cm)
Width: 15in (38.4cm)

FAX-160

CONTRAST	DELAY
2	3
5	6
8	9
0	#

COPY   STOP   START

The message window displays the current status of the machine

QuadMark PassPort portable copier 1993

When Xerox company QuadMark introduced this portable copier in 1993, it was the world's smallest plain paper copier. Battery-operated and cordless, it weighs just 4lb (1.8kg) and is diminutive enough to be stored in a briefcase or desk drawer. Despite its modest size, the reproduction quality is high, with copies printed at 400 dots per inch resolution.

Specifications

Country: US
Material: Plastic
Height: 2¾in (7cm)
Width: 11¾in (30cm)

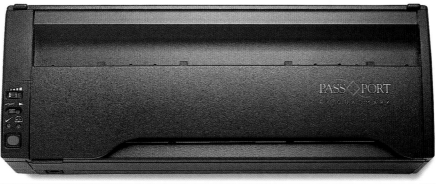

PASS◇PORT
BY QUADMARK

ADDING MACHINES

WE NOW TAKE FOR GRANTED the use of sophisticated, inexpensive electronic calculators. However, early calculating machines were heavy, slow, and had no stored memory. Computers with storage capacity became available for commercial use in the 1950s; they could be programmed to solve complex problems, but their size made them impractical for home use. It was the introduction of the microchip in the 1970s that facilitated massive reductions in the size, weight, and cost of calculators, while transforming their power beyond compare. Today, designers' increased sensitivity to the needs of the operator is reflected in the form of the machine, its graphics, and the grouping of keys.

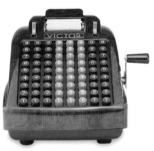

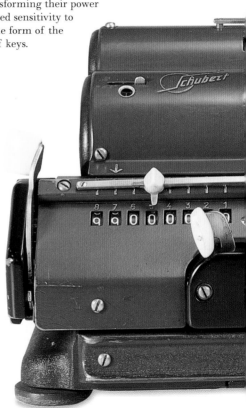

Victor adding machine c.1935

This mechanical calculator has a two-tone, typewriter-style keyboard, which allows the fast and efficient entry of numbers. Designed by W.A. Knapp for the Victor Adding Machine Co. of Chicago, it is housed in a lightweight Bakelite case. Relatively inexpensive and easy to mold into a modern shape, Bakelite was made popular in the 1930s by the likes of Raymond Loewy, Wells Coates, and Jean Heiberg.

Specifications

Country: US
Materials: Bakelite and metal
Height: 7in (18cm)
Width: 7¼in (18.5cm), Depth: 12¼in (31cm)

Schubert c.1950

Cumbersome and complicated to operate, the Schubert was one of the last dinosaurs of the adding machine world, doomed to extinction by the advent of the silicon chip.

The Schubert was able to compute figures with up to 10 digits

Specifications

Country: Germany
Materials: Metal and plastic
Height: 5¼in (13.2cm)
Width: 11¼in (28.5cm)
Depth: 5⅜in (13.8cm)

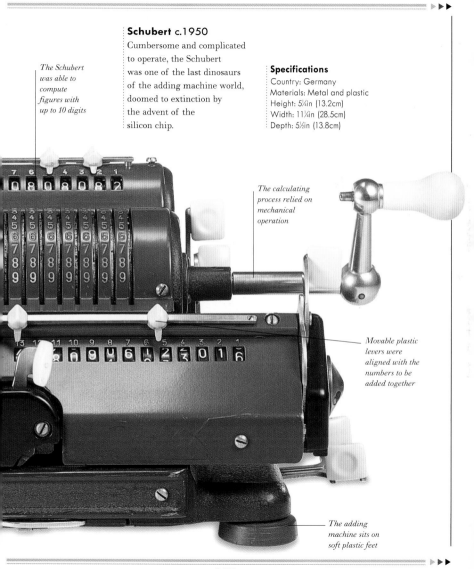

The calculating process relied on mechanical operation

Movable plastic levers were aligned with the numbers to be added together

The adding machine sits on soft plastic feet

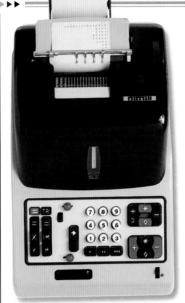

Olivetti Divisumma 18 1973

Like Marcello Nizzoli, Olivetti designer Mario Bellini responds to human requirements in his designs. Although he studies ergonomics, he stresses that they can be merely a starting point, as people are much more complex than a set of measurements. Divisumma 18 will be remembered as much for its feel as its appearance. Manufactured in brightly colored plastic and covered with a thin sheath of rubber, its soft, tactile keys and the rounded forms make it a pleasure to handle.

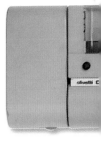

Olivetti Divisumma 24 1956

This calculator is the work of one of Olivetti's most celebrated designers, Marcello Nizzoli. Always mindful of those who will use and maintain his products, Nizzoli has considered the positioning of the keys, the coloring, and the graphics layout to make the machine easier to use. Note particularly the large addition and subtraction keys. To ease servicing, the two-part plastic casing is removable, allowing maximum access to the mechanism.

Specifications

Country: Italy
Materials: Plastic and metal
Height: 9½in (24cm)
Width: 9½in (24.4cm)
Depth: 17in (43cm)

POCKET CALCULATORS

The first pocket calculator was introduced in 1972 by Clive Sinclair. This model by Casio from the 1990s is typical of the millions now inexpensively available and in

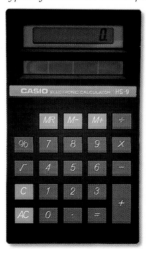

constant use in homes, offices, and schools across the world. It demonstrates the possibilities afforded by modern technology: in addition to its memory storage facility and multitude of mathematical functions, it is powered by a solar cell, and so requires no batteries. The model's simple, sleek form is a classic of modern design.

Casio pocket calculator, 1990s

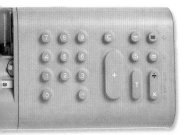

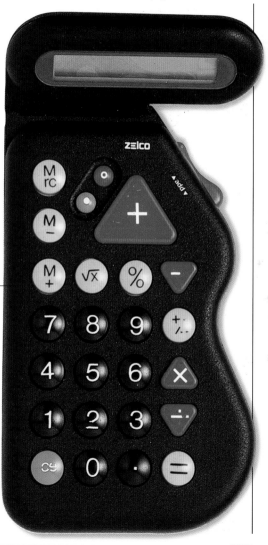

Specifications
Country: Italy
Materials: Plastic and rubber
Height: 1¾in (4.6cm)
Width: 12⅜in (30.9cm)
Depth: 4¾in (12cm)

Because of the ergonomic design, there are separate versions for right- and left-handed users

Zelco "Double Plus" calculator 1986
Designed by Donald Booty Jr. for Zelco Industries, this calculator is shaped to be gripped. The name "Double Plus" derives from the unusual feature of having two addition keys, allowing the addition function to be used more rapidly. These and the other keys are positioned, shaped, and colored to maximize efficiency.

Specifications
Country: US
Materials: Plastic and acrylic
Height: 5⅛in (14.4cm)
Width: 2½in (6.6cm), Depth: ½in (1.3cm)

GRAPHICS, ADVERTISING, & PACKAGING

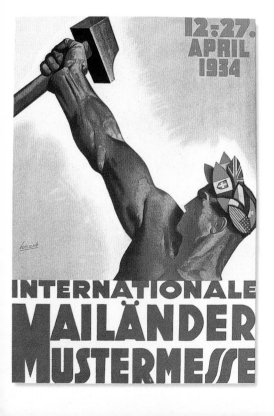

TYPEFACES

COUNTLESS PRODUCTS from the 20th century are instantly associated with a particular style of lettering, be it a cereal box, a newspaper, or a public transportation map. In fact, so powerful is the impact of many typefaces that words are often given expression even before the literal meaning becomes apparent. There are two basic divisions of typefaces: serif faces (those with terminal strokes) and sans serifs (those without terminal strokes), and a multitude of variations exist. Functional and geometric, sans serif letterforms were pioneered by Bauhaus designers in the 1930s, and labeled "new typography."

Even the verticals of Eckmann Schmuck curve organically

The letterforms are based on classical Roman proportions

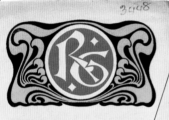

Eckmann Schmuck 1900

Organic and calligraphic influences are clearly evident in this Jugendstil typeface, designed by German typographer Otto Eckmann. The curvilinear strokes of each letter taper and swell, as if with the movement of an italic pen tip. Devised for the Rudhard Foundry, it was also adopted by Klingspor, with which it is most commonly associated.

The letter "O" is a perfect circle

Underground 1915

In 1915, Edward Johnston was commissioned by London Underground to design a display typeface. He produced a sans serif alphabet that is simple to read and easy to recognize; it is still used by London Underground today. The typeface is deployed to great effect on the roundel, which appears throughout the system to indicate each station name.

The roundel originally had a solid red disc with a blue bar

Each stroke is of an identical thickness

abcdefghi
jklmnopqr
stuvwxyz

HERBERT BAYER: Abb. 1. Alfabet
„a" und „k" sind noch als
unfertig zu betrachten

Beispiel eines Zeichens
in größerem Maßstab
Präzise optische Wirkung

sturm blond

Abb. 3. Anwendung

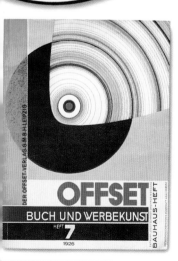

Universal 1925

During his time as head of the print department at the Bauhaus, Austrian Herbert Bayer produced this alphabet. An advocate of modernism, Bayer defended the sans serif typeface as an expression of its time. He denounced serifs as a hangover from handwriting, incompatible with modern typography and printing. His simple, geometric Universal alphabet also suspended the use of capital letters. It was employed in the Bauhaus publication *Offset*, but never released as a typeface.

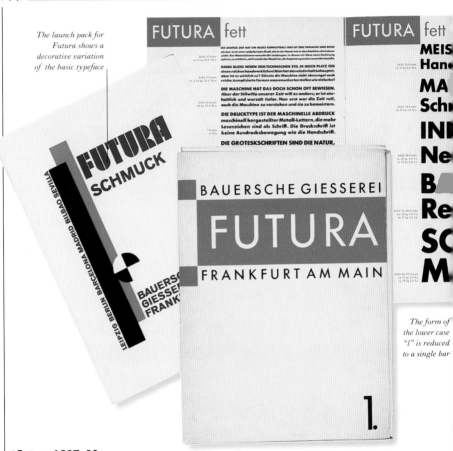

The launch pack for Futura shows a decorative variation of the basic typeface

The form of the lower case "l" is reduced to a single bar

Futura 1927–30

The design of the Futura typeface owes more to precision engineering than to the calligrapher's pen. Taking inspiration from Bayer's Universal face, German typographer Paul Renner was one of the first to utilize the revolutionary approach of a completely even stroke throughout the alphabet. Futura is notably more rigid in its geometry than its corresponding British typeface, Gill Sans. As with Universal, the letterforms are based on squares and circles; but, interestingly, the crossbar of the "E" and "F" is positioned above center. The typeface is still used today in a number of variations.

RSUS
kunſt

RIPT

ben

RIE

ten

EN

me

LE

rei

¶ANNUAL MEETING

FEDERATION

OF

MASTER

PRINTERS

THE LANSTON MONOTYPE CORPORATION LIMITED, LONDON
PRESENT
AN INTERIM PROOF OF THEIR
SANS-SERIF TITLING
DESIGNED BY ERIC GILL

CONGRESS

SELLING

AND

PUBLICITY

BLACKPOOL

MAY 31
COLLECT FOR
THE FEAST OF S. ANGELA MERICI

DEUS, QUI NOVUM PER BEATAM
ANGELAM SACRARUM VIRGINUM
COLLEGIUM IN ECCLESIA TUA FLOR-
ESCERE VOLUISTI: DA NOBIS, EIUS
INTERCESSIONE, ANGELICIS MORI-
BUS VIVERE; UT, TERRENIS OMNIBUS
ABDICATIS, GAUDIIS PERFRUI MERE-
AMUR AETERNIS · PER DOMINUM NOSTRUM
IESUM CHRISTUM FILIUM TUUM QUI TECUM
VIVIT ET REGNAT IN UNITATE SPIRITUS SANCTI
DEUS PER OMNIA SAECULA SAECULORUM

ABCDEFGHIJKLMN
OPQQRRSTUV
WXYZ

I.2,3:4;5-6!7?8§9*¶0[

Gill Sans 1928

British designer Eric Gill was a highly respected type designer, sculptor, and letter cutter. His namesake typeface is identified with modernism. Gill studied under Edward Johnston, whose guidance can be seen in the forms of this sans serif alphabet. Subtle stroke variations give the face greater fluidity, making it easy to read as continuous text. Gill Sans was created for the Monotype Company (renamed the Monotype Corporation in 1931), whose adviser for typography, Stanley Morison, had earlier supported Gill in the development of the typeface Perpetua.

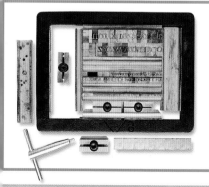

MOVABLE TYPE

Printing with metal type has its origins in the invention of movable type by the 15th-century German goldsmith Johannes Gutenberg. Each block has a single letter that can be set, inked, and the relief surface then impressed onto paper. The method was an improvement on woodblock printing, not least because one mistake no longer meant the replacement of an entire printing block. Here, a "forme" is made up of the inked type, wedges, and iron frame, or "chase."

Inked forme

THE TIMES NEW ROMAN

It may be claimed that *The Times*, with its new titling, its new device, and its new text types, possesses, from the headline on the front page to the tail imprint on the back, a visual unity. But this is no more than the beginning of typographical wisdom, for visual harmony, whatever its

It may be claimed that *The Times*, with its new titling, its new device, and its new text types, possesses, from the headline on the front page to the tail imprint on the back, a visual unity. But this is no more than the beginning of typographical wisdom, for visual harmony, whatever its significance for the artist, has little value for the general reader unless and until it accompanies

It may be claimed that *The Times*, with its new titling, its new device, and its new text types, possesses, from the headline on the front page to the tail imprint on the back, a visual unity. But this is no more than the beginning of typographical wisdom, for visual harmony, whatever its significance for the artist, has little value for the general reader unless and until it accompanies the basic factors of textual legibility. The reader needs a definite

It may be claimed that *The Times*, with its new titling, its new device, and its new text types, possesses, from the headline on the front page to the tail imprint on the back, a visual unity. But this is no more than the beginning of typographical wisdom, for visual harmony, whatever its significance for the artist, has little value for the general reader unless and until it accompanies the basic factors of textual legibility. The reader needs a definite plainness and familiarity of type design;

It may be claimed that *The Times*, with its new titling, its new device, and its new text types, possesses, from the headline on the front page to the tail imprint on the back, a visual unity. But this is no more than the beginning of typographical wisdom, for visual harmony, whatever its significance for the artist, has little value for the general reader unless and until it accompanies the basic factors of textual legibility. The reader needs a definite plainness and familiarity of type design; the greatest possible size and cleanness of impression; and that adjustment of the spacing, first, to the single letters, next to their combination in words, lines, paragraphs, columns, and pages which makes the whole "look right" to him. From this point of view,

Times New Roman 1931

As well as advising Monotype (see p.363), Stanley Morison was typographic consultant to *The Times*, London, for three decades, when he created this typeface for the newspaper. It was used exclusively for one year, replacing a Gothic type that had been favored for over 120 years. Simplifications to the formation of each letter meant that text could be condensed and remain legible, at the same time saving space.

Univers 1957

Swiss designer Adrian Frutiger earned his considerable reputation through the creation of this versatile typeface. Univers 65, shown here, is just one of 21 variations contributing to this universal lettering system, which permits a multitude of combinations and effects. Designed for the purpose of filmsetting, Univers is particularly compatible with printing in condensed spaces and has frequently been the preferred choice for timetables. In expanded, bolder format, it has been used for large-scale, public signage systems. The typestyle is sans serif, with the weight stress balanced on both vertical and diagonal strokes. Univers was taken up by the Monotype Corporation soon after it was launched.

Univers 65

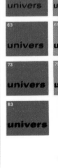

ABCDEFGH
IJKLMNOPQRS
TUVWXYZÇ
abcdefgh
jklmnopqrs
tuvwxyzæœ
'.,:;!?Æfbéœ£()§:;-
1234567890

DANS LA PREMIÈRE SÉRIE

Les efforts que l'homme fait pour mieux connaître et pour mieux comprendre assouplissent son esprit

POUR SERVIR D'ATTRIBUTION

Les efforts que l'homme fait pour comprendre et pour mieux connaître assouplissent son esprit et le rendent plus apte aux progrès

UNE IMPRESSION RÉCONFORTANTE SE DÉGAGE

Les efforts que l'homme fait pour mieux connaître et pour mieux comprendre assouplissent son esprit et le rendent plus apte aux progrès du lendemain. C'est un

LE MERVEILLEUX ESSOR DE LA PHYSIQUE

Les efforts que l'homme fait pour mieux connaître et pour mieux comprendre assouplissent son esprit et le rendent plus apte aux progrès du

UN SUJET ASSEZ DIFFICILE A TRAITER

Les efforts que l'homme fait pour mieux connaître et pour mieux comprendre assouplissent son esprit et le rendent plus

LES DISCIPLINES DE LA SCIENCE

Les efforts que l'homme fait pour mieux comprendre et pour mieux connaître assouplissent son esprit

UN MOUVEMENT RAPIDE

la réflexion de la lumière sur les miroirs et la propagation

RÉSUMONS UN PEU
maintenant que nous devons cesser pour un

BANQUEROUTE
une reproduction authentique de la

PERSUASION
le mouvement qui était prévu

FRANCHE
instruction

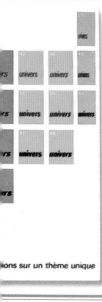

ABCDEFGHIJK
LMNOPQRSTUVW
XYZ ÄÖÜ MN
abcdefghijklmnopq
rstuvwxyz äöü

ÆŒÇ ÉÊÈÊ ÅØ åø
æœç chckfffiflftijß
£ 1234567890 $
.,-:;!?'()„"»«&–[]§†*
áâà éêèë íîïì óôò úûù

FIGURENVERZEICHNIS DER OPTIMA

Optima 1958

German type designer Hermann Zapf created this sans serif typeface, the Roman proportions of which have a hand-written quality. Elegant, flowing, and easy to read when reduced in size, the letters terminate in shallow cups. Initially, Optima was badly received by critics and designers, but soon became a highly popular choice for page text. Zapf is internationally recognized for his considerable contribution to the printmaking industry and his celebrated designs, including Palatino in 1949, Melior in 1952, Zapf Book in 1976, and Zapf International in 1979. More recently, he has been involved in the developmental design of digital type.

Recta 1958

This typeface was designed by Italian graphic artist Aldo Novarese, director of a production type foundry, the Società Nebiolo, in Turin. Linear and sans serif in design, the alphabet comprises a series of 21 variations designed to be compatible with the technical requirements of modern printing. This presentation document has been created to accentuate the geometric quality of Novarese's typeface.

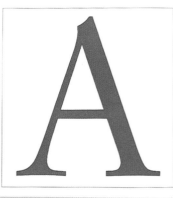

Sabon Antiqua

ABCDEFGHIJKLMNOPQ
RSTUVWXYZÄÖÜ
abcdefghijklmnopqrstuvwxyz
ßchckfffiflft&äöü
1234567890 1234567890
.,:;-!?·'()[]*†‹›«»„"/£$

Sabon Kursiv

Sabon 1964–66

Jan Tshichold began his career as a modernist, and his *Die Neue Typographie* (1928) had a significant impact on the Bauhaus. In the 1930s, he returned to a more traditional style of typography. His Sabon face (see mauve alphabet below) was the first typeface to be designed for linotype, monotype, and hand composition.

Bell Centennial 1978

Devised by British designer Matthew Carter, this typeface was commissioned for use in US telephone directories and was launched during Bell Directories' centennial year. Its key advantage was its ability to stand up to compression; unlike Bell Gothic or Helvetica.

655   WATERGATE—WATSON

DISTRICT OF COLUMBIA

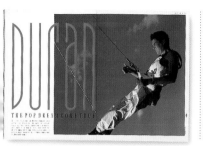

Typeface Six 1986

Postmodernist designer Neville Brody made his name while art editor of British music and style magazine *The Face* (see p.384). He is one of a number of designers who have taken advantage of technological developments in printing to produce typefaces and layouts that break the rules of traditional printsetting. Frequently aided by computer-generated manipulations, Brody uses letterforms as graphic devices, designing unconventional alphabets that make a dramatic impact, such as the "Duran" shown here.

EMIGRE №19:
Starting From
Zero

Abefgor

Template Gothic

Template Gothic
abcdefghijklmnopqrstuvwxyz
ABCDEFGHIJKLMNOPQRSTUVWXYZ
1234567890

Template Gothic 1990

This deconstructed modern typeface is taken from laundromat sign lettering. It was created by American designer Barry Deck and was acclaimed as "the typeface of the decade." Deck's mutilated and distorted typefaces first appeared on CD covers and in publications such as *Ray Gun* and *Emigré*. He uses computer software to create random destructive effects and is concerned with "removing conceit from typography" by parodying the functional and geometric forms of conventional typefaces.

Use of computer-manipulated typefaces reflects designers' increased comfort with screen-derived forms

STUVWXYZ

CORPORATE ID

PETER BEHRENS was the original "corporate designer," the first to consider the complete look of a company and the image that it projects to the public. Since his revolutionary program at AEG, most major corporations have paid designers vast sums to create for them a memorable visual identity. Ironically, one of the world's most successful works of corporate identity, the Coca-Cola script, was designed by the company's bookkeeper.

Shell 1900–71

Although primarily a petroleum company, Shell has many other commercial interests, and more than 90 percent of its businesses around the world use the time-honored logo. The picture of the shell has been altered several times over the years, but has been modified very little since 1971, when the name was repositioned below the stylized image.

The modern symbol is a crisp, symmetrical design in eye-catching primary colors

THE SHELL PECTEN AND LOGOTYPE

1900

1904

1909

1930

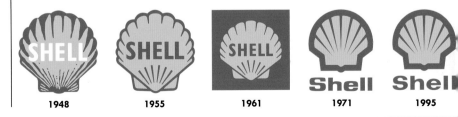

1948

1955

1961

Shell
1971

Shell
1995

MICHELIN MAN

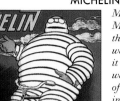

Monsieur Bibendum, the Michelin Man, has been the chief symbol of the French tire company since he was created in 1898. Legend has it that the designer, Mr. O'Galop, was inspired by the sight of a pile of rubber tires. In his earliest incarnations, Monsieur Bibendum had many more thinner rolls, as Michelin made bicycle tires at the beginning of the century. But as the company moved into the production of car tires, his shape changed accordingly. Always depicted as an active, friendly figure, Monsieur Bibendum has achieved lasting success, being both highly memorable and evocative of the product he represents.

Early 20th-century advertisement

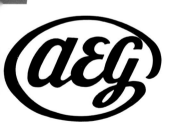

1908

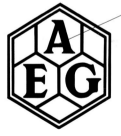

1908

The bold, authoritative style of lettering evokes the power of the company

AEG 1908–60

When, in 1907, Peter Behrens was appointed artistic director of the giant German industrial company AEG (Allgemeine Elektricitäts-Gesellschaft), one of his first challenges was to redesign the company logo. This he did by dramatically simplifying it to just three letters in a rectangle. The strong, simple lettering remains the basis of the logo used today.

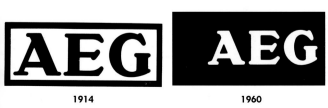

1914   **1960**

▶ ▶ ▶

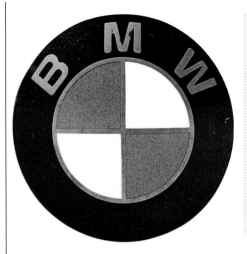

BMW 1930

Bayerische Motoren Werke was founded in 1916 in Munich, the capital of Bavaria. But it was not until 1929 that the Dixi became the first vehicle to carry the famous BMW emblem. The symbol is remarkably simple: silver lettering on a circular black band that encases four segments of solid blue and white – the colors of Bavaria. The image has its origins in World War I, when the Bavarian *Luftwaffe* flew planes painted in Bayern blue and white, affording the pilot a view through his propeller of blue and white segments. This inspired the stylized design we now recognize on vehicle emblems, such as the one pictured here, and on other BMW products. It has been updated to project an identity that is smart, clean-cut, sporty – and image conscious.

COCA-COLA

The famous Coca-Cola script was designed by an amateur: Frank Robinson, the fledgling company's bookkeeper. He devised both the Spencerian script and the brilliantly concise words beneath: "Delicious and Refreshing." The logo now appears across the globe in languages as diverse as Hebrew and Japanese. The bottle is also among the most recognizable icons in the world, a design that has come to symbolize the youthful exuberance of America. Countless variations have been released over the decades, but the enduring classic – which has been used as a logo on the company's cans – is the curved green glass vessel designed by the Root Glass Company of Terre Haute, Indiana, and introduced in 1915. A Coca-Cola dispenser was later designed by the famous American industrial designer Raymond Loewy.

A "Coke" variation of the famous corporate logo

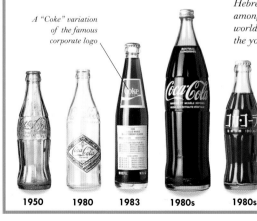

1950 **1980** **1983** **1980s** **1980s** **1992**

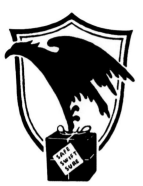

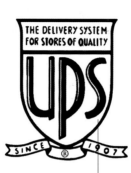

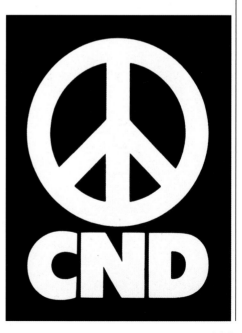

UPS 1920s–61

United Parcel Service developed its first shield logo in the 1920s, using the image of an eagle carrying a package labeled "Safe, Swift, Sure." This was simplified in 1937 to a shield outline containing the company initials. In 1961, the current logo was born, the work of Paul Rand. He shortened the shield, added a rectangular package, and clarified the lettering. The key to good design, he explained, was "taking the essence of something that is already there and enhancing its meaning by putting it into a form everyone can identify with."

The shield symbolizes integrity and quality

CND 1958

When Gerald Holtom designed what has become the symbol for the British Campaign for Nuclear Disarmament, he was told that it would never catch on. It has since been adopted as the universal image of peace. Designed originally for the Direct Action Committee Against Nuclear War, it works on two levels: it is semaphore for "N" and "D", and it is a self-portrait. Holtom explained: "I drew myself, the representative of an individual in despair, with hands outstretched outwards and downwards in the manner of Goya's peasant before the firing squad."

McDONALD'S

The famous McDonald's Golden Arches logo was introduced in 1962. It was created by Jim Schindler to resemble new arch-shaped signs on the sides of the McDonald's restaurants. He merged the two golden arches together to form the famous "M" logo that is now recognized throughout the world as the McDonald's trademark. Schindler's work was a development of the stylized "v" logo sketched by Fred Turner, which was conceived as a more stylish corporate symbol than the Speedee chef character that had previously been used. The McDonald's name was added to the Golden Arches logo in 1968.

McDonald's restaurant, Ipswich, England

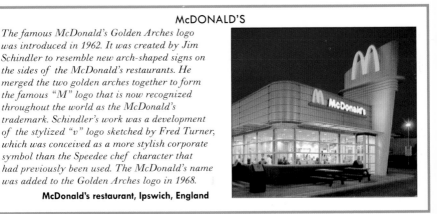

olivetti

Olivetti 1970

Like Sony, Olivetti eschews a corporate symbol, instead using the letters of its name as a logo. Devised by Walter Ballmer, this latest logo, with its rounded, lower-case letters, has evolved from three earlier designs, dating back to a 1934 version by X. Schawinsky.

SNCF 1970

Established in 1938, the French railway SNCF (Société Nationale des Chemins de Fer) has made two significant redesigns of its corporate image. The example shown here dates from 1970, before which the interwoven letters "SNF" were framed by the "C." Updated by Roger Tallon in 1985, a lighter, more fluid-looking logo emerged, based on the italicized outline of its letters.

SONY

Sony 1973

The visual simplicity of the Sony logo is pivotal to its design. Easy to
understand and pronounce, the name is readable in any language and
immediately recognizable. The name derives from the Latin *sonus*,
meaning "sound," and also recalls the English word "sonny," a term
of endearment for a small boy. The design of the logo has been
modified only minimally since 1957, when the strokes of the letters
were lighter and more expanded. The version shown here is from
1973, since when it has remained the same.

*The thick letters of
the Sony logotype
always appear in
a single color*

*Apple's image-only
logo has broken the
conventional rules of
computer industry
corporate imagery*

Apple 1984

The American company
Apple was the first
computer firm not to use
its name as its corporate
identity. The idea of
selling a computer under
the name and image of
a fruit was conceived by
Californian Steve Jobs
and his colleagues (even
"Macintosh" is the name of an
American apple variety). The motif
of a multicolored apple with a bite
taken out of it is a reference to the
biblical story of Adam and Eve, in
which the apple represents the
fruit of the Tree of Knowledge.

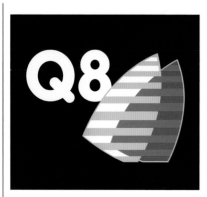

Q8 1986

In a bid to expand its retail petroleum business into the international market, Kuwait Petroleum took the radical step of completely changing the name of its subsidiary company, Gulf Oil. Gulf became Q8 in 1986, based on the English pronunciation of Kuwait. Its symbol of twin sails refers to traditional Kuwaiti trading ships, and the bright color combination is intended to improve the visibility of the gas stations in the dark. The new identity was created by Wolff Olins.

ICI 1987

When Nobel and three other large British chemical companies merged to form Imperial Chemical Industries in 1926, the existing black and orange Nobel roundel was adopted by the new company. It has been updated several times since, most notably in 1987, when the corporate identity design group Wolff Olins introduced the clean, modern combination of white letters against a blue background. The full name is now used only occasionally; otherwise, the company is universally identifiable by its initials.

The underlining waves are now smoother than in earlier versions

Here the logo Swoosh is reversed on the right-hand shoe

Nike 1989

The Nike logo is a classic case of a company gradually simplifying its corporate identity as its fame increases. The company's first logo appeared in 1971, when the word "Nike," the Greek goddess of victory, was printed in orange over the outline of the Swoosh, its mark of positivity. Used as a motif on sports shoes since the 1970s, this Swoosh is now so recognizable that the company name itself has become a superfluous addition. The solid, orange Swoosh was registered as a trademark in 1995.

Barcelona Olympic Games 1992

In 1988, José M. Trías, professor of design and director of Quod Design Company, won a competition that had been launched to select the symbol and logotype for the 1992 Olympic Games in Barcelona. The apparently abstract image above the words "Barcelona '92" is based on the stylized form of a leaping human figure. It faces the right, following the flow of the text, and expresses dynamism, victory, and joy. A shadow has been included to give a sense of height. The five interlocking Olympic rings were designed in 1913 by Pierre de Coubertin, each ring representing one of the five competing continents.

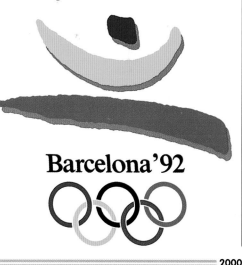

Barcelona'92

MAGAZINE COVERS

BEFORE THE 1930s, THE MAJORITY of magazines featured art illustrations rather than photographs on their covers. But during World War II, designers began to fully realize the power of the photographic image. Often used for political manipulation, pictures such as those showcased by the photojournalism magazine *Picture Post* had enormous impact. After the war, there was a boom in the market for women's journals; this was largely fashion led and started a trend, which continues today, for glossy, color cover shots of glamorous models. The advent of desktop publishing in the 1980s enabled designers to create pages on screen and to experiment with unusual typefaces. In some cases, the creative presentation of type and the frank content of the text make the cover lines as eye-catching as the image itself.

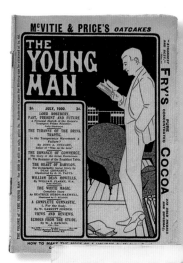

Magazines 1900–10

Figaro Illustré is a fine example of Art Nouveau design. It features the abstract floral motifs and organic forms typical of the French style. Elements of this style were adopted by Edward Penfield, who illustrated this edition of *Collier's*. Penfield was an influential figure in the evolution of the American art poster – a new genre of advertising that was typified by bold, flat colors and simple design. *The Young Man*, counterpart to the popular Victorian publication *The Young Woman*, shows elements of the Arts and Crafts style, the predecessor to European Art Nouveau.

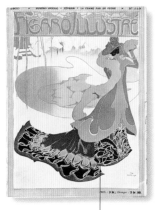

Abstract floral patterns were popular in French Art Nouveau graphics

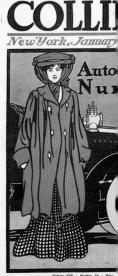

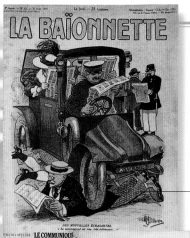

Magazines 1910s

There are several subjects that, when featured on the
cover of a magazine, are guaranteed to attract a readership.
Among these are political satire and the lifestyles of the
fashionable. The French publication *La Baïonnette* is a prime
example of the first, while *Millions* and *Every Week*, with
their cover images of chic women, demonstrate the second.
In early magazines, it was the illustration rather than the
words that conveyed the title's content. It was not really
until the 1980s that cover lines became equally as influential.

The cartoon style of La
Baïonnette *was influenced
by the popular weekly*
L'Assiette au Beurre

*The lifestyles of the
rich, fashionable, and
famous continued to
attract attention
through the decades*

*The classic Roman
alphabet contrasts
with the florid Art
Nouveau typefaces*

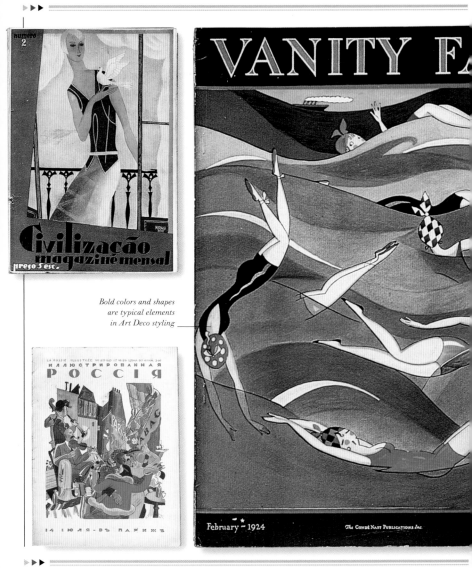

*Bold colors and shapes
are typical elements
in Art Deco styling*

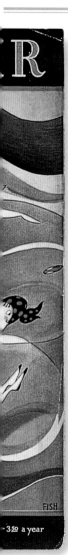

FISH

-3½⁰ a year

Magazines 1920s

The Art Deco style takes its name from the seminal *Paris Exposition Internationale des Arts Décoratifs et Industriels Modernes*, held in 1925. The style was quickly adopted worldwide and to such an extent that national origin is often difficult to identify. All of the magazines shown here demonstrate the combination of cubist and modernist elements with a bold use of color and stylized forms, which were hallmarks of the Art Deco style in the graphic arts. The images promote the glamorous high-living of the 1920s.

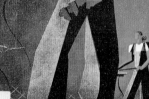

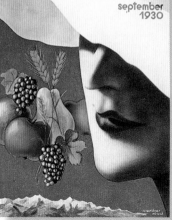

die neue linie

september 1930

Magazines 1930s

The Spanish Civil War turned Spain into a battleground of rival ideologies. Great political art grew from the conflict, in the form of literature, posters, and magazines. The propagandist cover of *Blanco y Negro* celebrates women's wartime role in industry. Germany continued to be a center for design excellence, exemplified by the assimilation of the Bauhaus school, and by a stream of great designers such as Herbert Bayer (see p.361), who was responsible for this beautiful cover of *die neue linie*.

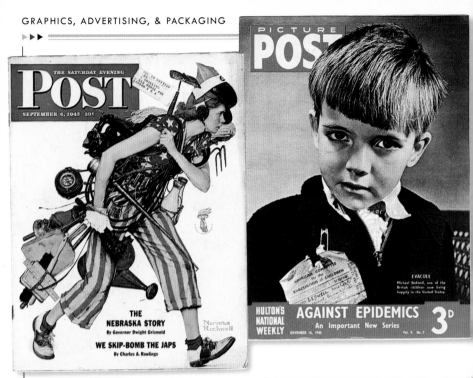

Magazines 1940s

World War II dominated design
in the 1940s, and is the subject of
both the covers shown here. Like
Blanco y Negro (see p.379), the witty
cover of *Saturday Evening Post*,
created by Norman Rockwell, pays
tribute to women war workers. Both
women hold a monkey wrench; but
Rockwell's woman, dressed in the
American flag, struggles with the
tools of many trades, from milk
delivery to nursing. *Picture Post* was
one of the first magazines to feature
photography – inside and out.

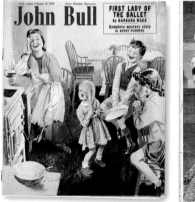

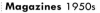
VOGUE

Holidays abroad :
where to go, what to pack

Magazines 1950s

American *Vogue* was
established in the early
1890s, followed by
the British and French
versions in 1916 and
1920 respectively. The
early covers showed
a commitment to
contemporary art
movements; but from the
1950s, color photographs
of the latest *haute couture*
fashions were increasingly
popular. This copy of the
photojournalism title *Look*
shows a grid of famous faces
that repeats the squares
of the masthead.

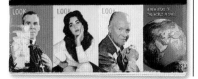

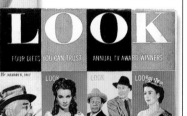

*The front cover of
Vogue has long been
associated with style
and glamour*

▶ ▶ ▶

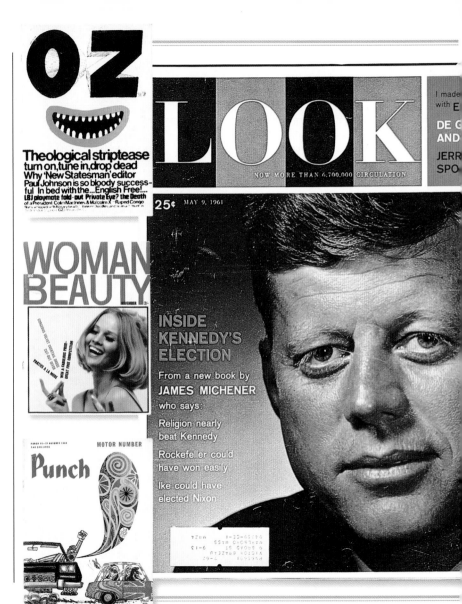

OZ

Theological striptease
turn on, tune in, drop dead
Why 'New Statesman' editor
Paul Johnson is so bloody successful. In bed with the...English Free!...
LBJ playmate fold-out **Private Eye**? the Death
of a President. Colin Marchmen & Malcolm X - Rupert Congo

WOMAN
BEAUTY

Punch MOTOR NUMBER

LOOK
NOW MORE THAN 6,700,000 CIRCULATION

25¢ MAY 9, 1961

I made
with E

DE G
AND

JERR
SPO

**INSIDE
KENNEDY'S
ELECTION**

From a new book by
JAMES MICHENER
who says:

Religion nearly
beat Kennedy

Rockefeller could
have won easily

Ike could have
elected Nixon

Magazines 1960s

Among the many underground publications that appeared in the 1960s was *OZ* magazine. Along with contemporaries such as Milton Glaser (see p.36), *OZ*'s designer Martin Sharp was instrumental in setting new standards in graphic design. Their experiments with typography even rubbed off on more conventional magazines like *Woman and Beauty*. While photographs were favored by news magazines like *Look*, *Time*, and *Paris Match*, the satirical journal *Punch* continued to use illustrations.

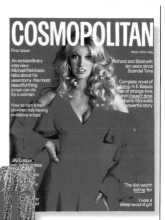

Magazines 1970s

By the 1970s, as more magazines appeared on the newsstands, sales became heavily reliant on an arresting cover image. The grainy, tinted photograph used on this edition of *Vanity Fair* demonstrates a technique favored by designers in the 1970s, which was intended to give a sense of realism. *Cosmopolitan*, launched in its present form in the US in 1965, is now an internationally successful title. Shown here, the first British issue prefigures the style of women's magazine covers of the 1980s – strong, vivid, and unmistakably confident.

▶ ▶ ▶

Magazines 1980s

From 1981 to 1986, graphic designer Neville Brody (see p.367) was responsible for the groundbreaking British style and music magazine *The Face*. Like Peter Saville (see p.388), Brody was influenced by the chaotic typography of Punk. He manipulated new and existing typefaces to create a unique visual language that challenged the editorial content of the text. Although *The Face* had a mixed readership, it was aimed more at men than women. *Vogue* took advantage of a gap in the market for a fashion-led men's magazine and launched *Hommes*, presaging the 1990s' craze for men's magazines.

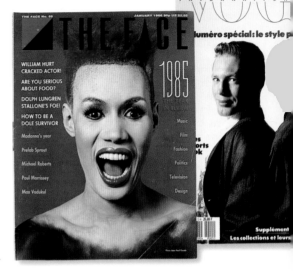

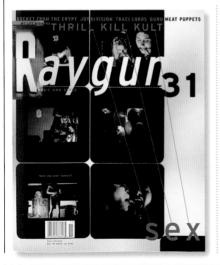

Magazines 1990s

Over the past decade, Terry Jones' *i-D* magazine and others, such as *Raygun*, have challenged the most basic concepts of magazine design, eschewing the grid (on which designers lay images and text), in favor of a seemingly random, anarchic

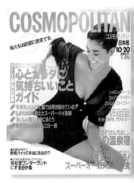

approach to layout. Desktop publishing has meant that designers can create pages on screen and are able to make immediate changes to typography, rather than sending corrections to a typesetter. The ability to manipulate and overlay type directly has resulted in the image almost taking second place to the text in magazines.

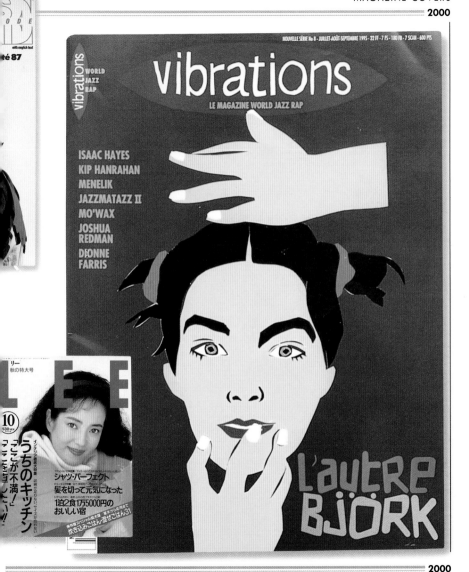

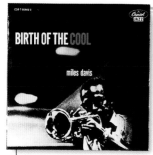

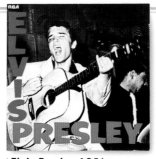

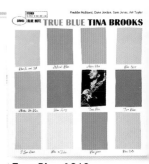

Birth of the Cool 1956

Amran Avakian created the atmospheric image on this record sleeve for *Birth of the Cool* by Miles Davis, released by Capitol Records. The black-and-white photograph is the perfect vehicle for cultivating the ultra-cool persona of this 1950s' jazz giant.

Elvis Presley 1956

The sleeve of Elvis Presley's eponymous first album, produced by RCA, captures the young "King of Rock 'n' Roll" during a live performance. Presley's pose and the red-and-green lettering that spells out his name were echoed two decades later on The Clash's *London Calling* (see p.388).

True Blue 1960

Blue Note Records is responsible for some of the greatest album cover concepts ever devised. This sleeve for Tina Brooks' album is a witty example by Reid Miles. Each song contains the word "blue" in its title, and each is represented by a rectangle in a different shade of blue.

RECORD COVERS

ALTHOUGH POPULAR MUSIC has been available on record since the beginning of the century, it is only since the 1950s that the design of record sleeves has emerged as an art form. The American record company Blue Note was one of the first to develop an apparent design brand, an idea taken to austere lengths in the 1980s by the British label Factory Records. In the 1990s, the significance of covers to the potential purchaser is recognized by all major record companies, who employ teams of designers to create competitive packaging for releases on vinyl, tape cassette, and compact disc.

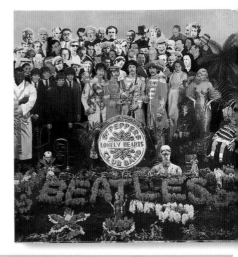

1900

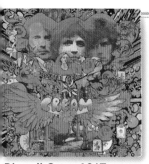

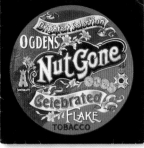

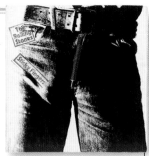

Disraeli Gears 1967

Martin Sharp's design for Cream's album combines peacocks, flowers, and clocks – all surrealist icons of drug-induced hallucination and 1960s psychedelic album illustration. In their midst float the band members' heads, photographed by Bob Whitaker. The album was released by Polydor.

Ogdens' Nut Gone Flake 1968

The British band the Small Faces released this album for the company Immediate Records. Created by P. Brown, the illustration on the sleeve resembles a circular can of tobacco. Developing this theme, the compact disc version of Ogdens' Nut Gone Flake was later released in a can.

Sticky Fingers 1971

Early editions of this sexually suggestive album cover for the Rolling Stones' *Sticky Fingers* incorporated a real, functioning zipper, while the back of the sleeve shows the rear view of the same denim-clad figure. The concept and photography were created by Andy Warhol.

Sgt. Pepper's Lonely Hearts Club Band 1967

Designed by Pop artists Peter Blake and Jann Haworth, this celebrated sleeve for the Beatles' seminal album, released by Parlophone, is probably the most famous ever created. The host of stars was made up of life-size cardboard cutouts and wax models. The famous figures included Marilyn Monroe, W.C. Fields, Oscar Wilde, and Mae West.

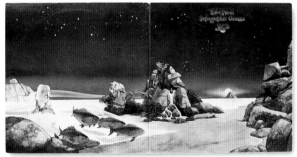

Tales from Topographic Oceans 1972

This fantasy landscape for the triple-fold cover of the album by supergroup Yes is by British artist Roger Dean. Using illustrations of famous English rocks, including those at both Stonehenge and Land's End, Dean has created a space-age, dreamlike plane with an infinite background. The album was released by Atlantic Records.

▶ ▶ ▶

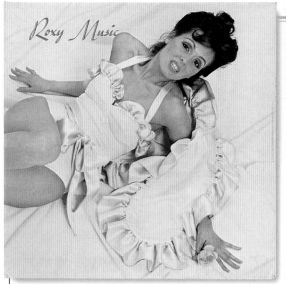

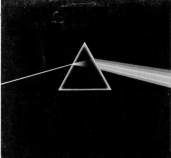

Dark Side of the Moon 1973

Released by EMI Records, this Pink Floyd album was one of the most successful of the 1970s. Its cover is a product of the influential British design group Hipgnosis. George Hardie produced the slick, enigmatic image of a light beam splitting into seven colors as it passes through a prism.

Roxy Music 1972

The term "Art Rock" was coined for Roxy Music, famed for the arty, image-conscious sophistication of their music and personal style. Released by Island Records, this was the first album to contain credits for art (Nicholas de Ville), clothes, makeup, and hair (Anthony Price), as well as photography (Karl Stoecker), and "cover concept" (Bryan Ferry).

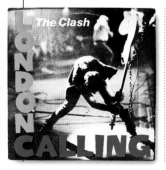

London Calling 1979

Designer Ray Lowry makes overt typographic and photographic references to Elvis Presley's album of 1956 (see p.386) in his sleeve design for the punk rock band The Clash. The powerful photograph by Penny Smith immortalizes vocalist/guitarist Joe Strummer in the act of smashing his guitar.

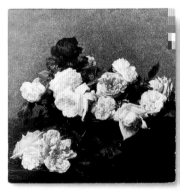

Power Corruption and Lies 1983

Inspired by the painting *Roses* by Henri Fantin-Latour (1836–1904), Peter Saville composed the cover for New Order's album *Power Corruption and Lies* for Manchester's Factory Records.

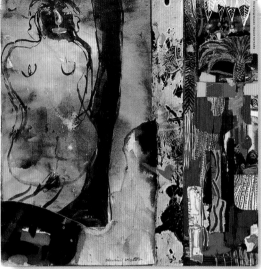

House Tornado 1988

Graphic artist Vaughan Oliver is renowned for his ability to reflect the style of music in the design of its accompanying record sleeve. He established the design studio 23 Envelope, known as v23 after 1988, to create packaging for the British record company 4AD. He designed this album sleeve for the group Throwing Muses, showing painterly influences.

Blue Lines 1991

Designed by Michael Nash Associates, this CD insert features the flame logo that has come to identify Massive Attack albums. The title *Blue Lines* appears in such tiny lettering it looks almost like a copyright mark.

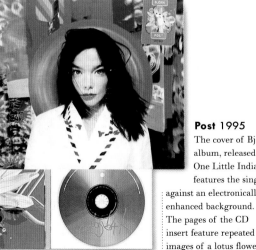

Post 1995

The cover of Björk's album, released on One Little Indian, features the singer against an electronically enhanced background. The pages of the CD insert feature repeated images of a lotus flower.

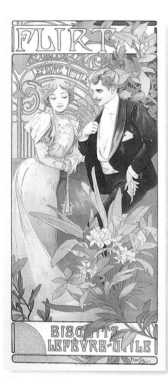

POSTERS 1900–19

THE DEVELOPMENT OF LITHOGRAPHIC PRINTING in the second half of the 19th century heralded the start of modern poster art. Work by Frenchmen Jules Chéret (1836–1932) and Henri de Toulouse-Lautrec (1864–1901) formed the background to the new art form. By the turn of the century, the most important movement in poster design was Art Nouveau; but William Morris and the Arts and Crafts Movement also had a marked impact on the two main centers of design – Glasgow, home to the Glasgow School, and Vienna, birthplace of the Vienna Secession.

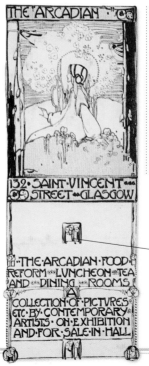

The Arcadian c.1906
During the 1890s and 1900s, the so-called Glasgow School was centered around Charles Rennie Mackintosh, and included Jessie M. King, who designed this poster for the Arcadian Tea Rooms. The Glasgow School took recognizable Art Nouveau elements and added rigid geometry and compositional decoration.

These stylized floral motifs are typical of Art Nouveau

Flirt c.1895
The Czech artist Alphonse Mucha is the most famous and flamboyant exponent of Art Nouveau poster design. His posters featured beautiful women, often with long flowing hair, framed by floral decoration and organic lines. Mucha's break came in Paris in 1894, when he designed a hugely successful life-size poster for Sarah Bernhardt. This example is one of many advertising posters he produced.

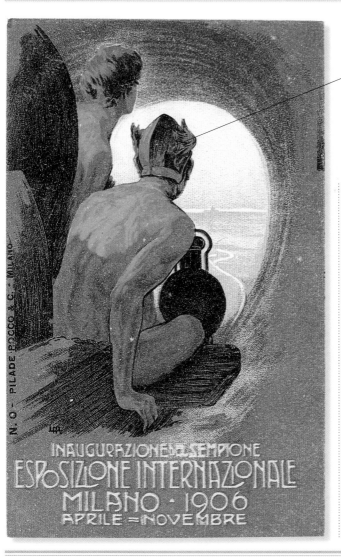

The figure of Mercury is identified by his winged helmet

Inauguration of the Simplon Tunnel 1906

Italian designer Leopoldo Metlicovitz (1868–1944) created this poster to mark the opening of the Simplon Tunnel at the Milan International Exhibition. The winged-helmeted figure of Mercury, the god of speed, sits at the front of the train as it is about to leave the tunnel. The poster's message is that "even Mercury finds it faster to take the train!" It typifies Metlicovitz's work, with the painterly figure of a muscular athletic young man, the allegorical subject matter, and subdued brown tones.

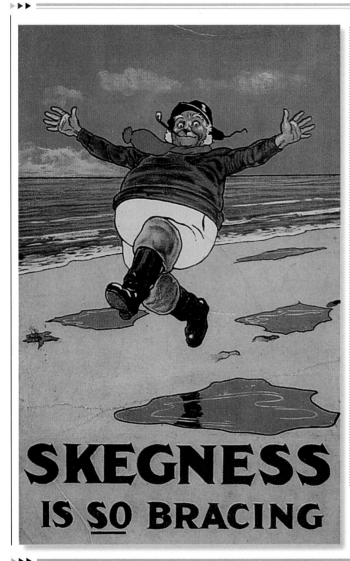

Skegness is so Bracing 1909

The growth of the British railroad at the start of the century is responsible for some quality posters commissioned by London Transport, various railroad companies, and tourist resorts served by the railroad. This famous poster by prolific graphic designer John Hassall (1868–1948) extols the virtues of the seaside resort of Skegness. Like many other seaside destinations, off-season was harder to sell; so Hassall resorts to the invigorating effect of the cold, fresh sea air. His comic image is of a portly gentleman skipping along the beach in Wellington boots, scarf, and hat. The poster was so successful that Hassall produced different versions of it. It is, in effect, a translation into English design of the French entertainment posters of the 1890s, typified by the work of Toulouse-Lautrec.

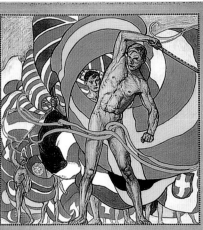

JEUX OLYMPIQUES
ᔕ STOCKHOLM 1912 ᔕ
LE 29 JUIN — 22 JUILLET

A. BÖRTZELLS TR. A. B. STOCKHOLM

Stockholm Olympic Games 1912

Throughout the century, the Olympic Games have given both athletes and poster designers the opportunity to prove their prowess. In this version, A. Börtzells places a young naked man center stage (his dignity preserved by a well-positioned streamer) swirling the Swedish flag above his head. He is followed by a host of naked men with undulating national flags.

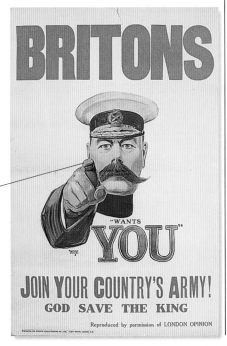

BRITONS

"WANTS"
YOU

JOIN YOUR COUNTRY'S ARMY!
GOD SAVE THE KING

Reproduced by permission of LONDON OPINION

The extreme perspective of the poster draws the viewer into the poster

Your Country Needs You 1914

During World War I, many governments made use of posters to aid the war effort. This one, designed by Alfred Leete (1882–1933), gave rise to many imitations, including a recruitment poster for the US Army by J.M. Flagg (1877–1960). Leete's poster features the inescapable gaze of Lord Kitchener, the Secretary of War.

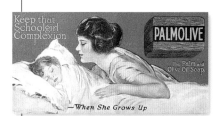

Palmolive early 1920s

This poster exemplifies the technique of selling a product with a slogan. American designer Clarence Underwood (1871–1929) was commissioned by J.B. Watson, head of the giant Walter Thompson agency, to produce a series of posters around the same slogan: "Keep that Schoolgirl Complexion." Watson had done extensive research into finding slogans that triggered the "buy impulse."

POSTERS 1920–39

THERE ARE AS MANY SCHOOLS and movements in poster design as there are in painting, and from 1920 to 1939 they abounded: Bauhaus, De Stijl, futurism, cubism, to name but four. Yet we should be wary of categorizing designers by movement. Certainly, the designer E. McKnight Kauffer, author of *The Art of the Poster* (1924), complained that the public placed "cubist" or "futurist" tags on anything modern. The majority of the posters produced during these two decades were designed to promote commercial products or cultural events; but propaganda pieces, including the El Lissitsky poster shown here, continued to appear in Russia and elsewhere to support particular causes such as the Spanish Civil War.

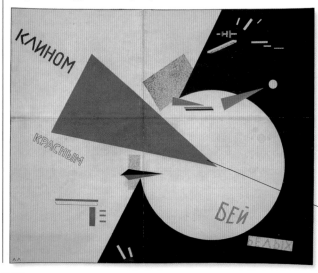

Beat the Whites with the Red Wedge c.1920

El Lissitsky's famous Soviet propaganda poster for the Red Army is an icon of Constructivist design. The poster is typical of Lissitsky's style: simple elements; sharp, dynamic diagonals contrasting with circles; and a bold use of limited color, in this case red, white, and black.

The Red Wedge represents the Red Army overcoming "White" opposition during the 1918–20 civil war

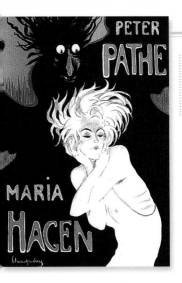

Hagen-Pathé 1920s

German designer, painter, theater set designer, and illustrator Walter Schnackenberg produced a number of high-quality posters, of which this atmospheric theater poster is typical.

Jyldis c.1925

Josef Binder (1898–1972) was an Austrian designer described in his day as "the biggest talent and the greatest hope of Austrian graphic arts." His highly individual, aggressively modern style was hugely successful. The basis of his theory was "everything moves faster today; we need the same speed to transmit the message effectively."

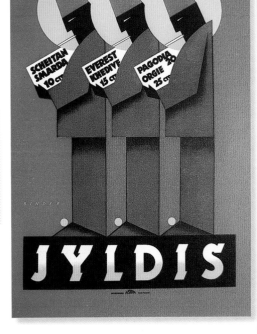

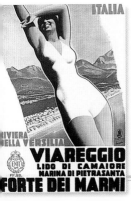

Forte dei Marmi 1930s

One of Italy's lesser-known poster artists, Gino Bocasile designed both the Internationale Mailänder Mustermesse poster (see p.359) and this travel work for the resort of Viareggio. The latter is an early example of using sexual imagery to sell.

▶ ▶ ▶

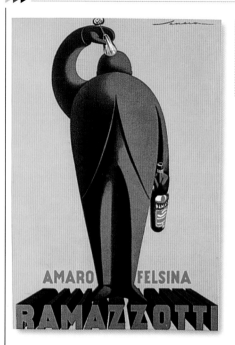

Ramazzotti 1930s

Federico Seneca (1891–1976), one of the most sought-after poster designers of his day, often featured stylized, Deco-style cartoon characters like this creation. Important clients included Buitoni pasta and Perugina chocolates.

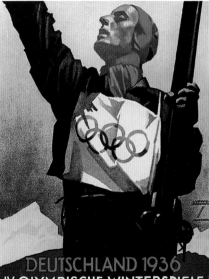

Winter Olympics 1936

Ludwig Hohlwein is the greatest German poster designer of the century, and his work prior to World War I has hardly been equaled. Hohlwein's style remained unchanged – usually one or two figures set against large areas of color, and the lettering confined to a rectangle. Sadly, it is for his last works, celebrating the Aryan race, that he is commonly remembered.

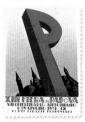

Futurist poster stamp 1931

Through their experiments in typography, the futurists had a direct influence on poster design. Their approach has been called "painterly typography": a visual onomatopoeia, where words look like their meaning. So *Speed* might be in italics, and **Shout** in bold type. Stamp-sized posters, allowed advertising through the mail.

Spanish Civil War 1936–37

The Spanish Civil War attracted the attention of artists and intellectuals the world over, and saw groups of designers collaborating in Madrid and Barcelona on the design of posters in support of the Republican cause. Many of them made use of photography rather than illustrations. This poster shows Constructivist influences with the powerful fist grasping a laurel wreath and sheltering the people in the foreground.

The fist is an inclusive graphic device, but also a symbol of strength

POR EL BIENESTAR, LA FELICIDAD Y LA LIBERTAD DEL PUEBLO ESPAÑOL, LUCHA EL EJERCITO POPULAR

SUBSECRETARIA DE PROPAGANDA

Shell 1937

E. McKnight Kauffer was one of several designers commissioned to produce posters for the Shell oil company in the 1930s. The poster shown is a good example of Kauffer's work, with modernist imagery, bold graphics, stark color contrast, and reductivist typography. The images suggest smooth movement. Kauffer devised the figure that was used throughout the campaign.

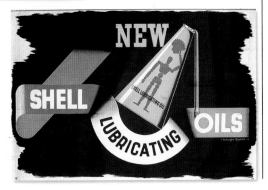

POSTERS 1940–59

DURING WORLD WAR II, posters advertising products were replaced by those helping the war effort, be they recruitment appeals or vehicles for issuing information. Governments that commissioned these posters urgently wanted direct, effective messages, and so took the risk of employing and giving free reign to young modernist designers. The results were often controversial, but from this period comes some of the most creative poster designs. The gates were also opened for more inventive commercial advertising after the war was over.

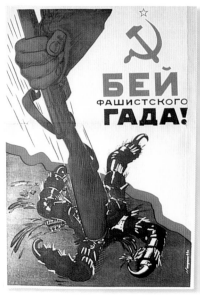

Kill the Fascist Reptile c.1940
Propaganda posters often lacked subtlety. This Soviet example shows the mighty arm of the red soldier smashing the enemy, here depicted as a swastika-shaped reptile. Symbols such as the hammer and sickle make the message easily identifiable.

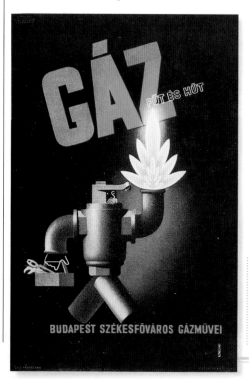

Budapest Gasworks 1940
This commercial poster makes effective use of color. Its focal point is the flame that forms the engineer's hand, and which illuminates the lettering above. It was designed by leading Hungarian graphic artist Georg Konecsni (1908–).

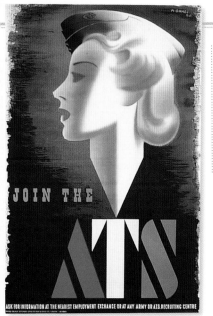

Join the ATS 1941

In his role as official war poster designer for Britain, Abram Games produced nearly 100 posters. This one is a good illustration of his personal maxim "maximum meaning, minimum means." It depicts a stylized profile of a glamorous woman soldier, with the simple message plastered across the bottom. The serifs that descend from the crossbar of the white letter "T" form the continuation of the woman's collar, and the post of the "T" suggests a tie.

7up family c.1945

This advertising poster portrays an archetypal American family enjoying the great outdoors. The fresh-faced beauty, wide smiles, relaxed attitude (the father is holding a fishing rod), and clear imagery present the drink as a healthy, refreshing product.

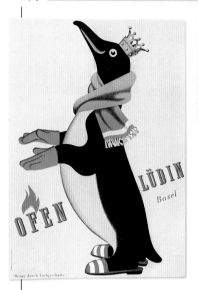

Ofen Lüdin 1949

One of Switzerland's most successful poster artists, Herbert
Leupin (1916–) first gained fame for his realistic commercial
advertising posters. However, after setting up his own studio in
1939, he developed a distinct style of illustration that earned
him commissions from both European and American clients.
Many of his posters were humorous, like this penguin
warming himself with a Lüdin company heater.

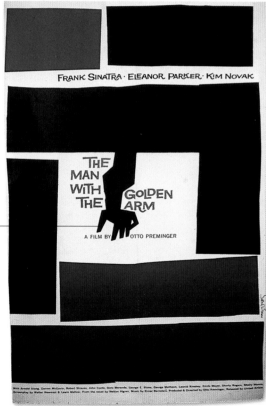

*Bass produced film
posters and titles,
combining type,
calligraphy, and
illustration*

The Man with the Golden Arm 1955

Saul Bass's poster for Otto
Preminger's film about a drug
addict marked a radical departure
in movie advertising. Instead
of depicting the storyline, the
jagged arm and stark imagery is
used to capture the film's essence.

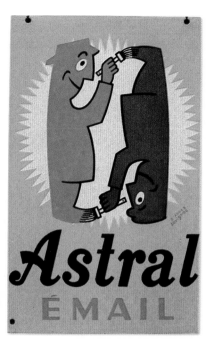

Astral Email 1955

Raymond Savignac was the master of the visual gag. His numerous posters, produced for clients around the world, are all characterized by their direct, simple, witty, and effective designs.

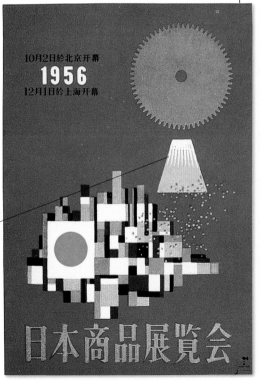

This cone shape represents a snow-capped Mount Fuji

Tokyo International Trade Fair 1956

Takashi Kono (1906–), who designed this poster, is one of the pioneers of modern Japanese graphic design. The simplified blocks of color incorporating the Japanese flag are reminiscent of 1950s' textile design.

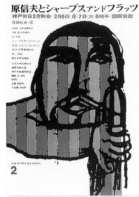

POSTERS 1960–79

THE PSYCHEDELIC ERA was one of the briefest, but most memorable, movements of this period. Its posters were designed for an exclusive audience with almost illegible lettering carrying the implied message "If you can't read it, it isn't for you." Psychedelia began on the West Coast of the US, but spread to Europe with the hippie movement. Elsewhere, Japanese designers were growing in international importance, being more willing than most to embrace new technology. In the 1970s, this gave designers far greater freedom through increased control of typesetting and image reproduction.

Kobe Workers' Music Council 1961

Tadanori Yokoo was one of the many innovative graphic artists to emerge from training at the Nippon Design Center, which was founded in 1959. His cultural and commercial posters of the 1960s and '70s drew on both traditional Japanese and Western imagery.

Arnhem Internationale Filmweek 1961

This was one of several screenprinted posters created by Dutchman Dick Elffers (1910–) to promote the Holland Festival of 1961. They featured abstract masked faces rendered with blocks of solid color. This particular example, advertising the Arnhem film week, displays a mixture of crude typography including some hand-rendered lettering. In addition to his work as a graphic artist and painter, Elffers taught at the Rotterdam Academy, and was an architect and set designer.

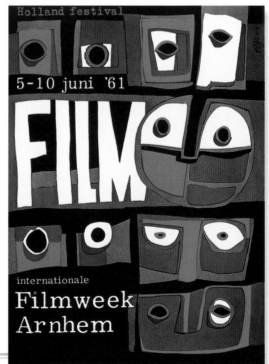

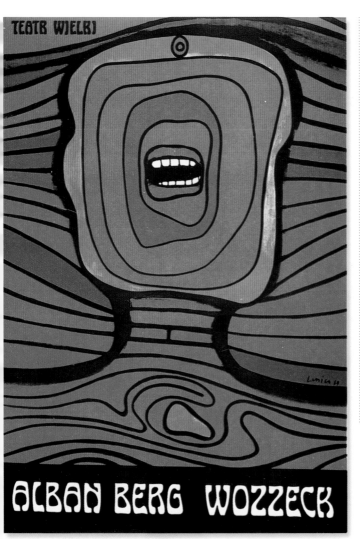

Wozzeck 1964
Jan Lenica's famed
poster for the opera
Wozzeck makes
direct reference to
the 1893 painting
The Scream by
the Norwegian
Expressionist artist
Edvard Munch
(1863–1944). In
both works, the
focal point of
the image is
a screaming
mouth, surrounded
by resonating
lines. Lenica,
a prodigiously
inventive Polish
designer, uses heavy
flowing lines that
divide the space
into solid bands
of color: in this
instance the whole
poster is designed
in vibrant shades of
red, split by varying
thicknesses of
black line.

▶ ▶ ▶

►►►

Captain Beefheart at the Fillmore 1966

The psychedelic artist Wes Wilson borrowed ideas from a variety of sources and fused them together into a style of his own. Using images and lettering from the Vienna Seccession (including the flowing hair), Art Nouveau ornamentation, and drug-inspired coloring, he created a language that was aimed at an exclusive "underground" audience. The swirling, multicolored lettering is barely legible.

The rich patterning evokes designs from the first years of the century

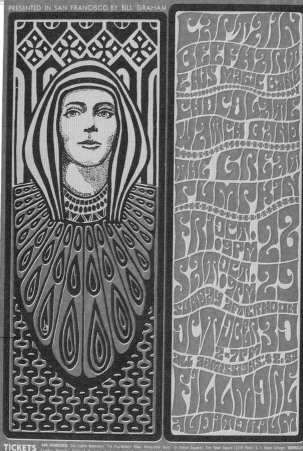

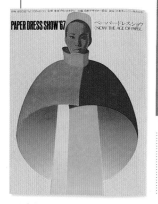

Paper Dress Show 1967

Designed by Hirokatsu Hijikata, this poster advertises a Japanese fashion show presenting dresses made of paper. It combines a photographic image (the woman's face) with artwork. The design makes striking use of bold graduated colors to evoke the woman's dress and cape.

►►►

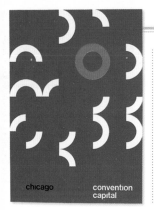

Chicago 1968

John Rieben's (1935–) poster is clearly influenced by the Swiss magazine *Neue Grafik* ("New Graphic Design"), which was launched in 1958 by Josef Müller-Brockmann and others. Its designers championed compositions based on grid systems, lower-case sans serif typography, and unornamented images.

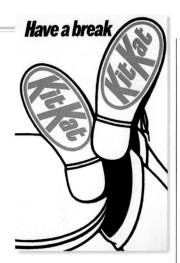

KitKat 1970s

The success of this commercial poster for a well-known chocolate bar relies on the power of the brand-name. Many things are suggested but not shown in the design. The owner of the feet is not shown, the viewer must imagine him. Likewise, the product itself does not appear, although the typography and color on the sole of the shoe is the same as the packaging on the bar of chocolate.

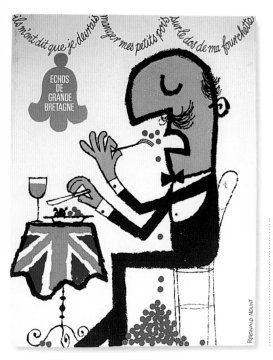

Echos of Great Britain 1970s

Reginald Mount was one of a number of graphic artists who made his name with work commissioned by the British Ministry of Information during World War II. After the war he produced many commercial and public service posters, including some for the "Keep Britain Tidy" campaign. Humorous, cartoon-like images, sometimes with Surrealist elements, are typical of his style.

1979

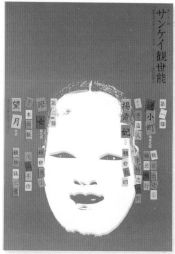

Noh 1981

Ikko Tanaka's posters are renowned for their subtle use of color; and while they are distinctly Japanese, they do show some influences of Western design. This performance poster is one of many he produced for the Kanze Noh drama. Here, calligraphic boxes suggest bunched hair.

Exhibition poster for Musée de l'Affiche 1981

This poster by the French design collective Grapus combines elements of three political philosophies: capitalism – the image of Mickey Mouse, and one eye made up of the US colors; fascism, suggested by the Hitler moustache and flick of bangs; and communism, represented by the hammer and sickle. Grapus was founded in 1970 by Pierre Bernard (1942–), Gérard-Paris Clavel (1943–), and Francois Miehe (1942–) to produce "social, political, and cultural images."

POSTERS 1980–99

DESPITE VAST SUMS OF MONEY being spent on television advertising campaigns, commercial companies and government agencies have by no means abandoned the poster as a direct and effective means of communication. The computer plays an increasingly important role in poster design, and new programs allow image manipulation to a degree not dreamed of even a decade ago. The resulting work may mix any combination of photography, illustration, and typography.

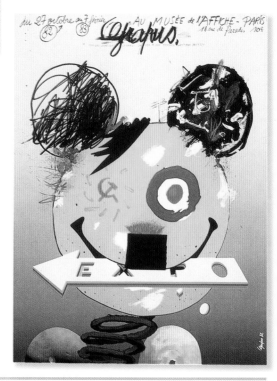

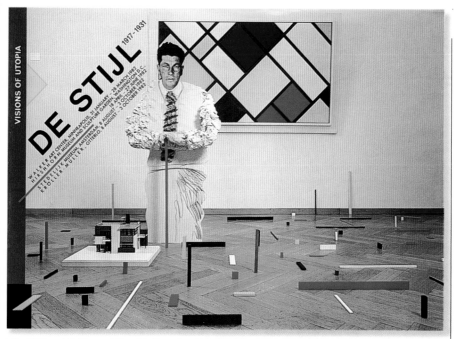

DE STIJL 1917-1931

WALKER ART CENTER, MINNEAPOLIS, 31 JANUARY - 28 MARCH 1982
HIRSHHORN MUSEUM AND SCULPTURE GARDEN, WASHINGTON D.C.,
18 APRIL - 27 JUNE 1982
STEDELIJK MUSEUM, AMSTERDAM, 8 AUGUST - 1 AUGUST 1982
KRÖLLER-MÜLLER, OTTERLO, 8 AUGUST - 3 OCTOBER 1982

De Stijl exhibition at the Walker Art Center, Minneapolis 1982

By photographing a created "scene," Gert Dumbar broke all the conventions of museum poster design. It advertises an exhibition of the Dutch art movement De Stijl. The movement's originator, Theo van Doesburg, appears; and there are references to De Stijl's ideas, including placing the text at the same angle as the lines in the painting.

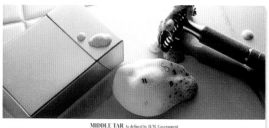

MIDDLE TAR As defined by H.M. Government
DANGER: Government Health WARNING: CIGARETTES CAN SERIOUSLY DAMAGE YOUR HEALTH

Benson and Hedges Shaved Pack 1985

The influential advertising campaign for Benson and Hedges cigarettes has featured a series of increasingly cryptic posters, of which this one, designed by Nigel Rose for the Collett Dickenson Pearce agency, is particularly successful. Although it is impossible to read the product's name (the letters have been shaved off the pack), the gold suggests it.

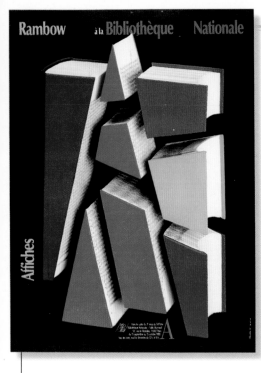

Rambow at the Bibliothèque Nationale 1987

This poster for an exhibition of Gunter Rambow's work was designed by the artist himself, and features a cut-up photograph of a book, rearranged to create a wedge shape that seems to split the book itself in half. Rambow, who typically employs photography and photomontage, is best known for his powerful political and social posters.

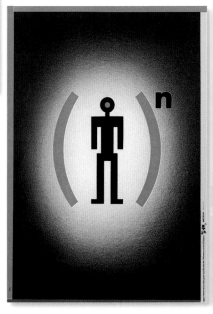

Bicentennial Exhibition for "The Human and The Citizens' Rights" 1989

Peret, born Pere Torrent, is a Spanish postmodernist designer. His work often consists of bold, simple graphics in strong colors. He has worked for many humanitarian organizations, including the Spanish Red Cross and Amnesty International. This simple, yet effective, poster plays on a mathematical equation putting a human pictogram in a bracket, multiplied to the power of "n," meaning humanity is all-important.

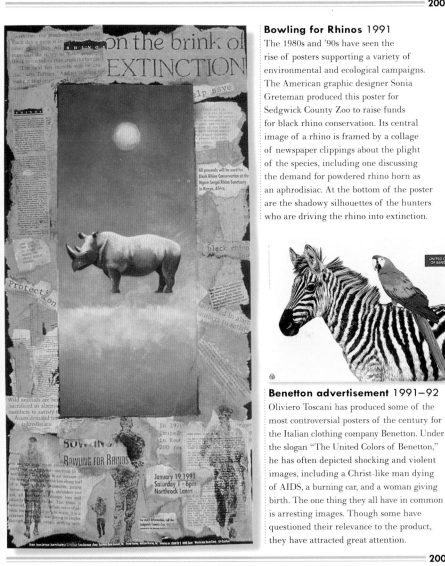

Bowling for Rhinos 1991

The 1980s and '90s have seen the rise of posters supporting a variety of environmental and ecological campaigns. The American graphic designer Sonia Greteman produced this poster for Sedgwick County Zoo to raise funds for black rhino conservation. Its central image of a rhino is framed by a collage of newspaper clippings about the plight of the species, including one discussing the demand for powdered rhino horn as an aphrodisiac. At the bottom of the poster are the shadowy silhouettes of the hunters who are driving the rhino into extinction.

Benetton advertisement 1991–92

Oliviero Toscani has produced some of the most controversial posters of the century for the Italian clothing company Benetton. Under the slogan "The United Colors of Benetton," he has often depicted shocking and violent images, including a Christ-like man dying of AIDS, a burning car, and a woman giving birth. The one thing they all have in common is arresting images. Though some have questioned their relevance to the product, they have attracted great attention.

PACKAGING 1900–09

UNLIKE MOST OTHER AREAS OF DESIGN, packaging can rarely be associated with individual designers. Instead, designs evolve with each new era: by 1900, shopping for groceries was changing from a traditional reliance on the grocer to recommend and wrap items to manufacturers' designs influencing choice. Many pack designs still reflected late 19th-century tastes, although toiletries and new brands were the exception, taking advantage of the flowing, organic style of the moment, Art Nouveau, to attract customers with a "modern" look.

This florid style was a hangover from the previous century

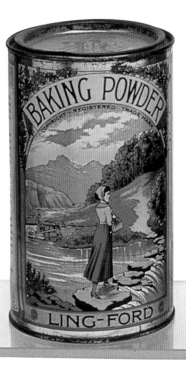

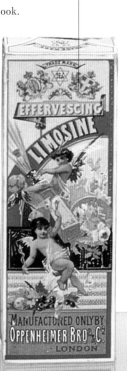

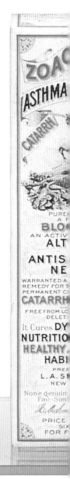

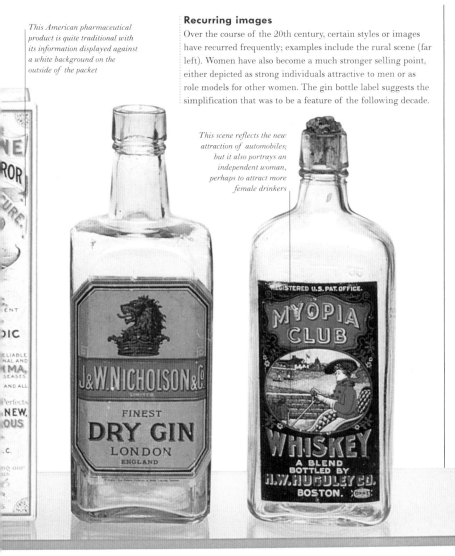

This American pharmaceutical product is quite traditional with its information displayed against a white background on the outside of the packet

Recurring images

Over the course of the 20th century, certain styles or images have recurred frequently; examples include the rural scene (far left). Women have also become a much stronger selling point, either depicted as strong individuals attractive to men or as role models for other women. The gin bottle label suggests the simplification that was to be a feature of the following decade.

This scene reflects the new attraction of automobiles; but it also portrays an independent woman, perhaps to attract more female drinkers

J&W.NICHOLSON&C?
LIMITED
FINEST
DRY GIN
LONDON
ENGLAND

REGISTERED U.S. PAT. OFFICE.
MYOPIA CLUB
WHISKEY
A BLEND
BOTTLED BY
H.W. HUBLEY CO.
BOSTON.

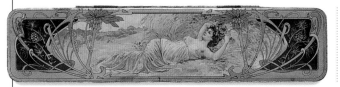

Le Furet corset

The stylish Art Nouveau graphics at either end of this corset box create a strong sense of refined elegance, echoing the figure's form.

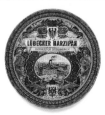

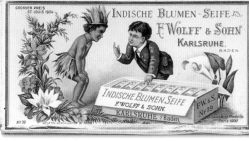

Lübecker marzipan

Somber colors and a picture of an industrial factory lend this box a heavy sense of the past. Two crests appear to give credence to the product.

Indische Blumen-Seife

The bright, eye-catching picture on this box of German Indian Flower soap illustrates the product quite literally. The luxuriantly detailed exotic flowers still reflect popular tastes of the late 19th century.

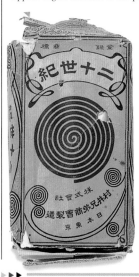

Soft pack cigarettes

At about this time, collectible pictorial cards became popular with cigarette companies as a promotional tool. The stiff cards helped to protect the cigarettes in the flimsy packs.

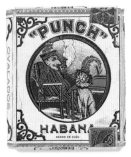

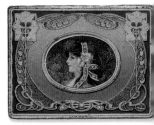

Turnwright's toffees

This gift-style box with its fashionable Art Nouveau graphics is an attempt to place these toffees in the same market as a box of chocolates.

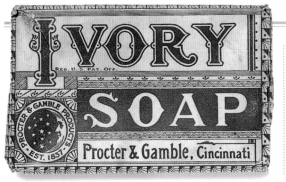

Ivory soap

The name "ivory" was first used for this soap by its American manufacturer Procter and Gamble in 1879. The traditional appearance of the monotone packaging remained quite constant until the company commissioned a utilitarian redesign in 1940 (see p.421).

Quality products

The arrival of individual, pre-wrapped, branded goods meant that for the first time the customer had to rely on the look of the manufacturer's packaging to suggest the freshness and quality of a product. Designs that appeared to change little were often meant to give the impression that a product was of a consistently good quality.

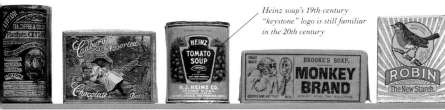

Heinz soup's 19th-century "keystone" logo is still familiar in the 20th century

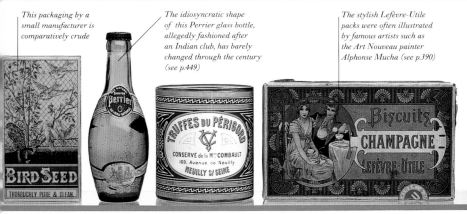

This packaging by a small manufacturer is comparatively crude

The idiosyncratic shape of this Perrier glass bottle, allegedly fashioned after an Indian club, has barely changed through the century (see p.449)

The stylish Lefèvre-Utile packs were often illustrated by famous artists such as the Art Nouveau painter Alphonse Mucha (see p.390)

PACKAGING 1910–19

WORLD WAR I ACCELERATED THE TREND toward individual packaging, for it was much easier to distribute and supply rations to the troops in small packets. The world was jolted into a new era by the war, and packaging reflected this. Many 19th-century brand labels were updated and, more importantly, better packaging techniques improved the possibilities of dispensing or resealing products. Art Nouveau was still popular until about 1915, its characteristic swirls and typography appearing on coffee labels and candy boxes.

Extraordinary claims

New household products for cleaning and washing made some extraordinary claims on their packaging: like those of Armour's Cleanser (below left). Reflecting this more pragmatic decade, the graphics are more ordered and controlled, with simple, straightforward colors and uncomplicated pictures.

This austere image reflects the practicality of the new era

This generic brand is typical of the off-the-shelf design packaging of the period

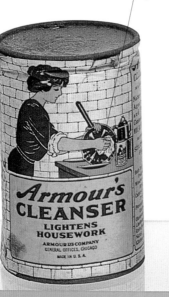

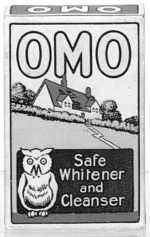

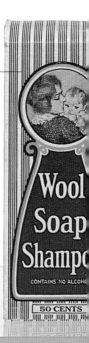

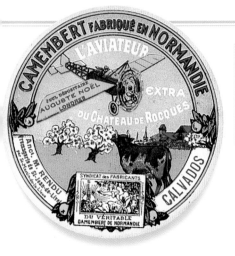

Camembert cheese

French Camembert cheese box labels traditionally depicted rural scenes or country maids. But this label reflects the world's new fascination with machinery and flight. The airplane skimming across this label is an exciting modern contrast to the image of a smiling dairy maid.

Packaging developments

By 1910, both the US and UK were producing aluminum foil; in 1908, a Swiss chemist had invented cellophane film. These new materials would revolutionize the way products could be sealed to retain their freshness, but it took time for them to become commonplace. More immediate were the advances made in resealing packages and dispensing the product.

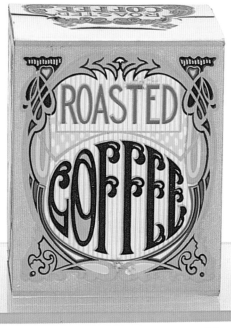

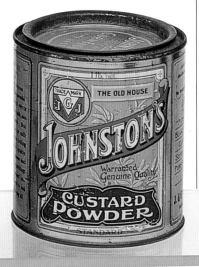

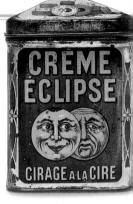

Crème Eclipse

Advertising came into its own as manufacturers jostled for the customer's attention. This can of string for tying packages would sit on the shop counter, its sides covered with advertisements, such as this one for Crème Eclipse boot polish.

Savon Tatiana

Images from nature were popular with exponents of Art Nouveau, as the snaking golden tendrils and buds on this French soap packet reveal. The embossed gold work and rich blue colors are particularly striking.

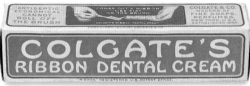

Colgate's ribbon dental cream

This toothpaste packet informs the user about the innovative and efficient nature of the product. Previously, tooth powder had been sold in a glazed pot or can; here, a cream is dispensed from a soft metal tube in a flat ribbon, making it more economical and preventing the toothpaste falling off the brush. Graphic instructions are included on the side of the packet.

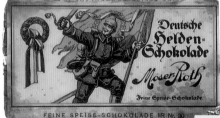

Chocolate wrappers

Commercially sold chocolate bars tasted so similar that the packaging had to attract the eye: this Vacantie wrapper (right), for instance, uses simple colors and looks elegant. By contrast, the German chocolate (above), which was distributed to troops during World War I, shows a patriotic image on a functional wrapper.

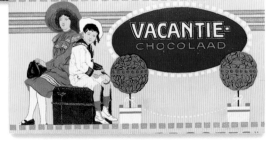

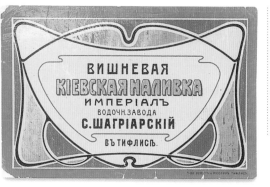

Cherry Kiev drink

This Russian beverage label, possibly for a schnapps drink, was manufactured by S. Shagriarskiy in Tbilisi. The simple pattern around the border has a strong Art Nouveau style and shows how much the popular style influenced all types of packaging internationally during this decade.

The side of this Horniman's cocoa packet illustrates the plantation where the product was grown

Exotic influences

Some brands, such as the talcum powder (bottom right), Horniman's cocoa (left), and the dates (bottom center) accentuated the setting of the product's origin or the mystique of the Far East. This set the brand apart from similar products and created an additional selling tool.

Lightweight cans gradually replaced many glazed pot containers and were especially popular for boot polish

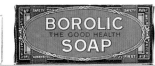

An elegant Art Nouveau design turns this packet of crystalized chestnuts into a sophisticated gift

Sprinkler tops were one of the new advances made in dispensing products

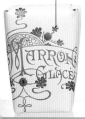

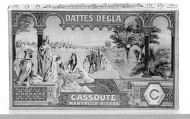

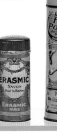

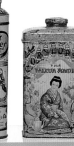

PACKAGING 1920–29

THE YEARS OF CHANGE after World War I continued into the 1920s as the number of servants in the home declined and the family unit reduced, encouraging a trend toward smaller pack sizes. Leisure time also increased, and with it came a new breed of snacks and "instant" packaged foods that saved time, such as shelled peas. A different style in packaging gradually emerged through the 1920s, with cleaner, fresher designs influenced by the popular, vivid colors and angular lines of the Art Deco movement.

This lettering shows the influence of modernist typefaces

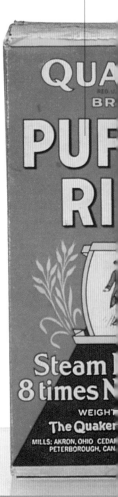

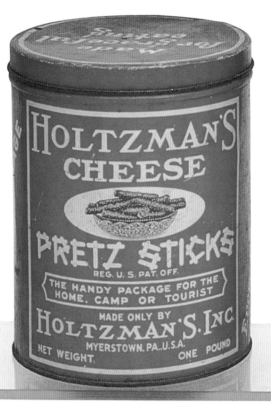

HOLTZMAN'S CHEESE PRETZ STICKS
REG. U. S. PAT. OFF.
THE HANDY PACKAGE FOR THE HOME, CAMP OR TOURIST
MADE ONLY BY
HOLTZMAN'S, INC.
MYERSTOWN, PA., U.S.A.
NET WEIGHT ONE POUND

QUA
REG. U.
BR
PUF
RI
Steam
8 times N
WEIGHT
The Quaker
MILLS: AKRON, OHIO CEDA
PETERBOROUGH, CAN.

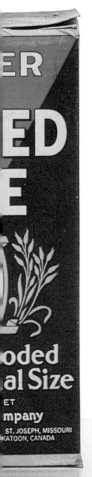

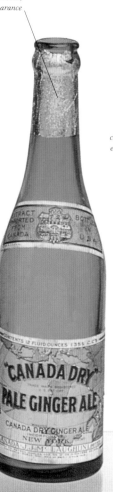

Launched in the US in 1923, this ginger ale bottle has a clean, fresh appearance

A time of change

The 1920s were a period when packaging stood at a crossroads between the more traditional designs of the earlier part of the century – seen here in the beer bottle below – and the influence of the Modern movement. Another innovation was the arrival of convenience foods and snacks, such as the Pretz Sticks (far left).

The label claims that it is exclusive to the manufacturer and the top of the bottle is sealed

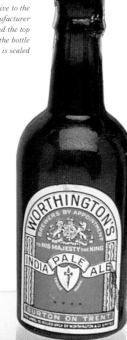

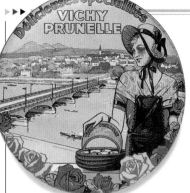

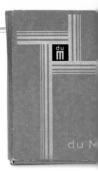

Women's cigarettes

With the increasing emancipation of women in the 1920s came a new breed of products targeted at their leisure time. Aimed at the female smoker, these cigarette packs are stylishly elegant or exotic. The du Maurier pack uses an impressive Art Deco design.

Vichy Prunelle gift can

This French gift can has adopted the bright colors of Art Deco. It is one version of a traditional design that is gradually adapting to the changing times; note for example the woman's fashionable dress under the conventional apron and bonnet.

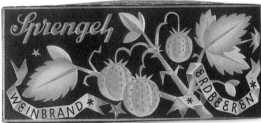

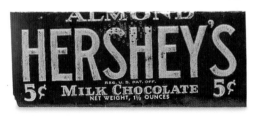

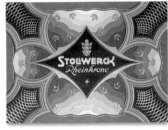

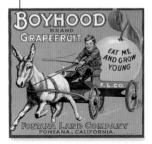

Boyhood fruit crate label

A flourishing fruit trade existed in California by the 1900s, and in order to identify different orchards, pictorial labels were pasted on to each wooden crate of fruit. This label is quite upbeat, the oversized grapefruit on the cart and the jolly colors create a bold, attractive impression.

Candy wrappers

This 1927 Stollwerck wrapper (above) and Sprengel label (top) are typical of the highly decorative nature of items intended as luxury products. Their extravagant graphics and strong colors contrast distinctively with the American Hershey bar (above left), its embossed monochrome packaging giving a mass market appeal.

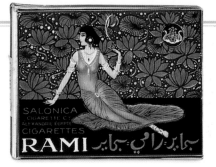

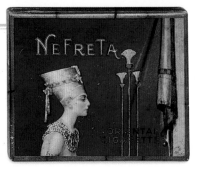

Appetizing images

Realistic illustrations printed on the front of packets were becoming commonplace, giving a better impression of what the product actually contained. The sumptuous display of fruit on the Rowntree's pastilles (bottom left) and the juicy marrowfat peas on the Thorn's packet (bottom right) make the brands seem far more enticing.

The carnation flower on this American evaporated milk can has been used to suggest freshness and sweetness

Strong, geometric shapes and intense colors defined Art Deco

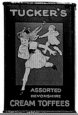

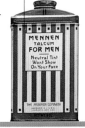

This American household cleaning product has been continually updated through the century (see p.432)

This potato chip pack design, which came out in 1920, lasted until the '50s

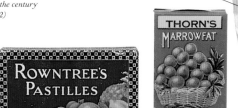

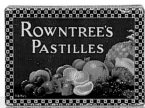

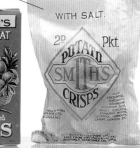

PACKAGING 1930–39

THE 1930S WAS THE DECADE when Art Deco influenced packaging and when graphics became noticeably bolder and simpler. Packing technology was also improving: cellophane was a hygienic overwrap for packed products, keeping them fresher; and plastic and aluminum, although still expensive, were lightweight replacements for heavy glass containers.

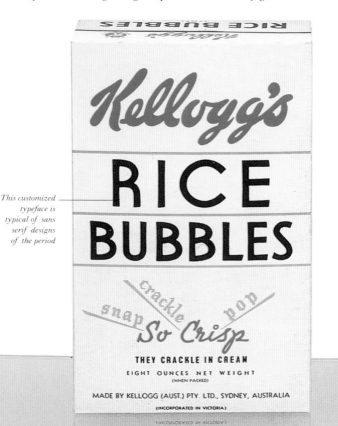

This customized typeface is typical of sans serif designs of the period

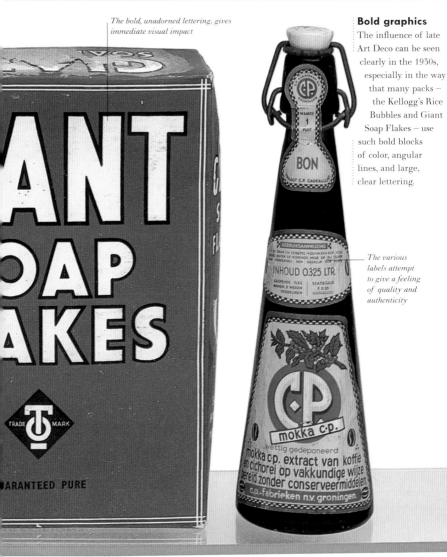

The bold, unadorned lettering, gives immediate visual impact

Bold graphics
The influence of late Art Deco can be seen clearly in the 1930s, especially in the way that many packs – the Kellogg's Rice Bubbles and Giant Soap Flakes – use such bold blocks of color, angular lines, and large, clear lettering.

The various labels attempt to give a feeling of quality and authenticity

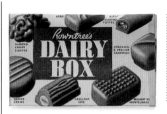

Rowntree's Dairy Box

The illustration on this box clearly explains its contents; labels to identify each chocolate are even printed alongside. This realistic format prefigures photographic packaging of the 1960s.

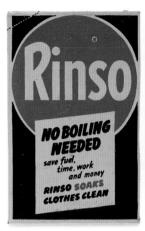

Petits Fours assortment

A classic example of two popular concepts in packaging at the time, this box of Petits Fours depicts a sunburst motif in the late Art Deco style using a range of limited, yet striking colors.

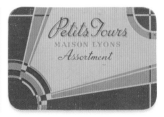

Rinso

A detergent, Rinso was first launched in 1910 by the American Lever Company to compete directly with Persil (opposite). This basic design was adapted slightly in successive decades.

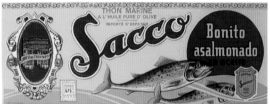

Sacco Bonito Asalmonado

All canned tuna fish tasted much the same, so it was the brand label that had to influence the customer's choice. This label is made more attractive by the realistic illustrations of tuna fish leaping through a stylized sea.

Purbeur butter cookies

Images of animals were often linked with certain products. This stylized illustration makes the cow licking a Purbeur look like a pat of butter.

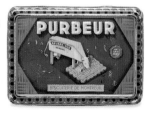

Japanese matchboxes

The stylish clothes, Art Deco colors, and simple graphic stripes on these elegant-looking Japanese matchbox covers illustrate the international influence of both Western fashions of the period and of Art Deco.

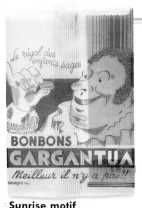

Gargantua candy bag

Although a cheap piece of packaging, this waxed paper bag is fun and vital with its simple illustration. Waxy paper cartons were also used for milk and waxed cardboard cartons for cream, honey, ice cream, and glacé cherries in the 1930s.

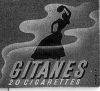

Cigarette packs

By the 1930s, cigarettes and tobacco were packed in aluminum containers, as well as round cans and cardboard boxes. Pack designs also changed: this 1930 Gitanes design by Max Ponty has become a classic.

Sunrise motif

Throughout the history of packaging, the sunrise motif has featured repeatedly as an immediately identifiable symbol. Here it manifests itself in the Gold Tint shortening (below left), Petits Fours (opposite), and Synergy light bulb pack (bottom).

Black Magic's Art Deco chocolate pack remained constant for years

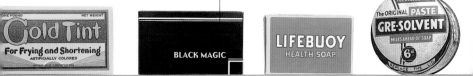

This fun light bulb pack substitutes a light bulb for the body of a butterfly

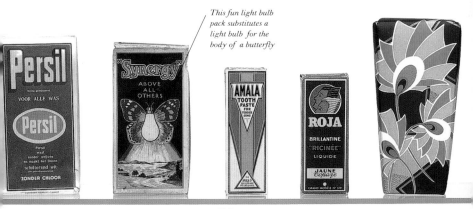

PACKAGING 1940–49

IN THE 1940S, LIFE WAS DOMINATED, once more, by a world war that affected every aspect of society. Packaging had to be adapted in some countries because the availability of printing ink and packing materials was in short supply. Labels were reduced in size, notably in Britain, in order to save paper. Limited natural resources and food shortages persisted in Europe after the end of the war in 1945, so relatively unaffected countries such as the US and Canada continued to export canned or dried produce overseas.

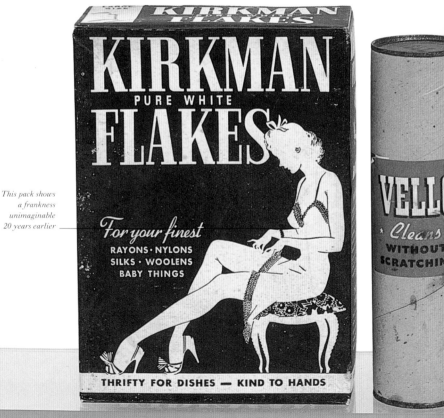

This pack shows a frankness unimaginable 20 years earlier

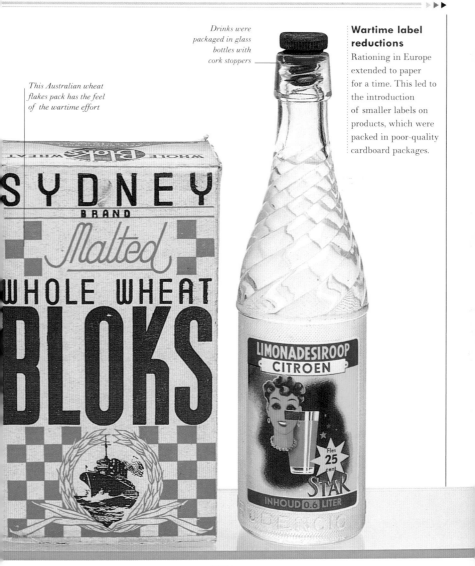

This Australian wheat flakes pack has the feel of the wartime effort

Drinks were packaged in glass bottles with cork stoppers

SYDNEY
BRAND
Malted
WHOLE WHEAT
BLOKS

LIMONADESIROOP
CITROEN
Fles 25 cent
STAR
INHOUD 0.6 LITER

Wartime label reductions

Rationing in Europe extended to paper for a time. This led to the introduction of smaller labels on products, which were packed in poor-quality cardboard packages.

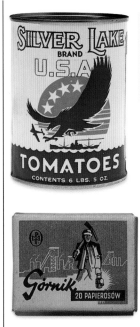

Silver Lake USA tomatoes

Part of the war effort, this can is minimalist in terms of its two-color printing.

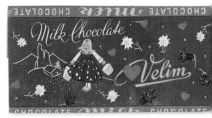

Velim paper wrapper

As a result of paper shortages in the 1940s, some items were sold without any wrapping. Chocolate bars, when they were available, were packaged without silver foil, and for a time even the paper wrappers were replaced by thin transparent ones.

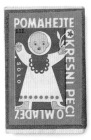

Matchbox

Friction matches first became available in 1827, and initally the labels tended to be plain. This label from Eastern Europe is just one example of the wide variety of designs that were produced.

Górnik cigarettes

The stark design on this pack has a strong utilitarian feel that is reminiscent of posters of the period.

Lucky Strike cigarettes

Lucky Strike cigarettes were introduced to the US in 1917, using the trademark red bull's-eye from the familiar Lucky Strike tobacco. The pack remained the same until 1942, when Raymond Loewy replaced the green background with a white one.

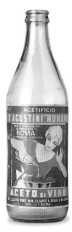

Aceto di Vino

The image on this wine vinegar label shows the consumer exactly how to use the product.

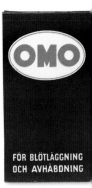

Omo

The austerity of the 1940s led to a reduction in the amount of ink printed on some brand packages – a more extreme example is the Rins packaging (right).

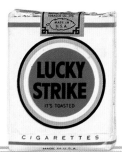

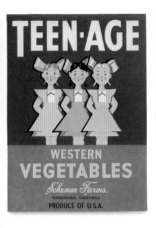

Teen-age Western Vegetables label

The airbrush technique and graphics of this label are typically 1940s. As with other American food crate labels of the period, this is attractive and colorful.

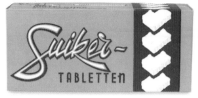

Suiker Tabletten

As the supply of raw materials dried up later in the decade, the quality of cardboard and paper deteriorated. This package of sugar cubes shows how simple designs and strong color contrasts became effective substitutes.

A typically British utilitarian 1940s' pack design

Utilitarian design

Economic restrictions and limited natural resources in Europe forced designers in the 1940s to adopt a utilitarian style for packaging. The products shown here clearly reflect the war years.

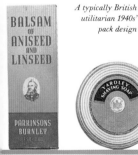

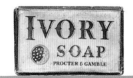

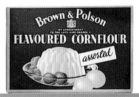

Heinz's shrunken keystone label is still recognizable

This dried product clearly states that it is wrapped in a "temporary pack"

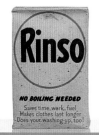

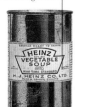

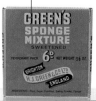

PACKAGING 1950–59

This Australian pack of Rinso makes good use of simple silhouetted figures for a contemporary feel

BIGGER, BOLDER, BRIGHTER – by the end of the 1950s, packaging could not have looked more different to that of the 1940s. This new incentive for packaging to be more competitive was due to the rise of the supermarket store: by 1950, the vast majority of goods sold were prepacked and the need for instantly recognizable products to sell themselves became imperative. Packaging was becoming a formal marketing tool, evoking a set of values in the consumer's mind through the images used.

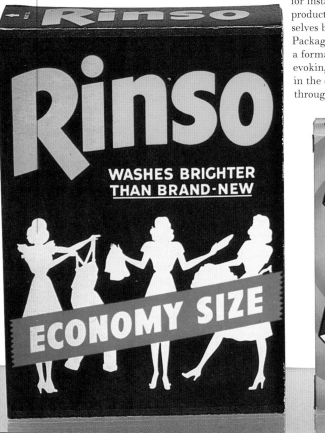

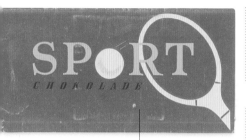

Sport chocolate

This Danish design relies on a clever visual association with the brand name to make a memorable image in the consumer's mind.

Tide and Surf (Suno) were part of a new type of soapless detergent packaged in active, or busy, bright designs

Here, a bold design is complemented by the use of bright colors

Consumerism in the 1950s

The commercial advertisements that first appeared on television in the 1950s were part of a new phase of consumerism. The range of frozen foods available expanded, as did the selection of products on the shelves. As the choice became wider, there was more competition and products had to compete for the "impulse buy." Graphics freshened up, becoming simpler and more recognizable with an emphatic logo or motif.

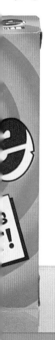

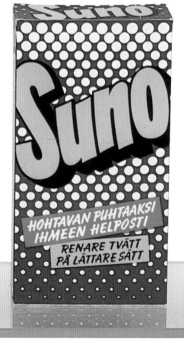

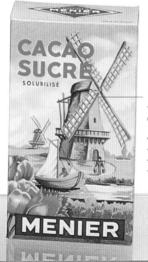

This French hot chocolate pack uses "modern" colors to liven up a traditional image

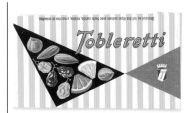

Tobleretti chocolate

Visually arresting, this wrapper has an "active" feel, relying on a combination of geometric shapes and detailed illustrations.

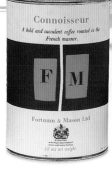

Connoisseur coffee

There is visually little to identify this product; but the simple, bold graphics designed by Ruth Gill make a strong impact.

Peek Freans Playbox cookies

The photo-realism of this illustration, displaying the contents of a can of cookies, was typical of the early 1950s. By the end of the decade, photographs were replacing drawn images (see Birds Eye peas opposite), as they were a cheaper means of producing an image.

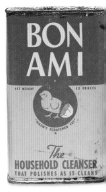

Bon Ami

The chick motif of the Bon Ami household cleaner, designed in 1901 by Louis H. Soule, was radically updated for the 1950s with new lettering.

Sophisticated packaging aimed at the female consumer

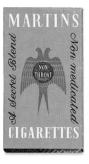

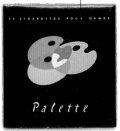

Cigarette packs

The manufacturers of products such as these capitalized on the 1950s' trend in graphics toward simpler, bolder images or cartoon characters to identify them. The painting palettes and bird visually refer to the products' brand names.

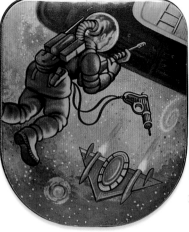

Sharpe's toffee box

This bright, space-age gift box lid is redolent of the 1950s' fascination with science fiction and popular children's comics. Interestingly, gift boxes rarely had the manufacturer's name printed on their lids.

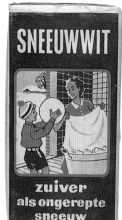

Sneeuwwit

Some well-known household products kept their traditional packaging, despite the new wave of soap and detergent designs emerging during the 1950s.

Like cartoon or comic characters, sales pitches using popular personalities proved successful

This American soap pack has a strong, bold design

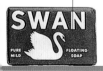

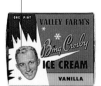

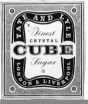

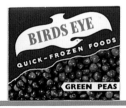

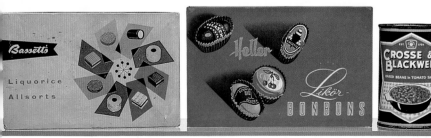

PACKAGING 1960–69

THE 1960S WERE TRULY AN AGE of modernity. Fast food, refrigerators, freezers, convenience food, diet products all became commonplace, influencing the eating habits and lifestyles of consumers throughout the world. Soft drinks were sold in "throwaway cans" with ring pulls, a dramatic departure from the traditional glass bottle and cork stopper. Cellophane, aluminum, and plastic now ensured the freshness of many products.

The packaging of liquor remained relatively unchanged (compare p.411)

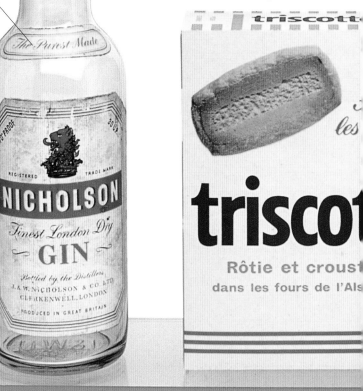

Consumer appeal

Packaging designers were preoccupied with conveying
a message to buy, while photography and promotional
incentives proliferated. Bold colors and striking images
were used to create visual appeal and, for the first time,
fun images were introduced to appeal directly to children.

The fresh, crisp colors of the packaging convey a sense of cleanliness

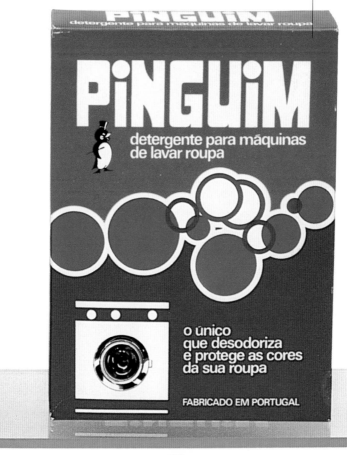

Siks diet cookies

The new fashions in clothes meant that women were more conscious of their figures. Diet packs used fashionable images to attract the consumer.

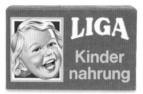

Liga rusks

Household packs used vibrant designs and active images to capture attention. This pack was designed to appeal to women who wanted their children to look as healthy as this one.

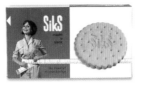

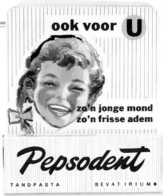

Pepsodent toothpaste

This toothpaste product competes for more shelf space, and therefore more customer awareness, by adding a tall cardboard back to the packet. The typography has been updated and the fresh-faced child added to give the product a sense of vitality.

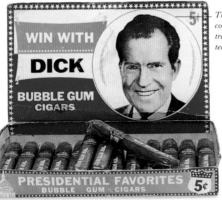

This cardboard counter box is a traditional selling technique

Presidential Favorites bubble gum cigars

Individually packed in cellophane, these bubble gum cigars are sold through another personality sales pitch, promoting Richard Nixon as a candidate for the presidential elections in 1969. Presumably they were aimed at politically aware adults buying treats for their children.

Cigarette pack

A stylized image of a spacecraft, this dramatic and visual design was influenced by the contemporary space race between the then Soviet Union and the US.

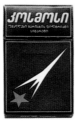

Dairy Box chocolates

The simple, rounded characters on the label of this box are modern and eye-catching. Designed by the artist Raymond Peynet (1908–91), the quirky scene was aimed at the gift market.

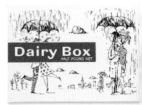

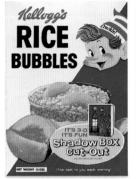

Kellogg's Rice Bubbles

An updated Australian pack (see p.422), this is a modern yet familiar version of Kellogg's designs. The healthy photographic image aims to convince the parent of its nutritional value, while the fun cartoon character and free promotion appeal directly to the child.

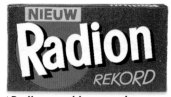

Radion washing powder

In order to stand out from other products, this pack has strong colors and bold, raised letters that appear to jump out from the two-dimensional design.

Stylish alternatives

Interestingly, some of the more successful designs of the decade were supermarket "own brand" packs, such as the British Sainsbury's peas pack (below), which were more experimental, despite being sold as cheap alternatives.

A free rattle is included in the lid of this can of talcum powder

The fun packaging represents a bird's head and beak with its cap and direction pointer

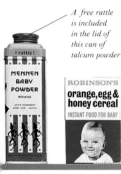

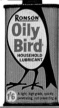

Disposable beverage cans

The 1960s was the era of the throwaway beverage can. Coca-Cola (left) was the first drink to be canned in 1960; the ring-pull opener was developed in the US in 1967.

Although displayed on a tin can, this design depicts a bottle cap from previous packaging

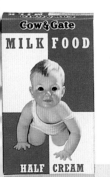

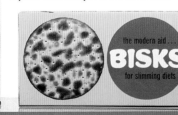

PACKAGING 1970–79

PACKAGING DESIGN REACHED A CROSSROADS in the 1970s, with a tremendous variety of different styles; and the stark new design of some products and supermarket "own brands" provided yet another alternative. Packing technology continued to improve with the arrival of the "Tetrapak" to hold milk, soft drinks, and juices, and molded plastic containers that were all lighter and cheaper to transport than heavy, breakable glass bottles. Consumer tastes were changing as people took more vacations abroad and tasted foreign food, while instant "TV dinners" proved popular alternatives to family meals around the table.

This British cereal pack – with sunrise motif and earthy colors – captures the essence of California, in the 1970s

This design by Dick Bruna was intended to appeal to both the mothers buying the product and the children eating it

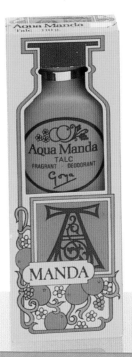

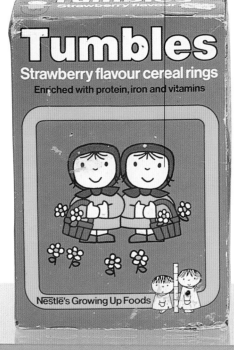

Psychedelic colors

Many of the packages on these pages make use of orange and brown, both strong fashion shades at the time. The garish plastic Aqua Manda container (below opposite) is dyed orange to accentuate the orange-scented talcum powder inside. Its yellow cardboard box creates a greater sense of value.

Another example of personality sales, this orange drink is promoted by comic book hero Superman

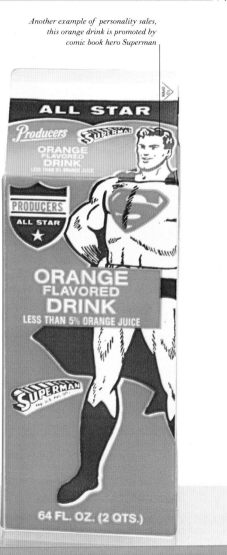

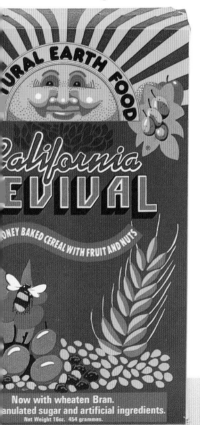

ALL STAR

Producers SUPERMAN
ORANGE FLAVORED DRINK
LESS THAN 5% ORANGE JUICE

PRODUCERS
ALL STAR
★

ORANGE FLAVORED DRINK
LESS THAN 5% ORANGE JUICE

SUPERMAN
Reg. U.S. Pat. Off.

64 FL. OZ. (2 QTS.)

URAL EARTH FOOD

California REVIVAL

HONEY BAKED CEREAL WITH FRUIT AND NUTS

Now with wheaten Bran.
anulated sugar and artificial ingredients.
Net Weight 16oz. 454 grammes.

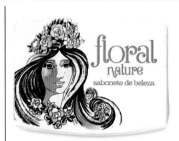

Floral Nature beauty soap

Toiletries continued to represent the latest fashions and popular styles on their packaging, as this line illustration on a pack of beauty soap shows. The white background is used to imply that this is a pure, natural product.

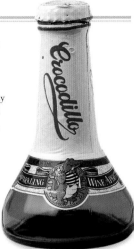

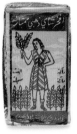

Brooke Bond Girl Brand Ceylon tea

This simply illustrated pack of Syrian tea uses a traditional image symbolically to create a sense of timelessness in the product.

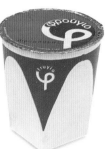

Fruyio yogurt

The Greeks started to package their yogurt in plastic containers in about 1970. Molded plastic containers could literally be produced in any size or shape as this square-bottomed, round-topped yogurt cup shows.

Crocodillo sparkling wine

Developed in 1979, this strangely shaped bottle prefigures some of the gimmicky containers that appeared in the 1980s and '90s. Shaped like the top part of a glass bottle, it looks as though the rest of the container is missing.

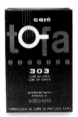

Café Tofa

The modern typography of this stylish Portuguese coffee pack has a clever motif of a full coffee cup, seen from above, incorporated into it.

Euro Coop hazelnut cookies

Packaging was generally becoming lightweight, while retaining a pack's freshness. Cookies were often now only packed in gift cans.

Antelope Brand mosquito coil incense

This conspicuous Indonesian pack design encapsulates the modern approach to selling a product: using bold graphics and colors to catch the eye.

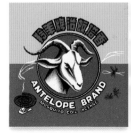

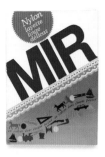

Mir detergent
The brightly-colored silhouettes on this pack of French detergent are displayed as examples of the free gifts available in every packet.

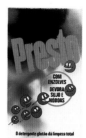

Presto detergent
The age of computer technology took off in the 1970s. These animated enzymes devouring dirt are similar to a popular computer game concept.

Minimalist design
The bewildering array of styles that appeared in the 1970s was capped by the "own brand" packs in supermarkets. The tea pack (below) takes the theme of a single color on a white ground to an extreme compared with the Welch's and Dannon brands.

Fruit yogurts were part of a flourishing range of healthy dairy products

This distinctive packaging is still in use today

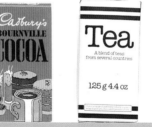

This ethnic TV dinner box is an extreme example of photographic packaging

This box of chocolate liqueurs uses retro-styled artwork more characteristic of the 1950s

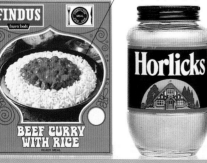

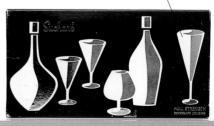

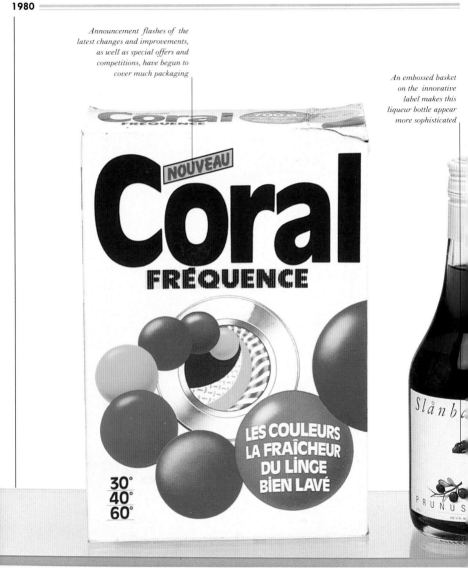

Announcement flashes of the latest changes and improvements, as well as special offers and competitions, have begun to cover much packaging

An embossed basket on the innovative label makes this liqueur bottle appear more sophisticated

PACKAGING 1980-89

IN THE 1980S, PACKAGING became a stronger selling vehicle for products. Designers realized that packaging could be integrated as part of a brand concept, conveying a total message to the consumer. The technology for cutting and folding materials and molding plastics became cheaper, leading to more innovative packaging ideas. While upbeat, contemporary graphics targeted a younger generation, nostalgia also came back into fashion to stress the wholesomeness and consistent quality of some products.

Glass bottles

Ironically, after disposable aluminum cans had almost universally dominated the soft-drink market for years, glass bottles (below) began to make a comeback with certain soft drinks. The hope was that the product would be imbued with a greater sense of quality and value.

This sunburst motif recalls earlier designs from the 1930s (see pp.424–25)

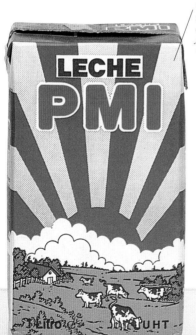

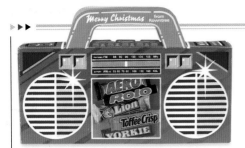

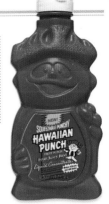

Hawaiian punch
This distinctive container is shaped as a character, a case where the product is identified with the form of the packaging.

Rowntree Christmas selection pack
A piece of novelty packaging aimed at the youth market, the dynamic graphics and vibrant colors make this molded plastic chocolate gift box an unusual and exciting one.

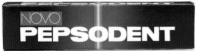

Pepsodent toothpaste
Gone are the pink candy stripes of previous decades; this "new" Portuguese version of the American product has precise graphic design, with strong, clean white typography.

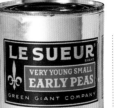

Le Sueur canned peas
Here the reflective silver label imitates a tin can with a kind of hyperealism, an influence from other areas of art and design in the 1970s and '80s.

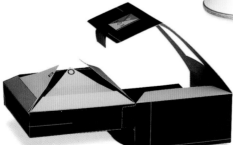

Pink orangeade
This small cartoon-character label allows the bright contents to show through.

The label's bright colors make the product appealing to children

Terry's Le Box
One of the more complicated packaging devices of the 1980s, this origami-inspired box for chocolates looked impressive as a concept on the drawing board, but in reality proved too impractical and expensive.

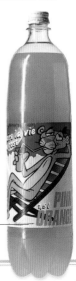

Recreating identities

Manufacturers use different strategies to create fresh identities for products. The Coca-Cola can (below) has a 1980s' fashion-led design that, although collectible, was intended to have a short shelflife. The traditional look of the gravy granules (below right) gives a nostalgic feel, harking back to a previous era; but it also makes the product stand out on a supermarket shelf. The classic Black Magic chocolates packaging (below) has been updated using a deep red rose.

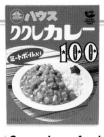

Convenience food

Prepacked ready-made meals such as these reflect a growing trend

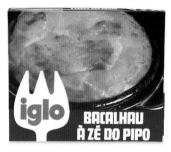

of 1980s and '90s consumers finding less time to shop and to cook basic ingredients. The growing popularity of microwaves has meant that these packs really can provide instant cooked food, a fact identified in their basic, slightly garish packaging.

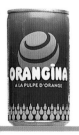
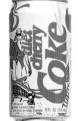

Use of a black background has always been the distinctive feature of this packaging

Gold lettering attempts to create a luxury feel

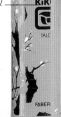
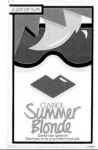
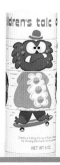

227g ½lb

PACKAGING 1990–99

CONSUMERISM IN THE 1990s has created a curious juxtaposition. On the one hand, excessive choice means that product designs adopt novel or gimmicky images to attract attention. On the other hand, increasing concern about environmental and ecological issues has put pressure on manufacturers to supply products in recyclable or biodegradable packaging. "International consumerism" rejects any regional product varieties; yet, at the same time, there is a trend toward minimalist packaging with cleaner, purer products that stress an independent and authentic identity.

International consumerism

Plastic packaging has made it possible to preserve, pack, and transport products from across the world for consumption or use elsewhere, inviting an element of international consumerism into our lives.

The Perrier bottle is now so familiar that it can be instantly recognized underneath the printed image

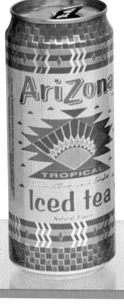

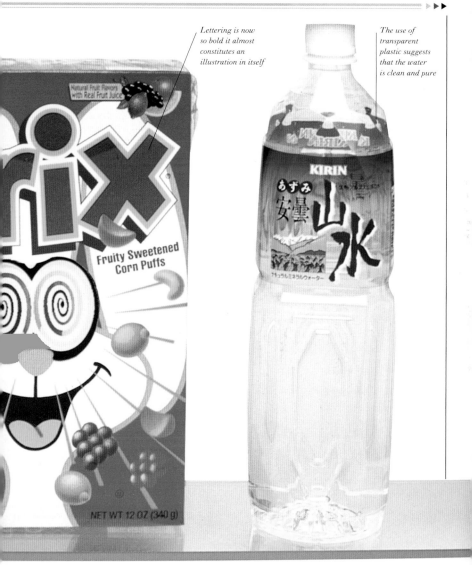

Lettering is now so bold it almost constitutes an illustration in itself

The use of transparent plastic suggests that the water is clean and pure

Natural Fruit Flavors with Real Fruit Juice

Fruity Sweetened Corn Puffs

NET WT 12 OZ (340 g)

KIRIN

あずみ
安曇山水

ナチュラルミネラルウォーター

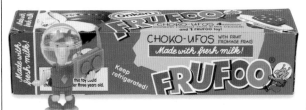

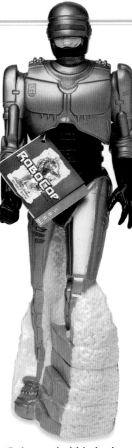

Frufoo Choko-UFOs

Having none of the sophisticated style of adult gift boxes, this pack of German children's chocolates uses every incentive to sell, including a free toy. As is the case with many products on these pages, children are specifically targeted.

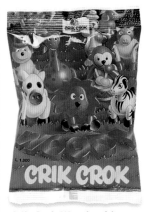

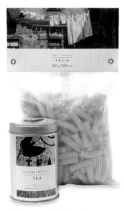

Crik Crok Woody chips

Printing methods are now so advanced that bright, fluorescent colors can be effectively printed on packing materials. This Italian potato chip packet, with its fun colors and cartoon characters, also contains a novelty toy to boost sales.

Harvey Nichols tea and pasta

Although these black and white photographs appear to have no direct relevance to the produce inside, they do give the utilitarian packaging a sophisticated, alternative image.

Robocop bubble bath

This is the ultimate example of state-of-the-art plastics technology used in the packaging industry. Aimed entirely at children, the container is molded in the shape of a popular film character, which, once empty, can also be used as a toy.

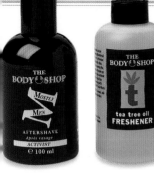

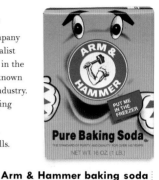

Body Shop toiletries

The identity and beliefs of this health and beauty company are embodied in its minimalist packaging. This is unusual in the cosmetics world, which is known as primarily a packaging industry. The majority of its packaging is also recyclable, enabling customers to return with their empty bottles for refills.

User-friendly

Even mundane household items now have complete packaging concepts. The shower gel container (bottom) is specially moulded to hook on to the shower unit.

This Japanese energy drink has a quirky, stylized image of a Samurai warrior on the label

Arm & Hammer baking soda

This American packaging for baking soda incorporates an older logo in a medallion superimposed over a jokey, modern design with an engaging character to encourage sales.

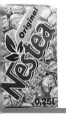

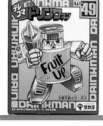

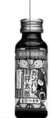

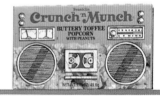

This disc top plastic dispenser allows the product to be opened and resealed easily with just one finger

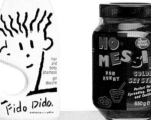

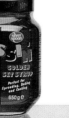

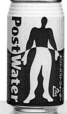

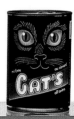

A–Z OF DESIGNERS

✎ **The use of this symbol and a cross-reference indicates the page(s) on which work by the particular designer appears in another section of the book.**

A

AALTO, Aino
1894–1949 **Finnish**
✎ pp.74–75
Aino Marsio was an architect and designer best-known for her glassware and interior designs. She was the wife of Alvar Aalto (see below), with whom she often collaborated.

AALTO, Alvar
1898–1976 **Finnish**
✎ pp.60, 74–75
One of Finland's most important designers, Aalto designed avant-garde buildings that reflected the close relationship of architecture with nature. During the 1920s, he experimented with wood, especially plywood, and in 1935 founded Artek to produce his furniture and lighting. The company still produces many of his original designs. His work includes the Paimio Tuberculosis Sanatorium, Finland (1929–32), the Viipuri Library (1927–35), the Paimio chair (1930), and the Savoy vase (1936).

AARNIO, Eero
1932– **Finnish**
✎ p.64
Aarnio studied industrial design before opening his own design studio. He is well-known for his chair design and use of synthetic materials. His early and late works make use of traditional materials; although during the 1980s he used computer-aided design and manufacture. His pieces include the Ball, or Globe, fiberglass chair

The Rover Chair, designed by Ron Arad, 1985

with built-in speakers or telephone (Asko, 1963), the Gyro fiberglass chair (Asko, 1968), and the Viking dining table and chairs (Polardesign, 1983).

AICHER, Otl
1922–91 **German**
A corporate identity specialist, Aicher studied sculpture before establishing a graphics studio. He was the consultant designer for the corporate identity of the 1972 Munich Olympic Games (see right), and produced many corporate identity and visual information systems, working for Braun, Lufthansa, and Frankfurt airport, among others. In the 1970s, he designed a new identity for the German town of Isny, using a series of geometric images. Aicher created the typeface Rotis, which combined serif and sans serif letters, in 1988.

ALBERS, Anni
1899–1994 **German**
Textile and industrial designer Albers (née Fleischmann) studied at the Bauhaus under Gunta Stölzl (see p.486). In 1933, she emigrated to the US with her husband, Josef

Aicher's 1972 Olympic Games pictograms

Albers (see below). There, she taught, experimented with weaving, and designed textiles for industry.

ALBERS, Josef
1888–1976 **German**
Albers was a painter, designer, and color theorist who taught at the Bauhaus from 1923. After its closure in 1933, he lectured at several universities in the US. A series of abstract paintings entitled *Homage to the Square* epitomize his color theories.

ALISON, Filippo
1930– **Italian**
✎ p.124
Alison is an architect with a special interest in interior design. Among his industrial designs is the Filumena 2 coffeepot (Sabattini, 1984).

AMBASZ, Emilio
1943– **Argentinian**
In 1972, while curator of design at New York's Museum of Modern Art, Ambasz organized an exhibition proposing that good design depended on many objects functioning together as an environment. His designs include the Vertebra chair (Cassina, 1977) and lighting for Artemide and Erco.

ARAD, Ron
1951– **Israeli/British**
✐ p.71
The design company One-Off was founded in 1981 by Ron Arad. Many of his furniture designs were made of metal, such as his stainless steel Big Easy Volume II armchair and sofa. Possibly his most famous design is the Rover Chair (1985; see left), consisting of a salvaged seat from a Rover car fitted into a tubular-steel frame. His later work includes hi-fi systems made of concrete (1985) and the interior design of the Tel Aviv Opera House (1990).

ARAI, Junichi
1932– **Japanese**
A textile designer and manufacturer, Arai gained fame for his experiments with unusual combinations of materials, including celluloid and metallic fibers. His highly complex patterns for weaving using computer punch cards have influenced other textile designers. He now works for his Tokyo-based retail company, Nuno.

ARMANI, Giorgio
1935– **Italian**
✐ p.253
One of the most highly acclaimed fashion designers to emerge from Milan, Armani pioneered a loosely tailored look of casual elegance in the 1980s. After working as a window dresser, he began designing for menswear company Nino Cerruti in 1961. Armani founded his own clothing firm in 1974. As well as his exclusive mens- and womenswear lines, he also mass produces clothing for Emporio Armani stores.

D'ASCANIO, Corradino
1891–1981 **Italian**
✐ p.305
In the 1920s, d'Ascanio worked at an aircraft factory as technical director. He soon started his own firm and designed a successful helicopter. In 1934,

Corradino d'Ascanio's Vespa scooter, 1946

he began working for the engineering company Piaggio, designing aircraft components and helicopters. But it is a 1946 design for which he is best-known – the eternally popular Vespa scooter (see above).

ASHBEE, Charles Robert
1863–1942 **British**
Ashbee was one of the leading figures in the English Arts and Crafts movement. He set up the Guild and School of Handicraft in 1888 and designed many pieces of jewelry, silverware, and furniture for it. His style was linked to Art Nouveau.

ASHLEY, Laura
1926–85 **British**
✐ p.219
From an inauspicious start as a cottage industry, Laura Ashley's company has become a worldwide commercial success. Aside from the trademark floral dresses and womenswear, the shops sell domestic interior furnishings, all marketing a nostalgic English "country" look.

ASPLUND, Erik Gunnar
1885–1940 **Swedish**
Although usually remembered for his contribution toward Scandinavian modernist architecture and for his interior designs, Asplund also designed furniture for the Nordiska Kompaniet. Reproductions of some pieces, such as his Senna chair (1925), are currently manufactured by Cassina.

B

BAHNSEN, Uwe
1930– **German**
Automobile designer Bahnsen was head of car design at Ford Europe from 1976 until the mid 1990s. He oversaw the design of the Fiesta, Granada, and Escort; but the most radical and admired of his cars is the Ford Sierra, launched in 1982.

BAIER, Fred
1949– **British**
The work of furniture designer and maker Baier is complex, often colorful, and always unconventional. For example, his Roll Top Drop Leaf Transforming Robot Desk (1989) owes as much to science-fiction imagery as traditional furniture design.

BAKKER, Gijs
1942– **Dutch**
✐ p.270
Together with his late wife, Emmy van Leersum, Bakker created a new look for contemporary jewelry. In the 1960s, they made aluminum collars and bracelets. Later, they moved into performance and sculpture, using the body as a part of jewelry design. Bakker has also designed items of furniture, including the Strip chair (1974) and the Finger chair (1979).

BALENCIAGA, Cristobal
1895–1972 **Spanish**

Balenciaga is thought by many to be the century's greatest couturier. At the age of 18, he opened his own shop in San Sebastián and began work as a couturier under the name Eisa. In the late 1930s, he opened a couture house in Paris and produced his first collection, consisting of full-skirted crinoline dresses. Like much of his later work, the designs were influenced by his Spanish background and featured brocades, ruffles, black lace, and embroidery. His dramatic evening clothes were strongly colored. In 1957, he produced the "sack" dress, a radical departure from Dior's close-fitting "New Look." He retired in 1968.

BALL, Douglas
1935– **Canadian**

Canada's most successful industrial designer, Ball is best-known for his Race office furniture and seating system (Sunar Hauserman, 1978). He has also designed wheelchairs.

BALMAIN, Pierre
1914–82 **French**

Balmain began his fashion career supplying drawings for the couturier Piguet. After a five-year stint for Molyneux, he worked for Lelong alongside Christian Dior (see p.462). Balmain founded his own house in 1945. His designs found favor with rich, older women and many celebrities. The house diversified into ready-to-wear, sportswear, and perfumes, while Balmain himself designed stewardess uniforms and numerous stage and film costumes.

BARNACK, Oskar
1879–1936 **German**
🖉 p.282

Barnack was the inventor of the Leica camera, the first successful 35mm camera, which provided the model for the later Leica A.

Mario Bellini's Class faucets for Ideal Standard, 1990s

BASS, Saul
1920–96 **American**
🖉 p.400

Design pioneer Bass established his graphic design company, Saul Bass Associates, in Los Angeles. In movie advertising and credit sequences, he produced groundbreaking work, most notably for Otto Preminger's film *The Man with the Golden Arm* (1955). In addition to Bass' film work, the company has developed many corporate identities including AT&T, Minolta, Quaker Oats, United Airlines, and Warner Communications.

BAYER, Herbert
1900–85 **Austrian/American**
🖉 pp.361, 379

The graphic designer most associated with the Bauhaus, Bayer designed and produced all its typography between 1925 and 1928. These lower-case, sans-serif typefaces became identified as the Bauhaus graphic style. Bayer left the school in 1928. In the years that followed, he art directed the German *Vogue*, designed typefaces, and introduced surrealism to the advertising style of the 1930s. In 1938, he moved to the US, where he designed graphics and buildings.

BECK, Henry C.
1903–74 **British**
🖉 p.26

In 1931, Beck designed a diagrammatic route map for London Underground.

Its geographically distorted and simplified lines were easier to follow than previous maps. Beck developed it until 1959.

BEDIN, Martine
1957– **French**

Bedin moved to Florence, Italy, in 1978. There, she worked for the Super-studio group before joining Ettore Sottsass at Alchimia, then Memphis. Her designs include the Super table or floor lamp (1981) and Charlotte sideboard (1987) for Memphis, and luggage for Louis Vuitton. In 1992, she cofounded La Manufacture familiale to produce mainly wooden furniture.

BEHRENS, Peter
1868–1940 **German**
🖉 p.126, 188, 332, 369

Industrial designer and architect associated with the electrical company AEG, Behrens epitomized the growing relationship between art and industry during the early 20th century. His early paintings and graphic work were influenced by Jugendstil. After joining the Munich Secession, and then the artists' colony in Darmstadt, Behrens worked for AEG between 1903 and 1914. He was responsible for its publicity, packaging, and later its architecture and general design. His many product designs include kettles and fans. Among his pupils at

AEG were Gropius (see p.468), Mies van der Rohe (see p.475), and Le Corbusier (see p.474).

BEL GEDDES, Norman

1893–1958 American
📎 p.161

After working as a window dresser and set designer, Bel Geddes began designing industrial objects in 1927. These included cars, radios, and aircraft interiors. Due to the futuristic nature of his designs, few went into production. However, his book *Horizons* helped popularize streamlining, and he was the first industrial designer to gain public notice.

BELLINI, Mario

1935– Italian
📎 pp.105, 153, 174–75, 356–57

One of Italy's leading industrial designers, Bellini studied architecture in Milan. Since 1963, he has been consultant to Olivetti, for whom he has designed typewriters, computers, calculators, and display terminals. Bellini's other work includes the Yamaha cassette deck (1973), the Figura chair (Vitra, 1987), consultancy for Renault cars, and editing *Domus* magazine.

BENNETT, Ward

1917– American
Artist, sculptor, and designer in many other capacities, Bennett has

also worked as an interior designer. He is now best-known for his furniture, textiles, and jewelry.

BERTOIA, Harry

1915–78 Italian/American
📎 p.63

Italian-born Bertoia moved to the US in 1930. After teaching metalwork, he worked with Charles Eames (see p.463) on plywood and wire chairs. In 1950, he set up a studio with help from Knoll International, for which he produced the Diamond Chair (1952).

BERTONE, Flaminio

1903– Italian
📎 p.313, 314, 318

The man behind the idiosyncratic shape and styling of the Citroën 2CV (1939), Bertone also styled the company's Traction Avant (1934) and DS (1960).

BERTONE, Giuseppe

1914–97 Italian
📎 p.319

"Nuccio" Bertone joined his father's car body shop in 1934 and went on to change it into a successful and influential auto design studio. He was responsible for the design of the Alfa Romeo Giulietta Sprint

(1954), Lamborghini Miura (1966), Ferrari Dino 308 (1973), and the Citroën BX (1982), among others.

BLACK, Misha

1910–77 British

Russian-born Black moved to the UK as a child. During the 1930s, he designed radios and televisions for

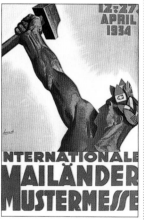

Bocasile's poster for a trade fair in Milan, 1934

Ekco, using new plastics. Much of his career was devoted to exhibition design, and he was responsible for part of the Festival of Britain (1951). Between 1959 and 1975 he taught industrial design.

BLAHNIK, Manolo

1943– Spanish

Known as the creator of original and extravagant shoes, Blahnik has

produced footwear collections for many important fashion houses, including Calvin Klein and Yves Saint Laurent.

BLAKE, Peter

1932– British
📎 p.386

Pioneer of the British Pop Art Movement, Blake's most famous design is the LP cover for the Beatles' *Sgt Pepper's Lonely Hearts Club Band* (1967). He is associate artist at the National Gallery, London.

BLOMBERG, Hugo

1897– Swedish
📎 p.226

As chief engineer and head of design at the Swedish telecommunications company Ericsson, Blomberg conceived and designed the Ericofon single-piece telephone (1940–54) with Ralph Lysell (see p.474).

BOCASILE, Gino

active 1930s Italian
📎 p.396

One of Italy's leading poster designers during the 1930s, Bocasile produced many advertising and tourism posters (see left).

BOERI, Cini

1924– Italian

After graduating in architecture, Boeri worked in the studio of Marco Zanuso (see p.491) until 1963, when she became a freelance designer. Although best-known for her furniture designs, including the Bobo (1967) and Strips (1972) seating sytems, she has designed showrooms for Knoll International (1976) and a series of prefabricated houses in Japan (1983).

BONETTO, Rodolfo
1929–91 Italian

A furniture and industrial designer, Bonetto first worked in the Pininfarina car design studio. Since setting up his own studio in 1958, he has designed products for Brionvega, Olivetti, Gaggia, Driade, Veglia Borletti, and Fiat. His original use of single-piece plastic molding in the interior of the Fiat 132 Bellini (1980) earned him much acclaim.

BOOTY JR., Donald
1956– American
✏ p.357

Before founding Booty Design Associates in 1988, Donald Booty Jr. had studied industrial design in Chicago. The company designs not only for other manufacturers, but also for its own production division, Phorm.

BORSANI, Osvaldo
1911–85 Italian

Borsani worked as both an architect and furniture designer. In 1954, with his twin brother Fulgenzio Borsani, he founded the furniture company Tecno. In the early years, Tecno produced Borsani's

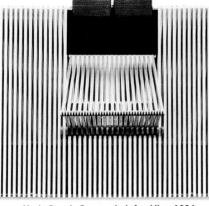

Mario Botta's Quarta chair for Alias, 1984

designs only, but later offered the work of other designers, such as Norman Foster (see p.465). Borsani's most famous pieces are the P40 chaise lounge (1954–55) and the D70 reclining sofa (1955).

BOTTA, Mario
1943– Swiss
✏ p.165

Botta studied architecture at the University of Venice, and his training included a stint in the Paris studio of Le Corbusier (see p.474). In 1969, Botta returned to Lugano and began work on various public and private buildings that would earn him recognition as an organic, rationalist architect. A recent commision was the San Francisco Museum of Modern Art (1995). Since 1982, Botta has designed a number of pieces of metal furniture for the Italian company Alias. These include the

Prima chair (1982), Quarta chair (see above), and Tesi table (1986).

BOUE, Michel
1936–71 French

Automobile designer Boué's career was cut short when he died of cancer at the age of 35. However, he had already produced one major design, the Renault 5 (known in the US as Le Car). The car, which appeared in 1972, was the first of the Superminis, and became the best-selling French car ever.

BOULANGER, Pierre
1886–1950 French
✏ pp.313, 314, 318

Boulanger, an engineer, worked for the French tire company Michelin until 1935, when it took over the car manufacturer Citroën. He became chief of the car company and was responsible for the concept of the Traction

Avant (1934), 2CV (1939), and DS (1960), all of which were styled by Flaminio Bertone (see p.455).

BRANDT, Marianne
1893–1983 German

Painter, designer, and metalworker, Brandt studied painting and sculpture in Weimar. She joined the Bauhaus in 1923 and, under the influence of László Moholy-Nagy (see p.476), became one of its best known metalwork students. She evolved from an Arts and Crafts worker to an industrial designer employing geometric principles. In 1925, she began designing metal lamps at the Bauhaus, and is particularly remembered for the Kandem bedside light (Körting and Matthiesen, 1928). Between 1928 and 1929, Brandt briefly worked for Walter Gropius' office (see p.467) in Berlin. After World War II she taught first in Dresden, then in Berlin.

BRANZI, Andrea
1938– Italian

An architect and designer, Branzi was an influential member of the Florence-based design group Archizoom Associati (founded in 1966). He moved to Milan in 1979 and worked with Studio Alchimia, then Memphis. His designs for Memphis include the Century couch and saucboat (1982), Foglia wall lamp (1988), and Magnolia bookcase (1985). In 1982, Branzi became educational director of the Domus Academy, a postgraduate design school in Milan.

BRAUN, Artur
1921–71 **German**
✐ p.92

Artur Braun took over the Frankfurt-based radio and record player company Braun on the death of his father in 1951, and turned it into the electronics giant it is today. He hired Fritz Eichler (see p.463) as design director. Together they designed the 1955 Phonosuper SK 4 and the SK 25 radio (see below). Eichler employed Otl Aicher (see p.452), Dieter Rams (see p.482), and Hans Gugelot (see p.468), designers with whom he had worked at the Ulm Hochschule für Gestaltung (Ulm College of Design). The Braun products they created displayed a strong company look, epitomized

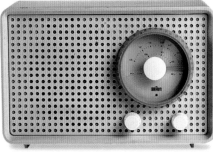

Artur Braun and Fritz Eichler's SK 25 radio, 1955

by an unadorned, industrialized style and geometric simplicity.

BREER, Carl
1883–1970 **American**

In the 1930s, Breer was chief engineer at the US car manufacturer Chrysler. He was responsible for the unconventional-looking Airflow (1934), which although a commercial failure, was widely commentated on at the time and influenced the design of many other automobiles. Breer retired in 1951.

BREUER, Marcel
1902–81 **Hungarian/American**
✐ pp.59, 221

After studying at the Bauhaus, Breuer opened an architect's office in Berlin in 1928. His most significant contribution to design this century is his revolutionary tubular-steel furniture. Inspired by the strength and lightness of his bicycle, he first made

use of tubular steel for the Wassily chair (1925). The Cantilever chair that followed (1928) was made with an unbroken length of tubing, and became a prototype for countless similar chairs. After a short time working for Isokon in England (for whom he produced a bent plywood chair), Breuer moved to the US, where he built his own house and produced experimental furniture. His major architectural works include the UNESCO headquarters in Paris (1953) and the Whitney Museum of American Art in New York (1966).

BROADHEAD, Caroline
1950– **British**

A prominent figure in European jewelry design, Broadhead first worked with ivory. In 1977, she produced bound-thread necklaces and, in 1978, innovative bracelets. She was one of the first designers to reject precious materials in favor of everyday materials such as cloth, rubber, and paper. In the 1980s, she created wearable pieces that combined jewelry, clothing, and sculpture.

BRODOVITCH, Alexey
1898–1971 **American**

Born in Russia, Brodovitch worked in Paris during the 1920s, where he designed books, posters, furnishings,

and advertising. He moved to the US in 1930, where he was art director of *Harper's Bazaar* for 25 years. Brodovitch revolutionized American magazine design by introducing cropped photographs, spare layouts with ample white space, and illusory effects.

BRODY, Neville
1957– **British**
✐ p.367, 384

A graphic designer who rose to fame in the 1980s, Brody studied fine art and graphic design at the London College of Printing. He began his career by designing record covers. In 1981, he was appointed art director of the magazine *The Face*, and experimented with unconventional typefaces, logos, and symbols. He continues to run his own design studio in London.

BÜLOW-HÜBE Vivianna Torun
1927– **Swedish**
✐ p.270

From 1951 to 1956, Bülow-Hübe worked in her own studio, concentrating on wooden and silver jewelry. From 1967, she produced various jewelry and watch prototypes for Georg Jensen Sølvesmedie. She later turned her hand to glassware, porcelain, and ceramics, and went on to design kitchen utensils, lamps, baskets, and office equipment.

BURYLIN, Sergei Petrovich
1876–1942 **Russian**
A textile designer, Burylin was active at various textile mills in Ivanovo-Vosnesensk. His most widely known fabric, the Tractor cotton print (1930), is typical of his strong, semi-abstract, constructivist style.

C

CAMPBELL, Sarah
1946– **British**
Textile designer Campbell works with her sister, Susan Collier (see p.460), with whom she founded Collier Campbell.

CAPUCCI, Roberto
1930– **Italian**
Capucci studied at the Accademia delle Belle Arti in Rome, and in 1950 opened a fashion house there. In 1962, he went to Paris, returning to Rome after seven years. He has produced many experimental and daring fashion items using bright colors and sculptural forms, including plastic garments filled with colored water. Capucci is renowned for the skilful cut of his garments.

CARDER, Frederick
1863–1963 **British**
In 1903, Carder moved to the US, where he co-founded the Steuben Glassworks in New York. Starting out by making iridescent glass, Aurene, in an Art Nouveau style, Steuben soon became a major player in the glass world. In 1918, the company was taken over by the Corning Glass Works. During the 30 years that Carder was art director there, he designed many of the most successful pieces himself.

CARDIN, Pierre
1922– **French**
Born in Italy to French parents, Cardin studied architecture in Paris after World War II, and then trained at the fashion houses of Paquin, Schiaparelli, and Dior. In 1950, he opened his own house, showing his first collection in 1953. During the 1960s, he moved into menswear and came to be considered one of France's most adventurous couturiers. His unusual designs used bright and patterned materials, some influenced by the space age, and had exaggerated features. Many of his designs were suitable for men or women, and he is said to have invented unisex clothing. Cardin's name is now also associated with cars, furniture, luggage, and wigs.

CARLU, Jean
1900–97 **French**
One of France's leading poster designers of the 1920s and '30s, Carlu was clearly influenced by cubism. Between 1940 and 1953, he lived in the US, and there produced the first US defense poster in 1941.

CARTER, Matthew
1937– **British**
🖉 p.366
Today considered to be a master of typography and its technology, Carter designed the Bell Centennial type for the US AT&T telephone directories in 1978. In 1981, he cofounded Bitstream Inc. to produce fonts for computers.

CARTIER, Louis
1875–1942 **French**
🖉 p.229
Grandson of the founder of the jewelers Cartier, Louis Cartier became its most important and innovative designer, improving the types of materials used in jewelry design. From around 1900, he utilized platinum, a suitably flexible metal, for his lace-like diamond-set jewelry.

CARWARDINE, George
1887–1948 **British**
🖉 p.87
As an automobile engineer, Carwardine was a suspension system specialist; as a lighting designer, he is famous for his 1934 Anglepoise lamp. The springs and hinges of the lamp were designed to replicate the muscles and movement of a human arm. Over 60 years later, the design is still in production and remains virtually unchanged.

CASSANDRE, A.M.
1901–68 **French**
A.M. Cassandre was the pseudonym of graphic artist Adolphe Jean-Marie Mouron. Between 1923 and 1936, he designed a series of highly successful and influential advertising posters using his idiosyncratic style of bold, geometric abstraction and broad planes of restricted color to integrate images

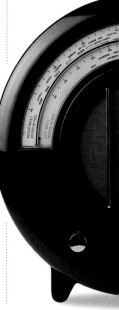

and words. He also created three new typefaces: Bifur (1929), Acier Noir (1930), and Peignot (1936). His Dubonnet poster (1934) and Etoile du Nord poster (1927) have become classics.

CASTIGLIONI, Achille
1918– **Italian**
🖉 p.64
Innovative industrial designer Castiglioni joined forces with his brothers Livio (1911–79) and Pier Giacomo (1913–68) in 1944, after graduating in architecture from Milan

Polytechnic. For more than 20 years, he collaborated closely with Pier Giacomo on lighting, exhibition, and product design. The brothers are best-known for their exploratory furniture design: the 1957 tractor seat stool Mezzadro, and the 1970 kneeling stool Primate.

CHANEL, Gabrielle (Coco)
1883–1971 **French**
🖉 p.184
From humble origins, Chanel had no formal fashion training, yet she is one of the most enduring fashion success stories. In 1914, she opened her first dress shop. During the 1920s, she responded to women's work and leisure fashion needs with practical but stylish wool jersey and corduroy clothing in neutral shades or red.
  Hers was a relaxed, simple style. Her evening wear was luxurious, with beading, embroidery, and fur. The look for which she is best-known is the jersey or soft tweed collarless suit, with braid trim and many pearls or gold chains. After her death, the House of Chanel remained open and was taken over by Karl Lagerfeld in 1983 (see p.473).

Wells Coates' AD 65 radio, 1932–34

CHASHNIK, Ilia Grigorevich
1902–1929 **Russian**
🖉 pp.22, 145
Chashnik collaborated with fellow suprematist painter Kazimir Malevich (see p.475) while working at the Lomonosov State Porcelain Factory design studios between 1922 and 1924. Chashnik designed the enameled decoration for Malevich's witty porcelain Half Cup.

CHERMAYEFF, Ivan
1932–96 **American**
A designer, illustrator, and painter, Chermayeff's major work was in partnership with Thomas Geismar (see p.466). The design group Chermayeff and Geismar Inc. became known for its bold, graphic work in corporate identity. He won many awards, both jointly and individually.

CLIFF, Clarice
1899–1972 **British**
Cliff is one of the foremost British ceramic designers of this century. She began as a lithographer in 1916 at A.J. Wilkinson Ltd, the Royal Staffordshire pottery with which she was associated for the rest of her working life. Her best-known design was the Bizarre range, produced from 1927, which was typified by brightly colored, stylized designs against a creamy background, giving a strong Art Deco feel. Despite

their unconventional look, Cliff's designs were sold in shops such as Harrods. Her work is enjoying renewed popularity.

COATES, Nigel
1949– **British**
An architect and furniture designer, Coates has achieved notoriety for his extravagant and unconventional designs for restaurant, bar, and club interiors in Japan and London. He has also designed fashion shops in London for Jasper Conran and Katherine Hamnett (see p.468). He launched his Metropole and Jazz furniture collections in 1987 and his Noah collection in 1988.

COATES, Wells
1895–1958 **Canadian**
🖉 p.91
Born in Tokyo and educated in Canada, Coates settled in the UK in 1929. He is most commonly associated with the Modern movement in England during the 1930s. His interest in new materials and technologies led him to form the Isokon company with Jack Pritchard in 1931 to design and build modern housing and furnishings. Most of Coates' industrial design work throughout the 1930s was for Ekco, and he is particularly remembered for his series of Bakelite radios, including the AD 65 (see left).

COLANI, Luigi
1928– **German**
📖 *p.147*

Colani's designs are largely influenced by aerodynamic styling, ranging in subject matter from transportation to fashion accessories. Most of his transport designs have never progressed beyond prototypes, although they have inspired other designers. Among his best-known designs are his 1971 Drop porcelain service for Rosenthal and his cameras for Canon.

COLLIER, Susan
1942– **British**

Susan Collier worked as the design and color consultant to Liberty of London Prints before founding her own textile company in 1979 with her sister, Sarah Campbell. Collier Campbell's philosophy was to grow away from the formal, organized graphic designs of the 1950s and produce painterly fabrics with strong colors and abstract patterns. Its concept of "design for now" is still apparent in its fashion and furnishing fabrics.

COLOMBO, Joe
1930–71 **Italian**
📖 *pp.112, 231*

A painter, sculptor, and designer, Colombo was a leading figure of post-World War II Italian design. He set up his own studio in Milan in 1962 and his works show a concern for the technical problems of design using new techniques and materials. His 1965 Chair 4860, made by Kartell, was one of the first one-piece injection molded chairs in ABS plastics. An interest in economy and scale led him to design a complete mobile kitchen in 1972. His other clients have included O'Luce, Italora, Zanotta, and Bieffeplast.

CONRAN, Terence
1931– **British**

Conran has greatly increased Britain's design awareness, bringing "good design" to the masses at affordable prices, largely through the Habitat stores he established in 1964. His early work was inspired by Italian and Scandinavian design. In 1989, the Conran Foundation funded a Design Museum in London devoted to mass-produced goods.

COOPER, Susie
1902–95 **British**

An enduring name in British ceramics, Cooper set up her own firm in 1929, producing popular tea and coffee sets and decorative items. Her designs feature patterns inspired by nature and strong shapes with clean lines and modern colors.

CORDERO, Toni
active 1980s & '90s **Italian**
📖 *p.195*

Designer of the dramatic Sospir bed, Cordero also built the Alpine Stadium (1985) and the Automobile Museum (1987), both in Turin, Italy. He designs for Artemide, Driade, and Sawaya & Moroni.

COURRÈGES, André
1923– **French**

Trained by Balenciaga (see p.454), Courrèges received great acclaim for his futuristic clothes. His 1964 Space Age collection and 1965 miniskirts and white and pastel trousers were copied worldwide.

D

DAY, Lucienne
1917– **British**

Day created her famous Calyx fabric design for the Festival of Britain in 1951:

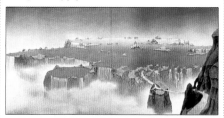

Roger Dean's Close to the Edge record sleeve, 1972

its thin black lines, precise graphics, and autumnal colors expressed a new approach to textile design. She has created many elegant screen-printed furnishing fabrics.

DAY, Robin
1915– **British**

Husband of Lucienne (see left), with whom he formed a design studio, Day won a low-cost furniture competition in 1948 at the Museum of Modern Art in New York. He subsequently designed one of the most successful post-World War II chairs for the non-domestic market, the Polyprop or Mark II stacking chair (Hille), in 1963.

DE BRETTEVILLE, Sheila Levant
1940– **American**

A typographer, graphic designer, and educator, de Bretteville is known for combining social and political attitudes with design. Her early inspiration came from feminist issues and much of her work promotes women's creative expression.

DE LUCCHI, Michele
1952– **Italian**
📖 *pp.41, 70*

De Lucchi was closely linked with the radical international design group, Memphis, from its initiation in 1981; previously he worked for Studio Alchimia. Like

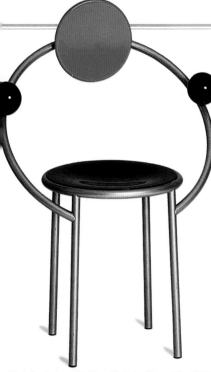

Michele de Lucchi's First Chair for Memphis, 1983

many Memphis designers, de Lucchi used bright, garish colors and asymmetry in his post-modernist work. His best-known piece for Memphis was the 1983 First Chair (see above). He set up his own studio in 1984 and went on to design plastic tableware for Bodum. He has also been a consultant to the office supplies manufacturer, Olivetti, and designed more than 50 Fiorucci shops.

DE PAS, D'URBINO, LOMAZZI
established 1966– **Italian**
Originally an architectural practice, the firm of Jonathan de Pas (1932–91), Donato d'Urbino (1935–), and Paolo Lomazzi (1936–) turned to furniture design, producing one of the most memorable pieces of Pop-inspired design, the PVC inflatable Blow chair, in 1967. The group have also created designs for Zanotta and Artemide.

DEAN, Roger
1942– **British**
✍ p.387
Dean has designed stage sets, Teddy Bear Chairs, and seating for a jazz club, as well as illustrating album covers. Characteristically, his work fuses natural images with fantastical, unworldly creations (see opposite). In 1979, he cofounded his own design company, Magnetic Storm, to specialize in product research and development, architectural and set design, illustration, and film.

DECK, Barry
1962– **American**
✍ p.367
Graphic designer Deck graduated from Northern Illinois University in 1986. Moving to New York in 1992, he quickly earned a reputation for his distorted, computer-manipulated typefaces, which epitomize the "new wave" of the early 1990s. He established his own New York-based company, Dysmedia, in 1995. His fonts include Template Gothic (1990), Caustic Biomorph (1992), and Cyberotica (1994).

DEGANELLO, Paolo
1940– **Italian**
After studying architecture, Deganello became a cofounder of the radical design group Archizoom Associati in Florence in 1966. He has also designed furniture for the Cassina and Driade companies: his

1982 Torso armchair, sofa, and bed for Cassina are important pieces.

DELAUNAY, Sonia
1885–1979 **French**
Delaunay's painter husband, Robert, influenced much of Sonia's work: with him she explored dynamism, rhythm, and movement through color. Her work incorporated interior design, fabrics, and theater, designing ballet costumes for Diaghilev's *Aida* and *Cleopatra* productions. By 1925, her bold, decorative clothing designs had become fashionable.

DESKEY, Donald
1894–1989 **American**
✍ p.69
An industrial and interior designer, Deskey was a pioneer design consultant and an important exponent of Art Deco in the 1930s. He began in advertising but was later commissioned to design items such as washing machines and printing presses. He was greatly interested in the new materials aluminum, cork, and linoleum. From 1927 to 1931 he worked in partnership with Phillip Vollmer, and his work expanded to include interiors, wallpapers, and fabrics. In 1932, he won a competition to design the interior of the Radio City Music Hall, New York, which is acknowledged as a piece of classic American Art Deco.

DIOR, Christian
1905–57 **French**
🖉 p.28
At his first
collection in 1947,
Dior launched a
totally new look that
transformed fashions
worldwide. His rise to
fame was meteoric: he
taught himself to draw,
selling his ideas to
couturiers and magazines,
and then trained formally
at the Piguet and LeLong
fashion houses. His 1947
"New Look" captured the
postwar mood; his famous
A-line collection appeared
in 1956. After Dior's death,
Yves Saint Laurent (see
p.484) became head of
design for a brief period.

DORN, Marion Victoria
1899–1964 **American**
After experimenting with
resist-dyed fabrics in the
US, Dorn moved to the UK
in the early 1920s, making
original batiks for interiors.
During the 1930s, she
became a leading
modernist designer,
achieving acclaim for her
textiles and tufted carpets.

DREYFUSS, Henry
1903–72 **American**
🖉 pp.190, 225
Industrial designer
Dreyfuss' interest in the
relationship between man
and society led him to
incorporate ergonomic
features in his work, an
approach that influenced
later designers. Apprenticed

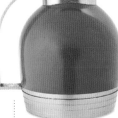

Dreyfuss' Thermos carafe, 1930s

to Norman Bel Geddes (see
p.455), he then established
his name in the 1930s
with the Bell Telephone
Company, designing its
classic Bell 300 in 1933. He
also designed for companies
such as American Airlines,
Lockheed, Thermos (see
above), and Hoover. His
autobiography, *Designing
For People*, was published
in 1955.

DU PASQUIER, Natalie
1957– French
A leading postmodern
textile designer, du
Pasquier worked first for
Rainbow Studio and then
Memphis from 1981 to
1988. She is known for
her vivid printed patterns.
In 1982, she joined the
creative staff of Fiorucci.
She has also designed
furniture, lamps (see right),
clocks, and ceramics.

DUFY, Raoul
1877–1953 **French**
The early work of painter
and decorative designer
Dufy was strongly

influenced by the bright,
strong colors of the Fauves.
Later, he designed dress
fabrics for couturier Paul
Poiret (see p.480) and
textiles for the Lyons-based
company Bianchini-Férier.

DUMAS, Rena
1937– **Greek**
🖉 p.330
After completing her
studies in Paris, Dumas
began working as a
designer of leather goods
for Hermès in 1962. She
set up her own office in
1971, designing office,
home, and shop interiors.
Working in collaboration
with Peter Coles
(1954–85), she produced
the Pippa collection of
folding furniture (Hermès,
1985) and has since created
shop interiors for Hermès.

DUMBAR, Gert
1940– **Dutch**
🖉 p.407
A graphic designer and
teacher, Dumbar studied
painting and graphic
arts before joining Tel
Design Associates in
The Hague in 1967.
Tel created the
internationally
acclaimed corporate
identity for the
Nederlands Spoorwegan
(Dutch Railways). In
1977, Dumbar left
the group to set up
his own practice.
Working in
association with

Total Design (established
1963), Studio Dumbar
produced the corporate
identity for PTT, the Dutch
Postal, Telegraph, and
Telephone authority. Other
commissions include the
celebrated signage system
for the Rijksmuseum and
the corporate identities for
Westeinde Hospital in The
Hague, and ANWB (Dutch
Automobile Association).

DUNAND, Jean
1877–1942 **Swiss**
Dunand studied art in
Geneva before moving to
Paris, where he worked as
a sculptor until 1902. He

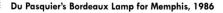

Du Pasquier's Bordeaux Lamp for Memphis, 1986

established his own metalwork studio in 1903. Best-known for his lacquer work, from 1912 he studied with the Japanese artist Seizo Sugawara, who also trained Eileen Gray (see p.467). He incorporated lacquering techniques into his metalwork designs, and later applied them to furniture, screens, and panels. Some of his finest Art Deco creations include the interior of the smoking room of the Ambassade Française at the Paris Expo in 1925, and lacquered panels for the *Normandie* ocean liner (1935).

D'URBINO, Donato

See de Pas, d'Urbino, Lomazzi

E

EAMES, Charles Ormond

1907–78 **American**
🖉 pp.64–65
Architect-designer Charles Eames studied architecture at Washington University before setting up in his own practice in St. Louis in 1930. In 1936, he was offered a fellowship at Cranbrook Academy of Art, Michigan, where he met Eero Saarinen (see p.483), and his future wife, Ray Kaiser (see right). Saarinen and Eames designed a series of molded plywood seats, which won the 1940 Organic Design in Home Furnishings competition at New York's Museum

of Modern Art. In 1941, he and Ray moved to California. The couple were in partnership from 1944, creating furniture designs which were mass produced by Herman Miller. They created several notable pieces, including the leather and rosewood Lounge chair and ottoman (1956). Later, they moved into film production, photography, and exhibition design. In 1949, they designed their own house in Pacific Palisades, California. Their client list included the US government and IBM.

EAMES, Ray

1912–88 **American**
🖉 pp.64–65
Ray Eames (née Kaiser) collaborated with her husband, Charles Eames (see left), on their magazines, exhibition, film, and furniture designs.

EARL, Harley

1893–1969 **American**
🖉 pp.32–33, 316–17
Earl was responsible for the styling of General Motors cars from 1927 until his retirement in 1959. His grounding in the glamorous world of Hollywood showed in his flamboyant styling. He was an innovator, introducing yearly model changes and the use of clay models for developing the shape of the bodywork. His most famous model is the Cadillac Eldorado (1959).

EBENDORF, Robert

c.1938– **American**
Ebendorf is a jeweler whose early work, including coffee pots and umbrella handles, showed both American and Scandinavian influences. In contrast to his early pieces, made from precious and semiprecious materials such as silver, ebony, and moonstone, his

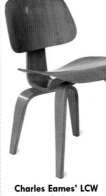

Charles Eames' LCW dining chair, 1946

jewelry from the 1980s was produced from a range of non-precious materials, including paper, wood, photographs, and Formica.

ECKMANN, Otto

1865–1902 **German**
🖉 p.360
After starting out as a painter, Eckmann turned his attention to the applied arts, producing illustrations for the magazines *Pan* and *Jugend*. In 1900, he created

the Art Nouveau typeface Eckmann Schmuck, one of several designed for the Klingspor foundry Offenbach. In addition to his work as a graphic artist, he also designed textiles, ceramics, and pieces of furniture.

EDISON, Thomas Alva

1847–1931 **American**
🖉 pp.100, 333
Edison is a key figure in the development of modern technology. Among his many inventions are the phonograph (1878), the incandescent light bulb (1879), and talking motion pictures (1912).

EICHLER, Fritz

1911–91 **German**
🖉 pp.92, 457
Eichler began his career in theater set design. In 1954 he was employed by Artur Braun (see p.457) as a program director. Together with the Braun design team, he was responsible for developing the austere functionalist style that has come to represent the company.

EISENLOEFFEL, Jan W.

1876–1957 **Dutch**
🖉 pp.142–43
After training in Amsterdam at the Hoeker en Zoon silver workshop, Eisenloeffel spent a year learning enameling in Russia. The metalwares

and ceramics that he created for various Dutch companies, including De Woning and De Distel, all demonstrate his preference for simple, industrial forms suited to mass production.

ERTÉ (Romain de Tirtoff)
1892–1990 **Russian**

Erté took his name from the French pronunciation of his initials, R.T. After studying at the Académie Julian, Paris, he was employed as a fashion illustrator by Paul Poiret (see p.480). From 1915, he created drawings for the covers of *Harper's Bazaar* and designed theatrical costumes and sets. Working briefly in Hollywood, he designed sets for Cecil B. de Mille and Louis B. Mayer. Later, he achieved renown when a retrospective of his drawings was shown in New York and London.

ESSLINGER, Hartmut
1945– **German**
✐ p.344

Industrial designer Esslinger founded frogdesign, an industrial design consultancy, in Altensteig in 1969. The firm's first client was Wega Radio, which was later bought out by Sony – establishing a presence for frogdesign in the Japanese market. Esslinger opened an office in Silicon Valley, California in 1982. His clients include Apple, for which he designed the Apple Macintosh (1984).

F

FARINA, Battista
1893–1966 **Italian**

Before setting up his own shop in Turin in 1930, car designer "Pinin" Farina

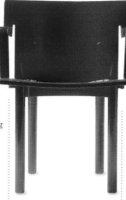

Ferrieri's stacking chair for Kartell, 1986

visited the US to study Ford's production methods. Generally associated with the classic Italian makers, such as Alfa-Romeo and Ferrari, he also designed for mass production. In 1961, the firm was renamed Pininfarina.

FATH, Jacques
1912–54 **French**

Trained at drama school, Fath worked briefly as an actor before establishing a fashion house in 1937. His career as a couturier was interrupted by World War II, but he emerged in peacetime as a successful *haute couture* designer. In 1948, he entered the American ready-to-wear market, creating biannual collections for Joseph Halpert. Fath was one of the first fashion houses to offer clothes in standardized sizes, which were sold through boutiques. In 1949, Fath received the prestigious Neiman-Marcus Award. The Jacques Fath house was relaunched in 1992.

FERRAGAMO, Salvatore
1898–1960 **Italian**
✐ p.255

The "shoemaker to the stars," Ferragamo found his vocation early in life, setting up his own studio in Bonito, Italy, at the age of 14. In 1914, he went to the US, where he opened a shop in Hollywood. He was appalled by the poor quality of mass-produced shoes and developed his own method of hand production, working directly from the wooden last. In 1927, he returned to Italy, where he continued to produce exciting designs, popularizing the wedge heel in the 1930s. He received the Neiman-Marcus Award in 1947, the year he invented the "invisible shoe."

FERRARI-HARDOY, Jorge
1878–1976 **Argentinian**
✐ p.61

Ferrari-Hardoy worked in collaboration with two fellow architects, Argentinian Juan Kurchan (1913–75) and Spaniard Antonio Bonet (1913–89), to produce the Hardoy chair, also referred to as the Butterfly chair, in 1938. Its inexpensive manufacture made it a popular choice for reproduction by many manufacturers, including Knoll and Artek-Pascoe.

FERRIERI, Anna Castelli
1920– **Italian**

Anna Ferrieri graduated in architecture from Milan Polytechnic in 1943. She married Giulio Castelli the same year and entered into the family business, Kartell, for which she produced plastic furniture, tableware, and modular storage systems. She set up her own architecture office in 1946, and from 1959 to 1973 worked in collaboration with architect-designer Ignazio Gardella (1905–) on furniture and public housing. She has received numerous awards.

FOLON, Jean-Michel
1934– **Belgian**

Illustrator and graphic artist Folon has produced drawings for various American journals,

Ford Model T, 1908

including *Time*, *Fortune*, and *The New Yorker*. His work, which highlights human alienation in a technological environment, has also been used extensively in posters and advertisements.

FORD, Henry
1863–1947 **American**
*p.312

Apprenticed to a machinist in Detroit in 1878, Ford had produced his first gasoline-driven car by 1893. In 1903, he founded the Ford Motor Company. The hugely successful Ford Model T (see above) of 1908 was the first car to be mass produced on the assembly line. The emphasis shifted from function to styling with the introduction of the streamlined V8 in 1952. Ford was eventually succeeded by his son and grandson.

FORNASETTI, Piero
1913–88 **Italian**

Fornasetti is recognized for his individualistic decoration. He collaborated on a number of projects with Gio Ponti (see p.480), after Ponti saw his work

exhibited at the Milan Triennale in 1940.

Famous for his black-and-white *trompe-l'oeil* designs, his most celebrated commission is the Casino, San Remo (1950).

FORTUNY Y MADRAZO, Mariano
1871–1949 **Spanish**

Working with hand-dyed silks and velvets, artist and dressmaker Fortuny made stunning aesthetic-style dresses, coats, and capes. His most famous garment is the Delphos dress (1909), for which he employed his patented pleating method. The body-sheathing dress maintained its pleats when twisted into a knot for storage.

FOSTER, Norman
1935– **British**
*p.330

Foster is best-known as a high-tech architect, reponsible for the Sainsbury Centre for the Visual Arts, University of East Anglia, Norwich (1978); the Hong Kong and Shanghai Bank, Hong Kong (1979–85); and the new Reichstag building, Berlin (1995–99). He also designed the Nomos set of office furniture (1983–87) with Tecno (see right), which has been used for the chancellor's office in the new Reichstag.

FRANCK, Kaj
1911–89 **Finnish**

An important ceramics and glassware designer, Franck worked for both Arabia pottery and Nuutajärvi glassworks (absorbed by Wärtsilä in 1950) between 1945 and the late 1970s. Through his work, such as the revolutionary Kilta tableware line (1952), he promoted a distinctly utilitarian aesthetic.

FRANK, Josef
1885–1967 **Austrian**

Austrian-born designer Frank became a lecturer at the Künstgewerbeschule, Vienna, in 1919. Between 1925 and 1934, he ran an interior design company called Haus und Garten. Moving to Sweden in 1934, he joined Svensk Tenn, where he designed textiles, furniture, and wallpaper. He was an early exponent of the Swedish Modern movement.

FRUTIGER, Adrian
1928– **Swiss**
*p.364

Graphic designer Frutiger earned his reputation in 1957, when he launched the versatile Univers typeface. Creator of more than 20 typefaces, he has also worked on signage, including Charles de Gaulle airport, Paris, and as a consultant for IBM, for which he developed both typewriter and computer faces.

FUKUDA, Shigeo
1932– **Japanese**

The witty posters, mosaics, and sculptures of Shigeo Fukuda all demonstrate his playful approach to design. He achieved international acclaim for his posters and signage for the Osaka World Expo in 1970, and since then has exhibited in many group and one-man shows throughout the world.

Work station by Norman Foster and Tecno, 1983

FULLER, Richard Buckminster
1895–1983 **American**
Radical architect and inventor Fuller trained in mathematics at Harvard and then at the Naval Academy, Maryland, where he began to develop his humanistic design concepts. His extensive research resulted in the Dymaxion house (1927) and car (1933). His foremost invention was the geodesic dome, which served as a model for future exhibition domes.

G
GALLIANO, John
1961– **British**
Gibraltan-born fashion designer Galliano graduated from London's St. Martin's School of Art in 1983. In his early collections, ethnic influence blended with his technique of spiral tailoring. When Hubert de Givenchy retired from his Paris couture house in 1995, Galliano became the first British fashion designer to head a French couture house.

GAMES, Abram
1914–96 **British**
✐ pp.123, 399
A leading Modernist graphic designer, Games is remembered for the posters he produced for the British War Office during World War II. His ideal of "maximum meaning, minimum means" is expressed in the cohesion

of stylized images and type. His more commercial designs include symbols for the 1951 Festival of Britain (designed in 1948), and BBC television (1952).

GATTI, PAOLINI, TEODORO
Established 1965– **Italian**
✐ p.66
This design association was founded by the Italian trio Piero Gatti (1940–), Cesare

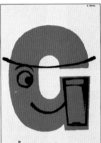

Poster by Games, 1958

Paolini (1937–83), and Franco Teodoro (1939–). They acquired early recognition with their Sacco beanbag seating (1968–69).

GAULTIER, Jean-Paul
1952– **French**
✐ pp.186–87
After early contact with fashion designer Pierre Cardin (see p.458), Gaultier established himself as a freelance

designer in 1976, creating ready-to-wear lines as well as his own exclusive label. His work, which often utilizes unusual materials, reveals the influence of London street style, particularly Punk. Gaultier has produced glamorous, nonconformist wear for men.

GEHRY, Frank O.
1929– **Canadian**
✐ pp.66–67
An internationally active architect and designer, Gehry has been prolific since the late 1970s. He studied architecture at the University of California and Harvard Graduate School of Design, setting up on his own in 1962. Characterized by irregular, layered shapes and volumes, his buildings have been termed deconstructivist. The fish is a recurrent theme, used in 1983 for his fish light, and in his Fish Dance restaurant in Kobe, Japan, 1987. The Vitra Design Museum in Germany (1989), and the Pito kettle (1988, see right) are among his works.

GEISMAR, Thomas
1931– **American**
Geismar is most commonly associated with New York graphic design consultancy Charmayeff & Geismar Inc., which he co-founded in 1960. Best-known for corporate identity and exhibition design, the

Mobil Oil logo (1964) and Xerox logo (1965) are among his works, as well as a number of exhibition advertisements. In 1985 he received a Presidential Design Award for his standardized transportation related symbols.

GIACOSA, Dante
1905–96 **Italian**
✐ p.316
One of Italy's greatest car designers, Giacosa joined Fiat in 1930. His Fiat 500A, launched in 1936, was the basis for several variations on this small car. He also created the Fiat 124, 128, and 130.

GILL, Eric
1882–1940 **British**
✐ p.363
Letter-cutter, illustrator, typeface designer, and writer, Gill studied at Chichester School of Art, and later under Edward Johnston (see p.471). After becoming involved with the Roman Catholic Church in 1913, he produced many religious illustrations. During the 1920s, Gill was commissioned by the Monotype Corporation, for whom he produced the typefaces Perpetua (1925–30) and Gill Sans (1928–30).

GIUGIARO, Giorgetto
1938– **Italian**
A prolific contributor to international car design, Giugiaro has produced

over 100 designs for several major manufacturers. In 1968, he set up ItalDesign. One of the cars the company worked on was the Volkswagen Golf (1974). Giugiaro's consumer products include appliances for Sony, cameras for Nikon, and lighting for Luci.

GIVENCHY, Hubert Taffin de
1927– French

One of the most highly respected fashion designers to emerge from Paris, Givenchy studied at the Ecole des Beaux-Arts and went on to work for the couture houses of Fath, Lelong, Piguet, and Schiaparelli. In 1952, he established his own house, designing traditional, elegant garments. He created Audrey Hepburn's wardrobes for the films *Funny Face* (1956), and *Breakfast at Tiffany's* (1961), and later expanded into the ready-to-wear clothing market.

GLASER, Milton
1929– American
✐ p.36

Illustrator and graphic designer, Glaser co-founded Pushpin Studio, New York, in 1954 with Seymour Chwast and Edward Sorel. Although he is often associated with 1960s' psychedelic graphic design, he also created the Twergi range of kitchenware for the Italian design group Alessi, and in 1987,

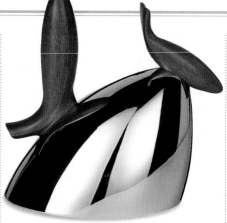

Frank Gehry's Pito kettle for Alessi, 1988

an international AIDS symbol for the World Health Organization.

GOLDMAN, Jonathan
1959– American
✐ p.89

Founder of the design consultancy GoldmanArts in 1986, Goldman has been described as an environmental sculptor. His novelty items include an inflatable Sawtooth lamp (1980s), and a 300-foot (91-metre) ribbon for the opening of the Trump Taj Mahal Casino, Atlantic City, in 1990.

GRANGE, Kenneth
1929– British
✐ pp.8, 136, 183

A London-based industrial designer, Grange advocates that the design of a product should be intrinsic to its manufacture. His

early creations include household appliances for Kenwood and the 1959 Brownie 44A for Kodak. He co-founded the design consultancy Pentagram in 1972. In the 1980s, he was influential in Japan, designing bathroom fixtures for Inax and sewing machines for Maruzen. One of his most recent innovative products is his Silk Effects razor for women, developed for Wilkinson Sword and launched by Schick in 1994.

GRAVES, Michael
1934– American
✐ pp.128–29

A key protagonist of postmodernism, Graves has been active as an architect and industrial designer. He graduated in architecture from Harvard University in 1959. From the late 1960s until 1977, he was a

member of the group of architects known as the "New York Five." His many buildings include the Public Services Building in Portland, Oregon (1982) and the Disney World Dolphin Hotel (1989). Among his most celebrated pieces are the Plaza dressing table for Memphis (1981) and the Kettle with a Bird Whistle for Alessi (1983).

GRAY, Eileen
1878–1976 British
✐ p.68

This Irish-born architect and designer studied at the Slade School of Art in London from 1898 to 1902, then moved to Paris. There she developed skills in Japanese lacquerwork. Gray's production of geometric furniture in aluminum and glass, such as her 1927 table, earned her much respect for her contribution to the Modern movement. Between 1926 and 1929, she designed a house in France for the architect Jean Badovici (1893–1956).

GROPIUS, Walter
1883–1969 German
✐ pp.19, 146–47

A leading figure in modern design, Gropius established the Bauhaus, the most influential design school this century. He assisted Peter Behrens (see p.454) from 1908 to 1910, became a member of the Deutsche Werkbund in 1910, and in

Lurelle Guild's bowl, 1934

1911 was one of the first to adopt the International Style with his Fagus factory at Alfeld in Germany. Director of the Weimar schools of fine and applied arts, he combined them in 1919 to form the Bauhaus, an exponent of unified arts. When it relocated to Dessau in 1925, Gropius designed the new building. He resigned from the Bauhaus in 1928 to concentrate on his own architecture and design practice. Nazi criticism forced him to England in 1934, where he designed furniture for Isokon. In 1937, he emigrated to the US. He taught at Harvard and, in 1945, founded The Architects' Collaborative (TAC) in Cambridge, Massachusetts.

GRUAU, René
1910– **Italian**
✎ p.267
After an international education, Gruau settled in Paris after World War II. He contributed regular illustrations to *Vogue*, but turned to poster design as fashion magazines began to make increasing use of photography.

GUGELOT, Hans
1920–65 **Dutch**
✎ p.102
An industrial designer and architect, Gugelot was an influential figure in reviving the functionalist ideology of the Bauhaus after World War II. Educated in Switzerland, he moved to Germany in 1954, where he became a designer for Braun. His chief works include Braun's Phonosuper record player (1956). From 1955 to 1965, he was head of product design at the Hochschule für Gestaltung in Ulm.

GUILD, Lurelle Van Arsdale
1898–c.1986 **American**
✎ p.122
Although he began his career in theatrical design, Guild is best-remembered for his industrial products. Among the most important is the Electrolux vacuum cleaner (1937). He produced several products for the Chase Brass and Copper Co. (see above).

GUIMARD, Hector
1867–1942 **French**
✎ pp.14, 58
A key proponent of Art Nouveau, Guimard studied at the Ecole des Beaux-Arts in Paris. Inspired by the style of the Belgian Victor Horta (1861–1947), he produced architecture, interior designs, and furniture. Many of the buildings featured cast iron. Florid, curvilinear forms found in his entrances for the Paris Métro system (1900) typify the style that is simply known as "Guimard."

H

HAFNER, Dorothy
1952– **American**
✎ pp.148–49
Primarily a ceramicist, Hafner's work is characterized by a lively, graphic style and vibrant colors. These are shown in her Roundabout punchbowl and ladle (see right). A number of her pieces have been produced by Rosenthal Studio Line.

HALD, Edvard
1883–1980 **Swedish**
✎ p.79
Hald's association with the famous Swedish glassworks Orrefors began in 1917, and continued for the rest of his life, including time spent as its managing director. At the 1925 Paris Expo, Hald won a grand prize for his work. Embracing the features of Swedish Modern design, his engraved wares, some of them colored, reveal a controlled, traditional influence. He also worked as a designer for the porcelain factories Rörstand (1917–24) and Karlskrona (1917–33).

HAMNETT, Katharine
1948– **British**
A fashion designer whose collections take inspiration from utilitarian workwear, Hamnett founded her own company in 1979 after freelancing for various foreign firms.

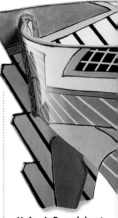

Hafner's Roundabout punchbowl, 1986

She is famous for bringing political and ecological issues to the forefront of fashion.

HANDLER, Laura
1947– **American**
✎ p.84
Active as an industrial designer in Italy, as well as her native US, Handler has created designs for

Sottsass Associati, and other Milan-based manufacturers. She received an award from *ID* magazine for her Cat's Eye candleholder (Design Ideas, 1991).

HAUSTEIN, Paul
1880–1944 **German**
✏ p.82
Active predominantly as an enameler, Haustein also worked as a

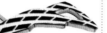

ceramicist, metalworker, graphic and furniture designer. He was a co-founder of the Darmstadt artists' colony in Germany in 1903, where he created silverware. From 1905 until his death, he taught metalwork at the School of Applied Art in Stuttgart

as well as producing silver- and metalware for various manufacturers.

HEIBERG, Jean
1884–1976 **Norwegian**
✏ p.225
Heiberg's training was as a painter, first in Munich, and then under Matisse, whose influence is clearly visible in his paintings. He was commissioned by the Swedish company L.M. Ericsson to produce a telephone design. It was instigated in 1931 and remained internationally the most common design until the 1950s.

HENNINGSEN, Poul
1895–1967 **Danish**
✏ pp.86–87
Henningsen's PH ceiling, wall, and table lamp line (1924), produced by Louis Poulsen & Co, is his most celebrated work, although he had won many prizes for earlier lighting designs. He initially trained as an architect, and later supported modernism while employed as editor of the magazine *Kritisk Revy* (1926–28). His architectural works include restaurants, theaters, and houses.

HILTON, Matthew
1957– **British**
✏ p.73
Best-known for his Antelope (1987) and Flipper (1988) side tables with animal legs, Hilton also designed high-tech products for the London-based design group CAPA. He established his own studio in 1984.

HOFFMANN, Josef Franz Maria
1870–1956 **Czech/Austrian**
✏ pp.18–19, 57, 78, 162–63
Architect and designer Josef Hoffmann trained as an architect under Otto Wagner (1841–1918), with whom he worked between 1896 and 1899. A founding member of the Vienna Secession (1897), he organized one of its early exhibitions. In 1903, inspired by the work of Charles Rennie Mackintosh (see p.474) and C.R. Ashbee (see p.453), Hoffmann,

Koloman Moser (see p.476), and arts patron Fritz Wärndorfer set up the Wiener Werkstätte (see p.16). His architectural achievements include the Purkersdorf Sanatorium (1904–05) and the Palais Stoclet in Brussels (1905–11), on which he collaborated with Gustav Klimt (see p.472). Furnishings for both buildings were created by the Wiener Werkstätte. Hoffmann also produced designs for other leading Viennese firms, including J. & J. Kohn and Lobmeyr.

HÖGLUND, Erik
1932– **Swedish**
✏ pp.84, 156–57
Glassware designer Höglund was employed at Boda from 1953 to 1973. His designs include anthropomorphic candle-holders and vases, bowls engraved with primitive figurative drawings, and hand-blown vessels with

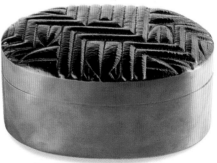

Brass box by Josef Hoffman, 1915

irregular bubbles (see right). Höglund's approach was unique in that it challenged the fashion for more formal glassware.

HOHLWEIN, Ludwig
1874–1949
German
✏ p.397

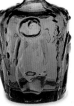

Decanter by Erik Höglund, 1950s

Hohlwein studied architecture in Munich before abandoning this discipline to become a poster artist. In his early work, including a series of posters for the Munich sports tailor Hermann Scherrer, he established a characteristic style that varied little over the next 40 years. His use of bold type, asymmetry, and large blank areas was influential on the work of Mcknight Kauffer (see p.472). Hohlwein created more than 3,000 posters during a career that spanned two world wars.

HULANICKI, Barbara
1936– **Polish/British**
Of Polish descent, Hulanicki moved to Britain in the 1940s. After studying at Brighton Art College, she worked briefly as a fashion illustrator. In 1963, she started a mail order fashion business aimed at teenagers. Encouraged by the response to these designs,

she opened a boutique called Biba, which marketed a look that typified the 1960s. In 1969, Biba took over an Art Deco building on Kensington High Street, London. It is for this chic store, with its all-black interior, that Hulanicki is best remembered.

IE, Kho Liang
1927–75 **Dutch**
✏ p.194
Architect and designer Kho Liang Ie trained at the Rietveld Academy of Arts, the Netherlands. Later, he produced furniture designs for the Dutch company, Artifort. His commissions have included the interior of the Schipol Airport, Amsterdam, and two rooms for the London home of Sir Robert and Lady Sainsbury.

INDIANA, Robert
1927– **American**
✏ pp.38, 270
Artist and designer Robert Clarke renamed himself after his home state. His most famous work, shown in his first one-man exhibition in New York (1962), is based on the word LOVE. The words HUG, ERR, and EAT have also inspired works.

IOSA GHINI, Massimo
1959– **Italian**
A designer of graphics and objects, Iosa Ghini has produced furniture designs for companies such as Moroso (see below) and Memphis. Since 1985, he has acted as a consultant to RAI, the Italian broadcasting service, and in 1988 designed the Bolidio discotheque in New York.

ISSIGONIS, Alec
1906–88 **British**
✏ p.317
Born in Turkey, Issigonis emigrated to

Britain in 1922. After training as a engineer in London, he worked as a draftsman at Rootes Motors in Coventry. In 1936, he joined Morris Motors, Oxford, for which he designed the Morris Minor (1948) and the celebrated Morris Mini (1959). The Mini, with its tiny wheels, transversely mounted engine, and front-wheel drive, was a radical departure from conventional car design.

J

JACKSON, Dakota
1949– **American**
✏ p.67
In the early 1970s, Jackson was commissioned by Yoko Ono to design some furniture for John Lennon. Since then, he has manufactured his own furniture, including the 'vik-ter range (1991).

JACOBSEN, Arne
1902–71 **Danish**
✏ pp.35, 63, 160
Born in Copenhagen, Jacobsen trained as an architect before opening his own practice in 1930.

New-tone sofas for Moroso by Massimo Iosa Ghini, 1989

Influenced by the work of Gunnar Asplund (see p.453), Le Corbusier (see p.474), and Mies van der Rohe (see p.475), he was an early exponent of the Modern style in Denmark. He worked as an architect and product designer, creating furniture for Fritz Hansen and tableware for Stelton (see right), among others. He earned wide acclaim for the SAS Hotel, Copenhagen (1956–60).

JEANNERET, Pierre
1896–1967 **Swiss**

Pierre Jeanneret, cousin of Le Corbusier (see p.474), moved to Paris in 1920. Together they designed various villas in the Parisian suburbs, before teaming up with Charlotte Perriand (see p.479) to create the company's iconic tubular-steel-framed furniture. Jeanneret produced some designs independently, such as the Scissor Chair (c.1947) for Knoll. After World War II, he collaborated on projects with Jean Prouvé (see p.480), as well as continuing his association with Le Corbusier.

JENSEN, Arthur Georg
1866–1935 **Danish**
✎ pp.126–27, 268

Early in the century, Georg Jensen established the famous silver company that bears his name. Together with Johan Rohde (1856–1935), he

designed a large proportion of the company's output, including jewelry, candlesticks, tea and coffee sets, cutlery, and other luxury items. By 1924, Jensen had outlets in Berlin, Paris, London, and New York. When he retired in 1926, his family took over the firm.

JENSEN, Jakob
1926– **Danish**
✎ p.102

Jensen graduated from and went on to become chief designer for the Copenhagen School of Arts, Crafts, and Design, working under Sigvard Bernadotte from 1952 to 1959. In 1961, he set up a design consultancy; by the late 1960s, his clients included Bang & Olufsen, for which he designed the sleek Beogram 4000 (1972).

JOHNSTON, Edward
1872–1944 **British**
✎ pp.360–61

Calligrapher and professor, Johnston is best-known for his typeface design for London Underground (1915): its geometric forms perfectly complemented the 1930s map designed by Henry Beck (see p.454). The sans serif alphabet served as a model for Gill Sans, the face created by his former pupil Eric Gill in 1928 (see p.466).

Johnston also published a classic calligraphy book, *Writing & Illuminating & Lettering* (1906).

JONES, Terry
1945– **British**

Jones worked on *Good Housekeeping* magazine before becoming art

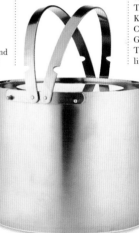

Arne Jacobsen's Cylinder line ice bucket for Stelton, 1967

director of the British *Vogue*. His *Not Another Punk Book*, produced in 1977, represented a turning point in his career. In this title, he first employed instant design, using collage, photocopied distortions, and typewriter print to convey a sense of energy. In 1980, he launched *i-D* magazine,

where he developed this approach. He has also worked in video production and acted as a consultant to Fiorucci.

K

KÅGE, Algot Wilhelm
1889–1960 **Swedish**

Trained as a painter, Kåge joined the Swedish Ceramic Company in Gustavsberg in 1917. There, he introduced a line of heat-resistant and stackable dinner sets, such as Pyro and Praktika (1930s); as well as more elegant and decorative pieces in the 1940s.

KAMALI, Norma
1945– **American**

Inspired by London designers like Barbara Hulanicki (see p.470), Kamali opened a shop selling imported European fashions in 1967, quickly introducing her own line. In 1978, she established OMO (On My Own), the showcase for her innovative garments. She popularized the use of sweatshirt fabric and Lycra for everyday wear.

KAN, Shui-Kay
1949– **British**

Born in Hong Kong, Shui-Kay Kan studied and still works in Britain. In the mid-1970s, he established SKK Lighting. He is

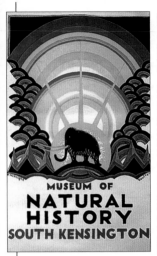

Poster by Kauffer, 1922

interested in new lighting techniques and has produced low-voltage and motorized systems. His 1988 Motorized Robotic Light was installed in the London Design Museum.

KAUFFER, Edward McKnight
1890–1954 **American/British**
✏ p.397
Edward Kauffer adopted the name McKnight in honor of the professor who sponsored his visit to Paris in 1913. In 1914, he moved to the UK, gaining his first commission as a poster designer from London Underground in 1915. His prolific output for clients including Shell and London Transport was greatly influenced by major artistic movements, such as cubism, Art Deco, vorticism, and surrealism.

KAWAKUBO, Rei
1942– **Japanese**
Having studied literature at Keio University, Tokyo, Rei Kawakubo joined the textile company Asaki Kasei. She founded Comme des Garçons in 1969. Her unconventional clothing, including wrapped, loosely structured garments, is based on Japanese workwear and ceremonial dress.

KENZO, (Kenzo Takada)
1939– **Japanese**
Kenzo was one of the first male students to be admitted to the leading Tokyo fashion school, where he was awarded a prestigious prize in 1960. In 1965, he moved to Paris, designing for various fashion houses before establishing his own shop, Jungle Jap, in 1970. Taking inspiration from Japanese and ethnic costume, Kenzo adapted the dramatic shapes and bright colors to suit Western tastes. By 1985, his international reputation was well established with shops in London, New York, and Milan.

KIESLER, Frederick
c.1890–1965 **Austrian**
An architect, sculptor, and designer of furniture, stage sets, and interiors, Kiesler is best-known for his biomorphic designs, including Two-Part Nesting Tables (1935–38). In 1923, he joined the De Stijl group and, in the same year, developed the blueprints for his Endless House, which although never realized was nevertheless influential for both architects and artists. In 1926, Kiesler moved to the US where he continued to work on a variety of projects.

KING, Jessie Marion
1875–1949 **Scottish**
✏ p.390
King is known primarily for her book illustrations. Her name, together with that of Mackintosh (see p.474), is linked with that Glasgow School. From 1905, she designed silverware for Liberty, and fabrics and wallpaper for other clients. Inspired by Léon Bakst's drawings for the Ballets Russes, she integrated bright hues into her pastel palette.

KING, Perry A.
1938– **British**
✏ p.342
An industrial designer, King undertook various projects for Olivetti and Praxis in Milan before teaming up with Ettore Sottsass (see p.485) in 1965. He worked with Sottsass on the design of the Valentine portable typewriter (1969). In collaboration with Spaniard Santiago Miranda (1947–), he designed typefaces for Olivetti. In 1975, King-Miranda became a formal partnership, concentrating on furniture, lighting, and graphic design.

KJAERHOLM, Poul
1929–80 **Danish**
Although he is known for his designs for mass-produced furniture, Kjaerholm trained in the traditional craft of cabinet-making. A proponent of the late International Style, he employed chromium and tubular steel in his furniture designs, which were made by Ejvind Kold Christensen and Hellerup, among others.

KLEIN, Calvin
1942– **American**
Inspired by Yves Saint Laurent (see p.484), Klein set up in business in 1968, specializing in classic designs in natural fabrics. His name is associated with jeans, which throughout the 1970s were sought after by the label-conscious. Klein is also known for his perfume, furs, shoes, and underwear.

KLIMT, Gustav
1862–1918 **Austrian**
✏ p.18
Painter and designer Klimt studied at the Vienna School of Arts and Crafts,

and was one of the founders of the Vienna Secession. He combined the stylized shapes of symbolism with rich, decorative backdrops inspired by Art Nouveau.

KNOLL, Florence Schust
1917– **American**
𝒪 p.222

A furniture designer, Knoll was greatly influenced by the Saarinens (see p.483). In 1943, she joined Hans Knoll (1914–55) in his furniture business, where she headed an interior design service for Knoll customers. With her financial backing, they formed Knoll Associates (now Knoll International) in 1946. The company manufactured many furniture classics, including designs by Bertoia (see p.455), Mies van der Rohe (see p.475), and Saarinen, as well as Florence Knoll.

KOMENDA, Erwin
1904–66 **German**
𝒪 pp.314, 320

An automobile engineer, Komenda was a designer for Daimler-Benz before joining Ferdinand Porsche's Stuttgart office (see p.480) in the 1930s. He was responsible for the styling of the original Volkswagen Beetle (1939), and the series of Porsche cars that commenced with the Type 356 (1949) and ended with the Type 911 (1963).

KOPPEL, Henning
1918–81 **Danish**

Koppel trained as a sculptor in Denmark before World War I, but during the Occupation he worked in Stockholm for the Orrefors glassworks. On his return to Denmark in 1945, he began his long association with Georg Jensen (see p.471). For Jensen he produced some of his finest designs – elegant, sculptural jewelry, flatware, and hollowware. He produced ceramics for

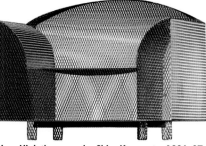

How High the moon by Shiro Kuramata, 1986–87

Bing Grøndahl from 1961 and glassware for Orrefors from 1971.

KURAMATA, Shiro
1934–91 **Japanese**
𝒪 p.40

Kuramata worked for the Teikokukizai furniture factory and the interior design departments of several major Tokyo stores before setting up on his own in 1965. His unconventional approach

to furniture design won him acclaim in the 1970s. His minimalist designs, executed in industrial materials, such as metal-mesh (see below), steel cables, and Plexiglass combine Japanese severity with the softer elements of Western design. Important works in the field of interior design include a series of boutiques for fashion designer Issey Miyake (see p.476) and the Seibu store, Tokyo (1987).

L

LAGERFELD, Karl
1939– **German**

A fashion designer best-known for his flamboyant evening wear and fur coats, Lagerfeld has been predominantly active in Paris. At the age of 14, he began working for the couturier Balmain, and later for Patou. In 1983, he became head of Chanel's ready-to-wear,

and since 1984 has also worked under his own name, producing 16 collections a year.

LALIQUE, René
1860–1945 **French**

An important designer known for his figurative jewelry in unusual combinations of base metals, stones, and enamel, and later for his glassware. He established Cristal Lalique in 1909, from where he created vases, bowls, perfume bottles, lighting, and other decorative glass designs produced by molding methods. He was particularly prolific in producing glass, often for architecture, between the wars.

LAND, Edwin Herbert
1909–91 **American**
𝒪 p.286

Physicist and businessman Edwin Land was educated at Harvard University. He is credited with the invention of the Polaroid-Land instant print-processing camera in 1947, and the Polaroid-Land SX-70 in 1972, an instant color-processing camera.

LAUREN, Ralph
1939– **American**

Born Ralph Lipschitz, Lauren had no formal training, but has become one of the most successful fashion designers in the US. Combining American prairie style with English tailoring, he creates a relaxed but elegant finish. His first menswear was for his company Polo in 1968. It has since expanded into womenswear.

LE CORBUSIER
1887–1965 **Swiss**

An instrumental figure in 20th-century architecture and design, Charles-Edouard Jeanneret-Gris adopted the pseudonym Le Corbusier in the 1920s. His first major piece was the Schwob house in Switzerland (1916). It indicated the purist, austere direction of modernism, setting the style for his future works. In 1922, he set up an architectural office with his cousin Pierre Jeanneret (see p.471). His book, *Vers Une Architecture* (1925), provided some of the fundamental theories of modernism, which were embodied in his Villa Savoye (1929–31) in France. Mainly concerned with urban design, he also produced furniture, and is particularly known for his range of Confort armchairs and sofas during the late 1920s.

LENICA, Jan
1928– **Polish**
✐ p.403

A graphic designer, Lenica studied architecture in Warsaw. In the 1950s and '60s, he designed posters and experimented with film animation. While his

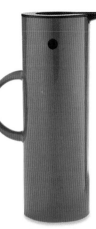

Magnussen's Thermos, 1977

earlier works are in keeping with the Polish school of design, his later works, such as the film *Adam 2* (1969), reveal a psychedelic influence.

LISSITZKY, Lazar Markovich
1890–1941 **Russian**
✐ p.394

An innovative typographer, architect, and designer, Lissitzky followed constructivist ideology. He was a key figure in adapting these theories to graphic design and internationalizing them through his teaching and traveling. He taught at VHkUTEMAS, the Moscow design institute (see p.23). In 1925, he produced *The Isms of Art*

1914–24, in collaboration with German artist Hans Arp (1887–1966).

LLOYD, Marshall B.
1858–1927 **American**
✐ p.60

Lloyd patented a twisted craft paper fiber strengthened with wire that imitated the appearance of wicker. Put into production by the furniture company Lloyd Loom, this method of creating inexpensive furniture became very popular during the 1920s and '30s.

LOEWY, Raymond
1893–1986 **French/American**
✐ pp.115, 139, 283, 350

Loewy is often heralded as the originator of the industrial design profession in the US. He studied engineering in Paris, then emigrated to New York, where he flourished as a designer. His redesign of the 1929 Duplicator 66 for Gestetner, the establishment of Raymond Loewy Associates in the same year, and the design of the 1934 Coldspot Super Six fridge for Sears Roebuck earned him early respect. His streamlined 1937 S1 locomotive for the Pennsylvania Railroad Company and the US Greyhound bus helped transform the image of American transportation. In the 1960s, he designed for NASA.

LOMAZZI
See de Pas, d'Urbino, Lomazzi

LYSELL, Ralph
1907– **Swedish**
✐ p.226

Lysell was the industrial designer who worked with Hugo Blomberg (see p.455) on the development of the Ericofon telephone (1940s).

M
MACKINTOSH, Charles Rennie
1868–1928 **Scottish**
✐ pp.4, 56, 138, 162, 192, 328

Mackintosh was a leading protagonist of Art Nouveau architecture in Britain. His work is unique in its combination of geometric Celtic design and Japanese decoration and shows the influence of the Arts and Crafts Movement. Born and educated in Glasgow, it was there that he executed one of his most definitive architectural projects, the Glasgow School of Art (1898–1909). In his early years, he often worked in collaboration with his wife, Margaret Macdonald (1865–1933), her sister, Frances Macdonald (1874–1921), and J. Herbert MacNair (1868–1953) as members of the Glasgow Four. In 1900, the group exhibited at the eighth Secession exhibition in Vienna. His architectural works were all in Britain.

MAGISTRETTI, Vico

1920– **Italian**

📎 p.88

An architect and designer, Magistretti benefited from Italy's postwar reconstruction, opening a studio in the 1950s. He developed the Selene chair from ABS plastic for Artemide in the 1960s, providing a new look for Italian plastic goods. His range of Sinbad chairs and sofas for Cassina (1981) emphasize the importance of structure.

MAGNUSSEN, Erik

1940– **Danish**

Magnussen studied ceramics before establishing his own workshop, producing lighting, kitchenware, and furniture. His line of containers for Stelton (1977, see left) were designed to be entirely functional. From 1978, he was employed at the Georg Jensen Sølvsmedie.

MAINBOCHER

1891–1976 **American**

Born Main Rousseau Bocher, Mainbocher embarked on his career as a fashion designer in Paris, illustrating for *Harper's Bazaar* (1922). He founded his own couture house in 1930, designing classic, understated clothing, and was the first to create boned, strapless evening dresses in 1934. He

retained his exclusive image by refusing the mass production of any of his designs.

MAJORELLE, Louis

1859–1926 **French**

📎 p.193

A leading exponent of Art Nouveau, Majorelle has become synonomous with the School of Nancy. He inherited his father's furniture business in 1879, updating the traditional styling of its products, and finishing them with naturalistic marqueteries. Mass produced at low cost, these designs were affordable to many.

After his factory was destroyed by fire in 1916, Majorelle's success dwindled.

MALEVICH, Kazimir Severinovich

1878–1935 **Russian**

📎 pp.22, 145

Influenced by the progressive movements of cubism and constructivism, Malevich was primarily an abstract artist. His work is characterized by strong colors against a white backgound, a style he described as suprematism.

In 1920, he founded the Unovis group, of which Lissitzky (see p.474) was also a member. Later, he diverted to product design, as well as architecture.

MARI, Enzo

1932– **Italy**

📎 p.339

Mari promoted the importance of communication through design. A prevailing interest in children's games began with a wooden puzzle he created for Danese in 1957. He continued to work with Danese, experimenting with ABS plastics and producing kitchen products (see above). He also created the 1972 Sof Sof chair.

Mari's salad servers, 1932

MARX, Enid

1902–93 **British**

Inspired by the patterns of wood engravings, Marx became a prolific fabric and wallpaper designer. She is best-remembered for her upholstery design for London Underground seating (1950s), and was awarded Royal Designer for Industry in 1944. She also created Utility furniture (1944–47) and book jackets for the British publisher Penguin (1950s).

MELLOR, David

1930– **British**

📎 pp.3, 139

Leading British kitchenware designer Mellor studied in Sheffield, where he founded a workshop in 1954. He is widely respected for his modestly simple but elegant designs for everyday use. He won an award in 1957 from the Design Council for his celebrated Pride cutlery.

MENDINI, Alessandro

1931– **Italian**

📎 pp.66, 221

After studying architecture in Milan, Mendini worked for Marcello Nizzoli (see p.478). He expounded radical design as editor of the Italian magazine *Casabella* (1970–76). He has produced furniture for the design group Alchimia, shown at the Milan Furniture Fair (1981), and silverware for Alessi.

MIES VAN DER ROHE, Ludwig

1886–1969 **German**

📎 p.59

Mies van der Rohe was trained by his father as a stonemason, and from 1908 to 1911 he was apprenticed to Peter Behrens (see p.454). Many of his early architectural concepts featured steel and glass, but were only realized in the form of the International Style after he moved to the US in 1938.

In the 1930s, his tubular-steel furniture was sold internationally through the German maker Thonet-Mundus. His Barcelona chair (1929) is one of his best-known works.

MIRANDA, Santiago
See Perry King

MIYAKE, Issey
1938– **Japanese**
Educated in graphic design in Tokyo, and fashion in Paris, Miyake founded couture house Issey Miyake International Inc. in 1971. He was among the first to exploit Eastern costume in the West, uniting natural fibers with traditional Japanese lines. He disregards transient fashions in favor of durable designs.

MOHOLY-NAGY, László
1895–1946 **Hungarian**
Forced to abandon his law studies by World War I, Moholy-Nagy began painting on recovering from a war injury. He moved to Berlin in 1920, pursuing an interest in photography. After Walter Gropius (see p.467) saw his work, he invited him to teach at the Bauhaus. Active as a stage

and exhibition designer from 1928 to 1933, he created the sets for the Kroll Opera in Berlin. He emigrated to the US in 1937, setting up a school in Chicago based on Bauhaus ideologies.

MOLLINO, Carlo
1905–73 **Italy**
✐ pp.164, 194
Mollino graduated in 1931 from his architectural studies in Turin, proceeding to design the Turin riding school, Ippica, in 1937. His preference for organic forms, epitomized by his Arabesque table (1947), reflect the influence of Spanish architect Antonio Gaudí (1852–1926). In the 1980s, a revival of interest in 1950s' style resulted in the reproduction of many of Mollino's designs.

MORISON, Stanley
1889–1967 **British**
✐ p.364
The typographer and type historian Stanley Morison did not have any formal

Jasper Morrison's Moon teaset, 1997

training in design. He acted as typographical advisor to the British Monotype Corporation from 1922 to 1967, during which time he directed the design of types Baskerville (1923), Gill Sans (1928), and Walbaum (1933), later using some of these more radical designs while working for the publisher Victor Gollancz as a book jacket designer. In 1922, he set up the typographic magazine *The Fleuron*, and from 1929 to 1959, acted as typographical advisor to *The Times* newspaper, creating its new face, Times New Roman (1931–1932).

MORRISON, Jasper
1959– **British**
✐ p.149
Educated at the Royal College of Art from 1982 to 1985, Morrison is a London-based designer of individual, offbeat items of furniture and accessories. He cofounded NATO (Narrative Architecture Today), creating designs for Vitra and Aram Designs, among others. His works have been

featured internationally in exhibitions, including the 1987 exhibition in Tokyo.

MOSER, Koloman
1868–1918 **Austrian**
Along with Gustav Klimt (see p.472), Josef Hoffmann (see p.469), Josef Maria Olbrich (see p.478), and others, Moser founded the Vienna Secession in 1897. Trained as a graphic artist and painter, he was involved in the launch of the group's journal *Ver Sacrum* in 1898. In the same year, he designed the stained glass and interior decoration for the Secession gallery, where the members' work was shown several times a year. Moser created furniture, ceramic, silver, and graphic designs for the Secession, as well as pieces for the Wiener Werkstätte, a commercial venture that he set up with Hoffmann in 1903.

MOULTON, Alex
1920– **British**
✐ pp.299, 317
An engineering graduate, Moulton worked as a researcher at the Bristol

Aeroplane Company during World War II. Later, he joined his family's rubber-manufacturing company, developing rubber suspension for cars. In collaboration with Alec Issigonis (see p.470), he designed the suspension for the Mini (1959). In the 1960s, Moulton developed an innovative line of bicycles.

MOURGUE, Olivier
1939– French
Mourgue's colorful, gently curvaceous, biomorphic forms epitomize the design aesthetic of the 1960s. Trained in interior architecture and the decorative arts in Paris, he designed his first prototype chair for Airborne while still a student. The Djinn line, which he created for Airborne in 1965, was used by Stanley Kubrick in the film *2001: A Space Odyssey*. Mourgue has also worked on various domestic projects, including a mobile studio (1970), as well as acting as a consultant to Renault and Air France.

MUCHA, Alphonse
1860–1939 Czech
🖉 p.390
Mucha began as a stage set designer in Vienna, moving to Munich in 1885 and Paris in 1887. Settling in Paris, he designed stamps and posters throughout the early 1890s, winning acclaim for a series of

posters of Sarah Bernhardt, produced from 1894. Over the next decade, he designed posters, magazine covers, packaging, textiles, and jewelry – all in a richly decorated Art Nouveau style. Between 1903 and 1909, he made several trips to America, where he collaborated on jewelry designs with Louis Tiffany (see p.486). Returning to his homeland in 1922, he produced a series of 20 murals, *Slav Epic*, depicting the history of Czechoslovakia.

MUIR, Jean
1933–95 British
Distinguished fashion designer Jean Muir served her apprenticeship at Liberty, London, before joining Jaeger in 1956. In 1962, she began to design under the Jane & Jane label, opening her own house in 1966. She is known for her classical, elegant, and superbly comfortable womenswear, made up in soft, flowing materials, such as silk jersey, crêpe, and suede. In 1983, she was awarded a CBE.

MÜLLER, Gerd Alfred
1932– German
Industrial designer Müller is best-known for the kitchen appliances (see right) and electric shavers that he created for Braun between 1955 and 1960. In 1960, he set up a design

studio in Eschborn, Germany, specializing in appliances and graphics.

MÜLLER-BROCKMANN, Josef
1914– Swiss
After studying and training in Zurich, Müller-Brockmann established his own studio in 1936, concentrating on corporate graphics, posters, and exhibition design. A key figure in the promotion of Swiss International Style, he was a cofounder of the journal *Neue Grafik* (1958), which championed this approach. During the 1950s, he received international recognition for a series of concert posters for the Zurich Tonhalle, and also created powerful public health and safety posters using photomontage. From 1966, he worked with Paul Rand (see p.482) as a consultant for IBM.

MUNARI, Bruno
1907– Italian
The early work of artist and designer Munari, from the 1920s and '30s, showed a strong futurist influence. After World War II, he began designing products and toys. In 1957, he created the Cube ashtray, the first of many products for Danese. He has taught at both Harvard University and Milan Polytechnic and written numerous texts, including *Design and Visual Communications* (1968).

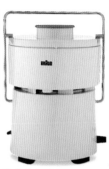

Muller's Multipress MP50 juicer for Braun, 1957

N
NELSON, George
1907–86 American
🖉 p.230
Architecture graduate Nelson won the Prix de Rome, which funded his visit to Europe in 1931. On his return to the US in 1933, he became an editor on *Architectural Forum*, where he was able to promote the modernist architecture and design that he had witnessed in Europe. His Storagewall of 1945, shown in *Life* magazine, led to a long association with furniture manufacturer Herman Miller, for which he executed many designs, including the unusual Marshmallow sofa (1956) and the Action Office (1961). Though a productive designer, Nelson was perhaps most influential in his writing and teaching.

NIELSEN, Harald
1892–1977 **Danish**
✐ p.155

Nielsen joined Georg Jensen's Solvsmedie as an apprentice in 1909, where he produced the Pyramid flatware service, one of the company's best-selling designs. When Jensen died in 1935, Nielsen became artistic director, a position that he retained for almost 30 years. His jewelry and tableware designs are characterized by smooth, unadorned forms inspired by the Bauhaus.

NIZZOLI, Marcello
1887–1969 **Italian**
✐ pp.341, 356

Nizzoli began as a painter, later turning to exhibition, poster, and textile design. During the 1920s and '30s, he worked with architects Edoardo Persico (1900–36) and Giuseppe Terragni (1904–43) on various exhibition and interior projects. In 1938, he was hired as a consultant by Olivetti, where he became the firm's most influential product designer. Among his best-known works are the Lettera 22 portable typewriter (1950) and the Divisumma 24 adding machine (1956), both for Olivetti.

NOGUCHI, Isamu
1904–88 **American**
✐ pp.27, 70

Born in Los Angeles, Noguchi trained as a cabinetmaker in Japan,

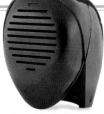

Noguchi's Radio nurse

returning to the US in 1918. During the 1920s and '30s, he worked as a sculptor, visiting Paris in 1927, where he studied under Constantine Brancusi (1876–1957). His first major product was the Radio Nurse of 1937 (see above), commissioned by Zenith. Throughout the 1940s and '50s, he developed a distinctive sculptural style, producing furniture designs for Herman Miller and Knoll, and lighting for Akari. His celebrated paper and bamboo lighting designs have been widely copied.

NOYES, Eliot Fette
1910–77 **American**
✐ p.343

After studying architecture at Harvard, Noyes joined the Cambridge office of Walter Gropius (see p.467) and Marcel Breuer (see p.457). In 1940, he became a curator at the Museum of Modern Art, New York. After the war, he joined the design consultancy of Norman Bel Geddes (see p.455), starting his long association with IBM. In 1947, he set up on his own, retaining IBM as a client,

and created the Model A typewriter, the first in a line of IBM products that established the company's corporate image. Another major client was Mobil, for which he designed the round gas pump in 1964.

NURMESNIEMI, Antti
1927– **Finnish**
✐ p.124

After studying interior design in Helsinki, Nurmesniemi worked for architect Viljo Revell, where he designed the interiors of banks, restaurants, and hotels. On his return to Finland in 1956, he set up his own office. He has produced popular designs for furniture, household objects – including the Finel coffee pot (1957) – and transportation. His client list includes Artek, Merivaara, and Cassina.

O

OLBRICH, Josef Maria
1867–1908 **Austrian**
✐ p.82

Having trained in architecture, Olbrich worked briefly for the Viennese architect Otto Wagner (1841–1918). He was a founding member of the Vienna Secession and, along with Gustav Klimt (see p.472), designed the Secession gallery. In 1899, he was invited by the Grand Duke of Hesse to join an artists' colony in Darmstadt, where he

designed numerous houses and exhibition halls, as well as textiles, furniture, metal- and glassware.

OLINS, Wally
1930– **British**
✐ p.370

Olins teamed up with graphic designer Michael Wolff (1933–) to form the London-based consultancy Wolff Olins in 1965. The company has created innovative corporate identity programs that have radically transformed major firms. Important clients include ICI, Q8, P&O, and British Telecom. When Wolff left the company in 1983, Olins became chairman.

OLIVER, Vaughan
1957– **British**
✐ p.389

A typographer and graphic designer, Oliver is a prominent figure in record sleeve art. In 1981, along with photographer Nigel Grierson (1959–), he formed a design studio called 23 Envelope, which was renamed v23 in 1988 when Oliver went freelance. He is best-known for his album sleeves for independent record label 4AD.

P

PANTON, Verner
1926– **Danish**
✐ pp.36–37, 64

After studying in Copenhagen, Panton worked briefly with Arne

Jacobsen (see p.470) before establishing a studio in Switzerland in 1955. His work covers the design spectrum, including architecture, textiles, furniture, lighting, and exhibitions. His most celebrated design, a cantilevered, plastic chair, produced by Herman Miller from 1967, was the first of its kind.

PAOLINI, Cesare

See Gatti, Paolini, Teodoro

PAPANEK, Victor

1925–98 **Austrian/American**

Born in Vienna, Papanek emigrated to the US in 1939, where he studied architecture under Frank Lloyd Wright (see p.490). From 1964, he ran his own consultancy and lectured widely. Through his teaching and writing, most strongly in his book *Design for the Real World* (1971), he criticized design's slavery to commercialism and the futile waste of resources, winning favor with the emerging ecological movement.

PATOU, Jean

1880–1936 **French**

After a false start, caused by the outbreak of World War I, Patou opened his fashion house to immediate acclaim in 1919. Like his rival Chanel (see p.459), Patou realized the marketing potential of simple clothing for the increasingly active woman.

Among Patou's clientele were actress Mary Pickford and French tennis star Suzanne Lenglen.

PECHE, Dagobert

1887–1923 **Austrian**
📖 *p.73*

After studying architecture in Vienna, Pêche established himself as a freelance designer in 1912, creating wallpaper, textiles, and ceramics. In 1915, he joined the Wiener Werkstätte, developing an ornamental style quite distinct from the geometry

of work by Hoffmann (see p.469) and Moser (see p.476). His designs for the Werkstätte include silver, textiles, furniture, ceramics, and glassware.

PERET, (Pere Torrent)

1945– **Spanish**
📖 *p.408*

Peret began as an illustrator and graphic designer in Barcelona, moving to Paris in 1970, where he worked in a freelance capacity for Citroën and Air France, among others. Returning

Gaetano Pesce's Umbrella Chair, 1992–95

to Barcelona in 1978, he created cultural posters for the city council and the regional government of Catalonia.

PERRIAND, Charlotte

1903– **French**

A graduate in decorative arts, Perriand exhibited her metal furniture at the 1927 Salon d'Automne, where it attracted the attention of Le Corbusier (see p.474). It marked the beginning of their productive collaboration, together with Pierre Jeanneret (see p.471), which lasted ten years. Acting as an industrial design advisor in Japan from 1940 to 1942, she mounted two exhibitions on French design. On her return to France, she continued her association with Jeanneret, as well as independent work.

PESCE, Gaetano

1939– **Italian**

Architect, designer, and artist Pesce is known for his radical approach to design. In the early 1960s, he worked on various experimental projects involving programed and kinetic art. In 1968, he began to explore furniture design, producing the Up series of chairs, made by B&B Italia in 1969. He is known for his multi-disciplinary approach – his Tramonto a New York, a sofa he designed for Italian furniture company

Cassina in 1980 is a good example of this. Pesce has worked on projects in Brazil, Japan, Europe, and the US, as well as teaching extensively.

PETERS, Michael
1941– **British**
Design entrepreneur Peters combines quality design with business acumen. He established Michael Peters & Partners in 1970, handling packaging designs for clients such

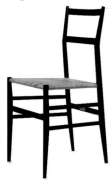

Ponti's 699 Superleggera Chair, 1956

as Winsor & Newton Inks, and Seagram. He is now chairman of a new firm called Michael Peters Ltd.

PETERSEN, Arne
1922– **Danish**
🖉 p.160
After serving as an apprentice in the gold and silver workshops of C.C. Herman, Copenhagen, Petersen joined Georg

Jensen Sølvsmedie in 1948. From 1976, he worked in the hollowware department.

PEZETTA, Roberto
1946– **Italian**
Pezetta worked for Zoppas and Nordica before joining the domestic appliance company Zanussi in the mid-1970s. In 1984, he was made head of the industrial design section. His best-known design is the Wizard refrigerator (1987).

POIRET, Paul
1879–1944 **French**
An influential fashion designer, Poiret pioneered the use of the brassière. In returning to the loose fit of the Empire-line, he freed women from the discomfort of the corset. After training at the houses of Doucet and Worth, he opened his own salon in 1904, designing lines which clearly show the influence of oriental costume. In 1911, he was the first couturier to launch his own perfume, and expand into other areas. He greatly encouraged creativity and spontaneity in students, and in 1911 founded the Ecole Martine decorative arts school.

POLI, Flavio
1900– **Italian**
🖉 p.80
An award-winning glass-ware designer, Poli joined the glass manufacturer Seguso Vetri d'Arte in the

1930s, becoming its director in 1963. The thick materials and vibrant colors that characterize his work are evident in his bowls and vases (1960s), made by Danese.

PONTI, Giovanni
1891–1979 **Italian**
🖉 p.170
Since the 1920s, Gio Ponti has contributed to the icons of Italian design. He studied architecture at Milan Polytechnic, and founded the magazine *Domus* in 1928, through which he promoted modernism. He cofounded a studio in 1927, seeking to achieve compatibility between tradition and industrial production. The Pirelli Tower in Milan (1956) is considered to be his finest architectural work, while the Superleggera chair for Cassina (see left) has become ubiquitous seating for Italian cafés, compromising between convention and innovation.

PORSCHE, Ferdinand "Butzi"
1935– **German**
🖉 p.89, 320–21
One of three designers in the Porsche family, the grandson of car designer Ferdinand Ferry Porsche (1875–1951), who founded Porsche in 1911, was nicknamed "Butzi." The 1963 Porsche 911 is his key car design. He established his own studio in 1972, and in the 1980s created

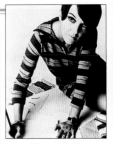

Mary Quant

furniture and lighting, including a line in 1985 for the company Luci.

PRICE, Anthony
1945– **British**
🖉 p.388
Educated in fashion at the Royal College of Art, London, Price was a prolific designer of 1970s' fashions. He is often associated with Bryan Ferry and the Rolling Stones, for whom he designed costumes, sets, and record covers. Since 1979, he has worked under his own name, continuing contact with media and rock stars.

PROUVE, Jean
1901–84 **French**
Metalwork designer Prouvé was the son of Victor Prouvé (1858–1943), a key figure of the Nancy School. He opened a studio in 1923, designing furniture made of bent sheet steel, suitable for industrial production. He created metal furnishings for Le Corbusier's buildings (see p.474) in 1925, and

in 1937, codesigned the Roland Garros flying club, acclaimed as the first truly industrialized building. In the 1950s, Prouvé explored the possibilities for mass-produced, prefabricated housing, schools, and offices.

PUCCI, Emilio
1914— **Italian**

A fashion designer who has concentrated on sportswear, Pucci opened Emilio, his own house, in 1950. He created boldly patterned, brightly colored silk jersey dresses, as casualwear for women. His international status earned him the Neiman-Marcus Award in 1954.

PUIFORCAT, Jean
1897–1945 **French**
✎ p.144

Puiforcat apprenticed to his father as a silversmith, and studied at the Central School of Arts and Crafts in London. He founded a workshop in 1921, producing clean-lined, unadorned silverware with contrasting materials, such as semiprecious stones and rare wood. The forms of his later works are based on careful mathematical calculations.

Q
QUANT, Mary
1934— **British**
✎ p.267

The name Mary Quant (see left) has become synonymous with the swinging London scene of the 1960s. She opened her Kings Road boutique, *Bazaar*, in 1955, responding to the youthful optimism of the time with ready-to-wear fashions for teenagers. Quant helped popularize the miniskirt in the 1960s, also introducing brightly colored tights. Several decades later, Quant's range has expanded to include makeup, jewelry, and accessories, many of which feature her trademark daisy motif.

QUISTGAARD, Jens
1919— **Danish**
✎ p.161

Educated as a silversmith during apprenticeship to Georg Jensen (see p.471), Quistgaard cofounded the Dansk International Designs with Ted Nierenberg in 1954, creating mainly table- and cookware. In the same year, he was awarded the Lunning Prize for his enameled cast-iron cooking pots, designed for the Danish manufacturer De Forenede Jerstøberier.

A poster by Rambow, 1995

R
RABANNE, Paco
1934— **Spanish**

This Spanish-born designer of avant-garde fashions was active in France. From 1960 to 1964, he designed fashion accessories for Balenciaga (see p.454), Givenchy (see p.467), and Dior (see p.462). In 1966, he launched a renowned line of body jewelry.

RACE, Ernest
1913–64 **British**
✎ p.62

An architect and designer of international reputation, Race took his inspiration from 18th-century craftsmanship. He founded Race Furniture in 1946, setting a precedent for the linear look created with steel rods. This is apparent in his 1951 Antelope and Gazelle chairs, displayed at the 1951 Festival of Britain. In the 1950s and '60s, he received various awards, including Royal Designer for Industry in England 1953, and several at the Milan Triennales.

RAMBOW, Gunter
1938— **German**
✎ p.408

Rambow cofounded a graphic design group with Gerhard Lienemeyer (1938–) in 1960. This was renamed Rambow/Lienemeyer/van de Sand, when Michael van de Sand (1945–) became a partner. The surreal effects of photomontage are evident in their award-winning 1978 theater poster for a production of *Othello*. The design group also created a corporate identity program for the German publisher S. Fischer Verlag (1976–83).

RAMS, Dieter
1932– German
✐ pp.92, 102

An industrial designer and architect, Rams played a pivotal role as a designer for the German manufacturer of durables, Braun. He joined in 1955, and by 1988 was the company's director. Together, Rams and Hans Gugelot (see p.468) developed a functionalist style (see right) that set a criterion for other producers. Among his most celebrated works are the SK4 Record Player (1956), and the KM 321 Kitchen Machine (1957). During the 1950s, he contributed to new forms of lighting, which initiated a change in interior design.

RAMSHAW, Wendy
1939– British

Following training in illustration and fabric design, Ramshaw established herself as a jeweler. She gained recognition in the 1970s with her designs in precious metals, and has since experimented with alternative materials, including paper and plastics.

RAND, Paul
1914–96 American
✐ p.371

The influential graphic designer Paul Rand is acclaimed for his adaptation of modernist design philosophies to suit graphic design. His

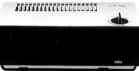

Dieter Rams' fan heater for Braun, 1969

corporate identity program for IBM (1956) set a style for future trademarks, and his influence has also been marked in advertising and editorial design. From 1935 to 1941, he directed magazines *Apparel Arts* and *Esquire*. His texts *Thoughts on Design* (1947), and *Paul Rand: A Designer's Art* (1985) are well respected among graphic designers.

REEVES, Ruth
1892–1966 American

A painter and textile designer, Reeves studied under the artist Fernand Léger (1881–1955) in Paris between 1922 and 1928. She is known for her printed fabrics and rugs, which show similarities to her cubist paintings. From 1931, she worked as a consultant for W. and J. Sloane's furniture store

in New York, which printed her famed Manhattan wallpaper design (1931). Reeves was inspired by her extensive travels, including visits to Guatemala in 1934 and India in the 1950s.

REICH, Tibor
1916–96 Hungarian

This textile designer united his native background with his formal education to achieve a unique style. His woven fabrics are inspired by the colored ribbons of peasant costume, while showing elements of modernism. In the 1930s, he settled in England, producing woven materials in Stratford, and also printed fabrics from the 1950s. His theory that "nature designs best" is visible in his 1957 Fotexur line of fabrics, rugs, and ceramics. In 1966, Reich created the upholstery for Concorde, the first supersonic plane.

RHODES, Zandra
1942– British

Rhodes graduated in textiles from the Royal College of Art, London, in the 1960s. Active as a fashion designer, her work reveals the influence of Pop Art. Combining her own textiles and fashions, she creates individual, romantic clothing influenced by her travels, featuring shells, feathers, and zebra motifs.

RIE, Lucie
1902–95 Austrian

The ceramicist Lucie Rie was born Lucie Marie Gomperz. Rich in ornamentation, her works embody the antithesis of modernism. She emigrated to London in 1938, where she established a pottery and button-making workshop. Her ceramics are recognizable by their cross-hatched sgraffito decoration, and subtly colored glazes, or textured white-tin surface. Rie has won various awards, and shown her works at several exhibitions.

RIEMERSCHMID, Richard
1868–1957 German

Progressive designer and architect Riemerschmid was one of the first designers to adjust his work to industrial production. In 1887, he cofounded the Verninigte Werkstätten für Kunst im Handwerk, Munich, producing simple works in metal. As an interior designer, he gained international recognition for his Room of an Art Lover for the Exposition Universelle in Paris (1900). He designed a variety of goods suitable for machine manufacture, including his Maschinenmöbel (1905). Among his architectural work is Germany's first garden city at Hellerau (1907–13). He directed the Kunstgewerbeschule in Munich from 1912 to 1924.

RIETVELD, Gerrit

1888–1964 Dutch
p.58

Architect and designer Gerrit Rietveld is best-known for his association with the De Stijl movement, which he joined shortly after its formation in 1917. The linear aesthetic with which his work is synonymous is expressed in his Red-and-Blue chair (1917–18), the Schröder house in Holland (1924), and his low-cost Zig-Zag chair for Metz & Company department store (1934). Although he favored wood as a material, Rietveld also created some experimental tubular-steel furniture during the 1920s. In the 1950s and '60s, he was mainly active as a lecturer and architect, designing the Rijksmuseum in Amsterdam between 1963 and 1972.

RODCHENKO, Aleksandr

1891–1956 Russian

A leading constructivist who was active as a painter and designer, Rodchenko brought the aesthetics of the machine age to these fields. He collaborated with fellow constructivists Kazimir Malevich (see p.475), and Vladimir Tatlin (1885–1953) from 1915 and, in 1921, co-founded the First Working Group of Constructivists. In the 1920s, he designed posters for the government, theaters, and journals *LEF* and *Novyi LEF*.

ROSSI, Aldo

1931– Italian
pp.125, 153

A leading postmodernist architect and designer, Rossi graduated from Milan Polytechnic in 1959. Formal and unornamented, his school library at Fagnano Olona in Italy (1972–76) typically draws inspiration from 18th-century neoclassicism. Rossi's product designs for Alessi are commonly based on architecture, such as his 1979 tea and coffee set, which is a scaled-down version of his floating Teatro del Mondo in Venice (1979).

RUHLMANN, Jacques-Emile

1869–1933 French
p.68

Ruhlmann is known for luxury Art Deco furniture and use of exotic materials. He first exhibited in 1913 at the Paris Salon d'Automne, and later played a significant role in the 1925 Paris Expo,

designing the Hotel du Collectionneur, which has been hailed as a high point in Art Deco design. His furniture for the Maharajah of Indore in the 1920s and '30s and his 1930 Soleil bed of rosewood veneer are typical of his furniture.

RUSSELL, Gordon

1892–1980 British

A proponent of the craft ethic, Russell began his education by repairing antique furniture for his father's business. In 1929, he set up Gordon Russell Ltd., working on designs of mass-produced radio sets for Murphy Ltd., and later a line of Utility furniture. In 1949, he became the director of the Council of Industrial Design.

S

SAARINEN, Eero

1910–61 Finnish/American
pp.62, 165

Saarinen's designs embrace a diverse selection of styles, from the organic to the

strictly geometric. Educated in Paris and New York, he was active mainly in the US. In the early 1960s, he designed Dulles Airport, Washington, and the TWA terminal at John F. Kennedy Airport, New York. He is also renowned for his use of bent plywood and fiberglass, the latter used for his famous Womb Chair (1947) and his Tulip chairs (1956), both created for Knoll (see p.473).

SABATTINI, Lino

1925– Italian
p.141

One of Italy's most inventive silversmiths, Sabattini is known for his fluid silverware; but he has also produced glass and ceramics. From 1956 to 1963, he was design director of French company Christofle, for whom he produced the Como tea set (1960). In 1964, he set up his own silver company in Italy, where he designed his Estro sauceboat (see below).

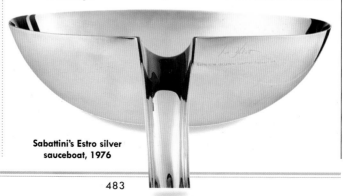

Sabattini's Estro silver sauceboat, 1976

SAINT LAURENT, Yves
1936– **French**

Algerian-born Saint Laurent won the International Wool Secretariat design contest in 1954 with a cocktail dress. The following year, he began work for Christian Dior (see p.462), and in 1957 he took over the great couture house on Dior's death. After fighting in the Algerian war, Saint Laurent opened his own house in 1962. His early collections were influenced by the Left Bank and the art world, most notably by the work of Piet Mondrian (evidenced in the 1965 collection) and Pop Art (1966). In 1966, he opened the Rive Gauche boutiques for ready-to-wear designs.

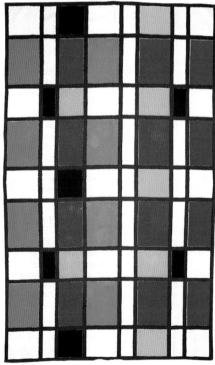

Geometric textile design by Sampe, c.1960

He has designed film and theater costumes as well as menswear, perfumes, and household goods.

SAMPE, Astrid
1909– **Swedish**

As head of the textile design studio at the Swedish fabric company Nordiska from 1937 to 1971, Sampe designed and commissioned many printed and woven textiles. She favored an abstract geometric style (see left). In 1972, she set up her own studio specializing in fabrics and interiors.

SAPPER, Richard
1932– **German**
✐ pp.88, 92, 226

After working in Germany as a designer for Mercedes-Benz, Sapper moved to Milan in 1957. There, he worked first for Gio Ponti (see p.480) and then the department store La Rinascente. Many of Sapper's most interesting designs have been created with Marco Zanuso (see p.491) with whom he began collaborating in 1960. Their work includes televisions and radios for Brionvega, and the Grillo telephone (1965). Among Sapper's other works are the Tizio lamp for Artemide (1972), which won a Compasso d'Oro award in 1979, kettles for Alessi, and car designs for Fiat. Since 1980, he has acted as a design consultant to IBM.

SARPANEVA, Timo
1926– **Finnish**

A leading figure in modern Scandinavian design, Sarpaneva has produced textiles, graphics, ceramics, and metalware. However, he is best known for his glass designs, particularly those for the Iittala factory.

SASON, Sixten
1912–69 **Swedish**

An industrial designer, Sason designed several cars for the Swedish company Saab, including the Saab 92, 96, and 99. He also acted as consultant designer for Hasselblad and Electrolux.

SAVIGNAC, Raymond
1907– **French**
✐ p.338

A former assistant to the great French poster artist A.M. Cassandre (see p.458), Savignac produced theatrical set designs and costumes, as well as posters. He was adept at choosing a single, often humorous, image to convey the message of his posters.

SCHIAPARELLI, Elsa
1890–1973 **Italian**
✐ p.185

Fashion designer Schiaparelli enjoyed phenomenal success in Paris during the 1930s. She started out by selling sweaters knitted by Armenian women. Later, she created interesting fabrics and garments, many decorated with surrealist-inspired features. Her most famous innovation was "shocking pink," a far more vibrant color than those used by other couturiers. In 1940, she moved to the US, and although she reopened in Paris in 1945, she did not recapture her former glory.

SCHRECKENGOST, Viktor

1906– **American**

⏿ pp.27, 79

Schreckengost's ceramics were heavily influenced by Viennese pottery. In 1930, while working at the Cowan Pottery Studio, he created a set of punch bowls for Eleanor Roosevelt. The bright blue bowls, which combined words and contemporary images, were later produced commercially. After Cowan closed in 1931, Schreckengost worked for a variety of other ceramic and industrial companies.

SERRURIER-BOVY, Gustave

1858–1910 **Belgian**

⏿ pp.220, 228

After initially working as an architect, Serrurier-Bovy began making furniture influenced by the Arts and Crafts movement. His Silex range of inexpensive self-assembled furniture was introduced in 1902. It featured wooden bedroom furniture, tables, and chairs, along with metalwork vases and lights.

SHIRE, Peter

1947– **American**

⏿ p.46

One of the many designers who produced pieces for the Italian Memphis group, Shire contributed brightly colored lamps, tables, a teapot, the Bel Air armchair (1982), and the Big Sur couch (1986). He has also designed silverware and glassware for other Italian companies.

SINCLAIR, Clive

1940– **British**

Sinclair worked as a technical journalist before setting up Sinclair Radionics in 1962. He developed miniaturized electronic goods, including the first pocket calculator (1972) and a miniature television (1977). In 1980, he launched the ZX80, the first of a series of home computers. His C5 electric car (1985) failed to sell.

ŠÍPEK, Bořek

1949– **Czech**

⏿ pp.77, 141, 221

Originally from Prague, Šípek studied architecture in Hamburg, taught in Hanover and Essen, and now works in Amsterdam. The design of his Bambi chair (1983) is typical of his individual poetic approach to functional items. For Vitra, he created the Ota Otanek chair

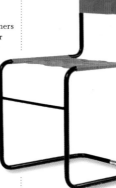

Mart Stam's chair, 1926

(1988), Wardrobe (1989–91), and a metal wastepaper basket (1989). Other works include tableware, glassware, and accessories.

SOGNOT, Louis

1892–1970 **French**

⏿ p.193

An architect and furniture designer, Sognot often worked with Charlotte Alix (1897–) designing interiors and metal and glass furniture.

SOTTSASS, Ettore

1917– **Austrian/Italian**

⏿ pp.222, 330

One of the best-known names in modern design, Sottsass began work as an architect, opening a design studio in Milan in 1947. In 1957, he became consultant designer to Olivetti for

which he produced various pieces of office equipment and furniture. He showed work with Studio Alchimia in 1979, then set up Sottsass Associati in 1980. The following year, he founded the Memphis group, which became a leader of the post-modernist movement. His own designs for Memphis include seating, sideboards, tables, and plates. He continues to design consumer products and exhibitions.

STAM, Mart

1899–1986 **Dutch**

After studying drawing, Stam worked for architectural practices in the Netherlands, Germany, and Switzerland, and as a town planner in the Soviet Union. He is usually remembered as the designer of the first tubular-steel cantilevered chair (see above left).

STARCK, Philippe

1949– **French**

⏿ pp.47, 171, 179, 331

Celebrated as one of the most exciting designers of the late-20th century, Starck shot to fame when he refurbished President Mitterrand's private rooms in the Elysée Palace (1982). Other interior designs include the Café Costes in Paris and the Royalton hotel in New York (both 1984). Starck's architectural projects range from the Nani Nani office building in Tokyo (1990) and the Angle in Antwerp (1991) to La Rue Starck in Paris. He has designed many pieces of furniture, much of it made from pressed metal, as well as products as diverse as motorcycles, lighting, clocks, lemon squeezers, and toothbrushes.

STICKLEY, Gustav

1857–1942 **American**

p.12

Stickley was the best-known American exponent of the Arts and Crafts movement. In 1901, he launched *The Craftsman* magazine to popularize the furniture made in his workshops using traditional construction methods. Stickley's company went bankrupt in 1915.

STÖLZL, Gunta

1897–1983 **German**

In 1927, textile designer Stölzl took charge of the Bauhaus weaving workshop in Dessau, where she had studied under the Swiss artist and teacher Johannes Itten (1888–1967). In 1931, she set up a textile studio in Zurich with two ex-colleagues from the Bauhaus. Among their commissions were commercial furnishing fabrics for Wohnbedarf furniture store.

STRAUB, Marianne

1909–94 **Swiss/British**

Straub played a major role in revitalizing the Welsh textile industry in the 1930s. Later, working for British firms Warner & Sons and Helios, she developed hand-woven fabrics for mass production. She created her famous Surrey textile for the 1951 Festival of Britain.

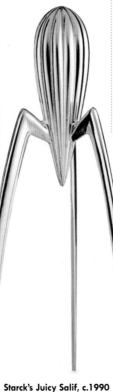

Starck's Juicy Salif, c.1990

SUMMERS, Gerald

1899–1967 **British**

p.61

In 1929, Summers set up a company called Makers of Simple Furniture, for which he designed molded plywood furniture similar to that of Alvar Aalto (see p.452). He is best known for the lounge chair he created from one piece of plywood (1933–34).

T

TALLON, Roger

1929– **French**

p.372

Industrial designer Tallon was one of France's first independent designers. His work includes furniture, lighting, and watches. Among his prestigious clients have been SNCF, General Motors, Daum, Lipp, and Erco.

TANAKA, Ikko

1930– **Japanese**

p.406

One of the foremost Japanese graphic and exhibition designers, Tanaka has produced some outstanding advertising and cultural posters.

TEAGUE, Walter Dorwin

1883–1960 **American**

pp.155, 283

Along with Raymond Loewy (see p.474) and Norman Bel Geddes (see p.455), Teague was a

pioneer professional industrial designer, and was one of the first to adopt streamlined styling. His many clients included Eastman Kodak, Corning Glass Works, Ford, Texaco, and Boeing. He designed pavilions for the 1939 New York World's Fair.

TEODORO, Franco

See Gatti, Paolini, Teodoro

THONET, Michael

1796–1871 **Austrian**

pp.56, 162–63

Thonet's influence extended long after his death through the designs of the furniture company he founded in 1853. Its bentwood chairs have become classics of 20th-century design. In the 1920s, the company began producing tubular-steel furniture.

THUN, Matteo

1952– **Austrian/Italian**

pp.140, 223

A partner in Sottsass Associati from 1980 to 1984, Thun was also a cofounder of Memphis. Although he has designed furniture, he is known for his ceramics and computer-aided manufacturing.

TIFFANY, Louis Comfort

1848–1933 **American**

pp.72–73

A well-known decorative artist of the early 20th-century, Tiffany set up an interior decorating firm in

1879, the Tiffany Glass Company in 1885, and Tiffany Studios in 1890. He designed pottery, jewelry, metalwork, furniture, lamps, and windows. His Favrile glass (see right) was hugely successful worldwide.

TSHICHOLD, Jan
1902–74 **German**
✎ p.366
Typographer Tshichold was the principle champion of the New Typography movement during the 1920s and '30s. He later adopted a more classical style. He also designed books.

TUSQUETS BLANCA, Oscar
1941– **Spanish**
✎ p.148
Tusquets trained as a painter, architect, and designer in Barcelona. In 1965, along with fellow students Lluís Clotet (1941–), Pep Bonet (1941–), and Christian Cirici (1941–), he formed the radical design and architecture group, Studio PER. In 1972, in collaboration with Lluís Clotet, he produced the controversial Belvedere de Regàs, which is generally regarded as one of the first postmodernist buildings. In 1973, Studio PER and other design offices formed B.d. Ediciones de Diseño to produce avant-garde designs. Tusquets created a tea and coffee set for Alessi in 1983.

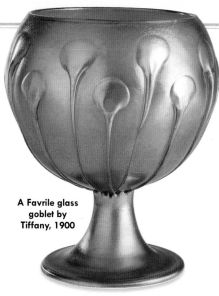

A Favrile glass goblet by Tiffany, 1900

U
UMEDA, Masanori
1941– **Japanese**
Umeda studied design in Tokyo. He worked at Studio Castiglioni, Milan, until 1969, joining Olivetti as a design consultant in 1970. His best-known piece is the Tawaraya boxing ring bed (Memphis, 1981). In 1986, he founded U-Meta Design in Tokyo, specializing in abstract furniture, crockery, and interior designs.

V
VALENTINO, (Valentino Garavani)
1932– **Italian**
Valentino studied fashion in Milan and Paris, returning to Rome in 1959, where he set up his own fashion house. His designs were in such demand that, in 1969, he opened a boutique for ready-to-wear women's clothing. This was followed in 1972 by a range of menswear. In the 1970s, he expanded his range to include perfume and accessories.

VENINI, Paolo
1895–1959 **Italian**
✎ p.76
Venetian law graduate Venini became a partner, together with Giacomo Capellin (1887–1968), in a Murano glassmaking business in 1921. Initially concentrating on traditional glassware, they began to show more modern pieces at the Monza Biennale in 1923 and later at the Milan Triennale. Venini assumed sole ownership in 1925. He worked with various designers, including Gio Ponti (see p.480), Massimo Vignelli (see p.488), and Fulvio Bianconi (1915–), who created the 1946 Handkerchief Vase, one of the company's most enduring designs.

VENTURI, Robert
1925– **American**
✎ p.148
In his book *Complexity and Contradiction in Modern Architecture* (1966), Venturi laid down the basic tenets of postmodernism. Although best-known for his architectural achievements, including the Sainsbury Wing extension for the National Gallery, London (1988), he has also designed a tea and coffee set for Alessi (1983) and furniture for Knoll (1984).

VERSACE, Gianni
1946–97 **Italian**
Versace learned his tailoring skills from his mother, who was a dressmaker. From 1972, he worked as a freelancer, producing a collection of women's ready-to-wear clothes under his own name in 1978. A menswear range followed in 1979. Versace was known for his original use of materials, particularly a soft metal fabric that he created for his 1983 collection.

Dinner set by Vignelli Associates, 1986

VIGELAND, Tone
1938– **Norwegian**
📖 p.271

One of Norway's foremost jewelry designers, Vigeland set up her own studio in 1961. Her striking designs evoke her Scandinavian heritage.

VIGNELLI, Lella
1934– **Italian**
📖 p.80

Husband and wife Massimo (1931–) and Lella Vignelli have introduced a European sophistication into American design through the graphics and products that they have produced since settling in the US in 1965. Working initially for Unimark International, in 1971 they founded Vignelli Associates. Massimo has been largely responsible for the graphic output, including Bloomingdale's corporate image and signage for the Washington subway system; while Lella

has headed the furniture and product design branch (see above).

VIGNELLI, Massimo
see Vignelli, Lella

VITRAC, Jean-Pierre
1944– **French**
📖 p.140

Vitrac set up in business in 1974, with offices in Milan, New York, and Tokyo. The company gained a reputation for exploring innovative design concepts, producing furniture, tableware, lighting, and sports equipment.

W
WAGENFELD, Wilhelm
1900–90 **German**

Entering the Weimar Bauhaus in 1923, Wagenfeld studied under László Moholy-Nagy (see p.476). He remained there, teaching in the metal workshop until 1927, when he went freelance.

Concerned with function, economy, and purity, Wagenfeld designed utilitarian ceramics, metal- and glassware (see right) for companies such as Rosenthal and the Jenaer Glassworks.

WARHOL, Andy
1928–87 **American**
📖 p.73

Although famed for his role in Pop Art, Warhol also created advertisements for *Vogue* and *Harpers Bazaar*, and record sleeves for Columbia Records. He was awarded the Annual Art Director's Club Medal in 1956 and 1957 for his I. Miller shoe and hat advertisement. His paintings and films drew on themes from the commercial world.

WEBER, Kem
1889–1963 **German**
📖 p.229

In 1914, Karl Emanuel Martin (KEM) Weber went to assist on Germany's exhibit in

the Panama-Pacific International Exposition in San Francisco. Trapped by the outbreak of war, he settled in the US. In 1927, he established himself as an industrial designer in Hollywood. Weber developed a distinctive style, openly embracing modernism.

WEGNER, Hans
1914– **Danish**
📖 p.163

Trained first as a cabinet-maker and later as a furniture designer, Wegner worked in the office of Arne Jacobsen (see p.470) from 1940 to 1943, when he set up his own studio. In 1940, he began his long and illustrious association with furniture maker Johannes Hansen, which produced his famous piece, The Chair, in 1949. Mostly executed in natural materials, Wegner's works stand out for their elegance and visual simplicity.

WEIL, Daniel
1953– **Argentinian**
📖 p.93

Born and trained as an architect in Buenos Aires, innovative industrial designer Weil went to London in 1978. He received recognition for a series of clocks, radios, and lights that he designed in 1981 as part of his degree show for the Royal College of Art, London. Together with Gerard Taylor, he has worked on various interior and product designs for Sottsass Associati, Knoll, and Alessi.

WEINGART, Wolfgang

1941– German

As a typography teacher at the Basel School of Arts and Crafts since 1968, the German compositor Wolfgang Weingart has been instrumental in overturning the conventional Swiss approach to graphics. He rejected strict adherence to the grid and introduced wide type spacing, step rules, and mixing of type weights. He is credited with bringing New Wave graphics to the US via his extensive teaching and through his cover designs for American journals such as *Visible Language*.

WEISS, Rheinhold

1934– German

p.190

Weiss remained at the Hochschule für Gestaltung, Ulm, as associate director of the product design section, after studying there. The products that he created for Braun in the 1960s reflect both his training at Ulm and Braun's functionalist aesthetic. In 1967, he moved to Chicago, setting up a studio in 1970.

WESTWOOD, Vivienne

1941– British

Generally recognized as the most influential and original British fashion designer of the 1970s and '80s, Westwood has played an important role in reasserting London on the international fashion stage. Inspired by the street style of rebellious urban youth and historical and ethnic costume, she has created a series of outrageous collections.

WEWERKA, Stefan

1928– German

pp.112–13

Artist, architect, filmmaker, and designer Wewerka worked initially as an architect and sculptor. He made his debut as a furniture designer in 1974, when he was commissioned by Tecta to design a classroom chair for its trade fair stand. Since then, he has produced a number of asymmetrical furniture

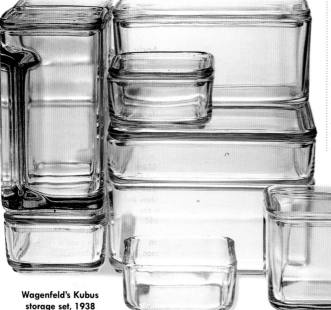

Wagenfeld's Kubus storage set, 1938

designs for Tecta and, from 1981, irregularly shaped clothing which he constructs on the body.

WIENER, Edward (Ed)
1918– **American**
🖉 p.269
Wiener began working as a jeweler in 1946, establishing himself in New York in 1947. Spirals, figures, and fish are familiar motifs in his work.

WILSON, Wes
1937– **American**
🖉 p.404
Underground cartoonist Wes Wilson was a chief exponent of Psychedelia. Drawing on Secessionist lettering, Art Nouveau ornamentation, and East Indian motifs, he produced numerous posters for West Coast rock concerts, principally at the Fillmore and Avalon venues in San Francisco.

WIRKKALA, Tapio
1915–85 **Finnish**
🖉 p.157
One of the finest postwar Scandinavian designers, Wirkkala won worldwide acclaim for his entries for the 1951 Milan Triennale. His glassware, produced by Iittala from 1946 to 1985, reflected his grounding in sculpture and his interest in organic forms. His famous Kantarelli vases, created in 1946, typify this approach. He also worked on a freelance basis, creating glassware

Iroquois carafe by Russel Wright, 1950

for Venini (see p.487), ceramics for Rosenthal, and lighting for Airam.

WORTH, Jean Philippe
1853–1924 **French**
When his father, English-man Charles Frederick Worth, died in 1895, Jean Philippe assumed responsibility for the house of Worth. Jean Philippe handled the creative output, while his brother Gaston (1856–1926) provided the business acumen, hiring designers such as Paul Poiret (see p.479). Retiring in 1910, Jean Philippe was succeeded by his nephew, who kept the name of Worth at the forefront of fashion during the 1920s. The house of Worth finally closed in 1954.

WRIGHT, Frank Lloyd
1867–1949 **American**
🖉 p.150
Primarily remembered as America's most creative architect, Wright was also an important design theorist. Working at the architectural office of Louis Sullivan (1856–1924), he was first exposed to the concept of functionalism. His interest in Japanese architecture led to the development of his own style of work, which he called "organic architecture." This was characteristically low and simple and made use of natural materials. He designed about 800 buildings, 380 of which were realized.

WRIGHT, Russel
1904–76 **American**
🖉 pp.138, 151, 156
Wright was born and raised as a Quaker in Lebanon, Ohio. His functional designs reflect his puritanical outlook. He began in theater design, but by 1930 he had established a studio in New York, producing metalware. He introduced his hugely successful Modern Living furniture line, which was mass produced by Conant-Ball and sold through Macy's store, in 1935. Wright is best-known for his ceramics (see left), particularly the American Modern dinnerware made by Steubenville Pottery from 1939.

Y
YAMAMOTO, Yohji
1943– **Japanese**
Yamamoto studied at Keio University and later at the prestigious Bunka College of Fashion in Tokyo. He founded his own company in 1972, showing his first collection in 1976. Like many Japanese fashion designers, Yamamoto concentrates on daywear. His garments are characterized by loose, asymmetrical forms.

YOKOO, Tadanori
1936– **Japanese**
🖉 p.402
Working as a freelance graphic designer, Yokoo's striking posters from the

1960s and '70s earned him international recognition. Mixing Western images with Eastern graphics, he explored the impact of pop culture on Japanese society.

Z

ZANUSO, Marco
1916– Italian
🖉 p.226

Zanuso studied architecture at Milan Polytechnic, where he later taught. He established his own design office in 1945. He is known for employing innovative materials, such as foam rubber and sheet metal, in his furniture designs for Arlex, among others. From 1958 to 1977, he worked with Richard Sapper (see p.484) on various projects for Siemens and Brionvega. Their 1965 folding Grillo telephone and 1962 Doney 14 television are two of the best-known pieces of Italian design from this period.

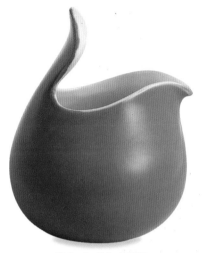

Pitcher by Zeisel, 1958

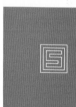

Optima typeface by Herman Zapf, 1958

ZAPF, Hermann
1918– German
🖉 p.365

An outstanding typeface designer, Zapf's work spans five decades. Self-taught from the writings of Rudolf Koch (1876–1934) and Edward Johnston (see p.471), he began his career at Paul Koch's foundry in Frankfurt. It was for the Stempel foundry, where he worked from about 1940, that he created his finest typefaces, such as Palatino (1949) and Optima

(1958). ZEISEL, Eva
1906– Hungarian
🖉 p.151

A Hungarian-born ceramicist, Zeisel worked extensively in Europe before settling in the US in 1938. Her early work reflects the prevailing trend for geometric patterns, but she adopted the emerging style of organic modernism (see above) with her move to the US.

GLOSSARY

ABS plastic

Acrylonitrile-butadiene-styrene thermoplastic has superior ductility, high-impact strength, good colorability, and a high gloss, making it suitable for molded and decorative objects. It is most commonly used in electrical goods, telephone handsets, and furniture.

Aesthetic movement

An artistic movement that evolved in the 1880s and was devoted to "art for art's sake." Leading to the Arts and Crafts movement, it adopted an extravagant ideal of beauty and led to freer expression in art and design.

Anti-design

A movement that emerged in the late 1960s and rejected established design theory. It reacted to the rise of consumerism in the 1950s and '60s, which was thought to promote "good design" to enhance sales. Anti-design sought to redefine design through its garish colors and unconventional shapes and proportions.

Art Deco

A decorative style, its name originated from the 1925 Paris *Exposition Internationale des Arts Décoratifs et Industriels Modernes*. Its influences were diverse, from cubism to Egyptian art to an appreciation of modern machinery. Characterized by simple geometric patterns, sharp edges, and bright colors, the style was applied to a wide range of disciplines.

Art Nouveau

An international decorative style that began in Europe in the 1880s and reached the height of its popularity by 1900. Based on forms of plantlife, the style created a new unity across the visual arts. It is characterized by the whiplash curve, suggestive of organic fluidity.

Arts and Crafts movement

An English and American movement, first established in England in 1882 and named after the Arts and Crafts Exhibition Society. In its prime, between 1888 and 1910, it sought to revive the ideal of the handcrafted object in an industrial age, a notion that had both social and aesthetic implications. Characterized by medieval and Gothic references, its products were often robust and simply constructed.

Austerity

A period during World War II when governments in Europe, Japan, and the US limited the use of strategic materials and instead commissioned a range of consumer products using basic or new materials.

Avant-garde

Meaning "the vanguard," a group of innovators. In art and design, the term refers to developments in the use of materials and styles.

Bakelite

The trade name for a thermosetting plastic, Phenol-Formaldehyde, invented and patented by Leo Baekeland in 1907. An early, brittle plastic, its streamlining qualities, cheapness, and similarity to wood made it ideal for consumer products such as radios and televisions.

Bauhaus

An influential art school founded in 1919 by Walter Gropius, which ran until 1933, when it was closed by the Nazis. One of its aims was to forge links between art and industry. In the 1920s, the Bauhaus became the leading intellectual and creative center of design, playing a key role in the development of modernism.

biomorphic design

A style of design in which an object is styled to imitate the appearance of a living organism.

Brussels Expo, 1958

A world's fair that was dominated by the Atomium, a huge structure built specifically for the exhibition, which accurately represented an atomic molecular structure.

cantilever

An engineering term to describe a projecting bracket that supports a load. The concept of a cantilever has been applied by innovative 20th-century designers to furniture, producing some highly original, modern chairs.

classicism

A design style based on abstract principles of organization and order found in Greek and Roman antiquity. The style is simple, harmonious, and well-proportioned.

Compasso d'Oro

Established in 1954, this design award for excellence is presented every year by the Italian chain store La Rinascente to Italian designers for outstanding products.

constructivism

A movement that emerged in Russia after the 1917 Russian Revolution. Partly influenced by cubism and futurism, it ignored fine art in favor of applied art: design for mass production was an important ideal. Its largely abstract, "sculptural" works were assembled rather than painted or carved, influencing design in the West.

cubism

Developed in France in 1907 by Pablo Picasso and Georges Braque, cubism was a reaction against the optical realism of Impressionism. Images were depicted in geometrical form from multiple viewpoints but displayed on one plane on the canvas. Though short-lived, the movement had a major influence on 20th-century art and design.

De Stijl

A multidisciplinary Dutch modernist movement founded in 1917 by Theo van Doesburg.

Its name derives from the *De Stijl* journal, meaning "the style." It used abstract geometrical forms, with neutral and primary colors in place of natural form, in the search for a visual language to express the new machine aesthetic.

deconstructivism

A term that emerged in the 1980s to describe visually complex forms with geometrically arranged areas of vibrant colors. Most designs never progressed beyond prototypes.

determinism

A philosophical theory that humans do not act out of free will, but are directed by external forces.

eclecticism

The term for borrowing from, often combining, a variety of historical sources. This practice was prevalent between 1900 and 1950, and later reemerged in postmodernism.

ergonomic design

A scientific approach to the relationship between humans and their environment. Products are designed to suit the human form.

Favrile glass

The trade name registered in 1894 for a high-quality glass produced by Louis Comfort Tiffany.

Festival of Britain, 1951

This festival reflected a new, postwar British approach to architecture and industrial design, characterized by light metal structures and modern materials.

functionalism

Louis Sullivan coined the phrase "form follows function" in 1896. The term embodied the belief that an object's function is of primary importance in determining its appearance.

futurism

An Italian movement launched in 1909 by Filippo Tommaso Marinetti. It extolled the virtues of modernity, demanding the inclusion of new technology and dynamism in art.

Glasgow School

A group led by the innovative Scottish architect and designer Charles Rennie Mackintosh. His interpretation of Art Nouveau in the 1890s and early 1900s resulted in a linear, less ornamental style.

graphic design

A generic term for photography, drawing, typography, and printing.

high-tech

An architectural and design style that rejects decorative elements in favor of industrial equipment.

International Style

An architectural style adopted worldwide that epitomized the simple, functional approach of modernism. Leading exponents were Walter Gropius, Mies van der Rohe, and Le Corbusier; and it was characterized by new materials such as steel, reinforced concrete, and plate glass windows.

Jugendstil

Meaning "young style," a term used in Austria, Germany, and Scandinavian countries for a style closely related to Art Nouveau.

kinetic art

A form of art that depends on movement for its effect.

kitsch

A critical term used to describe pretentious, cheap, ugly, or sentimental work. The style has flourished since the rejection of modernism by some designers in the 1960s. Gillo Dorfles' 1969 *Kitsch: An Anthology of Bad Taste* is the definitive book on the subject.

machine aesthetic

A term describing the appearance of an object that has been determined by its manufacturing process.

Milan Triennale

An art exhibition held every three years in Milan, it is a showcase for modern designs, generally Italian.

modernism

Not representative of one group, but a general reaction in art, design, technology, and society in the 20th century against traditional styles. Emphasizing the simple, functional aspect of forms without decoration, its aim was to produce high-quality designs for a mass population.

motif

A distinctive feature or dominant idea. Also an ornament identifying a maker or model.

Nancy School

The school of craftsmen set up in Nancy, France, by Art Nouveau exponent Emile Gallé in 1890 to promote naturalism in design.

New York World's Fair, 1939

The theme of this exhibition was "Building the World of Tomorrow." It was dominated by the American concept of streamlining, revealed in the cars, model buildings, and futuristic products on show. For the first time, the decorative arts were overshadowed by industrial designs strongly influenced by modernism.

Op Art

An abstract movement that developed in the 1960s and exploited various optical effects. Illusions of movement were produced by graphic processes or by overlapping patterns.

organic design

A style of design that echoes the curvilinearity of natural forms. In recent years, it has been aided by the improvements in plastics and computer technology in production.

pâte-de-verre

A glassmaking technique that involves grinding down glass and reforming it in a mold.

Paris Expo, 1925

This exhibition, also known as *Exposition Internationale des Arts Décoratifs et Industriels Modernes*, focused on the decorative arts and first introduced the Art Deco style.

Pop Art

An abbreviation of Popular Art. The movement grew in the 1950s and '60s, drawing its inspiration from aspects of commercial culture such as packaging, advertising, and comics. Its irreverent images were based on consumerism, and its exponents, such as Andy Warhol, were opposed to contemporary aesthetic standards.

postmodernism

In rejecting modernism, with its innovations that alienated the masses, the postmodernists relied on historical references. The movement became increasingly influential through the late 1960s, and can be characterized by a rejection of the logic and simplicity of the modernists. Instead, designers used an eclectic range of references, styles, and eras.

psychedelia

An influential 1960s' style that sought inspiration from mind-altering hallucinogenic drugs for its bright, bold, often abstract designs.

punk

A British street culture movement that developed in the 1970s, following a style of popular music.

rationalism
An Italian movement rejecting futurism that made efficient use of resources, space, and visual impact.

romanticism
Containing the distinctive qualities or spirit of the romantic movement. Considered a state of mind rather than a style, it encompassed diverse artists, whose use of grandeur and the picturesque aimed to invoke a powerful emotional response.

sgraffito
A ceramic decorative technique in which a different, underlying color is revealed by scratching through the surface of a material.

signage
The arrangement or design of graphic images, often involving text, in a sign that is intended to convey information to the public.

social realism
Expressing social or political tendencies as part of a practical approach in art and design.

Stile Liberty (or Stile Floreale)
Term used in Italy for Art Nouveau, deriving its name from the British decorative arts retailer, Liberty & Co., which sold the designs of its progressive craftsmen in Italy. The style was revived in design as Neo-Liberty in the 1960s.

streamlining
Aerodynamic experiments to reduce wind resistance on aircraft in America were subsequently applied to cars and other design work in the 1930s and '40s, giving objects gentle curves free of projections. Equated with functional excellence, the style was also used for purely visual effects, and by the 1950s often appeared in a highly exaggerated form.

suprematism
Developed by Kazimir Malevich in Russia, this concept was concerned with the reduction of forms to a simple geometric arrangement in pure colors to represent the "supremacy of pure emotion."

surrealism
Surrealists sought to go beyond the accepted conventions of reality and explore the subconscious mind. Representations were presented as depictions of a dreamworld, and objects were deliberately constructed in strange conjunctions. The play on the meanings of objects was picked up by the Anti-design movement.

Utility
Furniture and textiles produced in Britain between 1941 and 1951 in response to the economies of war.

Vienna Secession
Considered the Austrian version of Art Nouveau, the movement was founded in 1897 when a group of artists and designers seceded from the Vienna Academy. It utilized natural images and curving forms, but its designs were more geometric than those of French and Belgian Art Nouveau.

vitreous china
A type of china so fine, hard, and transparent it is almost glasslike.

vorticism
An aggressive movement between 1912 and 1915 that attacked sentimentality in favor of violence, energy, and machinery. Bold and abstract, it drew from cubism and futurism, often creating angular machinelike objects.

Wiener Werkstätte
A cooperative group of workshops that grew out of the Vienna Secession in 1903. Incorporating artists, designers, and craftsmen, it flourished as a center of progressive design until 1932. Although initially rectilinear, it later developed a more curvilinear, eclectic style.

zoomorphism
A style of designing objects that imitate or represent animal forms.

INDEX

A

Aalto, Aino, 452
Aalto, Alvar, 452
  furniture, 26, 27
  Paimio chair, 60
  Savoy vase, 75
Aarnio, Eero, 64, 452
ABC Skootamota, 302
Acer Aspire computer, 347
acrylic, 30
AD 65 radio, 459
adding machines, 354–57
Adidas, 245, 279
Adolph, Peter, 208
advertising, 36
  packaging, 410–49
AEG (Allgemeine Elektricitäts-Gesellschaft), 18–19
  corporate identity, 368, 369
  fan, 332
  hair dryer, 188
AEG Telefunken, 104
aerodynamics, 24
aerosols, 48
Aertex, 241
Aesthetic movement, 14
Africa, 48
African art, 20
Aga, 111
Aicher, Otl, 34, 452
"Air Clip" clippers, 190
Air France, 139
aircraft, 51
  aerodynamics, 24
  Blériot, 51
  Concorde, 36, 52
  superjets, 52
  Wright brothers, 12–13
alarm clocks, 228, 231
Albers, Anni, 452
Albers, Josef, 19, 452
Alchimia see Studio Alchimia

Alessi:
  cafetière, 125
  clocks, 231
  "Kettle with a Bird-shaped Whistle," 126, 128
  Pito kettle, 467
  tea service, 148
Alias, 456
Alison, Filippo, 124, 452
aluminum:
  candlesticks, 84
  foil, 415, 422
Alumo watch, 261
Amana SRDE520TBW refrigerator, 117
Ambasz, Emilio, 452
Amea Twin jacuzzi, 171
American Modern cutlery, 138
American Modern dinner service, 150, 151
American Telephone and Telegraph, 224
American Thermos, 159
AMi Continental jukebox, 295
Amstrad PC1512 computer, 346
Anderson, Gunnar Aagaard, 36
Andreasen, Henning, 337
Anglepoise lamp, 86, 87
Ant chair, 63
Antelope chair, 34, 62
anthropometrics, 26
Apelli & Varesio, 164
Apple Macintosh:
  computers, 44, 344
  corporate identity, 373
Aqualisa, 174
Arad, Ron, 45, 453
  Rover Chair, 452
  Three Thirds of a Table, 71
Arai, Junichi, 453
Arcadian Tea Rooms,

Glasgow, 390
architecture:
  Art Deco, 21
  environmental concerns, 50
  modernism, 19
  postmodernism, 41
Armani, Giorgio, 253, 275, 453
Armitage Shanks, 170
Armstrong, Neil, 32
Arnhem Internationale Filmweek (1961), 402
Art Deco, 20–21
  bathrooms, 169, 172
  beds, 192
  cameras, 283
  candlesticks, 82, 83
  ceramics, 144
  clocks, 229
  desks, 223
  drinks accessories, 158, 161
  jewelry, 268–69
  lighting, 86
  magazine covers, 379
  packaging, 418, 420, 421, 424
  radios, 90
  watches, 258
Art Nouveau, 13, 14–15, 16, 58
  bathrooms, 169
  beds, 192
  cupboards, 220
  drinks accessories, 158
  furniture, 58, 162
  glassware, 154
  lighting, 86
  magazine covers, 376
  packaging, 410, 414, 417
  perfume bottles, 184
  posters, 390, 404
  prams, 196
  vases, 72
L'Art Nouveau, Paris, 14
Artemide, 35, 88
Arts and Crafts movement, 13, 14, 15, 16, 28
  candlesticks, 82
  furniture, 195

magazine covers, 376
  posters, 390
  tea sets, 142
Artzt, Walter, 242
Ascanio, Corradino d', 453
  Vespa scooters, 30, 305, 453
Ashbee, Charles Robert, 453
Ashley, Laura, 219, 453
Asplund, Gunnar, 453
assembly lines, 17
Astral Email, 401
Atfield, Jane, 49, 220, 223
Atlantic Records, 387
Atom Wall Clock, 230
Atomium, Brussels Expo (1958), 230
Auburn 851 Speedster, 313
Audi Quattro Sport, 324
austerity designs, 28–29
Austin, 207
Austin Mini Cooper, 317
Austria:
  Art Nouveau, 15
  Vienna Secession, 14, 16, 18, 38
Autoped scooter, 302
Avakian, Amran, 386

B

B3 chair, 59
Baby Born, 213
Baby Daisy vacuum cleaner, 232
baby dolls, 210, 213
Babygro, 242
Baccarat, 184
Back to the Future, 322
Baekeland, Leo, 27
Bag Radio, 93
Bahnsen, Uwe, 453
Baier, Fred, 453
Baillodin, Claude, 259
La Baionnette, 377
Baird, John Logie, 31, 94

magazine covers, 376
  posters, 390
  tea sets, 142
Bakelite, 21, 27, 31
  hair dryers, 189
  jewelry, 269
  radios, 91
  telephones, 224, 225
  televisions, 94
Bakker, Gijs, 271, 453
Balans chair, 331
Balenciaga, Cristobal, 454
Ball, Douglas, 454
Ball chair, 64
ballpoint pens, 338
Balla, Giacomo, 17
Ballets Russes, 20, 266
Ballmer, Walter, 372
balls, footballs, 279
Balmain, Pierre, 454
Bandolero desk fan, 334
Bang & Olufsen, 100
Barbie doll, 210, 213
Barcelona chair, 59
Barcelona International Exhibition (1929), 59
Barcelona Olympic Games (1992), 375
Barnack, Oskar, 282, 454
baseball cap, 244
Basie, Count, 22
basins, 15, 169–71
Bass, Saul, 400, 454
bassinets, 198
bathing suits, 274
bathrooms, 167–91
  razors, 180–83
  toothbrushes, 176–79
baths, 168
Battaglin bicycle, 298
Bauhaus, 17, 19, 23, 34, 221
  magazine covers, 379
  posters, 394
  typefaces, 360, 361, 366
Bayer, Herbert, 361, 379, 454
BayGen Freeplay radio, 48, 93
Baylis, Trevor, 48, 93
bead shoes, 254
Beatles, 252, 387

ACKNOWLEDGMENTS

Picture Credits

Key: b=bottom; t=top; c=center; l=left; r=right; a=above

The publisher would like to thank the following for their kind permission to reproduce the photographs:

Jacket Front Cover: cra: **Swatch AG**; cl: **Ronald Grant Archive** (I Love Lucy picture), **Robert Opie Collection** (Television set); Back Cover: tr: **Chanel**; tl: **Sony UK Ltd**; c: **©DACS, 1999**; bl: **Robert Opie Collection**; 1l, 17l: (see p.370b); 12/13: **Arcaid/Richard Bryant**; 12l: **Vitra Design Museum**; 18l: **Bridgeman Art Library, London/New York/Neue Galerie, Linz, Austria**; 18/19b: **Hoffmann Foundation**; 19tr: **AKG London**; 20bl, 21l: **©Angelo Hornak**; 22l: **Robert Opie Collection**; 22tr: **Chanel**; 24b: **Peter Newark's American Pictures**; 25tl: **Robert Opie Collection**; 26cr, 26tl: **London Transport Museum**; 28tr: **Robert Opie Collection**; 28b: **E.T. Archive**; 29r: **Topham Picturepoint**; 32tr: **Robert Opie Collection**; 33tr: **Hulton Getty**; 35bl: **Vitra Design Museum**; 35tr: **Science Museum, London**; 36/37: **Verner Panton**, 36cb: **Milton Glaser Inc**; 37b: **Hulton Getty**; 38/39t: **Elizabeth Whiting & Associates**; 40l: **Courtesy of the Trustees of the V&A**; 41t: **Arcaid**; 41br, 41bl: **Michele de Lucchi**; 46br: **Ergonomi Design Gruppen**; 48tr: **Splash Communications**; 50l: **©Design**

Council, London; 51tl: **Arcaid**; 52bl: **Nokia (UK)**; 53tc: **©Design Council, London**/ Photographer: Richard Learoyd; 53br: **Zevco/ Semaphore Systems Limited**; 56l: **Hunterian Art Gallery/ University of Glasgow, Mark Fiennes**; 57tl, 57b: **Vitra Design Museum**; 58tl: **©DACS, 1999**; 58r, 60tr: **Vitra Design Museum**; 60bl: **Alvar Aalto Foundation/Vitra Design Museum**; 61tl: **Vitra Design Museum**; 61br, 62tc: **Knoll Archives/Vitra Design Museum**; 62bl, 63tr, 64cl, 65c, 66cl, 66/67cb: **Vitra Design Museum**; 68tr: **Christie's Images**; 70/1c: **Michele de Lucchi**; 71cr: **Christie's Images**; 74/75: **Alvar Aalto Foundation**; 81b: **Rebecca de Quin (RCA)**; 82l: **Photographie Giraudon**; 93br: **Splash Communications**; 94tl: **Glasgow Museums**; 94bc: **Ronald Grant Archive**; 96tl, 97t, 97b: **Sony UK Ltd.**; 98b: **Panasonic UK Ltd.**; 98tr: **Philips Consumer Electronics**; 99c: **Panasonic UK Ltd.**; 100/101c, 101br: **Robert Opie Collection**; 102cl, 103r: **Bang and Olufsen UK Ltd.**; 105tl, 104bl: **Interface Digital Library Ltd.**; 105br: **Sony UK Ltd**; 106cl: **Philips UK Ltd**; 111tr: **Robert Opie Collection**; 111bl: **Aga Rayburn**; 112bl: **Alternative Plans**; 112t: **Smithsonian Institute**; 112/113c: **Tecta**; 113tr: **Neff UK Limited**; 114bl: **Sears and Roebuck**; 116l, 116r, 117bl: **Publicity Engineers**; 117tr: **DRA Public Relations**; 119tl: **Robert Opie Collection**;

119bl: **Sears and Roebuck**; 119br, 120/121: **Science & Society Picture Library**; 121br: **Elizabeth Hindmarch Relations**; 126tl: **©DACS, 1999**; 128tl: **Robert Opie Collection**; 128/129c: **Alessi spa Italy/** Design by Michael Graves; 129tr: **Rowenta UK**; 129br: **©Design Council, London**; 134tr: **Science Museum, London**; 138tl: **Sotheby's Transparency Library**; 148tl: **Alessi**; 148cl: **Swid Powell**; 153br: **Robert Opie Collection**; 163tr: **Bridgeman Art Library, London/New York**; 164/ 165b: **Alias Design**; 164tc: **Christie's Images**; 170cl: **Ideal Standard Ltd**; 171tr: **Jacuzzi**; 171tl: **Larkspur Communications**; 174tl, 174/175, 175tr, 175br: **Ideal Standard Ltd.**; 184b: **Chanel**; 185c: **Robert Opie Collection**; 186tl: **©DACS, 1999**; 188tl: **EHG Elektroholding GmbH**; 192/193: **Bridgeman Art Library, London/New York/**Giraudon; 192cl: **Hunterian Art Gallery/ University of Glasgow**; 193tr: **Sotheby's Transparency Library**; 194tl, 194b: **Bonhams Auctioneers, London**; 195t: **Hulton Getty**; 195b: **Sawaya & Moroni**; 209br: **Sony UK Ltd.**; 211br: **Kathe Kruse**; 212tl: **Hasbro**; 212r: **Robert Opie Collection**; 213tr: **Zapf Creations**; 213b: Barbie photography reproduced with kind permission of **Mattel Toys**; 220c: **Christie's Images**; 221tc: **Bonhams Auctioneers, London**; 221tl: **Tecta**; 221br: **Vitra London**; 222r: **©Design Council**; 223c: **Bieffe di Bruno Ferrarese**; 224bl, 224tl, 225tl:

BT Archives; 225c: **Peter Williams**; 225cr: **©Design Council**; 226r, 227br: **BT Archives**; 227t: **Swatch AG**; 228l: **Christie's Images**; 233tl, 233tl: **Robert Opie Collection**; 241tr: **Hulton Getty**; 245tr: **Ladybird/Coates Viyella Group**; 247b: **Worthing Gallery and Art Museum**; 247tr: **Du Pont UK Ltd.**; 252tl: **Rex Features**; 253tl: **Katz Pictures**; 255tr: **Aurelia**; 256cl: **Worthing Museum Art Gallery**; 260tr: **Omega UK Ltd.**; 261bc: **Seiko Europe Ltd.**; 261tr: **Swatch AG**; 264cl: **Parker Pens**; 266tr: **Robert Opie Collection**; 267tl: **Retrograph Archive Ltd.**; 271bc: **Scott Wilson**; 275cr: **Swatch AG**; 279b, 279cr: **Adidas**; 297bl: **National Motor Museum, Beaulieu**; 298cl: **Robert Opie Collection**; 299cr: **Mark Hall Cycle Museum**; 302tl: **National Motor Museum, Beaulieu**; 303tr: **Hulton Getty**; 304tr: **National Motor Museum, Beaulieu**; 305br: **Piaggio Veicoli Europei SPA**; 306cl, 308cl: **Motorcycle Heritage Museum**; 312/313t, 312/313b, 312bl, 313br: **National Motor Museum, Beaulieu**; 324tl: **Roy E. Craig**; 324/325b: **Ford Motor Company Ltd.**; 328tl: **Bridgeman Art Library, London/New York /**The Fine Art Society; 329t: **Christie's Images**; 330tl: **Vitra Design Museum**; 330bl: **Tecno**; 331bl: **Vitra, London**; 332: **AEG Firmenarchiv/©DACS, 1999**; 338c: **Retrograph Archive Ltd.**; 340, 343tr: **Science & Society Picture Library**; 344bl, 344t: **Apple Macintosh/ Bite Communications Ltd.**; 345tl: **Hulton Getty**; 345bl: **I.B.M.**; 346bl: **Sony UK Ltd.**;

ACKNOWLEDGMENTS

346t: **Amstrad/Michael Joyce Communications**; 347b: **Acer Computers**; 348bl: **Apple Macintosh/Bite Communications Ltd.**; 350r: **Peter Williams**; 351tr: **USCO Marketing**; 361tl: **London Transport Museum**; 361bl: ©DACS, 1999; 368c: **Shell UK**; 369t: **Robert Opie Collection**; 369b: **EHG Elektroholding gmbH**; 370tl: **BMW**; 370b: The design of the Contour bottle is reproduced by kind permission of The Coca-Cola Company. "Coca-Cola", Coke, and the design of the contour bottle are registered trademarks of the Coca-Cola Company; 371b: **CND**; 371t: **UPS**; 372bl: **Jean-Loup Charmet**; 372tr: **McDonald's Restaurants Ltd.**; 372c: **Olivetti Lexikon Ltd.**; 373b: **Bite Communications Ltd.**; 373t: **Sony UK Ltd.**; 374b: **ICI**; 374tl: **Kuwait Petroleum (GB) Ltd.**; 375tr: **Colorsport**; 375t: **Nike UK Ltd.**; 379bl, 379tr: **Retrograph Archive Ltd.**; 386tl: **Capitol Records/Rays Jazz**; 386tr: **Blue Note/Gilles Peterson**; 387tl: **Polydor Records**; 387tc: **Immediate Records**/The Small Faces; 387br: **Atlantic Records**/Roger Dean/Yes; 387tr: **Virgin Records**; 388tr: **EMI Records**/ British Design Group Hipgnosis, George Hardie/ Pink Floyd; 388tl: **Island Records**/Roxy Music; 388bl: **Ray Lowry**/Penny Smith/The Clash; 388br: **Factory Records**/ *Roses* by Henri Fantin-Latour (1836-1904)/New Order; 389tl: **Vaughan Oliver**/4AD; 389tr: **Virgin Records**/Michael Nash Associates/Massive Attack; 390bc: **National Library of Scotland**; 390tl: **Robert Opie Collection**;

391l: **Retrograph Archive Ltd**; 392, 393br: **Robert Opie Collection**; 393tl: **Swatch AG**; 394bl: **Christie's Images**; 394b: ©DACS, 1996; 394tl, 395tl: **Robert Opie Collection**; 395tl: ©DACS, 1999; 395cr, 395bl, 396tl, 397b: **Robert Opie Collection**; 396b: **AEG Firmenarchiv**; 396bl, 396cr, 397tl, 398bl: **Retrograph Archive Ltd**; 398tr, 399b, 399tl: **Robert Opie Collection**; 403: ©DACS, 1999; 405bl, tr: **Robert Opie Collection**; 400r: **Ronald Grant Archive**; 400tl, 401tl, 401br, 402tl, 402br, 403l, 404bl, 404tr, 405tl: **Retrograph Archive Ltd**; 406tl: **Ikko Tanaka Design Studios**; 406br: **Atelier de Création Graphique**; 407t: **Studio Dumbar**; 407b: **Gallagher Ltd.**; 408br: **M. Espeus y Peret Asociados**; 408tl: **Rambow & van de Sand**; 409l: **Greteman Group**; 409cr: **Benetton/Modus publicity**; 452bl: **Ron Arad**; 454bl: **Ideal Standard Ltd.**; 455c: **Robert Opie Collection**; 456t: **Alias**; 462br: **Memphis**; 464c: **Kartell**; 465tl: **National Motor Museum, Beaulieu**; 465b: **Tecno GB Ltd.**; 466c: **Retrograph Archive Ltd**; 470br: **Atrium Ltd**; 472: **Robert Opie Collection**; 473c: **Vitra Design, London**; 479b: **Zero Disegno**; 480tr: **Mary Quant Ltd.**; 481b: **Rambow & van de Sand**; 486: **Alessi spa Italy**/Design by Philippe Starck, 1991.

The following were photographed at Cooper-Hewitt, National Design Museum, Smithsonian Institute: 1r: (see 139r); 2c: (see 141r); 2/3c: (see 161tl); 3l (see 139l); 4bc: (see 126tl); 5r: (see179l);

5bc: (see 86bl); 10c: (see 160tcl); 25br: (see 224cr); 27bl: (see 478); 27tr: (see 79tl); 30l: (see 465); 30/31c: (see 76bl); 34tl: (see 102tl); 38cl: (see 270cl); 43tr: (see 356/357ct); 46tl: Gift of Dennis Gallion and Daniel Morris; 47br: Gift of Clotilde Bacri; 58l: Gift of Mme. Hector Guimard; 59tr: Gift of Gary Laredo; 63bl: Gift of Knoll International; 64/65: Gift of Robert Blaich; 64br: Gift of International Contract Furnishings Inc.; 66tr: Gift of International Contract Furnishings Inc.; 67tr: Gift from the collection of Zoe and Pierce Jackson; 69: Museum purchase through the Decorative Arts Association Acquisition; 72/73: Gift of Stanley Siegel; 72bl: Gift of Mme. Hector Guimard; 73tr: Museum purchase; 73br: Gift of Ely Jacques Kahn; 74l: Museum purchase; 74tl: Museum purchase through the James Ford Fund; 74/75: Gift of Harmon Godstone; 75tr: Museum purchase; 75br: Gift of Jefferson Patterson; 76b: Gift of Christian Rohlfing; 76tr: Gift of Danese Milano; 77l: Museum purchase with James Ford Fund; 77br: Gift of Gallery 91; 78/79: Museum purchase; 78cl: Gift of Ely Jacques Kahn, approved and licensed by Josef Hoffmann; 78tr: Gift of Denis Gallion and Daniel Morris; 79tl: Gift of Mrs Homer D. Kripke; 79cr: Gift of Robert and Frances Diebboll; 80tl: Gift of the Italian Government; 80tr: Gift of Lella and Massimo Vignelli; 80br: Gift of Mel Byars; 81t: Gift of Ronald Kent; 82c: Gift of Denis Gallion and Daniel Morris; 82tl: Gift of Vivianna Torun Bülow-Hübe and Royal,

Copenhagen; 83cr: Gift of Julia and Fred Haiblen; 84cl: Gift of Design Ideas; 84t: Gift of Harry Dennis, Jr.; 84/85: Gift of Mel Byars; 86/87: Museum purchase; 86bl: Gift of Margaret Carnegie Miller; 87br: Gift of Anglepoise Ltd.; 88tl: Gift of Mel Byars; 89bl: Museum purchase through the Eleanor G. Hewitt Fund; 89tr: Gift of Coch & Lowy; 90cl: Gift of Barry Friedman and Patricia Pastor; 92br: Gift of Barbara and Max Pine; 92tr, 92tl, 102tl: Gift of Barry Friedman and Patricia Pastor; 105tr: Gift of John W. Fell; 122br: Gift of Mel Byars; 124tl: Gift of Antti Nurmesniemi; 124r: Gift of Maura Santoro; 126tl: Museum purchase through the Decorative Arts Association Acquisition Fund made possible by a gift from Theodore Dell; 126/127: Anonymous gift; 130, 131br, 135: Museum purchase through the Decorative Arts Association Acquisition Fund; 138br: Gift of Russel Wright; 139l: Gift of Mel Byars; 139r: Gift of Stephen and Dorothy Globus; 140tl: Gift of J.P. Vitrac Design; 140bl: Gift of Württembergische Metallwarenfabrik AG; 141r, 142/143: Museum purchase through the Decorative Arts Association Acquisition Fund; 143tr: The Henry and Ludmilla Shapiro Collection, Partial gift and purchase through the Decorative Arts Association Acquisition Fund and Smithsonian Collections Acquisition Program; 144/145: Purchase through the Decorative Arts Association Acquisition Fund; 144tl: Museum purchase; 145tc: The Henry and Ludmilla Shapiro Collection, Partial gift and purchase through the

Decorative Arts Association Acquisition Fund and Smithsonian Collections Acquisition Program; 146/147, 147tr: Gift of Rosenthal Glas and Porzelain AG; 150: Gift of Roger Kennedy; 151t: Gift of Russel Wright; 151c: Gift of Paul F. Walter; 151b: Anonymous gift; 154l: Gift of Justin G. Schiller; 154r: Gift of Mr. and Mrs. Burton Tremaine and Mrs. John McGrew; 155t: Gift of Mrs. Jefferson Patterson; 155b: Museum purchase through the Sir Arthur Bryan Fund; 156/157t: Gift of Harry Dennis Jnr; 156l: Gift of Paul F. Walter; 157r: Gift of Carlo Moretti; 157c: Gift of Iittala Glassworks; 158l: Anonymous gift; 159: Gift of Paul F. Walter; 160cla, 160tr: Gift of Mel Byars; 160tl: Gift of Peter Condu; 160cr: Gift of Gallery 91; 160b: The Henry and Ludmilla Shapiro Collection, Partial gift and purchase through the Decorative Arts Association Acquisition Fund and Smithsonian Collections Acquisition Program; 161tl: Gift of Rodman A. Herren; 161c: Gift of Paul F. Walter; 161r: Gift from Dansk Design Ltd.; 162/163: Purchased with combined funds and Crane and Co.; 177r: Anonymous gift; 179l: Gift of Julia and Fred Haiblen; 181r: Gift of Barry Friedman and Patricia Pastor; 182l: Gift of Diane and Mauro Genneretti, Italianissimo, Inc.; 183t: Museum purchase; 184tl: Anonymous Gift; 186l: Gift of Monique Fink in memory of Peter Fink; 188b: Gift of Barry Friedman and Patricia Pastor; 190t: Gift of Henry Dreyfuss; 190b: Anonymous gift; 216r: Gift of Mr. Henry Spencer; 171, 217r, 218l, 218r: Museum

purchase; 224cr, Museum purchase through the Decorative Arts Association Acquisition Fund; 226tl: Gift of Becker, Inc.; 229t: Gift of Mr. and Mrs. Arthur Wiesenberger; 229b: Museum purchase through the Decorative Arts Association Acquisition Fund; 230 Gift of Mel Byars; 231tr: Gift of Barry Friedman and Patricia Pastor; 231c: Gift of Ivy Ross and Richard Ebendorf in memory of Herbert Ross; 231b: Gift of REXITE; 268l, 268c: Museum purchase through the Decorative Arts Association Acquisition Fund; 268r: Gift of Sally Israel in memory of Fredricka Steibach; 269r: Gift of Michele Wiener; 269c, 270cl: Gift of Deane Granoff; 270c: Gift of Vivianna Torun Bülow-Hümbe and Royal, Copenhagen; 270br, 271tr: Purchase through the Decorative Arts Association Acquisition Fund; 283l: Gift of Mr. & Mrs. Maurice Zubatkin; 283cr: Gift of Barry Friedman and Patricia Pastor; 327br: Gift of the Arango Design Foundation; 330cr: Gift of Hermès, SA; 334cl: Anonymous gift; 335bl: Gift of Philips Dictation system USA; 336cl: Gift of Rodman A. Herren; 336/337: Gift of Rolodex Corporation; 357cr, 339tr: Gift of the Arango Design Foundation and Steelcase Design Partnership; 339tl: Gift of Max and Barbara Pine; 339b: Courtesy of Plus Corporation of America; 341t: Museum purchase through the Decorative Arts Association Acquisition Fund; 341b: Gift of Mel Byars; 342: Gift of Barry Friedman and Patricia Pastor; 351b: Gift of Olentangy Associates; 353b: Gift of

Quadmark; 354cl: Gift of Max and Barbara Pine; 354/5, 356tl, 356/357t: Gift of Barry Friedman and Patricia Pastor; 357r: Gift of the Arango Design Foundation; 457bl: (see 92tl); 463: Anonymous gift; 462tl: Gift of Paul F. Walter; 468tl: Gift of Mel Byars; 468/469c: Gift of Dorothy Hafner; 469br: Gift of Mr. Phelps Warren/Hoffmann Foundation; 470tl: Gift of Harry Dennis Jnr; 471c, 474: Gift of A/S Stelton; 475c: Gift of Smart Design; 477: Gift of Barry Friedman and Patricia Pastor; 478tl: Gift of Mel Byars; 483: Gift of Lino Sabattini; 486, 487: Gift of Joseph L. Morris; 488: Gift of Lella and Massimo Vignelli; 489: Museum purchase; 490: Gift of Dalmar Tifft; 491: Gift of Paul F. Walter.

Dorling Kindersley would like to thank the following for the kind loan of props for photography:
ABC Business Machines: 343bc; Simon Alderson, Twentieth Century Design: 36/37, 39br, 70, 93tr, 96b, 222tl, 329b, 484; Algerian Coffee Stores: 122tl, 125ct, 125br, 128/129, 467tc; Angels and Bermans: 248r, 249l, 250l, c, r, 251l; Apple Computer U.K. Ltd: 51br, 348/349; Laura Ashley: 219l; Jane Atfield, Made of Waste: 49c, 223r; The Back Shop: 331tr; BBC Costume Store: 242l (boots and coat), 243l, r; Andrea Black, Artistic Licence: 250–253 (make-up); The Business, 0181-963 0668: front jacket br, 5r, 249c; Butler & Wilson: 5r, 249c, (jewellery); Joe Carroll, Rare Camera Company: 23b, 282cl, 284tr, bl, 285l, r, 286t, c; François Chabat: 287b; The Contemporary

Wardrobe: **front jacket** cta, **back jacket** cbl, 255cr, cbr, 256tl; Cos Prop: **back jacket** cbl, 1cr, 246l, c, r; 247l, 248l, c; Classic Restorations: 313bl; Roy E. Craig: 324tl; Garry Derby, American '50s Car Hire: 32/33, 316/317; Donghia, Chelsea Harbour Design Centre, London: 219r; The Duffer of St. George: 280t; D.H. Evans: 102bl, 133tr, br, 182/183c, 191; Max & Beverly Floyd: 321t; Freuds: 4l, 162l; Ghost: 249r; Jack Hampshire Baby Carriage Collection: 196b, tr, 197tr, bl; c/o Hendon Way Motors: 320/321; Phil Hester: 318/319b; D. Howarth: **back jacket** cbr, 322tl; Nick Hughes & Tim Smith: 314tl; Ideal Standard: 170c, cr, 170/171b; Jenny Jordan: 246–249, 266/267 (make-up); The Juke Box Showroom, RS Leisure, 0181-451 6124/5: 293b, 294tr, tl, 295b; Austin Kaye & Co. Ltd.: 2r, 258c, r, 259l, c, r, 260c, 261l; Lawleys Ltd.: 146t; The London Toy and Model Museum, Paddington, London: 200tc, cl, br, 201tr, 202tl, c, br, 203l, cr, 204tl, 205tl, ct, tr, 206tl, tr, 207t, b, 208t; Anna Lubbock: 238–245 (make-up); Graham Mancha, Design for Modern Living: 59bl, 68bl, 164/165tc, 335r; Carlo Manzi Rentals: 2l, 11l, 251c, r, 252bl, br, 253bl, r; Dr. Martens: 237, 257cr; The Robert Opie Collection, The Museum of Advertising & Packaging, Gloucester, England: **front jacket** cl, **back jacket** bl, c, 10r, 27br, 31tr, 90tr, br 91cr, 93tl, 94br, 95, 100cl, 104/105c, 110r, 111tr, 114tr, 115tr, 118tl, br, 120tl, 132tl, 134bl, 158br, 176, 177l, 179ct, 180bl, 180/181c,

ACKNOWLEDGMENTS

185l, 186/187c,187r, 189bl, r, 232, 233c, r, 234, 273, 282t, 292tl, 292/293c, 293tr, 294/295c, 333r, 332/333c, 340, 376/377, 378, 380/381, 382/383, 410–49; Dennie Pasion: 246–49, 266–67 (hair styling); PCC Group plc: 48bl; Penfriend: **front jacket** ctl, 1cl, 262–65 (all pens); Pentagram Design Limited, London: **front jacket** cb, 8, 183br; AJ Pozner (Hendon Way Motors): 325tl; Kevin Price, Volvo Enthusiasts' Club: 320tl; Reckless Records: 387tl; Red or Dead: 257tr; Road Runner: 281l; Rosenthal/ Waterford Wedgwood, London: 141l, 148/149c, 149t, 152/153c, 153tr, cl, 476b; Courtesy of Peter Rutt: 323b; Gad Sassower, Decodence, 13 The Mall, 359 Upper Street, Islington, London N1 0PD: 3r, 7r, 91l, 131tr, 334r; 458/459c; Slam City Skates: 280l; St. Bride Printing Library: 360t, 361b; 362/363, 364/365, 366; Sunglass Hut: 275cra, crb, br; Le Tout Petit Musée/ Nick Thompson, director Sussex 2CV Ltd: 314cl; Tom Turkington (Hendon Way Motors): 317tr; Irene Turner: 323tr; The Water Monopoly, 16/18 Lonsdale Rd, London NW6: 15br, 168l, cr, br, 169l, cr, bc, 172/173; "57th Heaven" Steve West's 1957 Buick Roadmaster; Janet & Roger Westcott: 316c; Wig Specialities: 246/247, 248l, 249l, c, 266l, c, 267c; Margaret Wicks: 238/239, 240l, c, 241l, c; William Levene Ltd: 125bl; Courtesy of Mr. Willem van Aalst: 314bl; Lawrence Zeegen: 17l, 370bl (all bottles).

Cooper-Hewitt, National Design Museum, Smithsonian Institute is grateful to the following staff for their generous support on this project: Linda Dunne, Assistant Director for Administration; Brad Nugent, Head of Photo Services; Greg Heringshaw, Technician, Wallcoverings Department; Cynthia Trope, Technician, Department of Applied Arts and Industrial Design; Todd A. Olson, Assistant, Department of Applied Arts and Industrial Design; Cordelia Rose, Registrar; Steven Langehough, Associate Registrar; Larry Silver, art handler; Honor Mosher, art handler.

Thanks are also due to: Nell Cozens (Design Council), Lizanda Lucas, Alex Madina (NMEC), Hugo Wilson, Laurent Marceau, The British Dental Association, and *VolksWorld* Magazine for their help and advice; Boyd Annison, Helen Castle, Adrian Craddock, DNH Camcorder Repairers, Victoria Elvines, Sasha Howard, Gloria & John Jacobson, Tassy King, Eyal Lavi, Joanne Mitchell, Nicky Munro, and Andrew Pucher for the loan of props; models Sarah Foster, David Gillingwater, Emily Gorton, Thomas Green, Hayley Miles, Susannah Marriott, Jacqueline Phillips, David Terrey, Ryan Thomas, David Williams, and Patricia Wright; and Susannah Steel, particularly for her help with the packaging section. Additional thanks to Kirstie Hills, Caroline Hunt, Claire Legemah, Neil Lockley, Heather McCarry, Claire Naylor, Julie Oughton, Claire Pegrum, Nicola Powling, Catherine Shearman, Nichola Thomasson, Tracy Timson, and Joanna Warwick.

Additional photography: Lynton Gardiner, Clive Streeter, Gary Ombler, Sarah Ashun, Dean Belcher, Terence Sarluis, and Jonathan Keenan.

Author's acknowledgments I particularly thank the staff at Dorling Kindersley, who have shown dedication, and have encouraged and guided me with enthusiasm. I am especially grateful to Janice Lacock, who has managed the project with skill and commitment. I thank Carla De Abreu, Louise Candlish, Stephen Croucher, Jo Marceau, Tracy Hambleton-Miles, Claire Pegrum, Jane Sarluis, Susannah Steel, Dawn Terrey, and David Tombesi-Walton for their remarkable efforts. Finally at DK, a special thanks to Sean Moore for his support and advice. My thanks also to Deborah Sampson Shinn at Cooper-Hewitt Museum, New York; Mike Ashworth and David Ellis at the London Transport Museum; Peter Barnet; The Victoria and Albert Museum, London; Hamish MacGillivray at the London Toy and Model Museum; Robert Opie; the Vitra Museum; Julia Tambini; Patricia Wright; Sandra Millichip; Hal Haines; Shirley Finch; and Stephen Le Flohic.

Revised edition team: **Senior editor:** Peter Jones; **Senior art editor:** Rowena Alsey; **Editors:** Jo Marceau, Julie Oughton; **Art editors:** Joanne Mitchell, Dawn Terrey; **DTP designer:** Rob Campbell; **Senior managing editor:** Anna Kruger; **Senior managing art editor:** Steve Knowlden; **Additional design:** Carla De Abreu, Claire Legemah; **Picture researcher:** Mariana Sonnenberg; **US editor:** Gary Werner.